Spanish

for Health Care Professionals

THIRD EDITION

William C. Harvey, M.S.

BARRON'S

The author wishes to thank Anaheim Memorial Medical Center in Southern California, and his editor, Dimitry Popow, for their help during the creation of this book.

All inquiries should be addressed to:
Barron's Educational Series, Inc.
250 Wireless Boulevard
Hauppauge, NY 11788
www.barronseduc.com

ISBN-13: 978-0-7641-3928-4 (book only))
ISBN-10: 0-7641-3928-2 (book only)
ISBN-13: 978-0-7641-9446-7 (book and CD set)
ISBN-10: 0-7641-9446-1 (book and CD set)

Library of Congress Control Number: 2007019827

Library of Congress Cataloging-in-Publication Data
Harvey, William C.
  Spanish for health care professionals / William C. Harvey.
    p. cm.
  ISBN-13: 978-0-7641-3928-4 (alk. paper)
  ISBN-10: 0-7641-3928-2 (alk. paper)
  ISBN-13: 978-0-7641-9446-7
  ISBN-10: 0-7641-9446-1
 1. Spanish language—Conversation and phrase books (for medical personnel) I. Title.

  PC4120.M3H37 2007
    468.3′42102461—dc22   2007019827

PRINTED IN THE UNITED STATES OF AMERICA

Contents

Chapter Five

THE PREGNANCY

Chapter Six

MARGARITA ESPINOZA, AGE SIX

Introduction

The key to learning Spanish is self-confidence. To build self-confidence you must first realize that the entire learning experience is painless and fun. What they told you in the traditional foreign language classroom was wrong. In fact, research has revealed some startling information. Consider these tenets to acquiring basic Spanish skills:

- Thousands of words are similar in both Spanish and English, which makes it easier for you to remember vocabulary.
- Grammar and pronunciation don't have to be "perfect" in order to be understood.
- Messages in Spanish can be communicated with a few simple expressions.
- As the number of Hispanics in the United States increases, so do the opportunities to practice new Spanish skills.
- Motivation shouldn't be a problem. Businesses across the country are making efforts to recruit employees who speak two or more languages.
- People who relax and enjoy their learning experiences seem to acquire Spanish at a much faster pace than everyone else.
- Even a little Spanish allows doctors, nurses, technicians, and support staff to help people in need of medical assistance.

Feel better? Trust me. When it comes to learning a new language, believing in yourself can make all the difference.

Before you begin

This book provides all the practical vocabulary and phrases you need to communicate with non-English speaking patients and their families. Each chapter introduces several new language skills, along with suggestions on how to use these skills in everyday situations. Read along at your own pace. If you get frustrated, review the material from previous chapters.

In Chapter One you will learn basic vocabulary and a few rules related to the Spanish language. In Chapter Two you will learn all there is to know about the patient. In Chapters Three through Eleven, you'll be following various members of a Latino family, the Espinozas, as they receive medical treatment from various hospital departments. At the end of the book, there is a section on cognate words along with an index that lists, in alphabetical order, words and expressions for the health care professional. Use this list as a quick reference point for immediate conversation.

Throughout each chapter are signposts to help you find your way around the language. The **¡No Se Olvide!** *('noh seh ohl-'bee-deh)* (Don't Forget!) sections give you tips on how to learn Spanish more effectively. The **¿Cuánto Aprendió?** *('kwahn-toh ah-prehn-dee-'oh)* (How Much Did You Learn?) sections are for easy review and practice. You will often find these sections preceded by a number within a circle, indicating that the answers are located on pages 200–206. The **Dos Culturas** *(dohs kool-'too-rahs)* (Two Cultures) segments provide you with valuable information on Hispanic customs. You will also find sections titled **Más Acción** *(mahs ahk-see-'ohn)* (More Action). Use these signposts as tools to improve your skills and to better understand your patient's needs and desires.

So, let's get started . . . and have fun. **¡Diviértase!** *(dee-bee-'ehr-tah-seh)*.

Chapter One

Capítulo Uno

(kah-'pee-too-loh 'oo-noh)

Basic Information

Información Básica

(een-fohr-mah-see·'ohn 'bah-see-kah)

This first section is an easy-to-follow introduction to survival Spanish. Before you learn all the job-related words and expressions, take time to review how the Spanish language is put together. Focus on the inside tips and practice the suggestions for successful communication. You soon will discover that learning Spanish is really **no problema** *(noh proh-'bleh-mah).*

The sound system

One of the biggest concerns people have about acquiring a second language is speaking with improper pronunciation. Fortunately, Spanish is close enough to English that minor mistakes won't hurt communication. In fact, you need to remember only five sounds in order to speak well enough to be understood. Here are the vowels—each one is pronounced the way it is written:

a *(ah)* as in yacht
e *(eh)* as in met
i *(ee)* as in keep
o *(oh)* as in open
u *(oo)* as in spoon

1

Now, using your new sound system, try pronouncing these words:

a: **banana** *(bah-'nah-nah)*, **gas** *(gahs)*, **plasma** *('plahs-mah)*
e: **Pepe** *('peh-peh)*, **bebé** *(beh-'beh)*, **excelente** *(ehk-seh-'lehn-teh)*
i: **sí** *(see)*, **Trini** *('tree-nee)*, **sífilis** *('see-fee-lees)*
o: **loco** *('loh-koh)*, **no** *(noh)*, **doctor** *(dohk-'tohr)*
u: **mucho** *('moo-choh)*, **pus** *(poos)*, **Lulú** *(loo-'loo)*

¡No se olvide! *(noh seh ohl-'bee-deh)*
Don't forget!

- Did you notice the accent (´) mark on some words? That part of the word with the accent mark should always be pronounced LOUDER and with more emphasis (i.e., **Lulú** *[loo-'loo]*). If there's no accent mark, say the last part of the word LOUDER and with more emphasis (i.e., **doctor** *[dohk-'tohr]*). For words ending in a vowel, or in **n** or **s**, the next to the last part of the word is stressed **excelente** *(ehk-seh-'lehn-teh)*. You'll get the hang of this once you begin to practice.

- In some cases, the letter **u** doesn't make the "oo" sound as with **guitarra** *(gee-'tah-rrah)* or **guerra** *('geh-rrah)*. Don't worry about these words right now. They're few and far between.

- **Note:** The word **si** *(see)* without an accent mark means "if."

Now let's take a look at the other sounds you'll need to remember. And don't forget—these sounds are always the same:

Spanish Letter	English Sound
c (after an e or i)	s as in Sam (**cerebral,** *seh-reh-'brahl*)
g (after an e or i)	h as in Harry (**general,** *heh-neh-'rahl*)
h	silent, like the k in knife (**hombre,** *'ohm-breh*)
j	h as in hot (**Julio,** *'hoo-lee·oh*)
ll	y as in yellow (**tortilla,** *tohr-'tee-yah*)
ñ	ny as in canyon (**español,** *ehs-pah-'nyohl*)
qu	k as in kit (**tequila,** *teh-'kee-lah*)
rr	The "rolled" r sound (**burro,** *'boo-rroh*)
v	b as in blood (**viva,** *'bee-bah*)
z	s as in son (**Gonzales,** *gohn-'sah-lehs*)

The rest of the letters in Spanish are very similar to their equivalents in English. Although some dialects may vary, these will work fine:

b	**bueno** (*'bweh-noh*)	p	**papá** (*pah-'pah*)
d	**disco** (*'dees-koh*)	r	**tres** (*trehs*)
f	**flan** (*flahn*)	s	**salsa** (*'sahl-sah*)
l	**Lupe** (*'loo-peh*)	t	**taco** (*'tah-koh*)
m	**más** (*mahs*)	x	**México** (*'meh-hee-koh*)
n	**nada** (*'nah-dah*)		

Take a few minutes to practice your new sounds in Spanish. Read the following words aloud. You should have no trouble figuring out what they mean.

accidente (*ahk-see-'dehn-teh*) **medicina** (*meh-dee-'see-nah*)
anestesista (*ah-nehs-teh-'sees-tah*) **menopausia** (*meh-noh-'pow-see·ah*)
colesterol (*koh-leh-steh-'rohl*) **sexo** (*'sehk-soh*)
intestinos (*een-tehs-'tee-nohs*) **tableta** (*tah-'bleh-tah*)

Some words are spelled the same in both languages, but are pronounced differently. (Don't forget the rules about accent marks.) Most medical terms in Spanish are easy to remember because they share common roots.

abdomen (*ahb-'doh-mehn*) **hospital** (*hos-pee-'tahl*)
dental (*dehn-'tahl*) **saliva** (*sah-'lee-bah*)
doctor (*dohk-'tohr*) **tendón** (*tehn-'dohn*)
epidermis (*eh-pee-'dehr-mees*) **vertebral** (*behr-teh-'brahl*)

Here are some more words in Spanish you may already know. People who speak English use them all the time!

adiós (*ah-dee-'ohs*) **macho** (*'mah-choh*)
amigo (*ah-'mee-goh*) **más** (*mahs*)
amor (*ah-'mohr*) **muchacho** (*moo-'chah-choh*)
bueno (*'bweh-noh*) **mucho** (*'moo-choh*)
casa (*'kah-sah*) **patio** (*'pah-tee·oh*)
dinero (*dee-'neh-roh*) **plaza** (*'plah-sah*)
español (*ehs-pah-'nyohl*) **problema** (*proh-'bleh-mah*)
Feliz Navidad (*feh-'lees nah-bee-'dahd*) **pronto** (*'prohn-toh*)
fiesta (*fee-'ehs-tah*) **rancho** (*'rahn-choh*)
gracias (*'grah-see·ahs*) **señorita** (*seh-nyoh-'ree-tah*)
grande (*'grahn-deh*) **sí** (*see*)
hombre (*'ohm-breh*) **uno** (*'oo-noh*)

¡No se olvide!

> Here's another hot tip for learners: The trend to mix Spanish and English has created a new language called *"Spanglish."* Millions of immigrants use it so don't be afraid to stick in an English word whenever you forget a Spanish word. Here are a few examples:
>
> **La** "nurse"   **El** "hospital"
> **La** "maternity"   **El** "bill"

The Spanish alphabet

At some point during the early stages of learning the language you may be forced to spell out a word in Spanish. In case of an emergency, you should know the letters of the alphabet in Spanish:

a	*(ah)*	**n**	*('eh-neh)*
b	*(beh-'grahn-deh)*	**ñ**	*('eh-nyeh)*
c	*(seh)*	**o**	*(oh)*
ch*	*(cheh)*	**p**	*(peh)*
d	*(deh)*	**q**	*(coo)*
e	*(eh)*	**r**	*('eh-reh)*
f	*('eh-feh)*	**rr**	*('eh-rreh)*
g	*(heh)*	**s**	*('eh-seh)*
h	*('ah-cheh)*	**t**	*(teh)*
i	*(ee)*	**u**	*(oo)*
j	*('ho-tah)*	**v**	*(beh-'chee-kah)*
k	*(kah)*	**w**	*(beh-'doh-bleh)*
l	*('eh-leh)*	**x**	*('eh-kees)*
ll*	*('eh-yeh)*	**y**	*(ee-gree-'eh-gah)*
m	*('eh-meh)*	**z**	*('seh-tah)*

* These letters have been cut from the official Spanish alphabet. However, people sometimes refer to them when spelling out a word.

With each bit of new information, you should be growing in self-confidence. However, if you're still having problems with the sounds of Spanish, try listening to the language for a few minutes each day. Radio, audiocassettes, television, plays, and musical performances provide fun and effective ways to help you become familiar with the pronunciation patterns.

Beginner's babble

On page 3 we mentioned a few Spanish words you may already know: now read these popular expressions and practice them aloud.

Excuse me!	**¡Con permiso!** *(kohn pehr-'mee-soh)*
Go ahead!	**¡Pase!** *('pah-seh)*
Good afternoon.	**Buenas tardes.** *('bweh-nahs 'tahr-dehs)*
Good-bye.	**Adiós.** *(ah-dee-'ohs)*
Good evening or Good night.	**Buenas noches.** *('bweh-nahs 'noh-chehs)*
Good morning.	**Buenos días.** *('bweh-nohs 'dee-ahs)*
Hi.	**Hola.** *('oh-lah)*
How are you?	**¿Cómo está?** *('koh-moh eh-'stah)*
How's it going!	**¡Qué tal!** *(keh tahl)*
I'm sorry!	**¡Lo siento!** *(loh see-'ehn-toh)*
May I come in?	**¿Se puede?** *(seh 'pweh-deh)*
Nice to meet you!	**¡Mucho gusto!** *('moo-choh 'goos-toh)*
Please!	**¡Por favor!** *(pohr fah-'bohr)*
Thank you!	**¡Gracias!** *('grah-see·ahs)*
Very well.	**Muy bien.** *('moo·ee 'bee·ehn)*
What's happening?	**¿Qué pasa?** *(keh 'pah-sah)*
What's wrong?	**¿Qué pasó?** *(keh pah-'soh)*
You're welcome!	**¡De nada!** *(deh 'nah-dah)*

¿Cuánto aprendió? *('kwahn-toh ah-prehn-dee-'oh)*

(1) How much did you learn?

Can you fill in the blanks with the appropriate response?

¿Cómo está? *('koh-moh eh-'stah)* ¡ _____ !

¡Gracias! *('grah-see·ahs)* ¡ _____ !

¿Se puede? *(seh 'pweh-deh)* ¡ _____ !

* To check your answers to these practice questions, see the ANSWERS section at the back of the book.

It is important to learn as many friendly exchanges as possible:

I appreciate it!	**¡Muy amable!** *('moo·ee ah-'mah-bleh)*
See you tomorrow!	**¡Hasta mañana!** *('ah-stah mah-'nyah-nah)*
We'll see you!	**¡Nos vemos!** *(nohs 'beh-mohs)*

Check out these "Excuse me" phrases:

Excuse me, if you cough or sneeze.	**¡Perdón!** *(pehr-'dohn)*
Excuse me, if you need someone's attention.	**¡Disculpe!** *(dees-'kool-peh)*

Note: The upside-down exclamation point (¡) and question mark (¿) must be used when you write in Spanish.

Dos culturas *(dohs cool-'too-rahs)*
Two cultures

Friendly greetings in Spanish are used all day long. Being courteous is the key to establishing trust with your patient. Throughout the Spanish-speaking world, a smile and kind word can lead to respect and complete cooperation.

Do you understand?

¿Entiende? *(ehn-tee-'ehn-deh)*

Let's be honest. One of the reasons you may be hesitant to speak Spanish is that you're afraid people might try to answer back and you won't understand them. You fear that all sorts of information will be given in return and you'll be totally confused.

Instead of running for help, search for clues as to what the person in front of you might be saying. If necessary, use your hands and facial expressions to help convey meanings. Then ask them to speak more slowly. Here are some phrases that will help you:

Again.	Otra vez. *('oh-trah behs)*
Another word, please.	**Otra palabra, por favor.** *('oh-trah pah-'lah-brah, pohr fah-'bohr)*
Do you speak English?	**¿Habla inglés?** *(ah-blah een-'glehs)*
How do you say it?	**¿Cómo se dice?** *('koh-moh seh 'dee-seh)*

How do you write it?	**¿Cómo se escribe?** *('koh-moh seh ehs-'kree-beh)*
I don't understand!	**¡No entiendo!** *(noh ehn-tee-'ehn-doh)*
I speak little Spanish.	**Hablo poquito español.** *('ah-bloh poh-'kee-toh ehs-pah-'nyohl)*
More slowly!	**¡Más despacio!** *(mahs dehs-'pah-see·oh)*
Thanks for your patience.	**Gracias por su paciencia.** *('grah-see-ahs pohr soo pah-see-'ehn-see·ah)*
What does it mean?	**¿Qué significa?** *(keh seeg-nee-'fee-kah)*
Word by word!	**¡Palabra por palabra!** *(pah-'lah-brah pohr pah-'lah-brah)*

The key here is not to panic. No doubt, they're having as much trouble understanding you, as you are understanding them. Make an attempt, and between the two of you, some kind of communication will take place.

Simple expressions

Expresiones simples
(ehks-preh-see-'oh-nehs 'seem-plehs)

Beginning conversations usually consist of nothing more than a brief exchange of words. To sound more natural when you speak, try running your words together. Go ahead—express yourself.

Bless you!	**¡Salud!** *(sah-'lood)*
Congratulations!	**¡Felicitaciones!** *(feh-lee-see-tah-see-'oh-nehs)*
Don't worry!	**¡No se preocupe!** *(noh seh preh-oh-'koo-peh)*
Good luck!	**¡Buena suerte!** *('bweh-nah 'swehr-teh)*
Go with God!	**¡Vaya con Dios!** *('bah-yah kohn 'dee-ohs)*
Happy Birthday!	**¡Feliz cumpleaños!** *(feh-'lees koom-pleh-'ah-nyohs)*
Have a nice day!	**¡Que le vaya bien!** *(keh leh 'bah-yah 'bee·ehn)*
Sure!	**¡Claro!** *('klah-roh)*
Take it easy!	**¡Cúidese bien!** *('kwee-deh-seh 'bee·ehn)*
That's great!	**¡Qué bueno!** *(keh 'bweh-noh)*
Very good!	**¡Muy bien!** *('moo·ee 'bee·ehn)*
Welcome!	**¡Bienvenidos!** *(bee-ehn-beh-'nee-dohs)*
Wow!	**¡Caramba!** *(kah-'rahm-bah)*

¡No se olvide!

- To improve your vocabulary, try writing the name of an object on removable stickers and placing them on objects you're trying to learn.

- Notice that the names for people, places, and things have either **el** *(ehl)* or **la** *(lah)* in front. Generally, if the word ends in the letter **o** there's an **el** in front (i.e., **el cuarto** *[ehl 'kwahr-toh]*, **el niño** *[ehl 'nee-nyoh]*). Conversely, if the word ends in an **a** there's a **la** in front (i.e., **la mesa** *[lah 'meh-sah]*, **la persona** *[lah pehr-'soh-nah]*). Some Spanish words are exceptions: **el agua** *(ehl 'ah-gwah)*, **la mano** *(lah 'mah-noh)*, **el sofá** *(ehl soh-'fah)*. But relax. There aren't that many.

- Words not ending in either an **o** or **a** need to be memorized (i.e., **el hospital** *[ehl ohs-pee-'tahl]*, **la mujer** *[lah moo-'hehr]*). In the case of single objects, use **el** and **la** much like the word **"the"** in English: The hospital is big (**El hospital es grande** *[ehl ohs-pee-'tahl ehs 'grahn-deh]*).

- Remember too, that **el** and **la** are used in Spanish to indicate a person's sex. **El doctor** *(ehl dohk-'tohr)* is a male doctor, while **La doctora** *(lah dohk-'toh-rah)* is a female doctor. Here's how we change words to refer to the female gender: **la muchacha** *(lah moo-'chah-chah)*, **la niña** *(lah 'nee-nyah)*, **la enfermera** *(lah ehn-fehr-'meh-rah)*, **la paciente** *(lah pah-see-'ehn-teh)*, **la visitante** *(lah bee-see-'tahn-teh)*.

- Learn how to say "this" and "that" in Spanish.

that	**ese** *('eh-seh)* or **esa** *('eh-sah)*
these	**estos** *('eh-stohs)* or **estas** *('eh-stahs)*
this	**este** *('eh-steh)* or **esta** *('eh-stah)*
those	**esos** *('eh-sohs)* or **esas** *('eh-sahs)*

Vocabulary

El vocabulario *(ehl boh-kah-boo-'lah-ree·oh)*

Now that you're using hand signals, greeting people with simple expressions, and getting a general idea of what people are telling you, it's time to take on the next series of survival words and expressions. These are divided into separate lists for easy practice and review. No doubt you'll hear other words in Spanish that mean the same as the words being introduced here. Vocabulary often differs from one region to the next, but don't worry—these are general enough to be understood by most Hispanics.

Everyday things

Las cosas diarias *(lahs 'koh-sahs dee-'ah-ree·ahs)*

bathroom	**el baño** *(ehl 'bah-nyoh)*
bed	**la cama** *(lah 'kah-mah)*
book	**el libro** *(ehl 'lee-broh)*
chair	**la silla** *(lah 'see-yah)*
desk	**el escritorio** *(ehl ehs-kree-'toh-ree·oh)*
door	**la puerta** *(lah 'pwehr-tah)*
floor	**el piso** *(ehl 'pee-soh)*
food	**la comida** *(lah koh-'mee-dah)*
light	**la luz** *(lah loos)*
office	**la oficina** *(lah oh-fee-'see-nah)*
paper	**el papel** *(ehl pah-'pehl)*
pen	**el lapicero** *(ehl lah-pee-'seh-roh)*
pencil	**el lápiz** *(ehl 'lah-pees)*
room	**el cuarto** *(ehl 'kwahr-toh)*
table	**la mesa** *(lah 'meh-sah)*
trash	**la basura** *(lah bah-'soo-rah)*
water	**el agua** *(ehl 'ah-gwah)*
window	**la ventana** *(lah behn-'tah-nah)*

People

La gente *(lah 'hehn-teh)*

baby	**el bebé** *(ehl beh-'beh)*
boy, child	**el niño** *(ehl 'nee-nyoh)*
doctor	**el doctor** or **el médico** *(ehl dohk-'tohr, ehl 'meh-dee-koh)*
girl	**la niña** *(lah 'nee-nyah)*
in-patient	**el paciente interno** *(ehl pah-see-'ehn-teh een-'tehr-noh)*
man	**el hombre** *(ehl 'ohm-breh)*
nurse	**el enfermero** *(ehl ehn-fehr-'meh-roh)*
outpatient	**el paciente externo** *(ehl pah-see-'ehn-teh ehks-'tehr-noh)*
patient	**el paciente** *(ehl pah-see-'ehn-teh)*
person	**la persona** *(lah pehr-'soh-nah)*
teenager (male)	**el muchacho** *(ehl moo-'chah-choh)*

teenager (female)	**la muchacha** *(lah moo-'chah-chah)*
visitor	**el visitante** *(ehl bee-see-'tahn-teh)*
woman	**la mujer** *(lah moo-'hehr)*

The colors

Los colores *(lohs koh-'loh-rehs)*

black	**negro** *('neh-groh)*
blue	**azul** *(ah-'sool)*
brown	**café** *(kah-'feh)*
gray	**gris** *(grees)*
green	**verde** *('behr-deh)*
orange	**anaranjado** *(ah-nah-rahn-'hah-doh)*
pink	**rosado** *(roh-'sah-doh)*
purple	**morado** *(moh-'rah-doh)*
red	**rojo** *('roh-hoh)*
white	**blanco** *('blahn-koh)*
yellow	**amarillo** *(ah-mah-'ree-yoh)*

¿Cuánto aprendió?

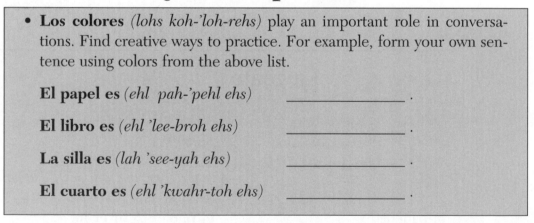

- **Los colores** *(lohs koh-'loh-rehs)* play an important role in conversations. Find creative ways to practice. For example, form your own sentence using colors from the above list.

  El papel es *(ehl pah-'pehl ehs)* _____ .

  El libro es *(ehl 'lee-broh ehs)* _____ .

  La silla es *(lah 'see-yah ehs)* _____ .

  El cuarto es *(ehl 'kwahr-toh ehs)* _____ .

The numbers

Los números *(lohs 'noo-meh-rohs)*

0	**cero** *('seh-roh)*	14	**catorce** *(kah-'tohr-seh)*
1	**uno** *('oo-noh)*	15	**quince** *('keen-seh)*
2	**dos** *(dohs)*	16	**dieciseis** *(dee-ehs-ee-'seh·ees)*
3	**tres** *(trehs)*	17	**diecisiete** *(dee-ehs-ee-see-'eh-teh)*
4	**cuatro** *('kwah-troh)*	18	**dieciocho** *(dee-ehs-ee-'oh-choh)*
5	**cinco** *('seehn-koh)*	19	**diecinueve** *(dee-ehs-ee-noo-'eh-beh)*
6	seis *('seh·ees)*	20	**veinte** *('beh·een-teh)*
7	siete *(see-'eh·teh)*	30	**treinta** *('treh·een-tah)*
8	**ocho** *('oh-choh)*	40	**cuarenta** *(kwah-'rehn-tah)*
9	**nueve** *(noo-'eh-beh)*	50	**cincuenta** *(seen-'kwehn-tah)*
10	**diez** *(dee-'ehs)*	60	**sesenta** *(seh-'sehn-tah)*
11	**once** *('ohn-seh)*	70	**setenta** *(seh-'tehn-tah)*
12	**doce** *('doh-seh)*	80	**ochenta** *(oh-'chehn-tah)*
13	**trece** *('treh-seh)*	90	**noventa** *(noh-'behn-tah)*

For all the numbers in-between just add **"y"** *(ee)*:

21   **veinte y uno** *('beh·een-teh ee 'oo-noh),*
22   **veinte y dos** *('beh·een-teh ee dohs),*
23   **veinte y tres** *('beh·een-teh ee trehs)* . . .

Practice your numbers in Spanish every day. Reciting addresses, phone numbers, and license plate numbers are just a few ways to learn them quickly.

Sooner or later, you'll also need to know how to say the larger numbers in Spanish. They aren't that difficult, so practice aloud:

100	**cien** *(see·'ehn)*
200	**doscientos** *(dohs-see-'ehn-tohs)*
300	**trescientos** *(trehs-see-'ehn-tohs)*
400	**cuatrocientos** *('kwah-troh-see-'ehn-tohs)*
500	**quinientos** *(keen-ee-'ehn-tohs)*
600	**seiscientos** *(seh·ees-see-'ehn-tohs)*
700	**setecientos** *(oh-choh-see-'ehn-tohs)*
800	**ochocientos** *(oh-choh-see-'ehn-tohs)*
900	**novecientos** *(noh-beh-see-'ehn-tohs)*
1000	**mil** *(meel)*
million	**millón** *(mee-'yohn)*
billion	**billón** *(bee-'yohn)*

(2) **¿Cuánto aprendió?**

- Translate the following:

200 rooms _____

80 tables _____

3 nurses _____

75 books _____

10 floors _____

361 babies _____

A beginner's list

appointment	**la cita** (lah 'see-tah)
care	**el cuidado** (ehl kwee-'dah-doh)
emergency	**la emergencia** (lah eh-mehr-'hehn-see·ah)
form	**el formulario** (ehl fohr-moo-'lah-ree·oh)
health	**la salud** (lah sah-'lood)
help	**la ayuda** (lah ah-'yoo-dah)
injury	**la herida** (lah eh-'ree-dah)
medicine	**la medicina** (lah meh-dee-'see-nah)
pain	**el dolor** (ehl doh-'lohr)
sickness	**la enfermedad** (lah ehn-fehr-meh-'dahd)

(3) **¿Cuánto aprendió?**

If you've been following closely, the following expressions should be easy for you to translate into English:

Mucho dolor ('moo-choh doh-'lohr)

_____

Tres formularios (trehs fohr-moo-'lah-ree·ohs)

_____

Herida y enfermedad (eh-'ree-dah ee ehn-fehr-meh-'dad)

_____

Dos citas (dohs 'see-tahs)

_____

Más ayuda (mahs ah-'yoo-dah)

_____

Commands

Las órdenes *(lahs 'ohr-deh-nehs)*

You could not survive in a medical situation without a set of command words that can quickly get the job done. Instead of trying to always speak perfect Spanish, you'll sometimes need to take control of a situation. Try using these phrases, and don't forget to emphasize the letter with the accent mark.

Calm down!	**¡Cálmese!** *('kahl-meh-seh)*
Get undressed.	**¡Desvístase!** *(dehs-'bees-tah-seh)*
Hurry up!	**¡Apúrese!** *(ah-'poo-reh-seh)*
Lie down!	**¡Acuéstese!** *(ah-'kwehs-teh-seh)*
Open your mouth.	**¡Abra la boca!** *('ah-brah lah-boh-kah)*
Sit down!	**¡Siéntese!** *(see-'ehn-teh-seh)*
Stand up!	**¡Levántese!** *(leh-'bahn-teh-seh)*
Take a deep breath.	**¡Aspire profundo!** *(ahs-'pee-reh proh-'foon-doh)*
Turn around!	**¡Voltéese!** *(bohl-'teh-eh-seh)*
Wait!	**¡Espérese!** *(ehs-'peh-reh-seh)*
Wake up!	**¡Despiértese!** *(dehs-pee-'ehr-teh-seh)*

¡No se olvide!

These two words can be used by themselves:

¡Venga! *('behn-gah)*   Come!
¡Vaya! *('bah-yah)*   Go!

The rules

Las reglas *(lahs 'reh-glahs)*

As you begin to describe things in Spanish, you will notice that the words are positioned in reverse order: The descriptive word goes <u>after</u> the word being described. Try to keep this general rule in mind, even though you'll still be understood if you should forget!

The big hospital	**El hospital grande** *(ehl ohs-pee-'tahl 'grahn-deh)*
The blue medicine	**La medicina azul** *(lah meh-dee-'see-nah ah-'sool)*

You'll need to make a few other changes when referring to more than one item. The words **el** and **la,** for example, as discussed on page 9, become **los** and **las,** respectively.

el cuarto *(ehl 'kwahr-toh)*	**los cuartos** *(lohs 'kwahr-tohs)*
la mesa *(lah 'meh-sah)*	**las mesas** *(lahs 'meh-sahs)*
el doctor *(ehl dohk-'tohr)*	**los doctores** *(lohs dohk-'toh-rehs)*
la mujer *(lah moo-'hehr)*	**las mujeres** *(lahs moo-'heh-rehs)*

In addition, not only do all the nouns and adjectives need **s** or **es** to make the sentence plural, but when they are used together, the **o**'s and **a**'s (masculine and feminine) must match as well. This may seem foreign at first, but you'll get the hang of it the more you listen and speak in Spanish.

Many good doctors	**Muchos doctores buenos** *('moo-chohs dohk-'toh-rehs 'bweh-nohs)*
Three white tables	**Tres mesas blancas** *(trehs 'meh-sahs 'blahn-kahs)*
Two yellow rooms	**Dos cuartos amarillos** *(dohs 'kwahr-tohs ah-mah-'ree-yohs)*

¡No se olvide!

- To say "a" in Spanish, use **un** or **una:**

A hospital	**un hospital** *(oon ohs-pee-'tahl)*
A nurse	**una enfermera** *('oo-nah ehn-fehr-'meh-rah)*

- To say some, use **unos** or **unas:**

Some hospitals	**unos hospitales** *('oo-nohs ohs-pee-'tah-lehs)*
Some nurses	**unas enfermeras** *('oo-nahs ehn-fehr-'meh-rahs)*

- Use these words to link everything together:

  y *(ee)*= and   **o** *(oh)* = or   **pero** *('peh-roh)* = but
  Thank you and goodbye!
  ¡Gracias y adiós! *('grah-see·ahs ee ah-dee-'ohs)*

Juan and María	**Juan y María** *(wahn ee mah-'ree-ah)*
money or love	**dinero o amor** *(dee-'neh-roh oh ah-'mohr)*

  Many patients, but few doctors.
  Muchos pacientes, pero pocos doctores.
  ('moo-chohs pah-see-'ehn-tehs, 'peh-roh 'poh-kohs dohk-'toh-rehs)

¡No se olvide!

- Are you ready to form a few phrases? You'll need the following:

for	**para** *('pah-rah)*	**para el paciente** *('pah-rah ehl pah-see-'ehn-teh)*
in, on, at	**en** *(ehn)*	**en el hospital** *(ehn ehl ohs-pee-'tahl)*
of, from	**de** *(deh)*	**de la doctora** *(deh lah dohk-'toh-rah)*
to	**a** *(ah)*	**a la oficina** *(ah lah oh-fee-'see-nah)*
with	**con** *(kohn)*	**con cuidado** *(kohn kwee-'dah-doh)*
without	**sin** *(seen)*	**sin la comida** *(seen lah koh-'mee-dah)*

- There are only two contractions in Spanish:

to the	**al** *(ahl)*	**al baño** *(ahl 'bah-nyoh)*
of the, from the	**del** *(dehl)*	**del paciente** *(dehl pah-see-'ehn-teh)*

Do you have a question?

¿Tiene una pregunta?
(tee-'eh-neh 'oo-nah preh-'goon-tah)

Understanding and using question words in Spanish is crucial in gathering information. The best way to learn how to use question words in a foreign language is to focus on the first word of each sentence, and then try to get a general feel for what the person might be asking. Attempting to translate every word will only lead to frustration.

In a medical situation, it is essential that staff members memorize as many of the following "question words" as they can:

How?	**¿Cómo?** *('koh-moh)*
How many?	**¿Cuántos?** *('kwahn-tohs)*
How much?	**¿Cuánto?** *('kwahn-toh)*
What?	**¿Qué?** *(keh)*
When?	**¿Cuándo?** *('kwahn-doh)*
Where?	**¿Dónde?** *('dohn-deh)*
Which?	**¿Cuál?** *(kwahl)*
Who?	**¿Quién?** *(kee-'ehn)*
Whose?	**¿De quién?** *(deh kee-'ehn)*

¡No se olvide!

- "There is" and "there are" are very simple: in both cases you use **hay** (*'ah·ee*).

There is one boy	**Hay un niño** (*'ah·ee oon 'nee-nyoh*)
There are two girls	**Hay dos niñas** (*'ah·ee dohs 'nee-nyahs*)

- **¿Por qué?** (*pohr keh*) means "why?" in English. To respond, simply repeat the word **porque** because it means "Because."

You soon will discover that daily conversations are filled with common question phrases. Take a look at these examples:

How are you?	**¿Cómo está?** (*'koh-moh eh-'stah*)
How much does it cost?	**¿Cuánto cuesta?** (*'kwahn-toh 'kwehs-tah*)
How old are you?	**¿Cuántos años tiene?** (*'kwahn-tohs 'ah-nyohs tee-'eh-neh*)
What's happening?	**¿Qué pasa?** (*keh 'pah-sah*)
Where are you from?	**¿De dónde es?** (*deh 'dohn-deh ehs*)

④ ¿Cuánto aprendió?

Match the following question with the appropriate response.

¿Qué pasa? (*keh 'pah-sah*)	**Verde.** (*'behr-deh*)
¿Cómo está? (*'koh-moh eh-'stah*)	**Kathy.**
¿Quién es la enfermera? (*kee-'ehn ehs lah ehn-fehr-'meh-rah*)	**Mucha.** (*'moo-chah*)
¿Cuál color? (*kwahl koh-'lohr*)	**Muy bien.** (*'moo-ee bee-'ehn*)
¿Cuántos visitantes? (*'kwahn-tohs bee-see-'tahn-tehs*)	**Nada.** (*'nah-dah*)
¿Cuánta medicina? (*'kwahn-tah meh-dee-'see-nah*)	**Seis.** (*'seh-ees*)

What's your name?

¿Cómo se llama? (*'koh-moh seh 'yah-mah*)

The popular phrase "**¿Cómo se llama?**" (*'koh-moh seh 'yah-mah*) is usually translated to mean "What's your name?" However, you may also hear "**¿Cual es su nombre?**" (*kwahl ehs soo 'nohm-breh*), which means "Which is your name?" You should also know these:

first name	**primer nombre** *(pree-'mehr 'nohm-breh)*
last name	**apellido** *(ah-peh-'yee-doh)*

It really helps if you are able to pronounce people's names correctly, as it makes patients feel much more at ease. Always remember that Spanish is pronounced the way it is written. Also, it is not uncommon for someone in Spain or Latin America to have two last names. Don't get confused. Here's the order:

First name	**Father's last name**	**Mother's last name**
primer nombre	apellido paterno	apellido materno
(pree-'mehr 'nohm-breh)	*(ah-peh-'yee-doh pah-'tehr-noh)*	*(ah-peh-'yee-doh mah-'tehr-noh)*
JUAN CARLOS	**ESPINOZA**	**GARCÍA**
(wahn 'kahr-lohs)	*(ehs-pee-'noh-sah)*	*(gahr-'see-ah)*

Dos culturas

- Not all Hispanic people have two first names, and there is no "middle name" as we know it.
- When a woman marries, she keeps her father's last name, followed by her husband's.
- Learn these abbreviations:

Mr.	**Sr.**	*(seh-'nyohr)*
Mrs.	**Sra.**	*(seh-'nyoh-rah)*
Miss	**Srta.**	*(seh-nyoh-'ree-tah)*

The missing link

Now that you're beginning to form simple questions and answers, it's time to link everything together. To accomplish this, you'll need to understand the difference between **está** and **es.** Both words mean "is," but they're used differently.

The word **está** *(eh-'stah)* expresses a temporary state, condition, or location.

The patient is fine.	**El paciente está bien.**
	(ehl pah-see-'ehn-teh eh-'stah 'bee·ehn)
The patient is in bed.	**El paciente está en la cama.**
	(ehl pah-see-'ehn-teh eh-'stah ehn lah 'kah-mah)

The word **es** expresses an inherent quality or characteristic, including origin and ownership.

The patient is big.	**El paciente es grande.** *(ehl pah-see-'ehn-teh ehs 'grahn-deh)*
The patient is Carlos.	**El paciente es Carlos.** *(ehl pah-see-'ehn-teh ehs 'kahr-lohs)*
The patient is Cuban.	**El paciente es cubano.** *(ehl pah-see-'ehn-teh ehs koo-'bah-noh)*
The patient is my friend.	**El paciente es mi amigo.** *(ehl pah-see'ehn-teh ehs mee ah-'mee-goh)*

Although this might seem confusing, these two wonderful words can really help put your Spanish together. You'll also need to talk about more than one person, place, or thing. To do so, replace **está** with **están,** and **es** with **son.** Don't forget that everything changes when you shift to plurals.

The patient is in the office.	**El paciente está en la oficina.** *(ehl pah-see-'ehn-teh eh-'stah ehn lah oh-fee-'see-nah)*
The patients are in the office.	**Los pacientes están en la oficina.** *(lohs pah-see-'ehn-tehs eh-'stahn ehn lah oh-fee-'see-nah)*
It's a child.	**Es un niño.** *(ehs oon 'nee-nyoh)*
They are children.	**Son niños.** *(sohn 'nee-nyohs)*

The best way to remember how to use these four words correctly is to follow them closely in sentences from real-life situations. Concentrate as you read aloud the following examples:

Dr. Ramírez is a big man.	**El Dr. Ramírez es un hombre grande.** *(ehl dohk-'tohr rah-'mee-rehs ehs oon 'ohm-breh 'grahn-deh)*
Hospitals are very important.	**Los hospitales son muy importantes.** *(lohs ohs-pee-'tah-lehs sohn 'moo·ee eem-pohr-'tahn-tehs)*
How are the patients?	**¿Cómo están los pacientes?** *('koh-moh ehs-'tahn lohs pah-see-'ehn-tehs)*
The medicines are in Chicago.	**Las medicinas están en Chicago.** *(lahs meh-dee-'see-nahs eh-'stahn ehn Chee-'cah-goh)*

The office is in the hospital.	**La oficina está en el hospital.** *(lah oh-fee-'see-nah eh-'stah ehn ehl ohs-pee-'tahl)*
When is the appointment?	**¿Cuándo es la cita?** *('kwahn-doh ehs lah 'see-tah)*
Where is the nurse?	**¿Dónde está la enfermera?** *('dohn-deh eh-'stah lah ehn-fehr-'meh-rah)*
Who are the doctors?	**¿Quiénes son los doctores?** *(kee-'eh-nehs sohn lohs dohk-'toh-rehs)*

To say "I am" and "We are" in Spanish, you must also learn the two different forms. **Estoy** *(eh-'stoh·ee)* and **Estamos** *(eh-'stah-mohs)* refer to the location or condition of a single person, place, or thing. **Soy** and **Somos** *('soh-mohs)* are used with everything else.

I am in the house.	**Estoy en la casa.** *(eh-'stoh·ee ehn lah 'kah-sah)*
I am well.	**Estoy bien.** *(eh-'stoh·ee 'bee·ehn)*
We are in the hospital.	**Estamos en el hospital.** *(eh-'stah-mohs ehn ehl ohs-pee-'tahl)*
We are sick.	**Estamos enfermos.** *(eh-'stah-mohs ehn-'fehr-mohs)*
I am Juan.	**Soy Juan.** *('soh·ee)*
I am a visitor.	**Soy un visitante.** *('soh·ee oon bee-see-'tahn-teh)*
We are Cuban.	**Somos cubanos.** *('soh-mohs koo-'bah-nohs)*
We are tall.	**Somos altos.** *('soh-mohs 'ahl-tohs)*

You also may hear people use the words **estás** or **eres**, which are the informal ways of saying "you" (**tú**). The "you" (**usted**) we are using in this book has a polite and respectful connotation, and is appropriate for communication between the health-care provider and the patient. The informal "you" is **tú**; it is used among friends and acquaintances, and requires additional verbal conjugation. For these reasons, **tú** has been left out. Let us see now the complete present tense of **estar** and **ser**.

TO BE	ESTAR *(eh-'stahr)*	SER *(sehr)*
I'm	estoy *(eh-'stoh·ee)*	soy *('soh·ee)*
you're, he's, she's, it's	está *(eh-'stah)*	es *(ehs)*
they're, you (plural) are	están *(eh-'stahn)*	son *(sohn)*
we're	estamos *(eh-'stah-mohs)*	somos *('soh-mohs)*

$\left(5 \right)$ ## ¿Cuánto aprendió?

Match the question with the appropriate answer.

¿Quiénes son? *(kee-'eh-nehs sohn)*

¿Dónde está? *('dohn-deh eh-'stah)*

¿Qué medicinas son blancas?
(keh meh-dee-'see-nahs sohn 'blahn-kahs)

¿Cuánta agua hay en el baño?
('kwahn-tah 'ah-gwah ah-ee ehn ehl 'bah-nyoh)

¿Qué comida es buena?
(keh koh-mee-dah ehs 'bweh-nah)

¿Cuántas camas hay en el hospital?
('kwahn-tahs 'kah-mahs ah-ee ehn ehl ohs-pee-'tahl)

Mucha. *('moo-chah)*

250. *(dohs-see-'ehn-tahs seen-'kwehn-tah)*

Estoy en el cuarto.
(eh-'stoh·ee ehn ehl 'kwahr-toh)

Pizza.

Somos enfermeros.
('soh-mohs ehn-fehr-'meh-rohs)

Las aspirinas.
(lahs ahs-pee-'ree-nahs)

Do you have problems?

¿Tiene problemas? *(tee-'eh-neh proh-'bleh-mahs)*

Another common linking verb is **tener,** which means "to have." You will need to use this word a lot as a health care professional. Although we'll be discussing **tener** in more detail later, here are the basic forms to get you started:

I have	**tengo** *('tehn-goh)*
you have, she has, he has, it has	**tiene** *(tee-'eh-neh)*
they have, you (plural) have	**tienen** *(tee-'eh-nehn)*
we have	**tenemos** *(teh-'neh-mohs)*

To practice, read these simple sentences aloud:

I have a lot of pain.	**Tengo mucho dolor.** *('tehn-goh 'moo-choh doh-'lohr)*
The doctor has the medicine.	**El doctor tiene la medicina.** *(ehl dohk-'tohr tee-'eh-neh lah meh-dee-'see-nah)*
The hospitals have many beds.	**Los hospitales tienen muchas camas.** *(lohs ohs-pee-'tah-lehs tee-'eh-nehn 'moo-chahs 'kah-mahs)*
We have an office.	**Tenemos una oficina.** *(teh-'neh-mohs 'oo-nah oh-fee-'see-nah)*

As you can see, the word **tener** (to have) is extremely practical. Also keep in mind that **tener** sometimes is used instead of the verb **estar** to express a temporary condition.

(I am) afraid	**(tengo) miedo** (*mee-'eh-doh*)
(we are) at fault	**(tenemos) la culpa** (*lah 'kool-pah*)
(they are) cold	**(tienen) frío** (*'free-oh*)
(she is) 15 years old	**(tiene) quince años** (*'keen-seh 'ah-nyohs*)
(I am) hot	**(tengo) calor** (*kah-'lohr*)
(they are) hungry	**(tienen) hambre** (*'ahm-breh*)
(he is) sleepy	**(tiene) sueño** (*'sweh-nyoh*)
(we are) thirsty	**(tenemos) sed** (*sehd*)

To say "not" in Spanish, interject the word **no** in front of the verb:

Kathy is a nurse.	**Kathy es una enfermera.**
	(*K. ehs 'oo-nah ehn-fehr-'meh-rah*)
Kathy is not a nurse.	**Kathy no es una enfermera.**
	(*K. noh ehs oo-nah ehn-fehr-'meh-rah*)
I have the paper.	**Tengo el papel.** (*'tehn-goh ehl pah-'pehl*)
I don't have the paper.	**No tengo el papel.** (*noh 'tehn-goh ehl pah-'pehl*)

(6) **¿Cuánto aprendió?**

Read the following story. How much of it can you understand?

Yo soy Roberto. (yoh 'soh·ee roh-'behr-toh) *Estoy en el hospital.* ('ch-stoh·ee ehn ehl ohs-pee-'tahl) *Tengo un dolor en el estómogo.* ('tehn-goh oon doh-'lohr ehn ehl eh-'stoh-mah-goh) *Hay una enfermera en el cuarto.* ('ah·ee 'oo-nah ehn-fehr-'meh-rah ehn ehl 'kwahr-toh) *Ella tiene la medicina blanca.* ('eh-yah tee-'eh-neh lah meh-dee-'see-nah 'blahn-kah)

Action!

¡Acción! (*ahk-see·'ohn*)

As we begin to express ourselves in Spanish, it becomes obvious that we're limited without verbs or "action words." Although **estar, ser,** and **tener** are extremely useful, they do not express action. Learning Spanish verbs will allow us to talk about what's going on in the hospital.

Fortunately, action words are easy to use. The best method is to first learn the basic forms, then practice them as parts of common expressions and commands. We'll acquire our action words through short practical phrases, and then use them in various forms as parts of our work-related comments and questions.

Let's open with a brief list of helpful beginning verbs. Please notice that Spanish action words end in the letters **ar, er,** or **ir.**

to drive	**manejar** *(mah-neh-'hahr)*
to eat	**comer** *(koh-'mehr)*
to go	**ir** *(eer)*
to read	**leer** *(lee-'ehr)*
to run	**correr** *(koh-'rrehr)*
to sleep	**dormir** *(dohr-'meer)*
to speak	**hablar** *(ah-'blahr)*
to write	**escribir** *(ehs-kree-'beer)*
to work	**trabajar** *(trah-bah-'hahr)*

Notice what happens when you place a verb after the following pattern: **tiene que** *(tee-'eh-neh keh)* (you have to, she/he has to):

You have to read the book.	**Tiene que leer el libro.**
	(tee-'eh-neh keh leh-'ehr ehl 'lee-broh)
You have to speak Spanish.	**Tiene que hablar español.**
	(tee-'eh-neh keh ah-'blahr ehs-pah-'nyohl)

Since we already have worked with the verb **tener** *(teh-'nehr)* (to have), you should have no trouble with **tener que** *(teh-'nehr keh)* (to have to). Here are the forms:

I have to	**tengo que** *('tehn-goh keh)*
you have to, she/he has to	**tiene que** *(tee-'eh-neh keh)*
you (plural)/they have to	**tienen que** *(tee-'eh-nehn keh)*
we have to	**tenemos que** *(teh-'neh-mohs keh)*

This is only one of the many patterns you'll encounter in this book. Soon you'll be introduced to a variety of verb phrases that target specific areas of medical care. Each new phrase will show how action words can be altered to communicate different messages.

In Spanish, one of the easiest verb forms to use is the Present Progressive. It refers to actions that are taking place at this moment. Simply combine the four forms of **estar** with any verb. Notice how the ending of the verb changes slightly.

eat	**comer** *(koh-'mehr)*
He is eating well.	**Está comiendo bien.**
	(eh-'stah koh-mee-'ehn-doh bee·'ehn)

gain	**ganar** *(gah-'nahr)*
They are gaining weight.	**Están ganando peso.**
	(eh-'stahn gah-'nahn-doh 'peh-soh)
leave	**salir** *(sah-'leer)*
We are leaving now.	**Estamos saliendo ahora.**
	(eh-'stah-mohs sah-lee-'ehn-doh ah-'oh-rah)

The **ndo** is similar to our "ing" ending. The **ar** verbs become **ando** while the **er** and **ir** verbs become **iendo.** Look at the first example and create "ing" phrases with the verbs that follow.

to cook	**cocinar** *(koh-see-'nahr)*
cooking	**cocinando** *(koh-see-'nahn-do)*
They are cooking	**Están cocinando sin sal.**
without salt.	*(eh-'stahn koh-see-'nahn-doh seen sahl)*
to cure	**curar** *(koo-'rahr)*
curing	**curando** *(koo-'rahn-doh)*

_____. _____.

to find	**encontrar** *(ehn-kohn-'trahr)*
finding	**encontrando** *(ehn-kohn-'trahn-doh)*

_____. _____.

to function	**funcionar** *(foon-see-oh-'nahr)*
functioning	**funcionando** *(foon-see-oh-'nahn-doh)*

_____. _____.

to gain	**ganar** *(gah-'nahr)*
gaining	**ganando** *(gah-'nahn-doh)*

_____. _____.

to lose	**perder** *(pehr-'dehr)*
losing	**perdiendo** *(pehr-dee-'ehn-doh)*

_____. _____.

to measure	**medir** *(meh-'deer)*
measuring	**midiendo** *(me-dee-'ehn-doh)*

_____. _____.

to follow	**seguir** *(seh-'geer)*
following	**siguiendo** *(see-ghee-'ehn-doh)*

_____. _____.

| to observe | **observar** *(ohb-sehr-'bahr)* |
| observing | **observando** *(ohb-sehr-'bahn-doh)* |

_____.

| to recuperate | **recuperar** *(reh-koo-peh-'rahr)* |
| recuperating | **recuperando** *(reh-koo-peh-'rahn-doh)* |

_____.

¡No se olvide!

A couple of verbs change in spelling when you add the **ndo** ending. Study this example:

to follow   **seguir** *(seh-'geer)*   Are you following the instructions?
¿Está siguiendo las instrucciones?
(eh-'stah see-gee-'ehn-doh lahs een-strook-see·'oh-nehs)

The majority of verbs used in medicine are similar to English. Look at these examples:

consult	**consultar** *(kohn-sool-'tahr)*
control	**controlar** *(kohn-troh-'lahr)*
disinfect	**desinfectar** *(dehs-een-fehk-'tahr)*
evaluate	**evaluar** *(eh-bah-loo-'ahr)*
recommend	**recomendar** *(reh-koh-mehn-'dahr)*

By now you may have noticed that some action words include the word **se,** which has many meanings. Here are some important action words in which **se** indicates that the action is self-directed (e.g., **lavar** means "to wash" but **lavarse** means "to wash oneself").

to bathe oneself	**bañarse** *(bah-'nyahr-seh)*
to brush oneself	**cepillarse** *(seh-pee-'yahr-seh)*
to fall down	**caerse** *(kah-'ehr-seh)*
to get better	**mejorarse** *(meh-hoh-'rahr-seh)*
to get dressed	**vestirse** *(behs-'teer-seh)*
to get sick	**enfermarse** *(ehn-fehr-'mahr-seh)*
to remember	**acordarse** *(ah-kohr-'dahr-seh)*

¿Cuánto aprendió?

- Practice the following dialogue with a friend.

  "Hola, Doctora Smith. ¿Cómo está?"
  ('oh-lah, dohk-'toh-rah S. 'koh-moh eh-'stah)

  "Buenos días, Francisco. Estoy bien. ¿Qué pasa?" *('bweh-nohs 'dee-ahs, frahn-'sees-koh. eh-'stoh·ee bee·'ehn. 'keh 'pah-sah)*

  "Mi amigo está en el hospital. Tiene muchos problemas."
  (mee ah-'mee-goh eh-'stah ehn ehl ohs-pee-'tahl. tee-'eh-neh 'moo-chohs proh-'bleh-mahs)

- If you were asked the following questions, what would you say?

  ¿Cómo se llama? *('koh-moh seh 'yah-mah)*

  ¿Cuántos años tiene? *('kwahn-tohs 'an-nyohs tee-'eh-neh)*

  ¿Quién es su amigo? *(kee-'ehn ehs soo ah-'mee-goh)*

  ¿Cómo está? *('koh-moh eh-'stah)*

  ¿De qué color es el hospital? *(deh keh koh-'lohr ehs ehl ohs-pee-'tahl)*

  ¿Tiene mucho dolor? *(tee-'eh-neh 'moo-choh doh-'lohr)*

  ¿Tiene que trabajar? *(tee-'eh-neh keh trah-bah-'hahr)*

Chapter Two

Capítulo Dos
(kah-'pee-too-loh dohs)

The Patient

El or La Paciente

(ehl/lah pah-see-'ehn-teh)

The head

La cabeza (lah kah-'beh-sah)

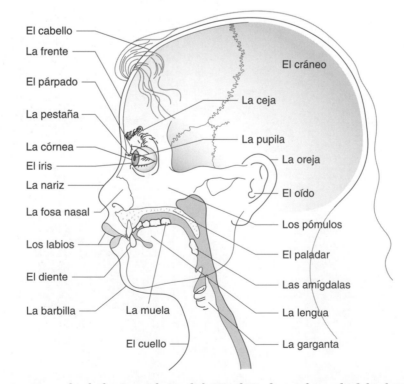

El cabello

La frente

El párpado

La pestaña

La córnea

El iris

La nariz

La fosa nasal

Los labios

El diente

La barbilla

La muela

El cuello

El cráneo

La ceja

La pupila

La oreja

El oído

Los pómulos

El paladar

Las amígdalas

La lengua

La garganta

For pronunciation, check the Spanish-English Word Finder at the end of this book.

The body

El cuerpo *(ehl 'kwehr-poh)*

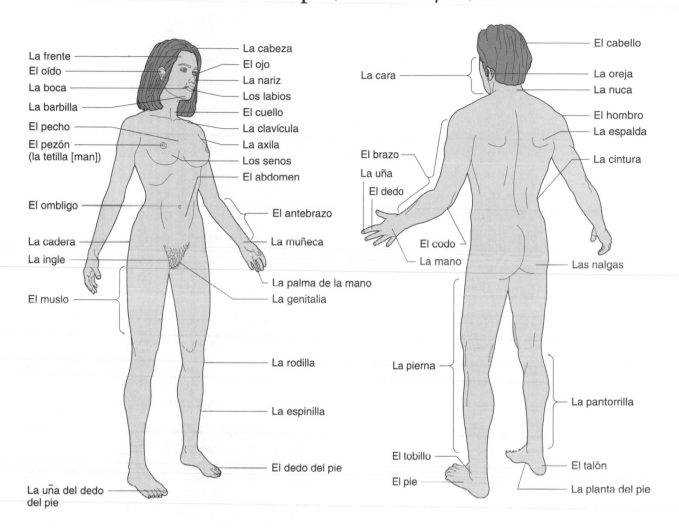

La frente — La cabeza
El oído — El ojo
La boca — La nariz
La barbilla — Los labios
 — El cuello
El pecho — La clavícula
El pezón — La axila
(la tetilla [man]) — Los senos
 — El abdomen
El ombligo
 — El antebrazo
La cadera — La muñeca
La ingle
El muslo — La palma de la mano
 — La genitalia
 — La rodilla
 — La espinilla
 — El dedo del pie
La uña del dedo
del pie

La cara — El cabello
 — La oreja
 — La nuca
 — El hombro
 — La espalda
El brazo — La cintura
La uña
El dedo
 — El codo
 — La mano — Las nalgas
La pierna
 — La pantorrilla
El tobillo — El talón
El pie — La planta del pie

Move the . . .	**Mueva** *(moo-'eh-bah)* . . .
Touch the . . .	**Toque** *('toh-keh)* . . .
Point to the . . .	**Señale** *(seh-'nyah-leh)* . . .

IMPORTANT: Learn these phrases as soon as you can.

Does it hurt?	**¿Le duele?** *(leh 'dweh-leh)*
Do they hurt?	**¿Le duelen?** *(leh 'dweh-lehn)*
It hurts!	**¡Me duele!** *(me 'dweh-leh)*
They hurt!	**¡Me duelen!** *(me 'dweh-lehn)*

It's the . . .

blood	**la sangre** *(lah 'sahn-greh)*
bone	**el hueso** *(ehl 'hweh-soh)*
skin	**la piel** *(lah pee-'ehl)*
muscle	**el músculo** *(ehl 'moos-koo-loh)*
nerve	**el nervio** *(ehl 'nehr-vee-oh)*
spine	**el espinazo** *(ehl ehs-pee-'nah-soh)*

(7) ¿Cuánto aprendió?

Can you translate these sentences?

Me duele la cabeza.	**Son los brazos.**
¿Le duelen los pies?	**La nariz está en la cara.**
¿Qué le duele?	**Hay muchos dientes en la boca.**
No me duelen los ojos.	**No tiene diez dedos.**

Who is it?

¿Quién es? *(kee-'ehn ehs)*

Now that you know what hurts, let's find out who needs your assistance. Some of the first words you'll hear as a beginner are those that designate the "who" of a sentence.

I **yo** *(yoh)*
You **usted** *(oo-'stehd)*
She **ella** *('eh-yah)*
They, feminine **ellas** *('eh-yahs)*

We **nosotros** *(noh-'soh-trohs)*
You, plural **ustedes** *(oo-'steh-dehs)*
He **él** *(ehl)*
They, masculine **ellos** *('eh-yohs)*

This is how they might appear in conversation:

He has big feet.	**Él tiene pies grandes.** *(ehl tee-'eh-neh 'pee-ehs 'grahn-dehs)*
How are you?	**¿Cómo está usted?** *('koh-moh eh-'stah oo-'stehd)*
I have blue eyes.	**Yo tengo ojos azules.** *(yoh 'tehn-goh 'oh-hohs ah-'soo-lehs)*
They are the patients.	**Ellos son los pacientes.** *('eh-yohs sohn lohs pah-see-'ehn-tehs)*
We are doctors.	**Nosotros somos doctores.** *(noh-'soh-trohs 'soh-mohs dohk-'toh-rehs)*
Where is she?	**¿Dónde está ella?** *('dohn-deh eh-'stah 'eh-yah)*

¡No se olvide!

- **Nosotras** *(noh-'soh-trahs)* is "We" feminine: We are female doctors **Nosotras somos doctoras** *(noh-'soh-trahs 'soh-mohs dohk-'toh-rahs).*

- You don't have to use the subject pronouns in every sentence. It's usually understood who's involved: **Nosotros somos** *(noh-'soh-trohs 'soh-mohs)* and **Somos** *('soh-mohs)* both mean "We are."

- **¿Y usted?** *(ee oo-'stehd)* "And you?" is a great expression. **¿Cómo está?** *('koh-moh eh-'stah)* "How are you?" **Bien. ¿Y usted?** *(bee·'ehn ee oo-'stehd)* "Fine. And you?"

Whose is it?

¿De quién es? *(deh kee-'ehn ehs)*

"¿De quién es?" *(deh kee-'ehn ehs)* means "Whose is it?" To answer this question in Spanish, you're going to need three new words. Look closely how each one functions:

It's my doctor.	**Es <u>mi</u> doctor.** *(ehs mee dohk-'tohr)*
It's your, his, her, or their doctor.	**Es <u>su</u> doctor.** *(ehs soo dohk-'tohr)*
It's our doctor.	**Es <u>nuestro</u> doctor.** *(ehs noo-'ehs-troh dohk-'tohr)*

Notice what happens when you talk about more than one.

mi doctor *(mee dohk-'tohr)*
mis doctores *(mees dohk-'toh-rehs)*
su doctor *(soo dohk-'tohr)*
sus doctores *(soos dohk-'toh-rehs)*
nuestro doctor *(noo-'ehs-troh dohk-'tohr)*
nuestros doctores *(noo-'ehs-trohs dohk-'toh-rehs)*

And don't forget the change when you refer to the feminine.

Our female friend	**nuestra amiga** *(noo-'ehs-trah ah-'mee-gah)*

Now try these other possessive words:

mine	**mío** *('mee-oh)*
yours, his, hers, or theirs.	**suyo** *('soo-yoh)*

If something "belongs to" someone else, use **de**:

It's Mary's.	**Es de María.** *(ehs deh mah-'ree-ah)*
It's the hospital's.	**Es del hospital.** *(ehs dehl ohs-pee-'tahl)*
It's his.	**Es de él.** *(ehs deh ehl)*

$\left(8 \right)$ **¿Cuánto aprendió?**

> Fill in the missing word.
>
> **Yo tengo <u>mi</u> papel.**
>
> **Sr. Pérez tiene _____ papel.**
>
> **Los niños tienen _____ papel.**
>
> **Nosotros tenemos _____ papel.**

A description, please

Una descripción, por favor.
('oo-nah dehs-kreep-see-'ohn, pohr fah-'bohr)

As you begin to describe people, places, and things in Spanish, it is important to add these words to your vocabulary. As you read this list, think of all the comments you can make about your patients.

alive	**vivo** *('bee-boh)*
asleep	**dormido** *(dohr-'mee-doh)*
available	**disponible** *(dees-poh-'neeb-leh)*
awake	**despierto** *(dehs-pee-'ehr-toh)*
bad	**malo** *('mah-loh)*
better	**mejor** *(meh-'hohr)*
big	**grande** *('grahn-deh)*
clean	**limpio** *('leem-pee-oh)*
cold	**frío** *('free-oh)*
correct	**correcto** *(koh-'rrehk-toh)*
crazy	**loco** *('loh-koh)*
dangerous	**peligroso** *(peh-lee-'groh-soh)*
dead	**muerto** *('mwehr-toh)*
deep	**profundo** *(proh-'foon-doh)*
difficult	**difícil** *(dee-'fee-seel)*
dirty	**sucio** *('soo-see·oh)*
dry	**seco** *('seh-koh)*
dull (edge)	**romo** *('roh-moh)*
dull (sound)	**sordo** *('sohr-doh)*
easy	**fácil** *('fah-seel)*
empty	**vacío** *(bah-'see-oh)*
fast	**rápido** *('rah-pee-doh)*

fat	**gordo** *('gohr-doh)*
full	**lleno** *('yeh-noh)*
good	**bueno** *('bweh-noh)*
hard	**duro** *('doo-roh)*
hot	**caliente** *(kah-lee-'ehn-teh)*
new	**nuevo** *(noo-eh-boh)*
old	**viejo** *(bee-'eh-hoh)*
older	**mayor** *(mah-'yohr)*
poor	**pobre** *('poh-breh)*
pretty	**bonito** *(boh-'nee-toh)*
quiet	**tranquilo** *(trahn-'kee-loh)*
restless	**inquieto** *(een-kee-'eh-toh)*
rich	**rico** *('ree-koh)*
safe	**seguro** *(seh-'goo-roh)*
sane	**cuerdo** *('kwehr-doh)*
severe	**severo** *(seh-'beh-roh)*
sharp (edge)	**afilado** *(ah-fee-'lah-doh)*
sharp (sound)	**agudo** *(ah-'goo-doh)*
short in height	**bajo** *('bah-hoh)*, in length **corto** *('kohr-toh)*
sick	**enfermo** *(ehn-'fehr-moh)*
slow	**lento** *('lehn-toh)*
small	**chico** *('chee-koh)*
soft	**blando** *('blahn-doh)*
strong	**fuerte** *('fwehr-teh)*
tall	**alto** *('ahl-toh)*
thick	**grueso** *(groo-'eh-soh)*
thin	**delgado** *(dehl-'gah-doh)*
ugly	**feo** *('feh-oh)*
weak	**débil** *(deh-'beel)*
well	**bien** *(bee·'ehn)*
wet	**mojado** *(moh-'hah-doh)*
worse	**peor** *(peh-'ohr)*
wrong	**equivocado** *(eh-kee-boh-'kah-doh)*
young	**joven** *('hoh-behn)*
younger	**menor** *(meh-'nohr)*

Notice how many descriptive words end in the same letters.

bent	**doblado** *(doh-'blah-doh)*
busy	**ocupado** *(oh-koo-'pah-doh)*
closed	**cerrado** *(seh-'rrah-doh)*
comfortable	**cómodo** *('koh-moh-doh)*

private	**privado** *(pree-'bah-doh)*
prohibited	**prohibido** *(proh-ee-'bee-doh)*
watery	**aguado** *(ah-'gwah-doh)*

To describe your actions in Spanish, try some of these:

completely	**completamente** *(kohm-pleh-tah-'mehn-teh)*
immediately	**inmediatamente** *(een-meh-dee-ah-tah-'mehn-teh)*
normally	**normalmente** *(nohr-mahl-'mehn-teh)*
quickly	**rápidamente** *(rah-pee-dah-'mehn-teh)*
slowly	**lentamente** *(lehn-tah-'mehn-teh)*

Don't forget the **o** at the end of a word has to change to **a** when you're referring to the feminine.

El muchacho es alto. *(ehl moo-'chah-choh ehs 'ahl-toh)*
La muchacha es alta. *(lah moo-'chah-chah ehs 'ahl-tah)*
El cuarto está lleno. *(ehl 'kwahr-toh eh-'stah 'yeh-noh)*
La oficina está llena. *(lah oh-fee-'see-nah eh-'stah 'yeh-nah)*

Also, remember to combine your words in reverse order:

It's a new house.	**Es una casa nueva.**
	(ehs 'oo-nah 'kah-sah noo-'eh-bah)

Finally, notice what you can do with these little words: I'm—**Estoy** *(eh-'stoh·ee)*

I'm sick	estoy **enfermo**
	(ehn-'fehr-moh)
I'm sicker	estoy **más enfermo**
	(mahs ehn-'fehr-moh)
I'm as sick as	estoy **tan enfermo como**
	(tahn ehn-'fehr-moh 'koh-moh)

These descriptions are easy to recall (but check out the stresses):

general *(heh-neh-'rahl)*
gradual *(grah-doo-'ahl)*
local *(loh-'kahl)*
normal *(nohr-'mahl)*
simple *('seem-pleh)*

(9) ### ¿Cuánto aprendió?

- Practice using your new vocabulary by reading and translating these sentences:

  Ella es alta y él es bajo.
  ('eh-yah ehs 'ahl-tah ee ehl ehs 'bah-ho)

  Los niños están dormidos.
  (lohs 'nee-nyohs eh-'stahn dohr-'mee-dohs)

  No somos muy ricos.
  (noh 'soh-mohs 'moo·ee 'ree-kohs)

  El doctor es viejo y delgado.
  (ehl dohk-'tohr ehs bee-'eh-hoh ee dehl-'gah-doh)

  ¿Dónde está el agua caliente?
  ('dohn-deh eh-'stah ehl 'ah-gwah cah-lee-'ehn-teh)

- Complete these sentences with the words you just learned.

  María es . . . *(mah-'ree-ah ehs)*

  as sick as her brother _____

  sick _____

  sicker _____

  El paciente es muy . . . *(ehl pah-see-'ehn-teh ehs 'moo·ee)*

  fat _____

  weak _____

  young _____

  Ustedes son . . . *(oo-'steh-dehs sohn)*

  older _____

  pretty _____

  thin _____

More important words

Más palabras importantes
(mahs pah-'lah-brahs eem-pohr-'tahn-tehs)

Let's learn some more practical terms that can be used as single-word responses. Add some of these to your vocabulary, and you'll begin to communicate:

all	**todo** *('toh-doh)*
almost	**casi** *('kah-see)*
alone	**solo** *('soh-loh)*
also	**también** *(tahm-bee-'ehn)*

different	**diferente** *(dee-feh-'rehn-teh)*
enough	**bastante** *(bah-'stahn-teh)*
few	**pocos** *(poh-kohs)*
first	**primero** *(pree-'meh-roh)*
last	**último** *('ool-tee-moh)*
less	**menos** *('meh-nohs)*
many	**muchos** *('moo-chohs)*
more	**más** *(mahs)*
next	**siguiente** *(see-gee-'ehn-teh)*
none	**ninguno** *(neen-'goo-noh)*
nothing	**nada** *('nah-dah)*
same	**mismo** *('mees-moh)*
some	**algunos** *(ahl-'goo-nohs)*
something	**algo** *('ahl-goh)*
too much	**demasiado** *(deh-mah-see-'ah-doh)*
very	**muy** *('moo·ee)*

They aren't the same patients.
No son los mismos pacientes.
(noh 'soh-mohs lohs 'mees-mohs pah-see-'ehn-tehs)

Something is in the stomach.
Algo está en el estómago.
('ahl-goh eh-'stah ehn ehl ehs-'toh-mah-goh)

There's enough medicine, too.
Hay bastante medicina, también.
('ah·ee bah-'stahn-teh meh-dee-'see-nah, tahm-bee-'ehn)

More action

Más acción *(mahs ahk-see·'ohn)*

Are you ready to expand your list of action words? Warm up by reviewing the following pattern.

Tengo que comer y dormir en el cuarto.
('tehn-goh keh koh-'mehr ee dohr-'meer ehn ehl 'kwahr-toh)
Tiene que escribir y leer en la mesa.
(tee-'eh-neh keh ehs-kree-'beer ee leh-'ehr ehn lah 'meh-sah)
Tienen que ir a la cita.
(tee-'eh-'nehn keh eer ah lah 'see-tah)
Tenemos que hablar más español en el hospital.
(teh-'neh-mohs keh ah-'blahr mahs ehs-pah-'nyohl ehn ehl ohs-pee-'tahl)

Now take a look at more survival action words.

to answer	**contestar** *(kohn-tehs-'tahr)*
to ask	**preguntar** *(preh-goon-'tahr)*
to come	**venir** *(beh-'neer)*
to do/make	**hacer** *(ah-'sehr)*
to leave	**salir** *(sah-'leer)*
to return	**regresar** *(reh-greh-'sahr)*
to say	**decir** *(deh-'seer)*
to understand	**entender** *(ehn-tehn-'dehr)*
to walk	**caminar** *(kah-mee-'nahr)*

The following verb is very important in helping a patient. Learn it and then combine it with a different set of words to create another pattern.

TO NEED	**NECESITAR** *(neh-seh-see-'tahr)*
I need	**necesito** *(neh-seh-'see-toh)*
I need to ask	**necesito preguntar**
	(neh-seh-'see-toh preh-goon-'tahr)
you need, he/she needs	**necesita** *(neh-seh-'see-tah)*
you/need, he/she needs to walk	**necesita caminar**
	(neh-seh-'see-tah kah-mee-'nahr)
you (plural) or they need	**necesitan** *(neh-seh-'see-tahn)*
you (plural), they need to return	**necesitan regresar**
	(neh-seh-'see-tahn reh-greh-'sahr)
we need	**necesitamos** *(neh-seh-see-'tah-mohs)*
we need to leave	**necesitamos salir**
	(neh-seh-see-'tah-mohs sah-'leer)

The verb **volver** *(bohl-'behr)* also means "to return." As in most languages, there is always more than one way to say the same thing.

By putting "No" in front of your verbs, you can tell "not to do" something.

no returning	**no regresar, no volver**
	(noh reh-greh-'sahr, noh bohl-'behr)
no running	**no correr** *(noh koh-'rrehr)*
no leaving	**no salir** *(noh sah-'leer)*

These words mean almost the same as **necesita.** Learn them:

necessary	**necesario** *(neh-seh-'sah-ree·oh)*
	Es necesario preguntar.
	(ehs neh-seh-'sah-ree·oh preh-goon-'tahr)
must	**debe** *('deh-beh)*
	Debe regresar.
	('deh-beh reh-greh-'sahr)

(10)   **¿Cuánto aprendió?**

Practice **necesitar** with your new vocabulary. Read the following aloud and translate the sentences.

Necesito una cita.
(neh-seh-'see-tah 'oo-nah 'see-tah)
¿Necesita usted la medicina?
(neh-seh-'see-tah oo-'stehd lah meh-dee-'see-nah)
Margarita y yo necesitamos camas.
(mahr-gah-'ree-tah ee yoh neh-seh-see-'tah-mohs 'kah-mahs)

Family

La familia *(lah fah-'mee-lee-ah)*

As you build conversations with your Latino patients, be aware of family and friends who lend their support and encouragement. Many of them will be relatives, **parientes** *(pah-ree-'ehn-tehs)*, who need to be greeted and kept informed. The names for family members in Spanish can be memorized easily by reading aloud the following words:

It's my . . .	**Es mi** *(ehs mee)* . . .
adopted child	**niño adoptado/niña adoptada** *('neen-yoh ah-dohp-'tah-doh/ 'neen-yah ah-dohp-'tah-dah)*
aunt	**tía** *('tee-ah)*
boyfriend	**novio** *('noh-bee·oh)*
brother	**hermano** *(ehr-'mah-noh)*
brother-in-law	**cuñado** *(koo-'nyah-doh)*
cousin	**primo** *('pree-moh)*
daughter	**hija** *('ee-hah)*
daughter-in-law	**nuera** *('nweh-rah)*
dependent	**dependiente** *(deh-pehn-dee-'ehn-teh)*
father	**padre** *('pah-dreh)*
father-in-law	**suegro** *('sweh-groh)*
foster child	**ahijado/ahijada** *(ah-ee-'hah-doh/ah-ee-'hah-dah)*
girlfriend	**novia** *(noh-'bee·ah)*
granddaughter	**nieta** *(nee-'eh-tah)*
grandfather	**abuelo** *(ah-'bweh-loh)*
grandmother	**abuela** *(ah-'bweh-lah)*

grandson	**nieto** (*nee-'eh-toh*)
guardian	**guardián** (*goo-ahr-dee-'ahn*)
husband	**esposo** (*ehs-'poh-soh*)
mother	**madre** (*'mah-dreh*)
mother-in-law	**suegra** (*'sweh-grah*)
nephew	**sobrino** (*soh-'bree-noh*)
next of kin	**pariente más cercano**
	(*pah-ree-'ehn-teh mahs sehr-'kah-noh*)
niece	**sobrina** (*soh-'bree-nah*)
sister	**hermana** (*ehr-'mah-nah*)
sister-in-law	**cuñada** (*koo-'nyah-dah*)
son	**hijo** (*'ee-hoh*)
son-in-law	**yerno** (*'yehr-noh*)
stepdaughter	**hijastra** (*ee-'hahs-trah*)
stepfather	**padrastro** (*pah-'drahs-troh*)
stepmother	**madrastra** (*mah-'drahs-trah*)
stepson	**hijastro** (*ee-'hahs-troh*)
uncle	**tío** (*'tee-oh*)
wife	**esposa** (*ehs-'poh-sah*)

For affection, add **-ito** and **-ita** to your words:

grandmother	**abuela** (*ah-'bweh-lah*)
granny	**abuelita** (*ah-bweh-'lee-tah*)
brother	**hermano** (*ehr-'mah-noh*)
little brother	**hermanito** (*ehr-mah-'nee-toh*)
baby	**bebé** (*beh-'beh*)
tiny baby	**bebito** (*beh-'bee-toh*)

Dos culturas

In-laws and godparents, **padrinos** (*pah-'dree-nohs*), are considered important family members and often assist in decision-making.

The extended family may include friends or neighbors who have lent their support to family members in the past. They may also want to be involved in hospital visits or procedures.

Latino families respect the elderly. Older children, too, are given more responsibilities and are treated differently. When dealing with a large family, it is usually a good idea to find out who is in charge.

Now, you're going to need more vocabulary and a few more Spanish skills before you can effectively communicate with non-English speakers.

Begin with these:

youth	**joven** (*'hoh-behn*)
elderly person	**anciano** (*ahn-see-'ah-noh*)
buddy	**compañero** (*kohm-pah-nee-'eh-roh*)
couple	**pareja** (*pah-'reh-hah*)
minor	**menor de edad** (*meh-'nohr deh eh-'dahd*)
partner	**socio** (*'soh-see-oh*)

¿Cuánto aprendió?

Start practicing today by making comments about various family members.

Do you have grandchildren?
¿Tiene usted nietos?
(*tee-'eh-neh oos-'tehd nee-eh-tohs*)

Her son-in-law has to drive.
Su yerno tiene que manejar.
(*soo 'yehr-noh tee-'eh-neh keh mah-neh-'har*)

His sisters are nurses.
Sus hermanas son enfermeras.
(*soos ehr-'mah-nahs sohn ehn-fehr-'meh-rahs*)

My son is in his room.
Mi hijo está en su cuarto.
(*mee 'ee-hoh ehs-'tah ehn soo 'kwahr-toh*)

Point to your girlfriend.
Señale a su novia.
(*seh-'nyah-leh ah soo 'noh-bee-ah*)

Our grandmother needs to return.
Nuestra abuela necesita regresar.
(*noo-'ehs-trah ah-'bweh-lah neh-seh-'see-tah*)

Who is your father?
¿Quién es su padre?
(*kee-'ehn ehs soo 'pah-dreh*)

Chapter Three

Capítulo Tres
(kah-'pee-too-loh trehs)

Admissions

Admisiones
(ahd-mee-see·'oh-nehs)

The Espinozas have been in this country for less than a year and they've suddenly required the services of a medical facility. There are six members of the Espinoza family. Juan Espinoza and his wife María are the parents of two young children, Margarita and Miguel. Juan's father, Carlos, lives next door, and María's grandmother, Guadalupe, is in a skilled nursing home nearby.

Each family member has a unique problem and needs to be followed from admissions through release. All of the words and expressions used to handle these cases have either already been introduced or will appear in the remaining text. Begin by greeting the Espinozas as they walk through the front doors of your medical facility.

Greetings

Saludos *(sah-'loo-dohs)*

Do you speak English?	**¿Habla inglés?** *('ah-blah een-'glehs)*
Good afternoon. What's going on?	**Buenas tardes. ¿Qué pasa?** *('bweh-nahs 'tahr-dehs keh 'pah-sah)*
Good evening. How's it going?	**Buenas noches. ¿Qué tal?** *('bweh-nahs 'noh-chehs keh tahl)*
Good morning. How are you?	**Buenos días. ¿Cómo está?** *('bweh-nohs 'dee-ahs 'koh-moh eh-'stah)*

Come.	**Venga.** *('behn-gah)*
Go with the nurse.	**Vaya con la enfermera.** *('bah-yah kohn lah ehn-fehr-'meh-rah)*
Sit on the chair.	**Siéntese en la silla.** *(see-'ehn-teh-seh ehn lah 'see-yah)*
Wait in the room.	**Espere en el cuarto.** *(ehs-'peh-reh ehn ehl 'kwahr-toh)*

As long as we're telling the Espinoza family what to do, let's add a few more commands to your vocabulary.

Bring	**traiga** *('trah·ee-gah)*
Bring the water.	**Traiga el agua.** *('trah·ee-gah ehl 'ah-gwah)*
Call	**llame** *('yah-meh)*
Call the doctor.	**Llame al doctor.** *('yah-meh ahl dohk-'tohr)*
Carry	**lleve** *('yeh-beh)*
Carry the baby.	**Lleve el bebé.** *('yeh-beh ehl beh-'beh)*
Get up	**súbase** *('soo-bah-seh)*
Get up on the table.	**Súbase a la mesa.** *('soo-bah-seh ah lah 'meh-sah)*
Sign	**firme** *('feer-meh)*
Sign your name.	**Firme su nombre.** *('feer-meh soo 'nohm-breh)*
Take	**tome** *('toh-meh)*
Take the medicine.	**Tome la medicina.** *('toh-meh lah meh-dee-'see- nah)*
Turn	**dese vuelta** *('deh-seh 'bwehl-tah)*
Turn, please.	**Dese vuelta, por favor.** *('deh-seh 'bwehl-tah pohr fah-'bohr)*

The information

La información *(lah een-fohr-mah-see·'ohn)*

This is the Espinoza's first trip to an American hospital. They're nervous, and they don't speak much English. You're the only one available to walk them through the registration process. Be patient, friendly, and courteous because it's going to take time. Use the expression **¿Cuál es su . . .?** (What is your . . .?) for virtually every question on the registration forms.

What is your . . .?	**¿Cuál es su . . .?** *(kwahl ehs soo)*
address	**dirección** *(dee-rehk-see·'ohn)*
age	**edad** *(eh-'dahd)*
blood type	**tipo de sangre** *('tee-poh deh 'sahn-greh)*
cell phone number	**número de teléfono celular** *('noo-meh-roh deh teh-'leh-foh-noh seh-loo-'lahr)*

date of birth	**fecha de nacimiento** *('feh-chah deh nah-see-mee-'ehn-toh)*
email address	**correo electrónico** *(kohr-'reh-oh eh-lehk-'troh-nee-koh)*
first language	**primer lenguaje** *(pree-'mehr lehn-'gwah-heh)*
first name	**primer nombre** *(pree-'mehr 'nohm-breh)*
full name	**nombre completo** *('nohm-breh kohm-'pleh-toh)*
group number	**número del grupo** *('noo-meh-roh dehl 'groo- poh)*
height	**altura** *(ahl-'too-rah)*
insurance company	**compañía de seguros** *(kohm-pah-'nyee-ah deh seh-'goo-rohs)*
last name	**apellido** *(ah-peh-'yee-doh)*
maiden name	**nombre de soltera** *('nohm-breh deh sohl- 'teh-rah)*
marital status	**estado civil** *(eh-'stah-doh see-'beel)*
middle initial	**segunda inicial** *(seh-'goon-dah ee-nee-see-'ahl)*
nationality	**nacionalidad** *(nah-see-oh-nah-lee-'dahd)*
place of birth	**lugar de nacimiento** *(loo-'gahr deh nah-see-mee-'ehn-toh)*
place of employment	**lugar de empleo** *(loo-'gahr deh ehm-'pleh-oh)*
policy number	**número de póliza** *('noo-meh-roh deh 'poh-lee-sah)*
race	**raza** *('rah-sah)*
relationship	**parentezco** *(pah-rehn-'tehs-koh)*
religion	**religión** *(reh-lee-'gee-'ohn)*
sex	**sexo** *('sehk-soh)*
social security number	**número de seguro social** *('noo-meh-roh deh seh-'goo-roh soh-see-'ahl)*
telephone number	**número de teléfono** *('noo-meh-roh deh teh-'leh-foh-noh)*
weight	**peso** *('peh-soh)*
zip code	**zona postal** *('soh-nah poh-'stahl)*

Perhaps the easiest way to learn more personal information about the Espinoza family is to ask simple questions that they can answer with **sí** or **no.**

Do you smoke?	**¿Fuma usted?** *('foo-mah oos-'tehd)*
Do you drink alcohol?	**¿Toma alcohol usted?** *('toh-mah ahl-koh-'ohl oos-'tehd)*
Do you use drugs?	**¿Usa drogas usted?** *('oo-sah 'droh-gahs oos-'tehd)*
Are you . . .?	**¿Es . . . ?** *(ehs)*
divorced	**divorciado** *(dee-bohr-see-'ah-doh)*
married	**casado** *(kah-'sah-doh)*
single	**soltero** *(sohl-'teh-roh)*

Do you have . . .?	**¿Tiene . . .?** *(tee-'eh-neh)*
allergies	**alergias** *(ah-'lehr-hee·ahs)*
documents	**los documentos** *(lohs doh-koo-'mehn-tohs)*
a driver's license	**una licencia de manejar** *('oo-nah lee-'sehn-see·ah deh mah-neh-'hahr)*
the forms	**los formularios** *(lohs fohr-moo-'lah-ree·ohs)*
high blood pressure	**alta presión sanguínea** *('ahl-tah preh-see-'ohn sahn-'gee-neh-ah)*
identification	**identificación** *(ee-dehn-tee-fee-kah-see-'ohn)*
a lot of pain	**mucho dolor** *('moo-choh doh-'lohr)*
medical insurance	**seguro médico** *(seh-'goo-roh 'meh-dee-koh)*
a question	**una pregunta** *('oo-nah preh-'goon-tah)*
the receipt	**el recibo** *(ehl reh-'see-boh)*
the results	**los resultados** *(lohs reh-sool-'tah-dohs)*
seizures	**ataques** *(ah-'tah-kehs)*
high temperature	**fiebre** *(fee-'eh-breh)*
Do you need . . .?	**¿Necesita . . . ?** *(neh-seh-'see-tah)*
an appointment	**una cita** *('oo-nah 'see-tah)*
a class	**una clase** *('oo-nah 'klah-seh)*
a consultation	**una consulta** *('oo-nah kohn-'sool-tah)*
a counselor	**un consejero** *(oon kohn-seh-'heh-roh)*
an exam	**un examen** *(oon ehk-'sah-mehn)*
an interpreter	**un intérprete** *(oon een-'tehr-preh-teh)*
a schedule	**un horario** *(oon oh-'rah-ree·oh)*
Are there . . .?	**¿Hay . . .?** *('ah-ee)*
problems with your heart	**problemas con su corazón?** *(proh-'bleh-mahs kohn soo koh-rah-'sohn)*
problems with your hearing	**problemas con sus oídos** *(proh-'bleh-mahs kohn soos oh-'ee-dohs)*
problems with your kidneys	**problemas con sus riñones** *(proh-'bleh-mahs kohn soos reen-'yoh-nehs)*
problems with your respiration	**problemas con su respiración** *(proh-'bleh-mahs kohn soo rehs-pee-rah-see-'ohn)*
problems with your stomach	**problemas con su estómago** *(proh-'bleh-mahs kohn soo ehs-'toh-mah-goh)*
problems with your vision	**problemas con su visión** *(proh-'bleh-mahs kohn soo bee-see-'ohn)*

(11) # ¿Cuánto aprendió?

Translate the English to form a complete sentence.

¿Cuál es su . . .? *(kwahl ehs soo)* (first name, father's last name, address)
¿Quién . . .? *(kee-'ehn)* (is the doctor, is sick)
¿Tiene. . .? *(tee-'eh-neh)* (medical insurance, the receipt)

A lot of work

Mucho trabajo
('moo-choh trah-'bah-hoh)

While you're taking the patient's personal information, you will occasionally pose questions related to his or her current occupation and employment status. Although this list refers to males only, do a "job" on all of these:

carpenter	**el carpintero** *(ehl kahr-peen-'teh-roh)*
cashier	**el cajero** *(ehl kah-'heh-roh)*
cook	**el cocinero** *(ehl koh-see-'neh-roh)*
employee	**el empleado** *(ehl ehm-pleh-'ah-doh)*
employer	**el empresario** *(ehl ehm-preh-'sah-ree-oh)*
farmer	**el campesino** *(ehl kahm-peh-'see-noh)*
firefighter	**el bombero** *(ehl bohm-'beh-roh)*
gardener	**el jardinero** *(ehl hahr-dee-'neh-roh)*
laborer	**el obrero** *(ehl oh-'breh-roh)*
landlord	**el propietario** *(ehl proh-pee-eh-'tah-ree-oh)*
lawyer	**el abogado** *(ehl ah-boh-'gah-doh)*
manager	**el gerente** *(ehl heh-'rehn-teh)*
mechanic	**el mecánico** *(ehl meh-'kah-nee-koh)*
painter	**el pintor** *(ehl peen-'tohr)*
plumber	**el plomero** *(ehl ploh-'meh-roh)*
police officer	**el policía** *(ehl poh-lee-'see-ah)*
priest	**el cura** *(ehl 'koo-rah)*
salesperson	**el vendedor** *(ehl behn-deh-'dohr)*
secretary	**el secretario** *(ehl seh-kreh-'tah-ree·oh)*
student	**el estudiante** *(ehl ehs-too-dee-'ahn-teh)*
teacher	**el maestro** *(ehl mah-'ehs-troh)*
truck driver	**el camionero** *(ehl kah-mee-'oh-neh-roh)*
waiter	**el mesero** *(ehl meh-'seh-roh)*

¡No se olvide!

- Don't forget to change the ending of the nouns when you are referring to females: Anne is the cook. **Ana es la cocinera.**
- **Jefe** means "boss." Who's your boss? **¿Quién es su jefe?** *(kee-'ehn ehs soo 'heh-feh)*

You may also need other work-related vocabulary words. These tell us where most people are employed:

I work in	Trabajo en . . . .
agency	**la agencia** *(lah ah-'hehn-see·ah)*
airport	**el aeropuerto** *(ehl ah·eh-roh-'pwehr-toh)*
bank	**el banco** *(ehl 'bahn-koh)*
building	**el edificio** *(ehl eh-dee-'fee-see·oh)*
business	**el negocio** *(ehl neh-'goh-see·oh)*
church	**la iglesia** *(lah ee-'gleh-see·ah)*
company	**la compañía** *(lah kohm-pah-'nyee-ah)*
factory	**la fábrica** *(lah 'fah-bree-kah)*
movie theater	**el cine** *(ehl 'see-neh)*
park	**el parque** *(ehl 'pahr-keh)*
restaurant	**el restaurante** *(oon rehs-tah·oo-'rahn-teh)*
school	**la escuela** *(lah ehs-'kweh-lah)*
station	**la estación** *(lah ehs-tah-see-'ohn)*
store	**la tienda** *(lah tee-'ehn-dah)*
warehouse	**el almacén** *(ehl ahl-mah-'sehn)*

¡No se olvide!

Just a reminder—while chatting about occupations, use **es** *(ehs)* instead of **está** *(eh-'stah)*: Frank is a chef. **Francisco es un cocinero.** *(frahn-'sees-koh ehs oon koh-see-'neh-roh)*. And use **está** *(eh-'stah)* to state where a person is located: He is at the restaurant. **Está en el restaurante.** *(eh-'stah ehn oon rehs-tah·oo-'rahn-teh)*.

Which illnesses?

¿Cuáles enfermedades?
('kwah-lehs ehn-fehr-meh-'dah-dehs)

As you continue to complete the registration forms, use the terms you need from the list below to learn the medical history of the Espinoza family. Again, have them answer with **sí** or **no**.

AIDS	**SIDA** *('see-dah)*
anemia	**anemia** *(ah-'neh-mee-ah)*
asthma	**asma** *('ahs-mah)*
cancer	**cáncer** *('kahn-sehr)*
chicken pox	**varicela** *(bah-ree-'seh-lah)*
cholera	**cólera** *('koh-leh-rah)*
diabetes	**diabetes** *(de-ah-'beh-tehs)*
diphtheria	**difteria** *(deef-'teh-ree·ah)*
epilepsy	**epilepsia** *(eh-pee-'lehp-see·ah)*
gallstones	**cálculos en la vesícula** *('kahl-koo-lohs ehn lah veh-'see-koo-lah)*
German measles	**rubéola** *(roo-'beh-oh-lah)*
hay fever	**rinitis alérgica** *(ree-'nee-tees ah-'lehr-hee-kah)*
high blood pressure	**alta presión sanguínea** *('ahl-tah preh-see-'ohn sahn-'ghee-neh-ah)*
high cholesterol	**colesterol alto** *(koh-lehs-teh-'rohl 'ahl-toh)*
HIV	**VIH** *(veh-ee-'ah-cheh)*
heart disease	**enfermedad del corazón** *(ehn-fehr-meh-'dahd dehl koh-rah-'sohn)*
hepatitis A, B, C	**hepatitis A, B, C** *(ehp-ah-'tee-tees ah, beh, seh)*
kidney stones	**cálculos en los riñones** *('kahl-koo-lohs ehn lohs ree-'nyoh-nehs)*
leukemia	**leucemia** *(leh-oo-'seh-mee·ah)*
Lyme disease	**enfermedad de Lyme** *(ehn-fehr-meh-'dahd deh Lyme)*
measles	**sarampión** *(sah-rahm-pee-'ohn)*
meningitis	**meningitis** *(meh-neen-'hee-tees)*
mumps	**paperas** *(pah-'peh-rahs)*
pneumonia	**pulmonía** *(pool-moh-'nee-ah)*
polio	**polio** *('poh-lee·oh)*
rheumatic fever	**fiebre reumática** *(fee-'eh-breh reh-oo-'mah-tee-kah)*
scarlet fever	**escarlatina** *(ehs-kahr-lah-'tee-nah)*
smallpox	**viruela** *(bee-roo-'eh-lah)*

tetanus	**tétano** *('teh-tah-noh)*
tonsillitis	**tonsilítis** *(tohn-see-'lee-tees)*
tuberculosis	**tuberculosis** *(too-behr-koo-'loh-sees)*
typhoid	**tifoidea** *(tee-foh·ee-'deh-ah)*
ulcers	**úlceras** *('ool-seh-rahs)*
whooping cough	**tos ferina, tos convulsiva** *(tohs feh-'ree-nah, tohs kohn-bool-'see-bah)*

Notice how similar these words are to English:

artritis *(ahr-'tree-tees)*
botulismo *(boh-too-'lees-moh)*
bronquitis *(brohn-'kee-tees)*
celulitis *(seh-loo-'lee-tees)*
cirrosis *(see-'rroh-sees)*
dermatitis *(dehr-mah-'tee-tees)*
disentería *(dee-sehn-teh-'ree-ah)*
encefalitis *(ehn-seh-fah-'lee-tees)*
enfisema *(ehn-fee-'seh-mah)*
hemofilia *(eh-moh-'fee-lee-ah)*
hipertiroidismo *(ee-pehr-tee-roh-ee-'dees-moh)*
hipoglicemia *(ee-poh-glee-'seh-mee-ah)*
infección viral *(een-fehk-see-'ohn vee-'rahl)*
influenza *(een-floo-'ehn-sah)*
lupus *('loo-poos)*
osteoporosis *(ohs-teh-oh-poh-'roh-sees)*
soriasis *(soh-ree-'ah-sees)*
trombosis *(trohm-'boh-sees)*
vértigo *('vehr-tee-goh)*

Do you recognize the following key words and acronyms?

bird flu	**influenza aviar** *(een-floo-'ehn-sah ah-vee-'ahr)*
CF	**fibrosis cística** *(fee-'broh-sees 'sees-tee-kah)*
CP	**parálisis cerebral** *(pah-'rah-lee-sees seh-reh-'brahl)*
Mad Cow Disease	**encefalopatía espongiforme bovina** *(ehn-seh-fah-loh-pah-'tee-ah ehs-pohn-gee-'fohr-meh boh-'vee-nah)*
MD	**distrofia muscular** *(dees-'troh-fee-ah moos-koo-'lahr)*
MS	**esclerosis múltiple** *(ehs-kleh-'roh-sees 'mool-tee-pleh)*
STDs	**enfermedades venéreas** *(ehn-fehr-meh-'dah-dehs veh-'neh-reh-ahs)*
West Nile virus	**virus del Nilo Occidental** *('vee-roos dehl 'nee-loh ohk-see-dehn-'tahl)*

The consent form

El formulario de consentimiento
(ehl fohr-moo-'lah-ree-oh deh kohn-sehn-tee-mee-'ehn-toh)

Do you have a consent form?
¿Tiene usted un formulario de consentimiento?
(tee-'eh-neh oos-'tehd oon fohr-moo-'lah-ree-oh deh kohn-sehn-tee-mee-'ehn-toh)

Would you like one?
¿Quisiera tener uno?
(kee-see-'eh-rah teh-'nehr 'oo-noh)

Who will bring me a copy of the form?
¿Quién me va a traer una copia del formulario?
(kee-'ehn meh bah ah trah-'ehr 'oo-nah 'koh-pee-ah dehl fohr-moo-'lah-ree-oh)

Do you have any special requests?
¿Tiene usted algunos pedidos adicionales?
(tee-'eh-neh oos-'tehd ahl-'goo-nohs peh-'dee-dohs ah-dee-see-oh-'nah-lehs)

Who is your legal healthcare agent?
¿Quién es su agente legal para el cuidado de la salud?
(kee-'ehn ehs soo ah-'hehn-teh leh-'gahl 'pah-rah ehl kwee-'dah-doh deh lah sah-'lood)

We need your permission.
Necesitamos su permiso.
(neh-seh-see-'tah-mohs soo pehr-'mee-soh)

Do you have insurance?

¿Tiene seguro? *(tee-'eh-neh seh-'goo-roh)*

Questions related to admitting often lead to health insurance coverage. As you read the following sentences, pay particular attention to those words you may already know.

Do you have insurance?
¿Tiene seguro? *(tee-'eh-neh seh-'goo-roh)*

Which is your insurance company?
¿Cuál es su compañía de seguros?
(kwahl ehs soo koh-pah-'nyee-ah deh seh-'goo-rohs)

What's your policy and group number?
¿Cuál es su número de póliza y grupo?
(kwahl ehs soo 'noo-meh-roh deh 'poh-lee-sah ee 'groo-poh)

If you need more information, learn these words and expressions:

employer	**empresario** *(ehm-preh-'sah-ree·oh)*
employment	**empleo** *(ehm-'pleh-oh)*
workman's compensation	**compensación de obrero**
	(kohm-pehn-sah-see·'ohn deh oh-'breh-roh)

What kind?	**¿Qué tipo?** *(keh 'tee-poh)*
An insurance for . . .	**Un seguro de . . .** *(oon seh-'goo-roh deh)*
accidents	**accidentes** *(ahk-see-'dehn-tehs)*
automobile	**automóvil** *(ow-toh-'moh-beel)*
Blue Cross	**Cruz Azul** *('kroos ah-'sool)*
Blue Shield	**Escudo Azul** *(ehs-'koo-doh ah-'sool)*
dental care	**cuidado dental** *(koo-ee-'dah-doh dehn-'tahl)*
disability	**incapacidad** *(in-kah-pah-see-'dahd)*
family	**familia** *(fah-'mee-lee-ah)*
health	**salud** *(sah-'lood)*
hospital	**hospital** *(ohs-pee-'tahl)*
life	**vida** *('bee-dah)*
mental health	**salud mental** *(sah-'lood mehn-'tahl)*
personal	**personal** *(pehr-soh-'nahl)*
vision care	**cuidado de la visión**
	(koo-ee-'dah-doh deh lah vee-see-'ohn)

Keep going:

federal grant	**beca federal**
	('beh-kah feh-deh-'rahl)
HMO	**Organización para el Mantenimiento de la Salud**
	(ohr-gah-nee-sah-see-'ohn 'pah-rah ehl mahn-teh-nee-mee-'ehn-toh deh lah sah-'lood)
PPO	**Organización de Proveedores Preferentes**
	(ohr-gah-nee-sah-see-'ohn deh proh-beh-eh-'doh-rehs preh-feh-'rehn-tehs)
special programs	**programas especiales**
	(proh-'grah-mahs ehs-peh-see-'ah-lehs)
state aid	**ayuda estatal**
	(ah-'yoo-dah ehs-tah-'tahl)

Dos culturas

Many immigrants aren't familiar with health insurance procedures in the United States. Don't be surprised if some patients attempt to pay cash for hospital services.

Once you've filled out the registration and insurance forms, your next concern is why the Espinoza family has come to your hospital. Here are some questions you can use to acquire more basic information.

Do you have a doctor?	**¿Tiene un doctor?** *('tee-'eh-neh oon dohk-'tohr)*
Who is sick?	**¿Quién está enfermo?** *(kee-'ehn eh-'stah ehn-'fehr-moh)*
Who is your doctor?	**¿Quién es su doctor?** *(kee-'ehn ehs soo dohk-'tohr)*
Whose child is it?	**¿De quién es el niño?** *(deh kee-'ehn ehs ehl 'nee-nyoh)*

More key words:

benefits	**beneficios** *(beh-neh-'fee-see-ohs)*
cash	**efectivo** *(eh-fehk-'tee-boh)*
charge	**cargo** *('kahr-goh)*
check	**cheque** *('cheh-keh)*
deposit	**depósito** *(deh-'poh-see-toh)*
discount	**descuento** *(dehs-'kwehn-toh)*
expenses	**gastos** *('gahs-tohs)*
free	**gratis** *('grah-tees)*
income	**ingreso** *(een-'greh-soh)*
loan	**préstamo** *('prehs-tah-moh)*
plan	**plan** *(plahn)*
resources	**recursos** *(reh-'koor-sohs)*

Continue to chat with the family about their insurance coverage:

Here is (the)...	**Aquí tiene...** *(ah-'kee tee-'eh-neh)*
claim form	**el formulario del reclamante** *(ehl fohr-moo-'lah-ree-oh dehl reh-klah-'mahn-teh)*
co-pay amount	**el co-pago** *(ehl koh-'pah-goh)*
coverage	**la cobertura** *(lah koh-behr-'too-rah)*
date of service	**la fecha de servicio** *(lah 'feh-chah deh sehr-'vee-see-oh)*
deductible	**el deducible** *(ehl deh-doo-'see-bleh)*
family policy	**la póliza para la familia** *(lah 'poh-lee-sah 'pah-rah lah fah-'mee-lee-ah)*
health plan	**el plan de salud** *(ehl plahn deh sah-'lood)*
insurance card	**la tarjeta de seguro** *(lah tahr-'heh-tah deh seh-'goo-roh)*

list of providers	**la lista de proveedores** *(lah 'lees-tah deh proh-veh-eh-'doh-rehs)*
premium	**la prima de seguro** *(lah 'pree-mah deh seh-'goo-roh)*
procedure code	**el código de procedimiento** *(ehl 'koh-dee-goh deh proh-seh-dee-mee-'ehn-toh)*

Are you (the)...?	**¿Es usted...?** *(ehs oos-'tehd)*
claimant	**el reclamante** *(ehl reh-klah-'mahn-teh)*
dependent	**la persona a su cargo** *(lah pehr-'soh-nah ah soo 'kahr-goh)*
patient	**el paciente** *(ehl pah-see-'ehn-teh)*
principal member	**el miembro principal** *(ehl mee-'ehm-broh preen-see-'pahl)*
provider	**el proveedor** *(ehl proh-veh-eh-'dohr)*
representative	**el representante** *(ehl reh-preh-sehn-'tahn-teh)*

Do you need (the)...	**¿Necesita...?** *(neh-seh-'see-tah)*
directions	**las instrucciones** *(lahs eens-trook-see-'oh-nehs)*
files	**los archivos** *(lohs ahr-'chee-vohs)*
pre-approval	**la aprobación previa** *(lah ah-proh-bah-see-'ohn 'preh-vee-ah)*
prices	**los precios** *(lohs 'preh-see-ohs)*
referral	**la referencia** *(lah reh-feh-'rehn-see-ah)*
second opinion	**la segunda opinión** *(lah seh-'goon-dah oh-pee-nee-'ohn)*
signature	**la firma** *(lah 'feer-mah)*

Now make sure that all questions are answered:

Do you understand (the)...?	**¿Entiende ...?** *(ehn-tee-'ehn-deh)*
coverage	**la cobertura** *(lah koh-behr-'too-rah)*
liability	**la responsabilidad legal** *(lah rehs-pohn-sah-bee-lee-'dahd leh-'gahl)*
monthly payments	**los pagos mensuales** *(lohs 'pah-gohs mehn-soo-'ah-lehs)*
restrictions	**las restricciones** *(lahs rehs-treek-see-'oh-nehs)*
rights	**los derechos** *(lohs deh-'reh-chohs)*
services	**los servicios** *(lohs sehr-'vee-see-ohs)*
terms	**las condiciones** *(lahs kohn-dee-see-'oh-nehs)*

Do you want...?	**¿Quiere...?** *(kee-'eh-reh)*
to cancel	**cancelar** *(kahn-seh-'lahr)*
to change	**cambiar** *(kahm-bee-'ahr)*
to check	**averiguar** *(ah-veh-ree-'gwahr)*
to enroll	**matricularse** *(mah-tree-koo-'lahr-seh)*
to file	**reportar** *(reh-pohr-'tahr)*
to verify	**verificar** *(veh-ree-fee-'kahr)*

The policy

La póliza *(lah 'poh-lee-sah)*

When necessary, explain all of the insurance policies and procedures:

We have (a)...	**Tenemos...** *(teh-'neh-mohs)*
24-hour service	**servicio de veinticuatro horas** *(sehr-'vee-see-oh deh veh-een-tee-'kwah-troh 'oh-rahs)*
affordable payments	**pagos a su alcance** *('pah-gohs ah soo ahl 'kahn-seh)*
comprehensive coverage	**una cobertura completa** *('oo-nah koh-behr-'too-rah kohm-'pleh-tah)*
easy access	**una ubicación conveniente** *('oo-nah oo-bee-kah-see-'ohn kohn-veh-nee-'ehn-teh)*
individual health plans	**planes de salud personales** *('plah-nehs deh sah-'lood pehr-soh-'nah-lehs)*
wide selection	**una selección amplia** *('oo-nah seh-lehk-see-'ohn 'ahm-plee-ah)*
special rates	**tarifas especiales** *(tah-'ree-fahs ehs-peh-see-'ah-lehs)*
statewide network	**una red de servicios interestatal** *('oo-nah rehd deh sehr-'vee-see-ohs een-tehr-ehs-tah-'tahl)*
It also includes...	**También incluye...** *(tahm-bee-'ehn een-'kloo-yeh)*
ambulance service	**el servicio de ambulancia** *(ehls sehr-'vee-see-oh deh ahm-boo-'lahn-see-ah)*
convalescent clinics	**las clínicas para convalescientes** *(lahs 'klee-nee-kahs 'pah-rah kohn-vah-lehs-see-'ehn-tehs)*
examinations	**los exámenes** *(lohs ehks-'ah-meh-nehs)*

home health care	**el cuidado médico en la casa**
	(*ehl koo-ee-'dah-doh 'meh-dee-koh ehn 'kah-sah*)
immunizations	**las vacunas** (*lahs vah-'koo-nahs*)
laboratory work	**el trabajo de laboratorio**
	(*ehl trah-'bah-hoh deh lah-boh-rah-'toh-ree-oh*)
major surgery	**la cirugía mayor** (*lah see-roo-'hee-ah mah-'yohr*)
office visits	**las visitas al médico**
	(*lahs vee-'see-tahs ahl 'meh-dee-koh*)
physical checkups	**los exámenes médicos periódicos**
	(*lohs ehks-'ah-meh-nehs 'meh-dee-kohs peh-ree-'oh-dee-kohs*)
prescriptions	**las recetas médicas**
	(*lahs reh-'seh-tahs 'meh-dee-kahs*)
treatments	**los tratamientos** (*lohs trah-tah-mee-'ehn-tohs*)

(12) ## ¿Cuánto aprendió?

Try to translate these sentences without using a dictionary.

¿Qué tipo de seguro tiene?
(*keh 'tee-poh deh seh-'goo-roh tee-'eh-neh*)

¿Cuál es la dirección de su empresario?
(*kwahl ehs lah dee-rehk-see·'ohn deh soo ehm-preh-'sah-ree·oh*)

Necesita seguro para accidentes.
(*'neh-seh-'see-etah seh-'goo-roh 'pah-rah ahk-see-'dehn-tehs*)

Parts of the hospital

Las partes del hospital
(*lahs 'pahr-tehs dehl ohs-pee-'tahl*)

Once the Espinoza family has been interviewed, you'll want to send the patient to the appropriate department, or at least give the family general directions to different parts of the hospital. Pointing helps, but it only sends them so far. Here's some beginning vocabulary for everyone who works in Admissions. To practice the names of any objects or locations, try labeling them in Spanish with removable stickers. For daily practice, begin your phrases with one of the most valuable phrases in medicine:

Do you need . . . ?	**¿Necesita . . . ?** (neh-seh-'see-tah)
Administration	**La administración** (lah ahd-mee-nee-strah-see-'ohn)
Cashier	**El cajero** (ehl kah-'heh-roh)
Chapel	**La capilla** (lah kah-'pee-yah)
Conference Room	**La sala de conferencias** (lah 'sah-lah deh kohn-feh-'rehn-see-ahs)
Delivery Room	**La sala de partos** (lah 'sah-lah deh 'pahr-tohs)
Emergency Room	**la sala de emergencia** (lah 'sah-lah deh eh-mehr-'hehn-see·ah)
Intensive Care	**la sala de cuidados intensivos** (lah 'sah-lah deh kwee-'dah-dohs een-tehn-'see-bohs)
Laboratory	**El laboratorio** (ehl lah-boh-rah-'toh-ree-oh)
Maternity Ward	**la sala de maternidad** (lah 'sah-lah deh mah-tehr-nee-'dahd)
Meditation Room	**La sala de meditación** (lah 'sah-lah deh meh-dee-tah-see-'ohn)
Nursery	**La guardería** (lah gwahr-deh-'ree-ah)
Operating Room	**la sala de operaciones** (lah 'sah-lah deh oh-peh-rah-see-'oh-nehs)
Radiology	**Radiología** (rah-dee-oh-loh-'hee-ah)
Recovery Room	**la sala de recuperación** (lah 'sah-lah deh reh-koo-peh-rah-see-'ohn)
Waiting Room	**la sala de espera** (lah 'sah-lah deh ehs-'peh-rah)

And when it comes to centers . . .

Blood Donor Center	**Centro de donación de sangre** ('sehn-troh deh doh-nah-see-'ohn deh 'sahn-greh)
Cancer Center	**Centro de cáncer** ('sehn-troh deh 'kahn-sehr)
Dialysis Center	**Centro de diálisis** ('sehn-troh deh dee-'ah-lee-sees)
Neuropsychiatric Center	**Centro neurosiquiátrico** ('sehn-troh neh-oo-roh-see-kee-'ah-tree-koh)
Orthopedic Center	**Centro ortopédico** ('sehn-troh ohr-toh-'peh-dee-koh)

Let's see the inside of the building . . .

ATM machine	**El cajero automático** (ehl kah-'heh-roh ow-toh-'mah-tee-koh)
basement	**el sótano** (ehl 'soh-tah-noh)
cafeteria	**la cafetería** (lah kah-feh-teh-'ree-ah)

department	**el departamento** *(ehl deh-pahr-tah-'mehn-toh)*
elevator	**el ascensor** *(ehl ah-sehn-'sohr)*
entrance	**la entrada** *(lah ehn-'trah-dah)*
exit	**la salida** *(lah sah-'lee-dah)*
gift shop	**la tienda de regalos** *(lah tee-'ehn-dah deh reh-'gah-lohs)*
hallway	**el corredor** *(ehl koh-rreh-'dohr)*
main lobby	**el salón principal** *(ehl sah-'lohn preen-see-'pahl)*
mailbox	**el buzón** *(ehl boo-'sohn)*
parking lot	**el estacionamiento** *(ehl eh-stah-see-oh-nah-mee-'ehn-toh)*
stairs	**las escaleras** *(lahs eh-skah-'leh-rahs)*
telephone	**el teléfono** *(ehl teh-'leh-foh-noh)*
toilet	**el excusado** *(ehl ehks-koo-'sah-doh)*
water fountain	**la fuente de agua** *(lah 'fwehn-teh deh 'ah-gwah)*

Directions

Las direcciones *(lahs dee-rehk-see·'ohn-nehs)*

If you're at a loss for words while giving directions to someone, try using these expressions:

Where is it/he/she?	**¿Dónde está?** *('dohn-deh eh-'stah)*
above	**encima** *(ehn-'see-mah)*
straight ahead	**adelante** *(ah-deh-'lahn-teh)*
behind	**detrás** *(deh-'trahs)*
down	**abajo** *(ah-'bah-hoh)*
first floor	**primer piso** *(pree-'mehr 'pee-soh)*
second floor	**segundo piso** *(seh-'goon-doh 'pee-soh)*
in front of	**en frente de** *(ehn 'frehn-teh deh)*
here	**aquí** *(ah-'kee)*
inside	**adentro** *(ah-'dehn-troh)*
to the left	**a la izquierda** *(ah lah ees-kee-'ehr-dah)*
near	**cerca** *('sehr-kah)*
next to	**al lado de** *(ahl 'lah-doh deh)*
outside	**afuera** *(ah-foo-'eh-rah)*
to the right	**a la derecha** *(ah lah deh-'reh-chah)*
there	**allí** *(ah-'yee)*
over there	**allá** *(ah-'yah)*
up	**arriba** *(ah-'rree-bah)*

north **norte** (*'nohr-teh*)

west **oeste** (*oh-'eh-steh*)   ◄✛►   east **este** (*'eh-steh*)

south **sur** (*soor*)

Remember that **en** (*ehn*) (in, on, at) is one of the most commonly used words in Spanish: She's at the hospital, on the third floor, in the bed. **Está en el hospital** (*eh-'stah ehn ehl ohs-pee-'tahl*), **en el tercer piso** (*ehn ehl tehr-'sehr 'pee-soh*), **en la cama** (*ehn lah 'kah-mah*).

Always use **estar** (*eh-'stahr*) instead of **ser** (*sehr*) to tell where someone is located. The doctor is here. **El doctor está aquí.**

Be familiar with as many location words as you can:

face down	**boca abajo** (*'boh-kah ah-'bah-hoh*)
face up	**boca arriba** (*'boh-kah ah-'rree-bah*)
on its way	**en camino** (*ehn kah-'mee-noh*)
on the side	**en el costado** (*ehn ehl kohs-'tah-doh*)
toward the back	**hacia atrás** (*'ah-see·ah ah-'trahs*)

⑬   **¿Cuánto aprendió?**

- Practice your location words by completing the following sentences. If you find this exercise difficult, refer back to the previous section.

  Vaya . . . (*'bah-yah*)   in front of the lobby:

  over there:

  outside:

  straight ahead:

- Translate the following sentence:

  Suba en el ascensor y dé vuelta a la derecha.
  (*'soo-bah ehn ehl ah-sehn-'sohr ee deh 'bwehl-tah ah lah deh-'reh-chah*)

Time

La hora (*lah 'oh-rah*)

While you're sending the Espinoza family this way and that way, be on the lookout for the common expression for "What time is it?" **¿Qué hora es?** (*keh 'oh-rah ehs*). Luckily, all that is needed to respond to this question is the hour, followed by the word **y** (*ee*) (and), and the minutes. For example, 7:15 is **siete y quince** (*see-'eh-teh ee 'keen-seh*). To say "It's . . .", use **Son las . . .** (*sohn lahs*)

For example, "It's 7:15" **Son las siete y quince** (*sohn lahs see-'eh-teh ee 'keen-seh*). You may want to go back and review your numbers in Spanish on page 11 before you try this. Here are a few more examples.

It's 12:30 A.M.	**Son las doce y trienta de la mañana.** (*sohn lahs doh-seh ee 'treh·een-tah deh lah mah-'nyah-nah*)
At 6:00 P.M.	**A las seis de la tarde.** (*ah lahs 'seh·ees deh lah 'tahr-deh*)
It's 3:45.	**Son las tres y cuarenta y cinco.** (*sohn lahs trehs ee 'kwah-'rehn-tah ee 'seen-koh*)

¡No se olvide!

- **A las** (*ah lahs*) refers to "At." At 7:15. **A las siete y quince.** (*ah lahs see-'eh-teh ee 'keen-seh*). At what time? **¿A qué hora?**

- A.M. is **de la mañana** (*deh lah mah-'nyah-nah*). P.M. is **de la tarde.** (*deh lah 'tahr-deh*).

- For 1:00–1:59, use **Es la** (*ehs lah*) instead of **Son las** (*sohn lahs*). For example, It's one o'clock. **Es la una.** (*ehs lah 'oo-nah*). It's one-thirty. **Es la una y treinta.** (*ehs lah 'oo-nah ee 'treh·een-tah*).

- Listen for the word, **¿Cuándo?** (*'kwahn-doh*) ("When?"). You will definitely need your time-telling skills to answer this question.

The calendar

El calendario (*ehl kah-lehn-'dah-ree·oh*)

You can't fill out all that paperwork without a calendar. Regardless of the forms you use, sooner or later the Espinozas will ask you questions about a specific day or date. Spend a few minutes looking over the following words and one-liners. These won't take you long to learn.

The days of the week

Los días de la semana
(lohs 'dee-ahs deh lah seh-'mah-nah)

Monday	**lunes** *('loo-nehs)*
Tuesday	**martes** *('mahr-tehs)*
Wednesday	**miércoles** *(mee-'ehr-koh-lehs)*
Thursday	**jueves** *('hoo·eh-behs)*
Friday	**viernes** *(bee-'ehr-nehs)*
Saturday	**sábado** *('sah-bah-doh)*
Sunday	**domingo** *(doh-'meen-goh)*
today	**hoy** *('oh·ee)*
tomorrow	**mañana** *(mah-'nyah-nah)*
yesterday	**ayer** *(ah-'yehr)*

Now practice some of the new expressions:

Today is Wednesday.	**Hoy es miércoles.** *('oh·ee ehsmee-'ehr-koh-lehs)*
Tomorrow is Thursday.	**Mañana es jueves.** *(mah-'nyah-nah ehs 'hoo·eh-behs)*
I have to work on Sunday.	**Tengo que trabajar el domingo.** *('tehn-goh keh trah-bah-'hahr ehl doh-'meen-goh)*

What is the date?

¿Cuál es la fecha? *(kwahl ehs lah 'feh-chah)*

Answering questions in Spanish concerning upcoming events, appointments, birthdays, and holidays can often be handled by pointing to dates on the calendar. However, it does help if you know the following. Notice how many of these look and sound like English:

The months of the year

Los meses del año *(lohs 'meh-sehs dehl 'ah-nyoh)*

January	**enero** *(eh-'neh-roh)*
February	**febrero** *(feh-'breh-roh)*
March	**marzo** *('mahr-soh)*
April	**abril** *(ah-'breel)*
May	**mayo** *('mah-yoh)*
June	**junio** *('hoo-nee·oh)*
July	**julio** *(hoo-lee·oh)*
August	**agosto** *(ah-'goh-stoh)*
September	**septiembre** *(sehp-tee-'ehm-breh)*
October	**octubre** *(ohk-'too-breh)*
November	**noviembre** *(noh-vee-'ehm-breh)*
December	**diciembre** *(dee-see-'ehm-breh)*

- To give the date, reverse the order of your words. For example, February 2nd is **El dos de febrero** *(ehl dohs deh feh-'breh-roh).*

  This is how you say "the first" in Spanish: **el primero.** *(ehl pree-'meh-roh)*

January 1st	**El primero de enero**
	(ehl pree-'meh-roh deh eh-'neh-roh)

- Several different **preguntas** *(preh-'goon-tahs)* can be used to ask "when." Learn the following:

How long ago?	**¿Hace cuánto?** *('ah-seh 'kwahn-toh)*
What day, month, year?	**¿Qué día, mes, año?**
	(keh 'dee-ah, mehs, 'ah-nyoh)
When is it?	**¿Cuándo es?** *('kwahn-doh ehs)*

- The year is built the same as in English:

2002	**dos mil dos** *(dohs meel dohs)*

- "On Friday" is **el viernes** *(ehl bee-'ehr-nehs)* but "on Fridays" is **los viernes** *(lohs bee-'ehr-nehs)*

  If you want, you can interject the following expressions:

the next one	**el próximo** *(ehl 'prohk-see-moh)*
the past one	**el pasado** *(ehl pah-'sah-doh)*
the weekend	**el fin de semana** *(ehl feen deh seh-'mah-nah)*

- How is the year divided in nature?

spring	**la primavera** *(lah pree-mah-'beh-rah)*
summer	**el verano** *(ehl beh-'rah-noh)*
fall	**el otoño** *(ehl oh-'tohn-yoh)*
winter	**el invierno** *(ehl een-bee-'ehr-noh)*

(14)   ¿Cuánto aprendió?

Fill in the missing words.

lunes, martes, _____ , jueves,
viernes, _____ , domingo.

enero, febrero, marzo, _____, mayo, junio,
julio, _____ .

Specialists

Los especialistas *(lohs eh-speh-see-ah-'lee-stahs)*

The Espinozas will probably need a variety of medical services. Choose what you need from the following list. Notice how many **especialistas** words look just like their English equivalents. Again, you'll need to change the final letter "o" to an "a" to indicate that it's a female:

You need . . .	Necesita un (una) . . .
anesthetist	**anestesista** *(ah-nehs-teh-'sees-tah)*
bacteriologist	**bacteriólogo** *(bahk-teh-ree-'oh-loh-goh)*
cardiologist	**cardiólogo** *(kahr-dee-'oh-loh-goh)*
chiropractor	**quiropráctico** *(kee-roh-'prahk-tee-koh)*
dermatologist	**dermatólogo** *(dehr-mah-'toh-loh-goh)*
gastroenterologist	**gastroenterólogo** *(gahs-troh-ehn-teh-'roh-loh-goh)*
gynecologist	**ginecólogo** *(hee-neh-'koh-loh-goh)*
neurologist	**neurólogo** *(neh-oo-'roh-loh-goh)*
obstetrician	**obstetriz** *(ohb-steh-'trees)*
ophthalmologist	**oftalmólogo** *(of-tahl-'moh-loh-goh)*
optometrist	**optometrista** *(ohp-toh-meh-'trees-tah)*
orthodontist	**ortodoncista** *(ohr-toh-dohn-'sees-tah)*
orthopedist	**ortopédico** *(ohr-toh-'peh-dee-koh)*
pathologist	**patólogo** *(pah-'toh-loh-goh)*
pediatrician	**pediatra** *(peh-dee-'ah-trah)*

podiatrist	**podiatra** *(poh-dee-'ah-trah)*
proctologist	**proctólogo** *(prohk-'toh-loh-goh)*
psychiatrist	**psiquiatra** *(see-kee-'ah-trah)*
psychologist	**psicólogo** *(see-'koh-loh-goh)*
radiologist	**radiólogo** *(rah-dee-'oh-loh-goh)*
surgeon	**cirujano** *(see-roo-'hah-noh)*
urologist	**urólogo** *(oo-'roh-loh-goh)*

Some other medical staff members are:

assistant	**ayudante** *(ah-yoo-'dahn-teh)*
dietician	**dietista** *(dee-eh-'tees-tah)*
nurse	**enfermero** *(enh-fehr-'meh-roh)*
orderly	**practicante** *(prahk-tee-'kahn-teh)*
paramedic	**paramédico** *(pah-rah-'meh-dee-koh)*
pharmacist	**farmacéutico** *(fahr-mah-'seh·oo-tee-koh)*
technician	**técnico** *('tehk-nee-koh)*
therapist	**terapeuta** *(teh-rah-peh-'oo-tah)*

REMEMBER: Use **el** for males, and **la** for females: **Bob es el dietista, Betty es la dietista.** *(B. ehs ehl dee-eh-'tees-tah, B. ehs lah dee-eh-'tees-tah)*

(15) # ¿Cuánto aprendió?

Translate the following:

¿Necesita. . .?

water fountain _____

mailbox _____

stairs _____

emergency room _____

pediatrician _____

gynecologist _____

therapist _____

More action!

¡Más acción! *(mahs ahk-see·'ohn)*

In order to communicate more effectively with the Espinoza family and other patients, you'll need to increase your list of action words. Read each word and sample sentence. Then see if you can translate their meanings.

to change	**cambiar** *(kahm-bee-'ahr)*
	No necesitan cambiar doctores.
	(noh neh-seh-'see-tahn kahm-bee-'ahr dohk-'toh-rehs)
to fill	llenar *(yeh-'nahr)*
	Necesita llenar el formulario.
	(neh-seh-'see tah yeh-'nahr ehl fohr-moo-'lah-ree·oh)
to learn	**aprender** *(ah-prehn-'dehr)*
	Necesitamos aprender inglés.
	(neh-seh-see-'tah-mohs ah-prehn-'dehr een-'glehs)
to look for	**buscar** *(boos-'kahr)*
	Tienen que buscar los libros.
	(tee-'eh-nehn keh boos-'kahr lohs 'lee-brohs)
to pay	**pagar** *(pah-'gahr)*
	Tengo que pagar el hospital.
	('tehn-goh keh pah-'gahr ehl ohs-pee-'tahl)
to register	**registrar** *(reh-hee-'strahr)*
	Tiene que registrarse el lunes.
	(tee-'eh-neh keh reh-hee-'strahr-seh ehl 'loo-nehs)
to smoke	**fumar** *(foo-'mahr)*
	No fumar en el cuarto.
	(no foo-'mahr ehn ehl 'kwahr-toh)
to study	**estudiar** *(eh-stoo-dee-'ahr)*
	¿Tiene que estudiar?
	(tee-'eh-neh keh eh-stoo-dee-'ahr)
to use	**usar** *(oo-'sahr)*
	Necesito usar el baño.
	(neh-seh-'see-toh oo-'sahr ehl 'bah-nyoh)
to verify	**verificar** *(beh-ree-fee-'kahr)*
	Tenemos que verificar la información.
	(teh-'neh-mohs keh beh-ree-fee-'kahr lah een-fohr-mah-see·'ohn)

What do you want?

¿Qué quiere? *(keh kee-'eh-reh)*

Ready to learn a new pattern? Earlier you learned **tener que** *(teh-'nehr keh)* (to have to) and **necesitar** *(neh-seh-see-'tahr)* (to need). Now practice the four forms of the verb **QUERER** *(keh-'rehr)* (TO WANT).

I want
> **quiero** *(kee-'eh-roh)*
> **Quiero hablar con el doctor.**
> *(kee-'eh-roh ah-'blahr kohn ehl dohk-'tohr)*

you want,
  he/she wants
> **quiere** *(kee-'eh-reh)*
> **¿Quiere usar el teléfono?**
> *(kee-'eh-reh oo-'sahr ehl teh-'leh-foh-noh)*

you (plural)
  want/they want
> **quieren** *(kee-'eh-rehn)*
> **Quieren trabajar en la oficina.**
> *(kee-'eh-rehn trah-bah-'hahr ehn lah oh-fee-'see-nah)*

we want
> **queremos**
> **Queremos verificar la información.**
> *(keh-'reh-mohs beh-ree-fee-'kahr lah een-fohr-mah-see·'ohn)*

Notice how action words change form according to who completes the action. The pattern is the same for most words:

HABLAR *(ah-'blahr)*	TO SPEAK
hablo *('ah-bloh)*	I speak
habla *('ah-blah)*	you, he, she speaks
hablamos *(ah-'blah-mohs)*	we speak
hablan *('ah-blahn)*	you (plural), they speak
COMER *(koh-'mehr)*	TO EAT
como *('koh-moh)*	I eat
come *('koh-meh)*	you, he, she eats
comemos *(koh-'meh-mohs)*	we eat
comen *('koh-mehn)*	you (plural) they eat
ESCRIBIR *(ehs-kree-'beer)*	TO WRITE
escribo *(ehs-'kree-boh)*	I write
escribe *(ehs-'kree-beh)*	you, he, she writes
escribimos *(ehs-kree-'bee-mohs)*	we write
escriben *(ehs-'kree-behn)*	you (plural), they write

¡No se olvide!

These words can be used in the same way as **quiere.**

desire   **desea** *(deh-'seh-ah)*

                  ¿Desea el doctor? *(deh-'seh-ah ehl dohk-'tohr)*

prefer   **prefiere** *(pre-fee-'eh-reh)*

                  ¿Prefiere el doctor? *(preh-fee-'eh-reh ehl dohk-'tohr)*

would like   **quisiera** *(kee-see-'eh-rah)*

                  Quisiera el doctor. *(kee-see-'eh-rah ehl dohk-'tohr)*

Chapter Four

Capítulo Cuatro

(kah-'pee-too-loh 'kwah-troh)

The Accident

El Accidente

(ehl ahk-see-'dehn-teh)

Juan Carlos Espinoza, age 34, has been in an automobile accident. He arrives at your hospital with a probable broken arm and bruises on his forehead. As the medical attendant, you need to evaluate his condition. Unfortunately, he doesn't speak English. It's probably best to begin with a few simple questions to make Juan feel relaxed. **¿Cómo está?** *('koh-moh eh-'stah)* (How are you?) will work. Juan could answer with almost anything. The key is to get him to keep it to one word. Let him know you speak only a little Spanish—**"Hablo poquito español"** *('ah-bloh poh-'kee-toh ehs-pah-'nyohl)*. If he speaks too quickly, get him to slow it down with **"Más despacio, por favor"** *(mahs dehs-'pah-see·oh, pohr fah-'bohr)*. Once he understands that communication is limited, his possible answers to your question may include the following:

How are you?

¿Cómo está usted? *('koh-moh eh-'stah oo-'stehd)*

I am. . .	**Estoy . . .** *(eh-'stoh·ee)*
dizzy	**mareado** *(mah-reh-'ah-doh)*
exhausted	**agotado** *(ah-goh-'tah-doh)*
nervous	**nervioso** *(nehr-bee-'oh-soh)*
sore	**dolorido** *(doh-loh-'ree-doh)*
sweaty	**sudoroso** *(soo-doh-'roh-soh)*
tired	**cansado** *(kahn-'sah-doh)*
uncomfortable	**incómodo** *(een-'koh-moh-doh)*
weak	**débil** *('deh-beel)*

Still More Emotions

Más emociones aún
('mahs eh-moh-see-'oh-nehs ah-'oon)

I feel . . .	**Me siento . . .** *(meh see-'ehn-toh)*
angry	**enojado** *(eh-noh-'hah-doh)*
bad	**mal** *(mahl)*
bored	**aburrido** *(ah-boor-'ree-doh)*
calm	**calmado** *(kahl-'mah-doh)*
confused	**confundido** *(kohn-foon-'dee-doh)*
excited	**emocionado** *(eh-moh-see-oh-'nah-doh)*
happy	**feliz** *(feh-'lees)*
relaxed	**relajado** *(reh-lah-'hah-doh)*
sad	**triste** *('trees-teh)*
scared	**espantado** *(ehs-pahn-'tah-doh)*
sleepy	**soñoliento** *(soh-nyoh-lee-'ehn-toh)*
surprised	**sorprendido** *(sohr-prehn-'dee-doh)*
worried	**preocupado** *(preh-oh-koo-'pah-doh)*

¡No se olvide!

- Instead of "How are you?" another popular expression that you can use is **¿Cómo se siente?** *('koh-moh seh see-'ehn-teh)* (How do you feel?).

More parts of the body

Más partes del cuerpo
(mahs 'pahr-tehs dehl 'kwehr-poh)

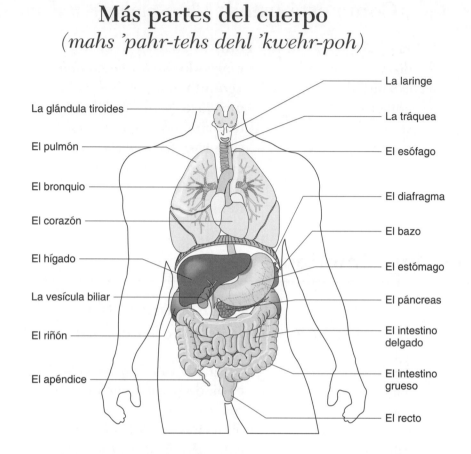

La glándula tiroides
El pulmón
El bronquio
El corazón
El hígado
La vesícula biliar
El riñón
El apéndice

La laringe
La tráquea
El esófago
El diafragma
El bazo
El estómago
El páncreas
El intestino delgado
El intestino grueso
El recto

Learn to inform about the following:

You have problems with the . . .	**Tiene problemas con . . .** *(tee-'eh-neh proh-'bleh-mahs kohn)*
artery	**la arteria** *(lah ahr-'teh-ree·ah)*
cartilage	**el cartílago** *(ehl kahr-'tee-lah-goh)*
glands	**las glándulas** *(lahs 'glahn-doo-lahs)*
hormones	**las hormonas** *(lahs ohr-'moh-nahs)*
immune system	**el sistema inmune** *(ehl sees-'teh-mah een-'moo-neh)*
joints	**las articulaciones** *(lahs ahr-tee-koo-lah-see-'oh-nehs)*
ligament	**el ligamento** *(ehl lee-gah-'mehn-toh)*
spinal column	**la columna vertebral** *(lah koh-'loom-nah behr-teh-'brahl)*
vein	**la vena** *(lah 'veh-nah)*

What happened?

¿Qué pasó? *(keh pah-'soh)*

Just naming body parts is not enough to handle every emergency that'll come your way. You need to also know phrases that will accomplish a lot more. Listen for the "yes" and "no"— **sí** and **no.**

Are you cut?	**¿Está cortado?** *(eh-'stah kohr-'tah-doh)*
Are you injured?	**¿Está herido?** *(eh-'stah eh-'ree-doh)*
Are you in pain?	**¿Tiene dolor?** *(tee-'eh-neh doh-'lohr)*
Are you pregnant?	**¿Está embarazada?** *(eh-'stah ehm-bah-rah-'sah-dah)*
Is it broken?	**¿Está roto?** *(eh-'stah 'roh-toh)*
Is it burned?	**¿Está quemado?** *(eh-'stah keh-'mah-doh)*
Is it infected?	**¿Está infectado?** *(eh-'stah een-fehk-'tah-doh)*
Is it inflamed?	**¿Está inflamado?** *(eh-'stah een-flah-'mah-doh)*
Is it irritated?	**¿Está irritado?** *(eh-'stah eer-ree-'tah-doh)*
Is it twisted?	**¿Está torcido?** *(eh-'stah tohr-'see-doh)*
Is it swollen?	**¿Está hinchado?** *(eh-'stah een-'chah-doh)*

Once you have examined Juan, you'll want to let him and the rest of the Espinoza family know what is wrong. Combine the word **tiene** *(tee-'eh-neh)* with the following vocabulary for a more extensive diagnosis.

He has . . .	**Tiene . . .** *(tee-'eh-neh)*
bruises	**contusiones** *(kohn-too-see-'oh-nehs)*
burns	**quemaduras** *(keh-mah-'doo-rahs)*
a concussion	**una concusión** *('oo-nah kohn-koo-see-'ohn)*
cuts	**cortadas** *(kohr-'tah-dahs)*
a dislocation	**una dislocación** *('oo-nah dees-loh-kah-see-'ohn)*
a fracture	**una fractura** *('oo-nah frahk-'too-rah)*
hemorrhage	**hemorragia** *(heh-mohr-'rah-hee-ah)*
a hernia	**una hernia** *('oo-nah 'ehr-nee-ah)*
lacerations	**laceraciones** *(lah-seh-rah-see-'oh-nehs)*
a pulled muscle	**una distensión** *('oo-nah dees-tehn-see-'ohn)*
punctures	**perforaciones** *(pehr-foh-rah-see-'oh-nehs)*
scrapes	**rasguños** *(rahs-'goo-nyohs)*
a sprain	**una torcedura** *('oo-nah tohr-seh-'doo-rah)*
a swelling	**una hinchazón** *('oo-nah een-chah-'sohn)*
tendonitis	**tendonitis** *(tehn-doh-'nee-tees)*

Is he conscious or unconscious?
¿Está él consciente o inconsciente?
(eh-'stah ehl kohn-see-'ehn-teh oh een-kohn-see-'ehn-teh)

Is she in a coma?
¿Está ella en estado de coma?
(eh-'stah 'eh-yah ehn ehs-'tah-doh deh 'koh-mah)

The emergency room

La sala de emergencias
(lah 'sah-lah deh eh-mehr-'hehn-see·ahs)

While emergency treatment is being applied, invaluable personal information can be collected. Ask the following questions of Juan or his family to further diagnose his condition.

How severe is the pain? **¿Cuán fuerte es el dolor?**
(kwahn foo-'ehr-teh ehs ehl do-'lohr)

Can you move? **¿Puede moverse?** (poo-'eh-deh moh-'behr-seh)

Is your pain . . . **¿Tiene un dolor . . . ?** (tee-'eh-neh oon doh-'lohr)
  burning **quemante** (keh-'mahn-teh)
  constant **constante** (kohn-'stahn-teh)
  deep **profundo** (proh-'foon-doh)
  dull **sordo** ('sohr-doh)
  intermittent **intermitente** (een-tehr-mee-'tehn-teh)
  mild **moderado** (moh-deh-'rah-doh)
  severe **muy fuerte** ('moo·ee 'fwehr-teh)
  sharp **agudo** (ah-'goo-doh)
  stable **estable** (ehs-'tahb-leh)
  throbbing **pulsante** (pool-'sahn-teh)
  worse **peor** (peh-'ohr)

Keep talking, but this time say: You need, she, he needs . . . **Necesita . . .** (neh-seh-'see-tah).

adhesive tape **cinta adhesiva** ('seen-tah ah-deh-'see-vah)
anesthesia **anestesia** (ah-nehs-'the-see-ah)
a bandage **un vendaje** (oon behn-'dah-heh)
a blood transfusion **una transfusión de sangre**
('oo-nah trahns-foo-see·'ohn deh 'sahn-greh)
a cast **una armadura de yeso**
('oo-nah ahr-mah-'doo-rah deh 'yeh-soh)

a compress	**una compresa** (*'oo-nah kohm-'preh-sah*)
CPR	**la resucitación cardiopulmonar** (*lah reh-soo-see-tah-see-'ohn kahr-dee-oh-pool-moh-'nahr*)
direct pressure	**presión directa** (*preh-see-'ohn dee-'rehk-tah*)
an ECG	**un electrocardiograma** (*oon eh-lehk-troh-kahr-dee-oh-'grah-mah*)
first aid	**primeros auxilios** (*pree-'meh-rohs owk-'see-lee-ohs*)
gauze	**la gasa** (*lah 'gah-sah*)
insulin	**insulina** (*een-soo-'lee-nah*)
intensive care	**el cuidado intensivo** (*ehl kwee-'dah-doh een-tehn-'see-boh*)
intravenous fluids	**líquidos intravenosos** (*'lee-kee-dohs een-trah-beh-'noh-sohs*)
a neck brace	**un collar de soporte** (*oon koh-'yahr deh soh-'pohr-teh*)
an operation	**una operación** (*'oo-nah oh-peh-rah-see-'ohn*)
oxygen	**oxígeno** (*ohk-'see-heh-noh*)
penicillin	**penicilina** (*peh-nee-see-'lee-nah*)
physical therapy	**la terapia física** (*lah teh-'rah-pee-ah 'fee-see-kah*)
serum	**el suero** (*ehl 'sweh-roh*)
a shot	**una inyección** (*'oo-nah een-yehk-see-'ohn*)
a sling	**un cabestrillo** (*oon kah-behs-'tree-yoh*)
a splint	**una tablilla** (*'oo-nah tah-'blee-yah*)
stitches	**puntadas** (*poon-'tah-dahs*)
a stretcher	**una camilla** (*'oo-nah kah-'mee-yah*)
a tourniquet	**un torniquete** (*oon tohr-nee-'keh-teh*)
X rays	**los rayos equis** (*lohs 'rah-yohs 'eh-kees*)

More orders

Más mandatos (*mahs mahn-'dah-tohs*)

You definitely will need to give Juan a few commands. Try using these phrases:

breathe	**respire** (*rehs-'pee-reh*)
Breathe more slowly.	**Respire más despacio.** (*rehs-pee-'reh mahs dehs-'pah-see-oh*)
follow	**siga** (*'see-gah*)
Follow instructions.	**Siga las instrucciones.** (*'see-gah lahs een-strook-see-'oh-nehs*)

grab	**agarre** *(ah-'gah-rreh)*
Grab my hand.	**Agarre mi mano.** *(ah-'gah-rreh mee 'mah-noh)*
listen	**escuche** *(ehs-'koo-cheh)*
Listen to the doctor.	**Escuche al doctor.** *(ehs-'koo-cheh ahl dohk-'tohr)*
look	**mire** *('mee-reh)*
Look here.	**Mire aquí.** *('mee-reh ah-'kee)*
lower	**baje** *('bah-heh)*
Lower your head.	**Baje la cabeza.** *('bah-heh lah kah-'beh-sah)*
raise	**levante** *(leh-'bahn-teh)*
Raise your leg.	**Levante la pierna.** *(leh-'bahn-teh lah pee-'ehr-nah)*
tell	**diga** *('dee-gah)*
Tell everything to the nurse.	**Diga todo a la enfermera.** *('dee-gah 'toh-doh ah lah ehn-fehr-'meh-rah)*

Emergencies

Las emergencias *(lahs eh-mehr-'henh-see·ahs)*

Unfortunately, certain dramatic situations may result in a patient being brought to the hospital. Become familiar with these expressions:

an anxiety attack	**un ataque de ansiedad** *(oon ah-'tah-keh deh ahn-see-eh-'dahd)*
a bad fall	**una mala caída** *('oo-nah 'mah-lah kah-'ee-dah)*
a bee sting	**una picadura de abeja** *('oo-nah pee-kah-'doo-rah deh ah-'beh-hah)*
chest pains	**dolor de pecho** *(doh-'lohr deh 'peh-choh)*
a convulsion	**una convulsión** *('oo-nah kohn-bool-see-'ohn)*
dehydration	**deshidratación** *(dehs-ee-drah-tah-see-'ohn)*
a dog bite	**una mordedura de perro** *('oo-nah mohr-deh-'doo-rah deh 'peh-rroh)*
a fainting spell	**un desmayo** *(oon dehs-'mah-yoh)*
fatigue	**fatiga** *(fah-'tee-gah)*
food poisoning	**intoxicación alimentaria** *(een-tohk-see-kah-see-'ohn ah-lee-mehn-'tah-ree-ah)*
frostbite	**congelamiento** *(kohn-heh-lah-mee-'ehn-toh)*
a gunshot wound	**una herida de bala** *('oo-nah eh-'ree-dah deh 'bah-lah)*

a heart attack	**un ataque al corazón** *(oon ah-'tah-keh ahl koh-rah-'sohn)*
heat stroke	**postración** *(pohs-trah-see·'ohn)*
a hemorrhage	**una hemorragia** *('oo-nah eh-moh-'rrah-hee-ah)*
an insect bite	**una mordedura de insecto** *('oo-nah mohr-deh-'doo-rah deh een-'sehk-toh)*
intoxication	**intoxicación** *(een-tohk-see-kah-see·'ohn)*
a knife gash	**una cuchillada** *('oo-nah koo-chee-'yah-dah)*
an overdose	**una dosis excesiva** *('oo-nah 'doh-sees ehk-seh-'see-bah)*
shock	**postración nerviosa** *(pohs-trah-see·'ohn nehr-bee-'oh-sah)*
a snake bite	**una mordedura de culebra** *('oo-nah mohr-deh-'doo-rah deh koo-'leh-brah)*
a spasm	**un espasmo** *(oon ehs-'pahs-moh)*
a stabbing	**una puñalada** *('oo-nah poo-nyah-'lah-dah)*
strangulation	**estrangulamiento** *(ehs-trah-goo-lah-mee-'ehn-toh)*
a stroke	**un ataque fulminante** *(oon ah-'tah-keh fool-mee-'nahn-teh)*
sun stroke	**insolación** *(een-soh-lah-see·'ohn)*
suffocation	**sofocación** *(soh-foh-kah-see·'ohn)*
trauma	**traumatismo** *(traw-mah-'tees-moh)*

On many of your commands, you can add the word **me** to direct the action toward yourself.

call me	**llámeme** *('yah-meh-meh)*
follow me	**sígame** *('see-gah-meh)*
help me	**ayúdeme** *(ah-'yoo-deh-meh)*
look at me	**míreme** *('mee-reh-meh)*
tell me	**dígame** *('dee-gah-meh)*

Dos culturas

Fear and apprehension may cause some accident victims to leave the scene prior to receiving medical treatment. Many non-English-speaking Hispanics do not trust facilities where only English is spoken. If possible, ask a translator to assist you during such an emergency. Patients need to be assured that their lives are in good hands.

More action!

¡Más acción! *(mahs ahk-see·'ohn)*

Once again, you may find yourself limited by what you can say. However, before you learn new action words, take a moment to review some of the verbs and patterns that already have been introduced.

I have to work at 8:00.	**Tengo que trabajar a las ocho.** *('tehn-goh keh trah-bah-'hahr ah lahs 'oh-choh)*
You have to work at 8:00.	**Tiene que trabajar a las ocho.** *(tee-'eh-neh keh trah-bah-'hahr ah lahs 'oh-choh)*
I need to fill out my form.	**Necesito llenar mi formulario.** *(neh-seh-'see-toh yeh-'nahr ehl fohr-moo-'lah-ree·oh)*
You need to fill out your form.	**Necesita llenar su formulario.** *(neh-seh-'see-tah yeh-'nahr soo fohr-moo-'lah-ree·oh)*
I want to return on Friday.	**Quiero regresar el viernes.** *(kee-'eh-roh reh-greh-'sahr ehl bee-'ehr-nehs)*
You want to return on Friday.	**Quiere regresar el viernes.** *(kee-'eh-reh reh-greh-'sahr ehl bee-'ehr-nehs)*

Now, using what you've already learned, think of ways to apply the following action words in real-life emergency situations. Change the endings of these when it's appropriate.

to help	**ayudar** *(ah-yoo-'dahr)*
They help a lot.	**Ayudan mucho.** *(ah-'yoo-dahn 'moo-choh)*
to examine	**examinar** *(ehk-sah-mee-'nahr)*
I examine the patient.	**Examino al paciente.** *(ehk-sah-'mee-noh ahl pah-see-'ehn-teh)*
to send	**mandar** *(mahn-'dahr)*
We send the papers.	**Mandamos los papeles.** *(mahn-'dah-mohs lohs pah-'peh-lehs)*
to drive	**manejar** *(mah-neh-'hahr)*
Do you drive?	**¿Maneja usted?** *(mah-'neh-hah oo-'stehd)*
to put	**poner** *(poh-'nehr)*
Put the forms there.	**Pongan los formularios allí.** *('pohn-gahn lohs fohr-moo-'lah-ree·ohs ah-'yee)*
to receive	**recibir** *(reh-see-'beer)*
We receive the medicine.	**Recibimos la medicina.** *(reh-see-'bee-mohs lah meh-dee-'see-nah)*

to suffer	**sufrir** (soo-'freer)
He isn't suffering.	**El no sufre.** (ehl noh 'soo-freh)
to live	**vivir** (bee-'beer)
We live in California.	**Vivimos en California.**
	(bee-'bee-mohs ehn Kah-lee-'fohr-nee·ah)

¿Cuánto aprendió?

Have you attempted to create any present tense verb forms on your own? By now, you should be able to understand them:

I don't walk much.	**No camino mucho.**
	(noh kah-'mee-noh 'moo-choh)
Tony doesn't smoke.	**Tony no fuma.** (T. noh 'foo-mah)
We run in the park.	**Corremos en el parque.**
	(koh-'rreh-mohs ehn ehl 'pahr-keh)

What are you going to do?

¿Qué va a hacer? (keh bah ah ah-'sehr)

Every health care professional needs to know this pattern, and it's easy to use. To tell Juan what's going to happen next, add your action words to one of these phrases:

I'm going to . . .	**voy a . . .** ('boh·ee ah)
you/he/she is going to . . .	**va a . . .** (bah ah)
they're going to . . .	**van a . . .** (bahn ah)
we're going to . . .	**vamos a . . .** ('bah-mohs ah)

We're going to help the patient.
Vamos a ayudar al paciente.
('bah-mohs ah ah-yoo-'dahr ahl pah-see-'ehn-teh)

I'm going to examine your leg.
Voy a examinar su pierna.
('boh·ee ah ehk-sah-mee-'nahr soo pee-'ehr-nah)

Everything is going to be fine.
Todo va a estar bien.
('toh-doh bah a eh-'stahr 'bee·ehn)

¡No se olvide!

- These words are forms of the verb **ir** *(eer)* (to go). They're usually spoken in reference to location. Observe:

  I'm going to my house.
  Voy a mi casa. *('boh·ee ah mee 'kah-sah)*

  Peter is going to his room.
  Pedro va a su cuarto. *('peh-droh bah ah soo 'kwahr-toh)*

  They're going to the right.
  Van a la derecha. *('bahn ah lah deh-'reh-chah)*

  We're going to the clinic.
  Vamos a la clínica. *('bah-mohs ah lah 'klee-nee-kah)*

- **Le** *(leh)* is another popular part of Spanish sentences. It simply refers to "you," "him," or "her." Notice its position in the following phrases.

  It hurts you.
  Le duele. *(leh 'dweh-leh)*

  We're going to call him.
  Vamos a llamarle. *('bah-mohs ah yah-'mahr-leh)*

  Tell her.
  Dígale. *('dee-gah-leh)*

- **Lo** *(loh)* and **la** *(lah)* are also active parts of Spanish sentences. However, they're used to refer to objects instead of people.

  We're going to examine it.
  Lo vamos a examinar. *(loh 'bah-mohs ah ehk-sah-mee'nahr)*

More emergencies

Más emergencias *('mahs eh-mehr-'hehn-see·ahs)*

Juan or another member of the Espinoza family may come into your facility for some other kind of emergency. Naturally, you can't learn every word in a Spanish/English dictionary. But you can focus on areas that are common. Here are lists of vocabulary for more emergencies, including burns and poisonings.

Burns

Las quemaduras *(lahs keh-mah-'doo-rahs)*

acid	**el ácido** *(ehl 'ah-see-doh)*
chemicals	**los productos químicos** *(lohs proh-'dook-tohs 'kee-mee-kohs)*
electric wires	**los cables eléctricos** *(lohs 'kah-blehs eh-'lehk-tree-kohs)*
fire	**el fuego** *(ehl 'fweh-goh)*
fireworks	**los fuegos artificiales** *(lohs 'fweh-gohs ahr-tee-fee-see-'ah-lehs)*
flames	**las llamas** *(lahs 'yah-mahs)*
gas	**el gas** *(ehl gahs)*
grease	**la grasa** *(lah 'grah-sah)*
hot water	**el agua caliente** *(ehl 'ah-gwah kah-lee-'ehn-teh)*
oil	**el aceite** *(ehl ah-'seh·ee-teh)*
smoke	**el humo** *(ehl 'oo-moh)*
steam	**el vapor** *(ehl vah-'pohr)*

Poisonings

Envenenamientos *(ehn-beh-neh-nah-mee-'ehn-tohs)*

alcohol	**el alcohol** *(ehl ahl-koh-'ohl)*
ammonia	**amoníaco** *(ah-moh-'nee-ah-koh)*
bleach	**el cloro** *(ehl 'kloh-roh)*
carbon monoxide	**el monóxido de carbono** *(ehl moh-'nohk-see-doh deh kahr-'boh-noh)*
cyanide	**el cianuro** *(ehl see-ah-'noo-roh)*
detergent	**el detergente** *(ehl deeh-tehr-'hehn-teh)*
food	**la comida** *(lah koh-'mee-dah)*
insecticide	**el insecticida** *(ehl een-sehk-tee-'see-dah)*
liquor	**el licor** *(ehl lee-'kohr)*
lye	**la lejía** *(lah leh-'hee-ah)*
medicine	**la medicina** *(lah meh-dee-'see-nah)*
mushrooms	**los hongos** *(lohs 'ohn-gohs)*
paint	**la pintura** *(lah peen-'too-rah)*
poison	**el veneno** *(ehl beh-'neh-noh)*
sleeping pills	**los tranquilizantes** *(lohs trahn-kee-lee-'sahn-tehs)*

Drug abuse

El abuso de las drogas
(ehl ah-'boo-soh deh lahs 'droh-gahs)

amphetamines	**las anfetaminas** *(lahs ahn-feh-tah-'mee-nahs)*
barbiturates	**los barbitúricos** *(lohs bahr-bee-'too-ree-kohs)*
capsules	**las cápsulas** *(lahs 'kahp-soo-lahs)*
cigar	**el puro** *(ehl 'poo-roh)*
cigarette	**el cigarrillo** *(ehl see-gah-'rree-yoh)*
cocaine	**la cocaína, la coca** *(lah koh-kah-'ee-nah, lah 'koh-kah)*
codeine	**la codeína** *(lah koh-deh-'ee-nah)*
crack	**el crack** *(ehl krahk)*
depressants	**los sedantes** *(lohs she-'dahn-tehs)*
ecstasy	**la éxtasis** *(lah 'eks-tah-sees)*
glue	**la goma, la cola** *(lah 'goh-mah, lah 'koh-lah)*
hashish	**el hachich** *(ah-'cheech)*
heroin	**la heroína** *(lah eh-roh-'ee-nah)*
inhalants	**los inhaladores** *(lohs een-ah-lah-'doh-rehs)*
LSD	**el ácido** *(ehl 'ah-see-doh)*
marijuana	**la marijuana, la mota, la hierba** *(lah mah-ree-'wah-nah, lah 'moh-tah, lah 'yehr-bah)*
mescaline	**la mescalina** *(lah mehs-kah-'lee-nah)*
morphine	**la morfina** *(lah mohr-'fee-nah)*
pills	**las píldoras** *(lahs 'peel-doh-rahs)*
pipe	**la pipa** *(lah 'pee-pah)*
speed	**la metadrina** *(lah meh-tah-'dree-nah)*
stimulants	**los estimulantes** *(lohs ehs-tee-moo-'lahn-tehs)*
tablets	**las tabletas** *(lahs tah-'bleh-tahs)*

When conversations get serious, these phrases may help:

It seems that . . .
Parece que . . . *(pah-'reh-seh keh)*

It seems that he is taking cocaine.
Parece que está tomando cocaína.
(pah-'reh-seh keh eh-'stah toh-'mahn-doh koh-kah-'ee-nah)

I believe that . . .
Creo que . . . *('kreh-oh keh)*

I believe that these tablets are very strong.
Creo que estas tabletas son muy fuertes.
('kreh-oh keh 'eh-stahs tah-'bleh-tahs sohn 'moo-ee 'fwehr-tehs)

Now make your own sentences with this vocabulary:

So . . .	**Así que** . . .	*(ah-'see keh)*
Therefore . . .	**Por eso** . . .	*(pohr 'eh-soh)*
However . . .	**Sin embargo** . . .	*(seen ehm-'bahr-goh)*

(16) **¿Cuánto aprendió?**

Translate the following terms. They're a lot like English:

convulsiones *(kohn-bool-see·'oh-nehs)*
náusea *('now-seh-ah)*
vómitos *('boh-mee-tohs)*
dilatación de las pupilas *(dee-lah-tah-see·'ohn deh lahs poo-'pee-lahs)*
pupilas reducidas *(poo-'pee-lahs reh-doo-'see-dahs)*
temperatura *(tehm-peh-rah-'too-rah)*
nerviosidad *(nehr-bee-oh-see-'dahd)*
depresión *(deh-preh-see·'ohn)*
tensión *(tehn-see·'ohn)*
ilusiones paranoicas *(ee-loo-see·'oh-nehs pah-rah-'noh·ee-kahs)*
alucinaciones *(ah-loo-see-nah-see·'oh-nehs)*
agresividad *(ah-greh-see-bee-'dahd)*
confusión *(kohn-foo-see·'ohn)*
dificultad respiratoria *(dee-fee-kool-'tahd rehs-pee-rah-'toh-ree·ah)*
irritabilidad *(ee-ree-tah-bee-lee-'dahd)*
insomnio *(een-'sohm-nee·oh)*

There may come a time when you are confronted with a natural disaster. Learn the following vocabulary for dealing with it:

Natural disasters

Los desastres naturales
(lohs deh-'sahs-trehs nah-too-'rah-lehs)

drought	**sequía**	*(seh-'kee-ah)*
earthquake	**terremoto**	*(teh-rreh-'moh-toh)*
epidemic	**epidemia**	*(eh-pee-'deh-mee·ah)*
flood	**inundación**	*(een-oon-dah-see·'ohn)*
forest fire	**incendio de bosque**	*(een-'sehn-dee-oh deh 'bohs-keh)*
hurricane	**huracán**	*(oo-rah-'kahn)*

landslide	**avalancha** *(ah-vah-'lahn-chah)*
tornado	**tornado** *(tohr-'nah-doh)*
tsunami	**sunami** *(soo-'nah-mee)*

Become familiar with these expressions:

Danger!	**¡Peligro!** *(peh-'lee-groh)*
Fire!	**¡Fuego!** *('fweh-goh)*
Help!	**¡Socorro!** *(soh-'koh-rroh)*

Here are some additional words you may need to know:

to beat **golpear** *(gohl-peh-'ahr)*
They want to beat my neighbor.
Quieren golpear a mi vecino. *(keh-'rehn gohl-peh-'ahr ah mee beh-'see-noh)*

to fight **pelear** *(peh-leh-'ahr)*
They fight a lot.
Ellos pelean mucho. *('eh-yohs peh-'leh-ahn 'moo-choh)*

to kick **patear** *(pah-teh-'ahr)*
He does not kick the door.
El no patea la puerta. *(ehl noh pah-'teh-ah lah 'pwehr-tah)*

to kill **matar** *(mah-'tahr)*
Drugs kill.
Las drogas matan. *(lahs 'droh-gahs 'mah-tahn)*

to rape **violar** *(bee-oh-'lahr)*
She was raped.
Ella fue violada. *('eh-yah foo-'eh bee-oh-'lah-dah)*

to shoot **disparar** *(dees-pah-'rahr)*
The police shoot.
La policía dispara. *(lah poh-lee-'see-ah dees-'pah-rah)*

Dos culturas

In many cultures, violence and tragedy are not uncommon. Do not be surprised by people's reaction to emergency situations. Also remember that families and friends will undoubtedly arrive to lend their support. Be aware that groups in the ER can be quite large, and that everyone will want to spend time with the patient.

X rays

Rayos equis *('rah-yohs 'eh-kees)*

It may become necessary to take x rays of Juan's injuries. To help alleviate some of his fear, you'll want to explain all this to Juan. Use the following sentences in Spanish to convey the appropriate information.

Calm down and breathe slowly.
Cálmese y respire más despacio.
('kahl-meh-seh ee rehs-'pee-reh mahs dehs-'pah-see·oh)

Follow my directions.
Siga mis instrucciones.
('see-gah mees een-strook-see·'oh-nehs)

Go to that room and wait.
Vaya a ese cuarto y espere.
('bah-yah ah 'eh-seh 'kwahr-toh ee ehs-'peh-reh)

I will send the information to your doctor.
Voy a mandar la información a su doctor.
('boh·ee ah mahn-'dahr lah een-fohr-mah-see·'ohn ah soo dohk-'tohr)

Move your leg closer and higher.
Mueva la pierna más cerca y más alto.
('mweh-bah lah pee-'ehr-nah mahs 'sehr-kah ee mahs 'ahl-toh)

Sit down on the table and turn around.
Siéntese en la mesa y voltéese.
(see-'ehn-teh-seh ehn lah 'meh-sah ee bohl-'teh-ee-seh)

Thanks for your cooperation.
Gracias por su cooperación.
('grah-see-ahs pohr soo koo-peh-rah-see·'ohn)

Take a deep breath and hold it.
Inspire profundamente y espere.
(een-'spee-reh proh-foon-dah-'mehn-teh ee ehs-'peh-reh)

The results are negative.
Los resultados son negativos.
(lohs reh-sool-'tah-dohs sohn neh-gah-'tee-bohs)

Chapter Five

Capítulo Cinco

(kah-'pee-too-loh 'seen-koh)

The Pregnancy

El Embarazo

(ehl ehm-bah-'rah-soh)

María Espinoza, Juan's wife, thinks she's pregnant with her third child. She has never received medical attention in this country, but her family has encouraged her to see an obstetrician. María needs to be informed about everything from family planning to the care of a newborn. She needs to know what services are available to her, and she needs to have some of her own questions answered. María, like her husband, speaks little or no English. Perhaps some of these Spanish words and phrases will get you started.

Important expressions

Expresiones importantes
(ehks-preh-see·'oh-nehs eem-pohr-'tahn-tehs)

Do you have . . .?	**¿Tiene . . .?** *(tee-'eh-neh)*
allergies	**alergias** *(ah-'lehr-hee·ahs)*
bleeding	**sangramiento** *(sahn-grah-mee-'ehn-toh)*
blisters	**ampollas** *(ahm-'poh-yahs)*
chills	**escalofríos** *(ehs-kah-loh-'free-ohs)*
constipation	**estreñimiento** *(ehs-treh-nyee-mee-'ehn-toh)*
contractions	**contracciones** *(kohn-trahk-see·'oh-nehs)*
convulsions	**convulsiones** *(kohn-bool-see·'oh-nehs)*

cramps · **calambres** *(kah-'lahm-brehs)*

cravings · **antojos** *(ahn-'toh-hohs)*

diarrhea · **diarrea** *(dee-ah-'rreh-ah)*

discharge · **flujo** *('floo-hoh)*

dizziness · **mareos** *(mah-'reh-ohs)*

emotional problems · **problemas emocionales** *(proh-'bleh-mahs eh-moh-see·oh-'nah-lehs)*

exhaustion · **agotamiento** *(ah-goh-tah-mee-'ehn-toh)*

fever · **fiebre** *(fee-'eh-breh)*

genital warts · **verrugas genitales** *(veh-'rroo-gahs heh-nee-'tah-lehs)*

hair loss · **pérdida de cabello** *('pehr-dee-dah deh kah-'beh-yoh)*

hemorrhoids · **hemorroides** *(eh-moh-'rroh·ee-dehs)*

high blood pressure · **presión alta** *(preh-see·'ohn 'ahl-tah)*

hot flashes · **bochornos** *(boh-'chohr-nohs)*

indigestion · **indigestión** *(een-dee-hehs-tee-'ohn)*

itching · **picazón** *(pee-kah-'sohn)*

labor pains · **dolores de parto** *(doh-'loh-rehs deh 'pahr-toh)*

lesions · **lesiones** *(leh-see-'oh-nehs)*

mucus · **mucosidad** *(moo-koh-see-'dahd)*

nausea · **náusea** *('now-seh-ah)*

palpitations · **palpitaciones** *(pahl-pee-tah-see·'oh-nehs)*

your period · **su regla** *(soo 'reh-glah)*

rash · **erupción** *(eh-roop-see·'ohn)*

severe pain · **dolores fuertes** *(doh-'loh-rehs 'fwehr-tehs)*

sexually transmitted disease · **enfermedad transmitida por relaciones sexuales** *(ehn-fehr-meh-'dahd trahns-mee-'tee-dah pohr reh-lah-see-'oh-nehs sehk-soo-'ah-lehs)*

swelling · **hinchazón** *(een-chah-'sohn)*

tender breasts · **senos adoloridos** *('seh-nohs ah-doh-loh-'ree-dohs)*

vaginal discharge · **descarga vaginal** *(dehs-'kahr-gah bah-hee-'nahl)*

varicose veins · **venas varicosas** *('beh-nahs bah-ree-'koh-sahs)*

visual problems · **problemas de visión** *(proh-'bleh-mahs deh bee-see·'ohn)*

weight gain · **aumento de peso** *(ow-'mehn-toh deh 'peh-soh)*

A very important question: When was your last period? **¿Cuándo fue su última regla?** *('kwahn-doh fweh soo 'ool-tee-mah 'reh-glah)*

Do you want to talk?

¿Quiere hablar? *(kee-'eh-reh ah-'blahr)*

María has received most of her medical advice concerning pregnancy from family and friends. When it comes to proper family planning, however, it may be best to bring in a professional. You can offer her counseling with the following information.

Do you want to talk about . . .?	**¿Quiere hablar de . . .?** *(kee-'eh-reh ah-'blahr deh)*
abortion	**el aborto** *(ehl ah-'bohr-toh)*
adoption	**adopción** *(ah-dohp-see-'ohn)*
AIDS	**el SIDA** *(ehl 'see-dah)*
cleanliness	**la limpieza** *(lah leem-pee-'eh-sah)*
your clothing	**su ropa** *(soo 'roh-pah)*
depression	**la depresión** *(lah deh-preh-see-'ohn)*
your diet	**su dieta** *(soo dee-'eh-tah)*
drug use	**el uso de drogas** *(ehl 'oo-soh deh 'droh-gahs)*
erectile dysfunction	**la disfunción eréctil** *(lah dees-foon-see-'ohn eh-'rehk-teel)*
exercise	**el ejercicio** *(ehl eh-hehr-'see-see-oh)*
family planning	**planificación familiar** *(plah-nee-fee-kah-see·'ohn fah-mee-lee-'ahr)*
frigidity	**la frigidez** *(lah free-hee-'dehs)*
hormone therapy	**la terapia hormonal** *(lah teh-'rah-pee-ah ohr-moh-'nahl)*
implants	**los implantes** *(lohs eem-'plahn-tehs)*
impotence	**la impotencia** *(lah eem-poh-'tehn-see-ah)*
infertility	**la infertilidad** *(lah een-fehr-tee-lee-'dahd)*
your job	**su trabajo** *(soo trah-'bah-hoh)*
Lamaze Method	**el método de Lamaze** *(ehl 'meh-toh-doh deh lah-'mah-seh)*
natural childbirth	**el parto natural** *(ehl 'pahr-toh nah-too-'rahl)*
premature ejaculation	**la eyaculación precoz** *(lah eh-yah-koo-lah-see-'ohn preh-'kohs)*
prenatal care	**la atención prenatal** *(lah ah-tehn-see·'ohn preh-nah-'tahl)*
your sexual relations	**sus relaciones sexuales** *(soos reh-lah-see·'oh-nehs sehk-soo-'ah-lehs)*

Birth control methods

Los métodos de anticoncepción
(lohs 'meh-toh-dohs deh ahn-tee-kohn-seh-pee·'ohn)

birth control pills	**las píldoras anticonceptivas** *(lahs 'peel-doh-rahs ahn-tee-kohn-seh-'pee-bahs)*
coitus interruptus	**la interrupción del coito** *(lah een-teh-rroop-see·'ohn dehl koh-'ee-toh)*
condoms	**los condones** *(lohs kohn-'doh-nehs)*
creams	**las cremas** *(lahs 'kreh-mahs)*
diaphragm	**el diafragma** *(ehl dee-ah-'frahg-mah)*
douching	**el baño de asiento** *(ehl 'bah-nyoh deh ah-see-'ehn-toh)*
foams	**las espumas** *(lahs ehs-'poo-mahs)*
hysterectomy	**la histerectomía** *(lah ees-teh-rehk-toh-'mee-ah)*
IUD	**el aparato intrauterino** *(ehl ah-pah-'rah-toh een-trah-oo-teh-'ree-noh)*
rhythm method	**el método del ritmo** *(ehl 'meh-toh-doh dehl 'reet-moh)*
sponge	**la esponja** *(lah ehs-'pohn-hah)*
tubal ligation	**la ligadura de los tubos** *(lah lee-gah-'doo-rah deh lohs 'too-bohs)*
vasectomy	**la vasectomía** *(lah bah-sehk-toh-'mee-ah)*

The reproductive systems

Los sistemas reproductivos
(los sees-'teh-mahs reh-proh-dook-'tee-vohs)

Here is the male reproductive system:

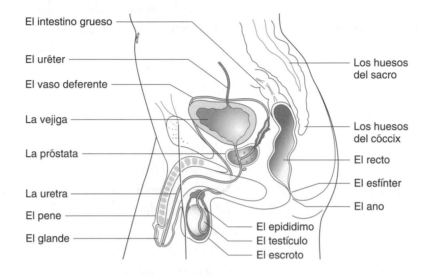

- El intestino grueso
- El uréter
- El vaso deferente
- La vejiga
- La próstata
- La uretra
- El pene
- El glande
- Los huesos del sacro
- Los huesos del cóccix
- El recto
- El esfínter
- El ano
- El epididimo
- El testículo
- El escroto

And here is the female reproductive system:

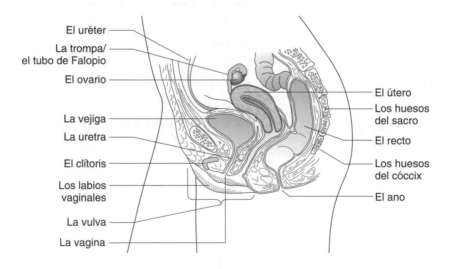

- El uréter
- La trompa/ el tubo de Falopio
- El ovario
- La vejiga
- La uretra
- El clítoris
- Los labios vaginales
- La vulva
- La vagina
- El útero
- Los huesos del sacro
- El recto
- Los huesos del cóccix
- El ano

Additional relevant terms:

embryo	**el embrión** *(ehl ehm-bree-'ohn)*
fertilization	**la fertilización** *(lah fehr-tee-lee-sah-see·'ohn)*
fetus	**el feto** *(ehl 'feh-toh)*
genes	**los genes** *(lohs 'heh-nehs)*
gestation	**la gestación** *(lah hehs-tah-see·'ohn)*

hormones	**las hormonas** *(lahs ohr-'moh-nahs)*
intercourse	**el coito** *(ehl 'koh·ee-toh)*
menstrual cycle	**el ciclo menstrual** *(ehl 'seek-loh mehn-stroo-'ahl)*
ovum	**el óvulo** *(ehl 'oh-voo-loh)*
placenta	**la placenta** *(lah plah-'sehn-tah)*
semen	**el semen** *(ehl 'seh-mehn)*
sperm	**la esperma** *(lah ehs-'pehr-mah)*
umbilical cord	**el cordon umbilical**
	(ehl kohr-'dohn oom-bee-lee-'kahl)

You are pregnant

Está embarazada *(eh-'stah ehm-bah-rah-'sah-dah)*

María will need to undergo several tests. The results from those tests must be made available to her in clear instructions. Use the following patterns to communicate this information.

Let's check the . . .

Verifiquemos . . . *(beh-ree-fee-'keh-mohs)*

area	**el área** *(ehl 'ah-reh-ah)*
liquid	**el líquido** *(ehl 'lee-kee-doh)*
organ	**el órgano** *(ehl 'ohr-gah-noh)*
pulse	**el pulso** *(ehl 'pool-soh)*
size	**el tamaño** *(ehl tah-'mahn-yoh)*

You need a . . .

Necesita un . . . *(neh-seh-'see-tah oon)*

AIDS test	**examen de SIDA** *(ehk-'sah-mehn deh 'see-dah)*
blood test	**examen de sangre** *(ehk-'sah-mehn deh 'sahn-greh)*
enema	**enema** *(eh-'neh-mah)*
pap smear	**examen de Papanicolao**
	(ehk-'sah-mehn deh pah-pah-nee-koh-'lah-oh)
pelvic exam	**examen pélvico** *(ehk-'sah-mehn 'pehl-bee-koh)*
pregnancy test	**examen de embarazo**
	(ehk-'sah-mehn deh ehm-bah-'rah-soh)

rectal exam	**examen del recto** (ehk-'sah-mehn dehl 'rehk-toh)
Rh factor test	**examen del factor Rhesus** (ehk-'sah-mehn dehl fahk-'tohr 'Reh-soos)
urine test	**examen de orina** (ehk-'sah-mehn deh oh-'ree-nah)

Use all the Spanish you've learned to conduct the following interview with María.

Did you ever have a miscarriage?
¿Perdió el bebé alguna vez? (perh-dee-'oh ehl beh-'beh ahl-'goo-nah behs)

Do you have other children?
¿Tiene otros hijos? ('tee-'eh-neh 'oh-trohs 'ee-hohs)

What are you going to need?
¿Qué va a necesitar? (keh bah a neh-seh-see-'tahr)

When is the date of birth?
¿Cuándo es la fecha de nacimiento?
('kwahn-doh ehs lah 'feh-chah deh nah-see-mee-'ehn-toh)

Who is the father?
¿Quién es el padre? (kee-'ehn ehs ehl 'pah-dreh)

There isn't time!

¡No hay tiempo! (noh 'ah·ee tee-'ehm-poh)

While you're handling María's pregnancy, time may become important to the conversation. Spend a few **momentos** scanning this next vocabulary list. These words are invaluable to health care professionals.

When?

¿Cuándo? ('kwahn-doh)

after	**después** (dehs-'pwehs)
already	**ya** (yah)
always	**siempre** (see-'ehm-preh)
before	**antes** ('ahn-tehs)
early	**temprano** (tehm-'prah-noh)
frequently	**con frecuencia** (kohn freh-'kwehn-see-ah)
late	**tarde** ('tahr-deh)
later	**luego** (loo-'eh-goh)

many times	**muchas veces** (*'moo-chahs 'beh-sehs*)
never	**nunca** (*'noon-kah*)
now	**ahora** (*ah-'oh-rah*)
once	**una vez** (*'oo-nah behs*)
right now	**ahorita** (*ah-oh-'ree-tah*)
sometimes	**a veces** (*ah 'beh-sehs*)
soon	**pronto** (*'prohn-toh*)
then	**entonces** (*ehn-'tohn-sehs*)
yet	**todavía** (*toh-dah-'bee-ah*)

Learn as many "time" words as you can:

day after tomorrow	**pasado mañana** (*pah-'sah-doh mah-'nyah-nah*)
day before yesterday	**anteayer** (*ahn-teh-ah-'yehr*)
last night	**anoche** (*ah-'noh-cheh*)
tomorrow	**mañana** (*mah-'nyah-nah*)
tonight	**esta noche** (*'eh-stah 'noh-cheh*)

(17)   ## ¿Cuánto aprendió?

Are you able to interpret the sample phrases below?

ago	**hace** (*'ah-seh*)
	hace una semana (*'ah-seh 'oo-nah seh-'mah-nah*)
between	**entre** (*'ehn-treh*)
	entre las tres y las cuatro
	(*'ehn-treh lahs trehs ee lahs 'kwah-troh*)
the following	**el siguiente** (*ehl see-gee-'ehn-teh*)
	el siguiente día (*ehl see-gee-'ehn-teh 'dee-ah*)
last	**el pasado** (*ehl pah-'sah-doh*)
	el pasado año (*ehl pah-'sah-doh 'ah-nyoh*)
the next	**el próximo** (*ehl 'prohk-see-moh*)
	el próximo mes (*ehl 'prohk-see-moh mehs*)
until	**hasta** (*'ah-stah*)
	hasta mañana (*'ah-stah mah-'nyah-nah*)
within	**dentro de** (*'dehn-troh deh*)
	dentro de dos horas (*'dehn-troh deh dohs 'oh-rahs*)

Match the words on the left with their opposites.

temprano *(tehm-'prah-noh)*   **muchas veces** *('moo-chahs 'beh-sehs)*
mañana *(mah-'nyah-nah)*   **siempre** *(see-'ehm-preh)*
el próximo *(ehl 'prohk-see-moh)*   **tarde** *('tahr-deh)*
una vez *('oo-nah behs)*   **después** *(dehs-'pwehs)*
nunca *('noon-kah)*   **ayer** *(ah-'yehr)*
antes *('ahn-tehs)*   **el pasado** *(ehl pah-'sah-doh)*

We need answers

Necesitamos respuestas
(neh-seh-see-'tah-mohs rehs-'pwehs-tahs)

Never give up on your standard **preguntas**. Use the basic question words to gather more information.

How much . . .?	**¿Cuánto . . .?** *('kwahn-toh)*
do you weigh	**pesa** *('peh-sah)*
did you gain	**subió** *(soo-bee-'oh)*
time	**tiempo** *(tee-'ehm-poh)*

How often?	**¿Cada cuánto tiempo?**
	('kah-dah 'kwahn-toh tee-'ehm-poh)

How long ago?	**¿Hace cuánto tiempo?**
	('ah-seh 'kwahn-toh tee-'ehm-poh)

How many . . .?	**¿Cuántos? ¿Cuántas . . .?**
	('kwahn-tohs, 'kwahn-tahs)
days	**días** *('dee-ahs)*
hours	**horas** *('oh-rahs)*
minutes	**minutos** *(mee-'noo-tohs)*
months	**meses** *('meh-sehs)*
seconds	**segundos** *(seh-'goon-dohs)*
weeks	**semanas** *(seh-'mah-nahs)*
years	**años** *('ah-nyohs)*

The past

El pasado (ehl pah-'sah-doh)

Gathering data on María's past requires working knowledge of Spanish verbs. Try to recall the changes that take place to most verb endings when we refer to <u>present</u> action.

to speak	**hablar** (ah-'blahr)
I speak a little Spanish.	**Hablo poquito español.** ('ah-bloh poh-'kee-toh ehs-pah-'nyohl)
to live	**vivir** (vee-'veer)
Where do you live?	**¿Dónde vive usted?** ('dohn-deh 'vee-veh oo-'stehd)
to eat	**comer** (koh-'mehr)
We eat at 6:00.	**Comemos a las seis.** (koh-'meh-mohs ah lahs 'seh·ees)

Although there are a variety of ways to state a <u>past</u> tense in Spanish, you need to start by learning the more commonly used form. Read the following examples and, just as you did with <u>present</u> actions, make the changes in your verbs. You won't be perfect at first, but María will know what you're trying to say.

- **ar** ending verbs—**HABLAR** (ah-'blahr) TO SPEAK

I spoke with the doctor.	**Hablé con el doctor.** (ah-'bleh kohn ehl dohk-'tohr)
You/he/she spoke a lot.	**Habló mucho.** (ah-'bloh 'moo-choh)
They spoke in English.	**Hablaron en inglés.** (ah-'blah-rohn ehn een-'glehs)
We spoke afterwards.	**Hablamos después.** (ah-'blah-mohs dehs-'pwehs)

- **er/ir** ending verbs—**BEBER** (beh-'behr) TO DRINK
  SALIR (sah-'leer) TO LEAVE

I left at eight.	**Salí a las ocho.** (sah-'lee ah lahs 'oh-choh)
I drank the medicine.	**Bebí la medicina.** (beh-'bee lah meh-dee-'see-nah)
You/he/she left late.	**Salió tarde.** (sah-lee-'oh 'tahr-deh)
You/he/she drank the coffee.	**Bebió el café.** (beh-bee-'oh ehl kah-'feh)

They left happy.	**Salieron contentos.**
	(sah-lee-'eh-rohn kohn-'tehn-tohs)
They drank water last night.	**Bebieron agua anoche.**
	(beh-bee-'eh-rohn 'ah-gwah ah-'noh-cheh)
We left in a car.	**Salimos en el carro.**
	(sah-'lee-mohs ehn ehl 'kah-rroh)
We drank the day before yesterday.	**Bebimos anteayer.**
	(beh-'bee-mohs ahn-teh-ah-'yehr)

Some common verbs have irregular past tenses, so be on the lookout.

To be—**Ser** *(sehr)* or To go—**Ir** *(eer)*

I was or went	**fui** *(fwee)*
you were or went	**fue** *(fweh)*
he/she was or went	**fue** *(fweh)*
you (plural)/they were or went	**fueron** *('fweh-rohn)*
we were or went	**fuimos** *('fwee-mohs)*

To have—**Tener** *(teh'nehr)*

I had	**tuve** *('too-beh)*
you/he/she had	**tuvo** *('too-boh)*
you (plural)/they had	**tuvieron** *(too-bee-'eh-rohn)*
we had	**tuvimos** *(too-'bee-mohs)*

Past tense isn't the only verb form you're going to need. Although these won't be discussed in detail, check out the spellings and meanings of these examples below:

I used to have	**tenía** *(teh-'nee-ah)*
I would have	**tendría** *(tehn-'dree-ah)*
I will have	**tendré** *(tehn-'dreh)*

(18) **¿Cuánto aprendió?**

Translate the following messages.

¿Qué comió? *(keh koh-mee-'oh)*

¿Tomó medicina? *(toh-'moh meh-dee-'see-nah)*

¿Fumó? *(foo-'moh)*

¿Se enfermó? *(seh ehn-fehr-'moh)*

¿Tuvo problemas? *('too-boh proh-'bleh-mahs)*

Build your commands

Construya sus órdenes
(kohns-'troo-yah soos 'or-deh-nehs)

A simple approach to forming a command in Spanish requires knowledge of the three different action word (verb) endings. As we stated above, the endings are:

ar as in **hablar**—to speak

er as in **comer**—to eat

ir as in **escribir**—to write

To make a command, drop the last two letters of the infinitive form and replace them as follows.

ar	**e**	
hablar *(ah-'blahr)*	**hable** *('ah-bleh)*	speak
er	**a**	
comer *(koh-'mehr)*	**coma** *('koh-mah)*	eat
ir	**a**	
escribir *(ehs-kree-'beer)*	**escriba** *(ehs-'kree-bah)*	write

But beware. Some verbs are strange and simply have to be memorized.

ir *(eer)*	**vaya** *('bah-yah)*	go
venir *(beh-'neer)*	**venga** *('behn-gah)*	come
decir *(deh-'seer)*	**diga** *('dee-gah)*	speak

More action!

¡Más acción! *(mahs ahk-see-see·'ohn)*

Add these action words to your list. They specifically target the needs of patients like María.

to be born	**nacer**
When were you born?	**¿Cuándo nació?** *('kwahn-doh nah-see-'oh)*
to begin	**comenzar** *(koh-mehn-'sahr)*
When did the pains begin?	**¿Cuándo comenzaron los dolores?** *('kwahn-doh koh-mehn-'sah-rohn lohs doh-'loh-rehs)*

to defecate	**defecar** *(deh-feh-'kahr)*
Did you defecate?	**¿Defecó?** *(deh-feh-'koh)*
to end	**terminar** *(tehr-mee-'nahr)*
Did the pains stop?	**¿Terminaron los dolores?** *(tehr-mee-'nah-rohn lohs doh-'loh-rehs)*
to grow	**crecer** *(kreh-'sehr)*
He grew very fast.	**Creció muy rápido.** *(kreh-see-'oh 'moo·ee 'rah-pee-doh)*
to menstruate	**menstruar** *(mehn-stroo-'ahr)*
When did you menstruate?	**¿Cuándo menstruó?** *('kwahn-doh mehn-stroo-'oh)*
to rest	**descansar** *(dehs-kahn-'sahr)*
Are you going to rest?	**¿Va a descansar?** *(bah ah dehs-kahn-'sahr)*
to urinate	**orinar** *(oh-ree-'nahr)*
Do you urinate a lot?	**¿Orina mucho?** *(oh-ree-'nah 'moo-choh)*
to visit	**visitar** *(bee-see-'tahr)*
I need to visit María.	**Necesito visitar a María.** *(neh-seh-'see-toh bee-see-'tahr ah mah-'ree-ah)*

Can I help you?

¿Puedo ayudarle? *('pweh-doh ah-yoo-'dahr-leh)*

Here's still another one of those incredible verb patterns that makes speaking Spanish so much easier. Combine your verbs with the forms of the word **poder**, which means "can."

I can	**puedo** *('pweh-doh)*
I can begin.	**Puedo comenzar.** *('pweh-doh koh-mehn-'sahr)*
You, she/he can	**puede** *('pweh-deh)*
She can visit.	**Puede visitar.** *('pweh-deh bee-see-'tahr)*
you (plural)/they can	**pueden** *('pweh-dehn)*
They can rest.	**Pueden descansar.** *('pweh-dehn dehs-kahn-'sahr)*
we can	**podemos** *(poh-'deh-mohs)*
We can finish.	**Podemos terminar.** *(poh-'deh-mohs tehr-mee-'nahr)*

María feels comfortable with her physician, and decides to visit the clinic at least once a month. As her time draws near, your questions may grow in intensity. Use your newly-acquired skill of using past tense to help you with these questions.

At what age did you begin to menstruate?
¿A qué edad comenzó a menstruar?
(ah keh eh-'dahd koh-mehn-'soh ah mehn-stroo-'ahr)

Do you have a hereditary disease?
¿Tiene una enfermedad hereditaria?
(tee-'eh-neh 'oo-nah ehn-fehr-meh-'dahd eh-reh-dee-'tah-ree·ah)

Do you have shortness of breath?
¿Respira con dificultad? *(rehs-'pee-rah kohn dee-fee-kool-'tahd)*

Do your breasts hurt?
¿Le duelen los senos?
(leh 'dweh-lehn lohs 'seh-nohs)

Is there blood or water?
¿Hay sangre o agua?
('ah·ee 'sahn-greh oh 'ah-gwah)

Were all your pregnancies normal?
¿Fueron todos sus embarazos normales?
('fweh-rohn 'toh-dohs soos ehm-bah-'rah-sohs nohr-'mah-lehs)

When it comes to multiple births, you should also learn these words:

second	**segundo** *(seh-'goon-doh)*
third	**tercero** *(tehr-'seh-roh)*
fourth	**cuarto** *('kwahr-toh)*
fifth	**quinto** *('keen-toh)*
sixth	**sexto** *('sehks-toh)*
seventh	**séptimo** *('sehp-tee-moh)*
eighth	**octavo** *(ohk-'tah-boh)*

Commands

Ordenes *('ohr-deh-nehs)*

The weeks are going by quickly. Check to see if María is following your instructions. Review your command words.

Bring the urine.	**Traiga la orina.** *('trah·ee-gah la oh-'ree-nah)*
Call the gynecologist.	**Llame al ginecólogo.** *('yah-meh ahl hee-neh-'koh-loh-goh)*

Come with your husband.	**Venga con su esposo.**
	('behn-gah kohn soo ehs-'poh-soh)
Follow the diet.	**Siga la dieta.** *('see-gah lah dee-'eh-tah)*
Take the medicine.	**Tome la medicina.**
	('toh-meh lah meh-dee-'see-nah)

Add a few more commands and create your own sentences.

pull	**jale** *('hah-leh)*
push	**empuje** *(ehm-'poo-heh)*
bend	**doble** *('doh-bleh)*
open	**abra** *('ah-brah)*
close	**cierre** *(see-'eh-rreh)*
eat	**coma** *('koh-mah)*

María is ready to deliver, and it's time for action. You probably won't have the opportunity to read these expressions at the time of the birth, so you may want to memorize them before it's too late.

Breathe deeply.	**Respire profundamente.**
	(rehs-'pee-reh proh-foon-dah-'mehn-teh)
Grab my hand.	**Agarre mi mano.** *(ah-'gah-rreh mee 'mah-noh)*
Move your leg.	**Mueva la pierna.**
	('moo·ee-bah lah pee-'ehr-nah)
Raise your head.	**Levante la cabeza.**
	(leh-'bahn-teh lah kah-'beh-sah)
Rest.	**Descanse.** *(dehs-'kahn-seh)*
This is for the pain.	**Esto es para el dolor.**
	('ehs-toh ehs 'pah-rah ehl doh-'lohr)
You need anesthesia.	**Necesita anestesia.**
	(neh-seh-'see-tah ah-nehs-'teh-see·ah)
You need a Cesarean section.	**Necesita una operación cesárea.**
	(neh-seh-'see-tah 'oo-nah oh-peh-rah-see-'ohn seh-'sah-reh-ah)

While giving orders to María, use the word **así,** *(ah-'see)* which means "like this." Breathe like this. **Respire así.** *(rehs-'pee-reh ah-'see)*

Remember to always say **por favor** *(pohr fah-'bohr)* (please) and **gracias** *('grah-see·ahs)* (thanks) with your commands. They help!

Note: Many Hispanics use the expression **dar a luz** *(dahr ah loos)* when referring to childbirth: María gave birth. **María dio a luz.** *(mah-'ree-ah dee-'oh ah loos)*

Dos culturas

Babies are sacred creatures in most cultures. In many Hispanic homes, the traditions and rituals of childbearing are not easily changed. Some family customs are centuries old, even though they may contradict modern science. Keep these things in mind as you give advice to expectant mothers.

The newborn

El recién nacido *(ehl reh-see-'ehn nah-'see-doh)*

Congratulations! It's a girl! **¡una niña!** *('oo-nah 'nee-nyah)* The delivery went well, the baby is healthy, and mother is doing fine. After she rests, María is going to need some information about proper care of the newborn. Although this is her third child, she needs to know what is best for her new baby girl. By the way, her name is Angelina.

Do you want to go home?
¿Quiere ir a la casa?
(kee-'eh-reh eer ah lah 'kah-sah)

She must eat a lot every day.
Tiene que comer mucho todos los días.
(tee'eh-neh keh koh-'mehr 'moo-choh 'toh-dohs lohs 'dee-ahs)

They eat every 3 or 4 hours.
Comen cada tres o cuatro horas.
('koh-mehn 'kah-dah trehs oh 'kwah-troh 'oh-rahs)

You must prepare the formula.
Tiene que preparar la fórmula.
(tee-'eh-neh keh preh-pah-'rahr lah 'fohr-moo-lah)

You will need a pediatrician.
Va a necesitar un pediatra.
(bah a neh-seh-see-'tahr oon peh-dee-'ah-trah)

Will you be breast feeding?
Va a amamantar?
(bah ah ah-mah-mahn-'tahr)

Describe her!

Describála (dehs-'kree-bah-lah)

Some of the first words you'll want to express to María will be descriptive words relating to her new baby, Angelina. Try these:

She is . . .	**Es . . .** (ehs)
bald	**calvita** (kahl-'bee-tah)
blond	**rubia** ('roo-bee·ah)
brunette	**morena** (moh-'reh-nah)
dark-skinned	**prieta** (pree·'eh-tah)
redhead	**pelirroja** (peh-lee-'roh-hah)
a twin	**una gemela** ('oo-nah heh-'meh-lah)

How much does the baby weigh? **¿Cuánto pesa el bebé?** ('kwahn-toh 'peh-sah ehl beh-'beh) Study these terms:

grams	**gramos** ('grah-mohs)
inches	**pulgadas** (pool-'gah-dahs)
liters	**litros** ('leet-rohs)
meters	**metros** ('meht-rohs)
ounces	**onzas** ('ohn-sahs)
pounds	**libras** ('lee-brahs)

Bad news

¡Malas noticias! ('mah-lahs noh-'tee-see·ahs)

Not all news is good news. Sometimes patients are not as fortunate as María when it comes to the health of their baby.

It is . . .	**Es** (ehs) . . .
or It has . . .	**Tiene** (tee-'eh-neh) . . .
a birth defect	**un defecto de nacimiento** (oon deh-'fehk-toh deh nah-see-mee-'ehn-toh)
blind	**ciego** (see-'eh-goh)
a cleft lip	**el labio leporino** (ehl 'lah-bee-oh leh-poh-'ree-noh)
cross-eyed	**bizco** ('bees-koh)
deaf	**sordo** ('sohr-doh)
fetal alcohol syndrome	**el síndrome de alcohol fetal** (ehl 'seen-droh-meh deh ahl-koh-'ohl feh-'tahl)

an induced abortion	**un aborto inducido**
	(oon ah-'bohr-toh een-doo-'see-doh)
jaundice	**ictericia** *(eek-teh-'ree-see·ah)*
malnutrition	**desnutrición** *(dehs-noo-tree-see-'ohn)*
a miscarriage	**una pérdida** *(oo-nah 'pehr-dee-dah)*
premature	**prematuro** *(preh-mah-'too-roh)*
SIDS	**el síndrome de muerte infantil súbita**
	(ehl 'seen-droh-meh deh 'mwehr-teh een-fahn-'teel 'soo-bee-tah)
stillborn	**nacido muerto** *(nah-'see-doh 'mwehr-toh)*

¡No se olvide!

Remember how the words change based upon the child's sex:

The baby girl is premature.
La bebé es prematura. *(lah beh-'beh ehs preh-mah-'too-rah)*

The baby boy is premature.
El bebé es prematuro. *(ehl beh-'beh ehs preh-mah-'too-roh)*

Visiting hours

Las horas de visita
(lahs 'oh-rahs deh bee-'see-tah)

Family and friends will no doubt want to come visit María and her new child. Prepare yourself by learning the phrase for "I'm sorry, but . . ." **"Lo siento, pero . . ."** *(loh see-'ehn-toh 'peh-roh)*

Children do not visit patients.
Los niños no visitan a los pacientes.
(lohs 'nee-nyohs noh bee-'see-tahn ah lohs pah-see-'ehn-tehs)

She needs rest.
Ella necesita descansar.
('eh-yah neh-seh-'see-tah dehs-kahn-'sahr)

The patient isn't seeing any visitors.
El paciente no recibe visitantes.
(ehl pah-see-'ehn-teh noh reh-'see-beh bee-see-'tahn-tehs)

There are too many visitors in the room.
Hay demasiados visitantes en el cuarto.
('ae·ee deh-'mah-see-ah-dohs bee-see-'tahn-tehs ehn ehl 'kwahr-toh)

Visitors during visiting hours only, please.
Visitantes solamente durante las horas de visita, por favor.
(bee-see-'tahn-tehs soh-lah-'mehn-teh doo-'rahn-teh lahs 'oh-rahs deh bee-'see-tah, pohr fah-'vohr)

Visiting hours are over.
Las horas de visita terminaron.
(lahs 'oh-rahs de bee-'see-tah tehr-mee-'nah-rohn)

Infants

¡Los infantes! *(lohs een-'fahn-tehs)*

Care to know more about babies? These words will definitely get it done.

bottle nipple or pacifier	**el chupete** *(ehl choo-'peh-teh)*
The bottle nipple is very big.	**El chupete es muy grande.** *(ehl choo-'peh-teh ehs 'moo·eeh 'grahn-deh)*
colic	**el cólico** *(ehl 'koh-lee-koh)*
The baby has colic.	**El bebé tiene cólico.** *(ehl beh-'beh tee-'eh-neh 'koh-lee-koh)*
diaper	**el pañal** *(ehl pah-'nyahl)*
He urinated in the diaper.	**Orinó en el pañal.** *(oh-ree-'noh ehn ehl pah-'nyahl)*
formula	**la fórmula** *(lah 'fohr-moo-lah)*
We have the formula.	**Tenemos la fórmula.** *(teh-'neh-mohs lah 'fohr-moo-lah)*
incubator	**la incubadora** *(lah een-koo-bah-'doh-rah)*
He/she is still in the incubator.	**Todavía está en la incubadora.** *(toh-dah-'vee-ah ehs-'tah ehn lah een-koo-bah-'doh-rah)*
milk	**la leche** *(lah 'leh-cheh)*
Do you want more milk?	**¿Quiere más leche?** *(kee-'eh-reh mahs 'leh-cheh)*
nap	**la siesta** *(lah see-'ehs-tah)*
She needs a nap.	**Necesita una siesta.** *(neh-seh-'see-tah 'oo-nah see-'ehs-tah)*
nursing bottle	**el biberón** *(ehl bee-beh-'rohn)*
Use the nursing bottle.	**Use el biberón.** *('oo-seh ehl bee-beh-'rohn)*

rash	**la erupción** *(lah eh-roop-see·'ohn)*
I am going to examine the rash.	**Voy a examinar la erupción.** *('boh·ee ah ehk-sah-mee-'nahr lah eh-roohp-see·'ohn)*
talcum powder	**el talco** *(ehl 'tahl-koh)*
Where is the talcum powder?	**¿Dónde está el talco?** *('dohn-deh eh-'stah ehl 'tahl-koh)*

And don't forget: Hugs and kisses! **¡Abrazos y besos!** *(ah-'brah-sohs ee 'beh-sohs)*

Dos culturas

Jewish religion requires the rite of circumcision—**circuncisión** *(seehr-coon-see-see·'ohn)*—and this practice also has become common among non-Jews in the United States. The opposite is true for Latin people. They often are surprised and shocked when the hospital nurse or physician asks them, as a matter of fact, about performing the procedure. Be aware that the overwhelming majority of Latin people are neither circumcised nor do they wish their babies to be circumcised.

At home

En casa *(ehn 'kah-sah)*

María is grateful for all your efforts, and can't wait to tell all her friends about the outstanding care she received. Here are some phrases you can use to let her know about some of your other programs.

There are . . .	**Hay** *('ah-ee)* . . .
classes for mothers	**clases para las madres** *('klah-sehs 'pah-rah lahs 'mah-drehs)*
exercise classes	**clases para ejercicios** *('klah-sehs 'pah-rah eh-hehr-'see-see·ohs)*
flu shots	**vacunas contra la influenza** *(vah-'koo-nahs 'kohn-trah lah een-floo-'ehn-sah)*
free vaccination	**vacunación gratuita** *(bah-koo-nah-see-'ohn grah-too-'ee-tah)*
services for teen-age pregnancies	**servicios para adolescentes embarazadas** *(sehr-'bee-see·ohs 'pah-rah ah-doh-leh-'sehn-tehs ehm-bah-rah-'sah-dahs)*

Chapter Six

Capítulo Seis
(kah-'pee-too-loh 'seh·ees)

Margarita Espinoza, Age Six

Little Margarita has had a chest cold for several days. Home remedies have been tried, but her condition has only gotten worse. She now has acute bronchitis and needs a physician's care. A pediatrician has recently opened a small office in the neighborhood and everyone says she is great with children—**los niños.** Juan and María have just made an appointment for their ailing daughter.

Young children require special care and, in order to communicate properly, lots of special Spanish vocabulary is required. Let's observe what goes on in the pediatrician's office, and discover what is being used to nurse the little ones back to good health.

The visit

La visita *(lah vee-'see-tah)*

Office or clinic visits will also be required, so notice how these key words are used:

Is this your first visit?	**¿Es su primera visita?** *(ehs soo pree-'meh-rah vee-'see-tah)*
Is it an emergency?	**¿Es una emergencia?** *(ehs 'oo-nah eh-mehr-'hehn-see-ah)*
What time is your appointment?	**¿A qué hora tiene cita?** *(ah keh 'oh-rah tee-'eh-neh 'see-tah)*

Please…	**Por favor…** (*pohr fah-'vohr*)
come back later	**regrese más tarde** (*reh-'greh-seh mahs 'tahr-deh*)
fill out these forms	**llene estos formularios** (*'yeh-neh 'ehs-tohs fohr-moo-'lah-ree-ohs*)
sign here	**firme aquí** (*'feer-meh ah-'kee*)
take a seat	**siéntese** (*see-'ehn-teh-seh*)
wait a moment	**espere un momento** (*ehs-'peh-reh oon moh-'mehn-toh*)
May I see your…?	**¿Puedo ver su/sus…?** (*'pweh-doh vehr soo/soos*)
ID	**identificación** (*ee-dehn-tee-fee-kah-see-'ohn*)
insurance card	**tarjeta de seguro médico** (*tahr-'heh-tah deh seh-'goo-roh 'meh-dee-koh*)
lab results	**resultados del laboratorio** (*reh-sool-'tah-dohs dehl lah-boh-rah-'toh-ree-oh*)
prescription	**receta médica** (*reh-'seh-tah 'meh-dee-kah*)
X rays	**radiografías** (*rah-dee-oh-grah-'fee-ahs*)
The doctor…	**El doctor…** (*ehl dohk-'tohr*)
is a little behind schedule	**está un poco atrasado** (*ehs-'tah oon 'poh-koh ah-trah-'sah-doh*)
is not in the office today	**no está en la oficina hoy** (*noh ehs-'tah ehn lah oh-fee-'see-nah 'oh-ee*)
is with another patient	**está con otro paciente** (*ehs-'tah kohn 'oh-troh pah-see-'ehn-teh*)
will see you in two weeks	**lo verá en dos semanas** (*loh veh-'rah ehn dohs seh-'mah-nahs*)
will see you now	**lo verá ahora mismo** (*loh veh-'rah ah-'oh-rah 'mees-moh*)

Margarita cannot get proper care until you have more answers about her past history. As usual, everything is divided into similar patterns.

Begin by asking the parents to respond to your questions about the patient with a simple **sí** (*see*) or **no** (*noh*).

Does she have pain?	**¿Tiene dolor?** (*tee-'eh-neh doh-'lohr*)
Is it an injury?	**¿Es una herida?** (*ehs oonah eh-'ree-dah*)
Is she sick?	**¿Está enferma?** (*eh-'stah ehn-'fehr-mah*)

Remember the *present* tense verb form? It works great during office visits.

It burns...	**Me quema . . .** *(meh 'keh-mah)*
It hurts...	**Me duele . . .** *(meh doo-'eh-leh)*
It itches...	**Me pica . . .** *(meh 'pee-kah)*

Does he/she breathe well?	**¿Respira bien?** *(reh-'spee-rah bee·'ehn)*
Does he/she drink milk?	**¿Toma leche?** *('toh-mah 'leh-cheh)*
Does he/she eat well?	**¿Come bien?** *('koh-meh bee·'ehn)*
Does he/she talk?	**¿Habla?** *('ah-blah)*
Does he/she walk?	**¿Camina?** *(kah-'mee-nah)*

More action

Más acción *(mahs ahk-see·'ohn)*

Eventually, you are going to run out of things to say. As you have already discovered, certain verbs target the language needs in specific areas of medicine. The following list and sample sentences will help you get children's background information:

to be constipated	**estar estreñido** *(ehs-'tahr ehs-treh-'nyee-doh)*
Is she constipated?	**¿Está estreñida?** *(eh-'stah ehs-treh-'nyee-dah)*
to burp	**eructar** *(eh-roohk-'tahr)*
Does she burp?	**¿Eructa?** *(eh-'rook-tah)*
to cough	**toser** *(toh-'sehr)*
Does she cough?	**¿Tose?** *('toh-seh)*
to cry	**llorar** *('yoh-'rahr)*
Does she cry?	**¿Llora?** *('yoh-rah)*
to feed	**alimentar** *(ah-lee-mehn-'tahr)*
When do you feed the child?	**¿Cuándo alimenta al niño?** *('kwahn-doh ah-lee-'mehn-tah ahl 'nee-nyoh)*
to sneeze	**estornudar** *(ehs-tohr-noo-'dahr)*
Does she sneeze?	**¿Estornuda?** *(ehs-tohr-'noo-dah)*
to swallow	**tragar** *(trah-'gahr)*
Does she swallow her food?	**¿Traga la comida?** *('trah-gah lah koh-'mee-dah)*
to vomit	**vomitar** *(boh-mee-'tahr)*
Does she vomit?	**¿Vomita?** *(boh-'mee-tah)*

The verb form is the same for most actions. A few words change slightly. Review these examples:

to play	**jugar** *(hoo-'gahr)*
Does she play much?	**¿Juega mucho?** *('hweh-gah 'moo-choh)*
to understand	**entender** *(ehn-tehn-'dehr)*
Does she understand?	**¿Entiende?** *(ehn-tee-'ehn-deh)*

Use **es** *(ehs)* to refer to the child's nature. **Está** *(eh-'stah)* only refers to her present condition.

She is sick (has a chronic illness).
Ella es enferma. *('eh-yah ehs ehn-'fehr-mah)*

She's feeling sick.
Ella está enferma. *('eh-yah eh-'stah ehn-'fehr-mah)*

Beber *(beh-'behr)* and **tomar** *(toh-'mahr)* may both be used to mean "to drink," although **beber** *(beh-'behr)* is more specific.

Here's another suggestion: Stick some of your base action forms **(ar, er, ir)** next to one of these:

Is he/she going to . . .?	**¿Va a . . .?** *(bah ah)*
Does he/she want to . . .?	**¿Quiere . . .?** *(kee-'eh-reh)*
Does he/she need to . . .?	**¿Necesita . . .?** *(neh-seh-'see-tah)*
Does he/she have to . . .?	**¿Tiene que . . .?** *(tee-'eh-neh keh)*
Can you . . .?	**¿Puede . . .?** *('pweh-deh)*
defecate	**defecar** *(deh-feh-'kahr)*
drink	**beber** *(beh-'behr)*
get up	**levantarse** *(leh-bahn-'tahr-seh)*
sit down	**sentarse** *(sehn-'tahr-seh)*
stand	**pararse** *(pah-'rahr-seh)*
swallow	**tragar** *(trah-'gahr)*
urinate	**orinar** *(oh-ree-'nahr)*

Continue to search for action words that you need. In the world of pediatrics, these verbs are always useful:

to bite	**morder** *(mohr-'dehr)*
to chew	**masticar** *(mah-stee-'kahr)*
to crawl	**gatear** *(gah-teh-'ahr)*
to nurse	**lactar** *(lahk-'tahr)*
to suck	**chupar** *(choo-'pahr)*

Symptoms

Los síntomas *(lohs 'seen-toh-mahs)*

Keep focusing on the "yes-no" questions. Feel free to mix in a few expressions with **tiene:**

Does he/she have . . .?	**¿Tiene . . .?** *(tee-'eh-neh)*
blisters	**ampollas** *(ahm-poh-yahs)*
bumps	**protuberancias** *(proh-too-beh-'rahn-see-ahs)*
bunions	**juanetes** *(hwah-'neh-tehs)*
calluses	**callos** *('kah-yohs)*
canker sores	**úlceras en la boca** *('ool-seh-rahs ehn lah 'boh-kah)*
constipation	**estreñimiento** *(ehs-treh-nyee-mee-'ehn-toh)*
convulsions	**convulsiones** *(kohn-boohl-see·'oh-nehs)*
a cough	**tos** *(tohs)*
diarrhea	**diarrea** *(dee-ah-'rreh-ah)*
fever	**fiebre** *(fee-'eh-breh)*
fleas	**pulgas** *('pool-gahs)*
hiccups	**hipo** *('ee-poh)*
hives	**urticaria** *(oor-tee-'kah-ree-ah)*
infection	**infección** *(een-fehk-see·'ohn)*
an ingrown toenail	**una uña encarnada** *('oo-nah 'oon-yah ehn-kahr-'nah-dah)*
lice	**piojos** *(pee-'oh-hohs)*
loss of appetite	**falta de apetito** *('fahl-tah deh ah-peh-'tee-toh)*
phlegm	**flema** *('fleh-mah)*
pimples	**granos** *('grah-nohs)*
pus	**pus** *(poohs)*
a rash	**erupción** *(eh-roop-see·'ohn)*
scabs	**costras** *('koh-strahs)*
a splinter	**una astilla** *('oo-nah ahs-'tee-yah)*
sweating	**sudor** *(soo-'dohr)*
swelling	**hinchazones** *(een-chah-'soh-nehs)*
temperature	**temperatura** *(tehm-peh-rah-'too-rah)*
ticks	**garrapatas** *(gahr-rah-'pah-tahs)*
warts	**verrugas** *(beh-'rroo-gahs)*

Does he/she have problems . . .?	**¿Tiene dificultades para . . .?** (tee-'eh-neh dee-fee-kool-'tah-dehs 'pah-rah)
breathing	**respirar** (rehs-pee-'rahr)
chewing	**masticar** (mah-stee-'kahr)
crawling	**gatear** (gah-teh-'ahr)
defecating	**defecar** (deh-feh-'kahr)
eating	**comer** (koh-'mehr)
sleeping	**dormir** (dohr-'meer)
swallowing	**tragar** (trah-'gahr)
walking	**caminar** (kah-mee-'nahr)
urinating	**orinar** (oh-ree-'nahr)

To get all the details, you will probably have to throw in a few verbs that refer to *past* action. Use your question words to find out what caused Margarita's condition. And see how much vocabulary you can string together:

When did he/she get sick?
¿Cuándo se enfermó?
('kwahn-doh seh ehn-fehr-'moh)

When was the last doctor's visit?
¿Cuándo fue la última visita al doctor?
('kwahn-doh fweh lah 'ool-tee-mah bee-'see-tah ahl dohk-'tohr)

What color was his/her stool?
¿De qué color fue su excremento?
(deh keh koh-'lohr fweh soo ehks-kreh-'mehn-toh)

(19) ¿Cuánto aprendió?

Answer the following questions:

- **¿Tiene...?** (tee-'eh-neh) (blisters, hiccups, phlegm)
- **¿Quiere...?** (kee-'eh-reh) (nurse, get up, sit down)
- Try these from memory:

Does she sleep? _____

Does she cry? _____

Does she walk? _____

The appointment

La cita *(lah 'see-tah)*

Are you learning all the new vocabulary? Here is only a sample of the many new words you'll need as you handle cases such as this one. These items will work well with your commands:

Bring . . .	**Traiga . . .** *('trah-ee·gah)*
bottle	**la botella** *(lah boh-'teh-yah)*
catheter	**el catéter** *(ehl kah-'teh-ter)*
chart	**el gráfico** *(ehl 'grah-fee-koh)*
cup	**la copa** *(lah 'koh-pah)*
instrument	**el instrumento** *(ehl eens-troo-'mehn-toh)*
light	**la luz** *(lah loos)*
needle	**la aguja** *(lah ah-'goo-hah)*
pan	**el bacín** *(ehl bah-'seen)*
scale	**la báscula** *(lah 'bahs-koo-lah)*
stethoscope	**el estetoscopio** *(ehl ehs-teh-tohs-'koh-pee-oh)*
syringe	**la jeringa** *(lah heh-'reen-gah)*
thermometer	**el termómetro** *(ehl tehr-'moh-meh-troh)*
tongue depressor	**la pisa-lengua** *(lah pee-sah-'lehn-gwah)*
tube	**el tubo** *(ehl 'too-boh)*

Dos culturas

A healer or **curandero** *(koo-rahn-'deh-roh)* is believed to have magic powers to heal the sick. In some neighborhoods, families prefer to send their ailing children to a healer first. You may want to check on where your patients are receiving their medical advice.

Medical history

La historia médica *(lah ees-'toh-ree·ah 'meh-dee-kah)*

Perhaps there's something **en la familia** that is part of Margarita's problem. Dig deeper into the past. Most of these words you should already know:

What did the . . . die of?	**¿De qué se murió . . .?**
	(deh keh seh moo-ree-'oh)
father	**el padre** *(ehl 'pah-dreh)*

mother	**la madre** *(lah 'mah-dreh)*
grandfather	**el abuelo** *(ehl ah-'bweh-loh)*
grandmother	**la abuela** *(lah ah-'bweh-lah)*

As long as you're doing family research, see if you can remember any of the following diseases in Spanish. They were introduced in **Capítulo Tres** when the Espinoza family first came to the hospital:

Did they have . . .

¿Tuvieron . . .? *(too-bee-'eh-rohn)*
difteria *(deef-'teh-ree·ah)*
fiebre escarlatina
(fee-'eh-breh ehs-kahr-lah-'tee-nah)
fiebre reumática
(fee-'eh-breh reh-oo-'mah-tee-kah)
fiebre tifoidea *(fee-'eh-breh tee-foo·ee-'deh-ah)*
hipoglicemia *(ee-poh-glee-'seh-mee-ah)*
paperas *(pah-'peh-rahs)*
sarampión *(sah-rahm-pee-'ohn)*
varicela *(bah-ree-seh-lah)*

Here are a few that you may not know:

another major illness	**otra enfermedad grave** *('oht-rah ehn-fehr-meh-'dah 'grah-beh)*
contagious diseases	**enfermedades contagiosas** *(ehn-fehr-meh-'dah-dehs kohn-tah-hee-'oh-sahs)*
emotional problems	**dificultades emocionales** *(dee-fee-kool-'tah-dehs eh-moh-see·oh-'nah-lehs)*
heart disease	**enfermedades del corazón** *(ehn-fehr-meh-'dah-dehs dehl koh-rah-'sohn)*
high blood pressure	**presión alta** *(preh-see-'ohn 'ahl-tah)*
low blood pressure	**presión baja** *(preh-see-'ohn 'bah-hah)*
mental problems	**dificultades mentales** *(dee-fee-kool-'tah-dehs mehn-'tah-lehs)*
respiratory problems	**problemas respiratorios** *(proh-'bleh-mahs rehs-pee-rah-'toh-ree·ohs)*
venereal disease	**enfermedades venéreas** *(ehn-fehr-meh-'dah-dehs beh-'neh-reh-ahs)*

Here are three ways to say "Does she have a cold?" In some Spanish-speaking countries, the words differ slightly:

¿Tiene resfrío? *(tee-'eh-neh rehs-'free-oh)*
¿Tiene catarro? *(tee-'eh-neh kah-'tah-rroh)*
¿Está resfriado? *(eh-'stah rehs-free-'ah-doh)*

¿Cuánto aprendió?

Guess the meanings of these terms. Many were also presented earlier.

anemia *(ah-'neh-mee·ah)*
angina *(ahn-'hee-nah)*
apendicitis *(ah-pehn-dee-'see-tees)*
arteriosclerosis *(ahr-teh-ree·oh-ehs-kleh-'roh-sees)*
artritis *(ahr-'tree-tees)*
asma *('ahs-mah)*
bronquitis *(brohn-'kee-tees)*
cáncer *('kahn-sehr)*
cirrosis *(see-'rroh-sees)*
cólera *(koh-'leh-rah)*
colon espástico *('koh-lohn ehs-'pahs-tee-koh)*
diabetes *(dee-ah-'beh-tehs)*
disentería *(dee-sehn-teh-'ree-ah)*
enfisema *(ehn-fee-'seh-mah)*
epilepsia *(eh-pee-'lehp-see·ah)*
glaucoma *(glah·oo-'koh-mah)*
gonorrea *(goh-noh-'rreh-ah)*
halitosis *(ah-lee-'toh-sees)*
hepatitis *(eh-pah-'tee-tees)*
hemorroides *(eh-moh-'rroh·ee-dehs)*
herpes *('ehr-pehs)*
indigestión *(een-dee-hehs-tee·'ohn)*
influenza *(een-floo-'ehn-sah)*
laringitis *(lah-reen-'hee-tees)*
leucemia *(lee-oo-'seh-mee·ah)*
mononucleosis *(moh-noh-noo-kleh-'oh-sees)*
nefritis *(neh-'free-tees)*
pancreatitis *(pahn-kreh-ah-'tee-tees)*
parálisis *(pah-'rah-lee-sees)*
pleuresía *(pleh-oo-ree-'see-ah)*
polio *('poh-lee·oh)*
reumatismo *(reh-oo-mah-'tees-moh)*
sífilis *('see-fee-lees)*
sinusitis *(see-noos-'ee-tees)*
tétanos *('teh-tah-nohs)*
tuberculosis *(too-behr-koo-'loh-sees)*
úlceras *('ool-seh-rahs)*

Have you had problems?

¿Ha tenido problemas?
(ah teh-'nee-doh proh-'bleh-mahs)

Bear in mind that all of the verb forms you have learned so far work wonders throughout the medical facility. Yet, you cannot communicate properly until a few more verb changes are made. For example, to ask the Espinozas if anyone in the family "has had" a certain disease before, you must use the phrase, **"Ha tenido,"** which translates "Have you...?" or "Has he or she had...". Try it:

Have you had a cough?
¿Ha tenido tos? *(ah teh-'nee-doh tohs)*

Have you had the illness?
¿Ha tenido la enfermedad? *(ah teh-'nee-doh lah ehn-fehr-meh-'dahd)*

Have you had mumps?
¿Ha tenido paperas? *(ah teh-'nee-doh pah-'peh-rahs)*

Study this two-part verb pattern. It's important in health care because it refers to actions that have already taken place. Practice these examples:

Have you had this pain before?
¿Ha tenido este dolor antes? *(ah teh-'nee-doh 'eh-steh doh-'lohr 'ahn-tehs)*

Have you spoken with the doctor?
¿Ha hablado con el doctor? *(ah ah-'blah-doh kohn ehl dohk-'tohr)*

Notice that in Spanish, you need both parts of the verb. Here is all you need to get started:

I have . . .	**he** . . . *(eh)*	had . . .	**tenido** *(teh-'nee-doh)*
you, he, or she has . . .	**ha** . . . *(ah)*	eaten	**comido** *(koh-'mee-doh)*
they or you (plural) have . . .	**han** . . . *(ahn)*	drunk	**tomado** *(toh-'mah-doh)*
we have . . .	**hemos** . . . *('eh-mohs)*	gone	**ido** *('ee-doh)*

This next series is an overview of actions that "have happened." Read them aloud:

Has he/she had an accident?
¿Ha tenido un accidente?
(ah teh-'nee-doh oon ahk-see-'dehn-teh)

Has he/she taken any medicines?
¿Ha tomado alguna medicina?
(ah toh-'mah-doh ahl-'goo-nah meh-dee-'see-nah)

Has he/she vomited?
¿Ha vomitado? *(ah boh-mee-'tah-doh)*

<hr>

(20) **¿Cuánto aprendió?**

Fill in the following:

- Did they have . . .?　　**¿Tuvieron . . .?** *(too-bee-'eh-rohn)*

  mumps
  heart disease
  major illnesses
  whooping cough

- Can you list three Spanish words for diseases that look a lot like the English words?

  1. _____

  2. _____

  3. _____

Allergies

Las alergias *(lahs ah-'lehr-hee·ahs)*

One of the most common ailments is a simple allergic reaction to the world around us. Find out from Mr. and Mrs. Espinoza if these things are of any concern:

Are you allergic to . . .?　　**¿Tiene alergia a . . .?**
　　　　　　　　　　　　　　(tee-'eh-neh ah-'lehr-hee·ah ah)

any food	**alguna comida** *(ahl-'goo-nah koh-'mee-dah)*
any medicine	**alguna medicina**
	(ahl-'goo-nah meh-dee-'see-nah)
dust	**el polvo** *(ehl -pohl-boh)*
fleas	**las pulgas** *(lahs 'pool-gahs)*
flowers	**las flores** *(lahs flohr-ehs)*
grass	**la hierba** *(lah 'yehr-bah)*

insect bites	**las picaduras de insectos** *(lahs pee-kah-'doo-rahs deh een-'sehk-tohs)*
lice	**los piojos** *(lohs pee-'oh-hohs)*
penicillin	**la penicilina** *(lah peh-nee-see-'lee-nah)*
poison ivy	**la hiedra venenosa** *(lah 'yeh-drah beh-neh-'noh-sah)*
poison oak	**la encina venenosa** *(lah ehn-'see-nah beh-neh-'noh-sah)*
pollen	**el polen** *(ehl 'poh-lehn)*
shots	**las inyecciones** *(lahs een-yehk-see·'oh-nehs)*
trees	**los árboles** *(lohs 'ahr-bohl-ehs)*

Some people may be allergic to animals or may have been bitten by one. Learn the following vocabulary:

The animals	**Los animales** *(lohs ah-nee-'mah-lehs)*
ant	**la hormiga** *(lah ohr-'mee-gah)*
bee	**la abeja** *(lah ah-'beh-hah)*
bird	**el pájaro** *(ehl 'pah-hah-roh)*
cat	**el gato** *(ehl 'gah-toh)*
dog	**el perro** *(ehl 'peh-rroh)*
lizard	**el lagarto** *(ehl lah-'gahr-toh)*
mosquito	**el zancudo** *(ehl sahn-'koo-doh)*
mouse	**el ratón** *(ehl rah-'tohn)*
rat	**la rata** *(lah 'rah-tah)*
scorpion	**el escorpión** *(ehl ehs-kohr-pee-'ohn)*
snake	**la víbora** *(lah 'bee-boh-rah)*
spider	**la araña** *(lah ah-'rah-nyah)*
squirrel	**la ardilla** *(lah ahr-'dee-yah)*

How's the weather?

¿Cómo está el tiempo?
('koh-moh eh-'stah ehl tee·'ehm-poh)

There are some things in life we can't control. Unfortunately, they are often the cause of our physical problems. Here's how we comment on the current weather conditions:

It's . . .	**Hace . . .** *('ah-seh)*
cold	**frío** *('free-oh)*
hot	**calor** *(kah-'lohr)*

nice weather	**buen tiempo** *('bwehn tee-'ehm-poh)*
sunny	**sol** *(sohl)*
windy	**viento** *(bee-'ehn-toh)*

It's . . .	**Está . . .**
clear	**despejado** *(dehs-peh-'hah-doh)*
cloudy	**nublado** *(noo-'blah-doh)*
drizzling	**lloviznando** *(yoh-bees-'nahn-doh)*
raining	**lloviendo** *(yoh-bee-'ehn-doh)*
snowing	**nevando** *(neh-'bahn-doh)*

There's (a) ...	**Hay...** *('ah-ee)*
bad weather	**mal tiempo** *(mahl tee-'ehm-poh)*
fog	**neblina** *(neh-'blee-nah)*
frost	**escarcha** *(ehs-'kahr-chah)*
humidity	**humedad** *(oo-meh-'dahd)*

What is bothering you?

¿Qué le molesta? *(keh leh moh-'leh-stah)*

Margarita is old enough to tell you what is bothering her. Listen for **tengo** as she complains of a bad cold:

Do you have . . .?	**¿Tienes . . .?** *(tee-'ehn-ehs)*
I have . . .	**Tengo . . .** *('tehn-goh)*
backaches	**dolores de espalda** *(doh-loh-rehs deh ehs-'pahl-dah)*
chest pains	**dolores en el pecho** *(doh-'loh-rehs ehn ehl 'peh-choh)*
chills	**escalofríos** *(ehs-kah-loh-'free-ohs)*
constipation	**estreñimiento** *(ehs-treh-nee-mee-'ehn-toh)*
diarrhea	**diarrea** *(dee-ah-'rreh-ah)*
earache	**dolor de oído** *(doh-lohr deh oh-'ee-doh)*
a fever	**fiebre** *(fee-'eh-breh)*
headache	**dolor de cabeza** *(doh-lohr deh kah-'beh-sah)*
phlegm	**flema** *('fleh-mah)*
a runny nose	**goteo nasal** *(goh-'teh-oh nah-'sahl)*
a sore throat	**dolor de garganta** *(doh-'lohr deh gahr-'gahn-tah)*

a sprained ankle	**un tobillo torcido** *(oon toh-'bee-yoh tohr-'see-doh)*
stomachache	**dolor de estómago** *(doh-lohr deh eh-'stoh-mah-goh)*
a stuffed nose	**la nariz tapada** *(lah nah-'rees tah-'pah-dah)*
swollen glands	**glándulas hinchadas** *('glahs-doo-lahs een-'chah-dahs)*
a toothache	**dolor de muela** *(doh-'lohr deh 'mweh-lah)*
watery eyes	**los ojos llorosos** *(lohs 'oh-hohs yoh-'roh-sohs)*
I have problems . . .	**Tengo problemas . . .** *('tehn-goh proh-'bleh-mahs)*
after eating	**después de comer** *(dehs-'pwehs deh koh-'mehr)*
in this weather	**en este clima** *(ehn 'eh-steh 'klee-mah)*
when I urinate	**cuando orino** *('kwahn-doh oh-'ree-noh)*
The pain is . . .	**El dolor es . . .** *(ehl doh-'lohr ehs)*
burning	**quemante** *(keh-'mahn-teh)*
deep	**profundo** *(proh-'foon-doh)*
dull	**sordo** *('sohr-doh)*
sharp	**agudo** *(ah-'goo-doh)*

¡No se olvide!

> Keep in mind that the action words directed at "you" may also refer to "he" or "she." Study the translations below:
>
> | | |
> |---|---|
> | you drink; he or she drinks | **toma** *('toh-mah)* |
> | you, he, or she drank | **tomó** *(toh-'moh)* |
> | you have drunk, he or she has drunk | **ha tomado** *(ah toh-'mah-doh)* |

The physical exam

El examen físico *(ehl ehk-'sah-mehn 'fee-see-koh)*

Margarita needs to be examined thoroughly. Most physical exams do not require much communication but it might be in your best interest to look over the following. Begin by informing the patient about the procedures:

I'm going to . . .	**Voy a . . .** *('boh·ee ah)*
listen to your chest	**escuchar su pecho**
	(ehs-koo-'chahr soo 'peh-choh)
make a diagnosis	**hacer un diagnóstico**
	(ah-'sehr oon dee-ahg-'nohs-tee-koh)
read your chart	**leer su gráfico** *(leh-'ehr soo 'grah-fee-koh)*
roll up your sleeve	**levantarle la manga**
	(leh-bahn-'tahr-leh lah 'mahn-gah)
take your temperature	**tomar su temperatura**
	(toh-'mahr soo tehm-peh-rah-'too-rah)

Now let the patient know that the exam is quite painless. Create your own comments utilizing the Spanish you already know:

Are you comfortable?	**¿Está cómodo?** *(eh-'stah 'koh-moh-doh)*
Everything will be OK.	**Todo va a estar bien.**
	('toh-doh bah ah eh-'stahr bee·'ehn)
It doesn't hurt.	**No duele.** *(noh 'dweh-leh)*

More commands!

¡Más ordenes! *(mahs 'ohr-deh-nehs)*

How can you give an exam without telling the patient what to do? As you instruct Margarita, try putting several Spanish words in a row:

Bring a sample in this cup.
Traiga una muestra en este vaso.
('trah·ee-gah 'oo-nah 'mweh-strah ehn 'eh-steh 'bah-soh)
Go to the scale.
Vaya a la báscula. *('bah-yah ah lah 'bahs-koo-lah)*
Put the thermometer in your mouth.
Ponga el termómetro en la boca.
('pohn-gah ehl tehr-'moh-meh-troh ehn lah 'boh-kah)
Take a deep breath.
Aspire profundo. *(ahs-'pee-reh proh-'foon-doh)*

Remember these? They send messages all by themselves:

move	**muévase** *(moo-'eh-bah-seh)*
relax	**relájese** *(reh-'lah-heh-seh)*
sit down	**siéntese** *(see-'ehn-teh-seh)*
turn	**voltéese** *(bohl-'teh-eh-seh)*
stand up	**levántese** *(leh-'bahn-teh-seh)*

Now combine your command words with some body parts:

Make a fist.	**Haga un puño.** (*'ah-gah oon 'poon-yoh*)
Bend your arm.	**Doble el brazo.** (*'doh-bleh ehl 'brah-soh*)
Close your mouth.	**Cierre la boca.** (*see-'eh-reh lah 'boh-kah*)
Lie on your back.	**Acuéstese de espalda.** (*ah-'kweh-steh-seh deh eh-'spahl-dah*)
Open your hand.	**Abra la mano.** (*ah-'brah lah 'mah-noh*)
Touch your head.	**Tóquese la cabeza.** (*'toh-keh-seh lah kah-'beh-sah*)

You can never have enough of the "command words." Review this new list carefully, repeat them aloud, and experiment with a few during your next exam:

cross	**cruce** (*'kroo-seh*)	_____
describe	**describa** (*dehs-'kree-bah*)	_____
exhale	**expire** (*ehk-'spee-reh*)	_____
extend	**estire** (*ehks-'tee-reh*)	_____
inhale	**aspire** (*ah-'spee-reh*)	_____
say	**diga** (*'dee-gah*)	_____
try	**trate** (*'trah-teh*)	_____

(21) ## ¿Cuánto aprendió?

Fill in the following:

- He... **Él** (drank the medicine, had an accident, spoke with the doctor)
- **Tiene alergia a...** (*tee-'eh-neh ah 'lehr-gee·ah ah*) (pollen, insect bites, cats)
- **Tengo...** (*'tehn-goh*) (a headache, a cold, problems with this weather)
- **Voy a...** (*'boh·ee ah*) (take your blood pressure, move your head)
- How do you express these comments?

  It's cloudy. _____

  It's sunny. _____

  It's snowing. _____

- Now give the following commands in Spanish:

  Drink the medicine!

  Extend your leg!

  Write your name!

  Describe the pain!

  Sit down on the bed!

Analysis, examination, and test!

¡Análisis, examen y prueba!
(ah-'nah-lee-sees, ehk-'sah-mehn ee proo-'eh-bah)

Special tests are needed for the young patient. Try to determine what the physician has decided to do:

I need . . .	**Necesito . . .** *(neh-seh-'see-toh)*
a blood sample	**una muestra de sangre** *('oo-nah 'mweh-strah deh 'sahn-greh)*
a count	**un recuento** *(oon reh-'kwehn-toh)*
a smear	**un frotis** *(oon 'froh-tees)*
a sputum sample	**una muestra de esputo** *('oo-nah 'mweh-strah deh ehs-'poo-toh)*
a stool sample	**una muestra de excremento** *('oo-nah 'mweh-strah deh ehks-kreh-'mehn-toh)*
a urine sample	**una muestra de orina** *('oo-nah 'mweh-strah deh oh-'ree-nah)*
an X ray	**una radiografía** *('oo-nah rah-dee-oh-grah-'fee-ah)*

Fortunately, many of the words that surface in your discussions about the test results sound a lot like English.

albúmina *(ahl-boo-'mee-nah)*
bacteria *(bahk-'teh-ree·ah)*
coagulación *(koh-ah-goo-lah-see·'ohn)*
defensas *(deh-'fehn-sahs)*
globular *(gloh-boo-'lahr)*
laboratorio *(lah-boh-rah-'toh-ree·oh)*
metabolismo *(meh-tah-boh-'lees-moh)*
microscopio *(mee-kro-'skoh-pee·oh)*
negativo *(neh-gah-'tee-boh)*
positivo *(poh-see-'tee-boh)*
saliva *(sah-'lee bah)*
virus *('vee-roos)*

The results

Los resultados
(lohs reh-sool-'tah-dohs)

Results indicate there is an infection, but Margarita's health can be restored easily through medication, rest, and appropriate care. Take note of what the doctor has to say:

She needs . . .	**Necesita . . .**
an antibiotic	**un antibiótico** *(oon ahn-tee-bee-'oh-tee-koh)*
cough medicine	**medicina para la tos** *(meh-dee-'see-nah 'pah-rah lah tohs)*
a good diet	**una buena dieta** *('oo-nah 'bweh-nah dee-'eh-tah)*
more liquids	**más líquidos** *(mahs 'lee-kee-dohs)*
a specialist	**un especialista** *(oon eh-speh-see·ah-'lee-stah)*
vitamins	**las vitaminas** *(lahs bee-tah-'mee-nahs)*

Kids!

¡Los niños! *(lohs 'nee-nyohs)*

Margarita is feeling much better. Chances are, the pediatrician will see her again in the future. The following questions, comments, and commands are designed for conversations with younger children. This relationship is an informal one, where friendly conversation and humor are blended with your job-related language skills. As you have learned, you can accomplish a great deal with very little language.

These phrases all mean "How cute!"

¡Qué bonito! *(keh boh-'nee-toh)*
¡Qué precioso! *(keh preh-see-'oh-soh)*
¡Qué lindo! *(keh 'leen-doh)*

Remember that the above phrases are for male subjects. Change to "a" endings when talking about female subjects.

And, they can be added to any item:

What a cute . . .	**¡Qué bonita . . .!**
	(keh boh-'nee-tah)
face	**cara** *('kah-rah)*
haircut	**corte de pelo** *('kohr-teh deh 'peh-loh)*
outfit	**ropa** *('roh-pah)*
smile	**sonrisa** *(sohn-'ree-sah)*
voice	**voz** *(vohs)*

Now, learn some vocabulary for a baby's or young child's personal belongings:

Where is the . . .?	**¿Dónde está . . .?**
	('dohn-deh eh-'stah)
ball	**la pelota** *(lah peh-'loh-tah)*
bassinet	**el bacinete** *(ehl bah-see-'neh-teh)*
blanket	**la cobija** *(lah koh-'bee-hah)*
crib	**la cuna** *(lah 'koo-nah)*
doll	**la muñeca** *(lah moo-'nyeh-kah)*
game	**el juego** *(ehl 'hweh-goh)*
infant car seat	**el asiento para infantes**
	(ehl ah-see-'ehn-toh 'pah-rah een-'fahn-tehs)
storybook	**el librito de cuentos**
	(ehl lee-'bree-toh deh 'kwehn-tohs)
stroller	**el cochecillo** *(ehl koh-cheh-'see-yoh)*
toy	**el juguete** *(ehl hoo-'geh-teh)*

¡No se olvide!

- The word **tú** is the informal way of saying "you" or "your" in Spanish. The "informal" form is also exchanged between family and friends. Here are some examples.

  You are my friend.
  Tú eres mi amigo. *(too 'eh-rehs mee ah-'mee-goh)*

  You must move.
  Tú debes moverte. *(too 'dee-behs moh-'behr-teh)*

  It's your hand.
  Es tu mano. *(ehs too 'mah-noh)*

  Your heart is all right.
  Tu corazón está bien. *(too koh-rah-'sohn eh-'stah 'bee·ehn)*

  Did you notice that "your" is **tu**, but without the accent?

- The command words take on a slightly different form when you address children. Memorize these examples:

Say "ah."	**Di "ah."** *(dee ah)*
Open your mouth.	**Abre la boca.** *('ah-breh lah 'boh-kah)*
Go to sleep.	**Duérmete.** *('dwehr-meh-teh)*
Stand up.	**Levántate.** *(leh-'bahn-tah-teh)*

Don't . . .	No . . .
be afraid	**tengas miedo** *('tehn-gahs me-'eh-doh)*
be naughty	**seas malcriado** *('seh-ahs mahl-kree-'ah-doh)*
cry	**llores** *('yoh-rehs)*
move	**te muevas** *(teh 'mweh-bahs)*

- All verb forms require changes when you talk to kids. Most can be recognized because they end in the letter "s."

Do you have . . .?	**¿Tienes . . .?** *(tee-'eh-nehs)*
Do you want . . .?	**¿Quieres . . .?** *(kee-'eh-rehs)*
Do you need . . .?	**¿Necesitas . . .?** *(neh-seh-'see-tahs)*

Dos culturas

Don't be afraid to touch the baby! In some Spanish-speaking countries, people believe that children can get sick if you stare at them without making physical contact. A brief stroke, hug, or light caress will make everyone feel more comfortable.

Remedies

Los remedios *(lohs reh-'meh-dee·ohs)*

As Margarita and her parents prepare to leave for home, you will have to write a prescription and then provide them with instructions. To do so, you will need the proper Spanish terminology and phrases. Fortunately, most medicines are spelled similarly in both languages:

Just as you did with previous lists, try to guess at the meanings of these:

antiácido *(ahn-tee-'ah-see-doh)*
antibiótico *(ahn-tee-bee-'oh-tee-koh)*
antídoto *(ahn-'tee-doh-toh)*
antihistamínicos *(ahn-tee-ees-tah-'mee-nee-kohs)*
antiséptico *(ahn-tee-'sehp-tee-koh)*
aspirina *(ah-spee-'ree-nah)*
astringente *(ahs-treen-'hehn-teh)*
codeína *(koh-deh-'ee-nah)*
cortisona *(kohr-tee-'soh-nah)*
demerol *(deh-meh-'rohl)*
desinfectante *(dehs-een-fehk-'tahn-teh)*
insulina *(een-soo-'lee-nah)*
morfina *(mohr-'fee-nah)*
nitroglicerina *(nee-troh-glee-seh-'ree-nah)*
penicilina *(peh-nee-see-'lee-nah)*
tranquilizantes *(trahn-kee-lee-'sahn-tehs)*
vitaminas *(bee-tah-'mee-nahs)*

These key words should be learned quickly. To make it easy on yourself, practice first with those words that you use most often:

capsules	**las cápsulas** *(lahs 'kahp-soo-lahs)*
lozenges	**las pastillas** *(lahs pah-'stee-yahs)*
pills	**las píldoras** *(lahs 'peel-doh-rahs)*
tablets	**las tabletas** *(lahs tah-'bleh-tahs)*

Try them out:

Pills for . . .	**Las píldoras para . . .**
	(lahs 'peel-doh-rahs 'pah-rah)
birth control	**anticoncepción** *(ahn-tee-kohn-sehp-see·'ohn)*
sleeping	**dormir** *(dohr-'meer)*

How about a few over-the-counter remedies? Some of them will be very easy to remember. As a matter of fact, if you mention a drug in English, they will probably understand what you are saying:

adhesive tape	**cinta adhesiva** *('seen-tah ah-deh-'see-bah)*
bandage	**venda** *('behn-dah)*
Band-Aid®	**curita** *(koo-'ree-tah)*
bicarbonate	**bicarbonato** *(bee-kahr-boh-'nah-toh)*
cough syrup	**el jarabe para la tos**
	(ehl hah-'rah-beh 'pah-rah lah tohs)
decongestant	**descongestionante**
	(dehs-kohn-hehs-tee-oh-'nahn-teh)
Epsom salt	**la sal de Epsom** *(lah sahl deh ehp-sohm)*
gauze	**gasa** *('gah-sah)*
ice pack	**bolsa de hielo** *('bohl-sah deh ee-'eh-loh)*
iodine	**yodo** *('yoh-doh)*
laxative	**laxante** *(lahk-'sahn-teh)*
hydrogen peroxide	**agua oxigenada**
	('ah-gwah ohk-see-heh-'nah-dah)
sedative	**sedante** *(seh-'dahn-teh)*
stimulant	**estimulante** *(ehs-tee-moo-'lahn-teh)*
vaseline	**vaselina** *(bah-seh-'lee-nah)*

These words allow you to explain the medication in detail:

drops	**las gotas** *(lahs 'goh-tahs)*
They are drops for the eyes.	**Son gotas para los ojos.**
	(sohn 'goh-tahs 'pah-rah lohs 'oh-hohs)
mixture	**la mezcla** *(lah 'mehs-klah)*
It is an aspirin and tranquilizer mixture.	**Es una mezcla de aspirina y sedante.**
	(ehs 'oo-nah 'mehs-klah deh ahs-pee-'ree-nah ee seh-'dahn-teh)
solution	**la solución** *(lah soh-loo-see·'ohn)*
The white solution is for the hair.	**La solución blanca es para el pelo.**
	(lah soh-loo-see·'ohn 'blahn-kah ehs 'pah-rah ehl 'peh-loh)

Now, it's your turn. Use the following words in sentences:

creams	**las cremas** *(lahs 'kreh-mahs)*
jelly	**la jalea** *(lah 'hah-'leh-ah)*
liniment	**el linimento** *(ehl lee-nee-'mehn-toh)*
lotion	**la loción** *(lah loh-see·'ohn)*
ointment	**el ungüento** *(ehl oon-'gwehn-toh)*
powder	**el talco** *(ehl 'tahl-koh)*
soap	**el jabón** *(ehl hah-'bohn)*
syrup	**el jarabe** *(ehl hah-'rah-beh)*
suppositories	**los supositorios** *(lohs soo-poh-see-'toh-ree·ohs)*

Dos culturas

Millions of people in the United States do not believe in pharmaceutical drugs. Many Hispanics still rely on **medicinas caseras** or home remedies. Certain **especias** *(eh-'speh-see·ahs)* (spices), for example, are taken to cure everything from a headache to heart disease. You may want to read up on such methods, not only to learn more about their culture, but also to find out if what they are taking at home has any real medicinal value.

The gift shop

La tienda de regalos
(lah tee-'ehn-dah deh reh-'gah-lohs)

Hospital gift shops play a significant role in recovery. Juan and María decide to do a little shopping to make Margarita happy and, also, to get a few things for home use.

I need . . .	**Necesito . . .** *(neh-seh-'see-toh)*
batteries	**pilas** *('pee-lahs)*
candy	**dulces** *('dool-sehs)*
CDs	**discos compactos** *('dees-kohs kohm-'pahk-tohs)*
a comb	**un peine** *(oon 'peh·-ee-neh)*
cosmetics	**cosméticos** *(kohs-'meh-tee-kohs)*
a deodorant	**un desodorante** *(oon dehs-oh-doh-'rahn-teh)*
envelopes	**sobres** *('soh-brehs)*
feminine napkins	**paños** *('pah-nyohs)*

flowers	**flores** *('floh-rehs)*
gifts	**regalos** *(reh-'gah-lohs)*
greeting cards	**tarjetas de saludo** *(tahr-'heh-tahs deh sah-'loo-doh)*
a hairbrush	**un cepillo de pelo** *(oon seh-'pee-yoh deh 'peh-loh)*
magazines	**revistas** *(reh-'bee-stahs)*
a needle	**una aguja** *('oo-nah ah-'goo-hah)*
newspapers	**periódicos** *(peh-ree-'oh-dee-kohs)*
a pin	**un alfiler** *(oon ahl-fee-'lehr)*
postcards	**tarjetas postales** *(tahr-'heh-tahs poh-'stah-lehs)*
razor blades	**navajas para afeitar** *(nah-'bah-hahs 'pah-rah ah-'feh·ee-tahr)*
rolls of film	**rollos de foto** *('roh-yohs deh 'foh-toh)*
scissors	**tijeras** *(tee-'heh-rahs)*
stamps	**estampillas** *(ehs-tahm-'pee-yahs)*
tape	**una cinta** *('oo-nah 'seen-tah)*
thread	**hilo** *('ee-loh)*
a toothbrush	**un cepillo de dientes** *(oon seh-'pee-yoh deh dee-'ehn-tehs)*
toothpaste	**pasta de dientes** *('pah-stah deh dee-'ehn-tehs)*

Margarita cries out when she sees one of these! Juan rewards his exhausted little girl with her favorite toy.

Stuffed animals	**Animales de peluche** *(ah-nee-'mah-lehs deh peh-'loo-cheh)*
bear	**el oso** *(ehl 'oh-soh)*
cat	**el gato** *(ehl 'gah-toh)*
dog	**el perro** *(ehl 'peh-rroh)*
duck	**el pato** *(ehl 'pah-toh)*
elephant	**el elefante** *(ehl eh-leh-'fahn-teh)*
giraffe	**la jirafa** *(lah hee-'rah-fah)*
monkey	**el mono** *(ehl 'moh-noh)*
mouse	**el ratón** *(ehl rah-'tohn)*
pig	**el puerco** *(ehl poo-'ehr-koh)*
rabbit	**el conejo** *(ehl koh-'neh-hoh)*
sheep	**la oveja** *(lah oh-'beh-hah)*
zebra	**la cebra** *(lah 'seh-brah)*

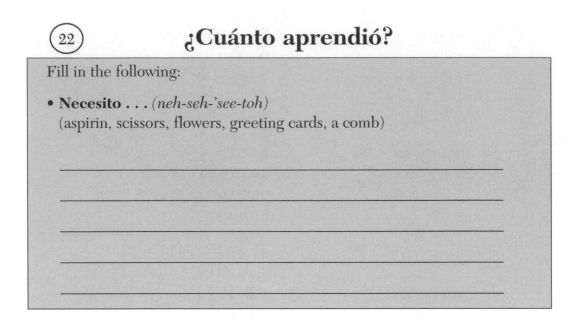

(22) **¿Cuánto aprendió?**

Fill in the following:

- **Necesito . . .** *(neh-seh-'see-toh)*
  (aspirin, scissors, flowers, greeting cards, a comb)

_____

_____

_____

_____

_____

The prescription

La receta médica *(lah reh-'seh-tah 'meh-dee-kah)*

Telling the Espinozas what medication they need to buy isn't enough. In order to administer the drug properly, clear and concise instructions must be given. Always begin by telling them what they have to do:

You have to . . .	**Tiene que . . .** *(tee-'eh-neh keh)*
bathe	**bañarse** *(bah-'nyahr-seh)*
gargle	**hacer gárgaras** *(ah-sehr 'gahr-gah-rahs)*
inhale	**inhalar** *(in-ah-'lahr)*
measure carefully	**medir con cuidado** *(meh-'deer kohn kwee-'dah-doh)*
read the label	**leer la etiqueta** *(leh-'ehr lah eh-tee-'keh-tah)*
refrigerate it	**refrigerarlo** *(reh-free-heh-'rahr-loh)*
rinse	**enjuagar** *(ehn-hwah-'gahr)*
swallow	**tragar** *(trah-'gahr)*
take the medicine	**tomar la medicina** *(toh-'mahr lah meh-dee-'see-nah)*
wash	**lavarse** *(lah-'bahr-seh)*

Use **tome** *('toh-meh)* (take) with all of your new vocabulary!

Take the medicine . . .	**Tome la medicina . . .**
	(toh-meh lah meh-dee-'see-nah)
after meals	**después de las comidas**
	(dehs-'pwehs deh lahs koh-'mee-dahs)
before meals	**antes de las comidas**
	('ahn-tehs deh lahs koh-'mee-dahs)
between meals	**entre las comidas**
	('ehn-treh lahs koh-'mee-dahs)
when you have pain	**cuando tiene dolor**
	('kwahn-doh tee-'eh-neh doh-'lohr)
with water	**con agua** *(kohn 'ah-gwah)*
___ times every ___	**___veces cada ___** *('beh-sehs 'kah-dah)*

Make sure the patient takes the correct amount of medication. Review these words used for measurement:

Take . . .	**Tome . . .** *('toh-meh)*
a cup	**una copa** *('oo-nah 'koh-pah)*
a glass	**un vaso** *(oon 'bah-soh)*
half	**la mitad** *(lah mee-tahd)*
one tablespoon	**una cucharada** *('oo-nah koo-chah-'rah-dah)*
one teaspoon	**una cucharadita**
	('oo-nah koo-chah-rah-'dee-tah)

¡No se olvide!

* Keep in mind that **no** means "don't." Be sure to tell the Espinozas what *not* to do:

Don't take the capsules.	**No tome las cápsulas.**
	(noh 'toh-meh lahs 'kahp-soo-lahs)
Don't drink alcohol with this.	**No tome alcohol con esto.**
	(noh 'toh-meh ahl-koh-'ohl kohn
	'eh-stoh)
It isn't for children.	**No es para niños.**
	(noh ehs 'pah-rah 'nee-nyohs)

Get well soon!

¡Que se alivie pronto!
(keh seh ah-'lee-bee-eh 'prohn-toh)

As the family heads for the pharmacy on their way home, make sure all the instructions are clear. Please add your own comments to the ones below:

Do you need something stronger?
¿Necesita algo más fuerte?
(neh-seh-'see-tah 'ahl-goh mahs 'fwehr-teh)

Have you had a bad reaction to the medicine?
¿Ha tenido una mala reacción a la medicina?
(ah teh-'nee-doh 'oo-nah 'mah-lah reh-ahk-see-'ohn ah lah meh-deh-'see-nah)

I need to explain the prescription.
Necesito explicar la receta.
(neh-seh-'see-toh ehks-plee-'kahr lah reh-'seh-tah)

Let's lower the dosage.
Vamos a bajar la dosis.
('bah-mohs ah bah-'hahr lah 'doh-sees)

Take this prescription to the pharmacy.
Lleve la receta a la farmacia.
('yeh-beh lah reh-'seh-tah ah lah fahr-'mah-see·ah)

You have to talk to the pharmacist.
Tiene que hablar con el farmacéutico.
(tee-'eh-neh keh ah-'blahr kohn ehl fahr-mah-'seh-oo-tee-koh)

You need to return in one week.
Necesita regresar en una semana.
(neh-seh-'see-tah reh-greh-'sahr ehn 'oo-nah seh-'mah-nah)

(23)   **¿Cuánto aprendió?**

Finish the following:

- **Necesita . . .** (*neh-seh-'see-tah*)
  (a blood sample, a test, more liquids)

  _____

  _____

  _____

- **Tiene que . . .** (*tee-'eh-neh keh*)
  (read the label, drink half)

  _____

  _____

- Translate: Take the pills with water.
              Take two tablespoons three times every day.
              You need to bathe in hot water.
              We are going to lower the dosage.

Chapter Seven

Capítulo Siete
(kah-'pee-too-loh see-'eh-teh)

Miguel Espinoza,
Age 12

Early one morning, young Miguel cries out in great pain and is immediately rushed to the hospital by his father. Upon further examination, the doctor determines that Miguel has appendicitis. With no time to lose, an operation is scheduled. Although his admission forms have already been completed, there are a variety of other questions that need to be answered prior to Miguel's surgery. Since his English is not good and he will be staying in the hospital for awhile, specialized words and phrases are going to be needed in order to exchange information and communicate requests.

The operation

La operación (lah oh-peh-rah-see·'ohn)

The Espinoza family needs to be informed of Miguel's condition as soon as possible. Here are some terms you'll need to communicate information about surgery in general:

It's very . . .	**Es muy . . .** (ehs 'moo·ee)
common	**común** (koh-'moon)
complicated	**complicada** (kohm-plee-'kah-dah)
dangerous	**peligrosa** (peh-lee-'groh-sah)
necessary	**necesaria** (neh-seh-'sah-ree·ah)
risky	**arriesgada** (ahr-ree-ehs-'gah-dah)

| serious | **grave** *('grah-beh)* |
| simple | **sencilla** *(sehn-'see-yah)* |

He needs . . .	**Necesita** . . . *(neh-seh-'see-tah)*
an appendectomy	**una apendectomía** *(ah-pehn-dehk-'to-mee·ah)*
a biopsy	**una biopsia** *('oo-nah bee-'ohp-see·ah)*
a blood transfusion	**una transfusión de sangre** *('oo-nah trahs-foo-see·'ohn deh 'sahn-greh)*
an exploratory operation	**una operación exploratoria** *('oo-nah oh-peh-rah-see·'ohn ehks-ploh-rah-'toh-ree·ah)*

Although they don't pertain to Miguel's condition, here are some other operations you may some day need to discuss in Spanish:

an amputation	**una amputación** *('oo-nah ahm-poo-tah-see·'ohn)*
a hysterectomy	**una histerectomía** *('oo-nah ees-teh-rehk-'tom-mee·ah)*
a mastectomy	**una mastectomía** *('oo-nah mahs-tehk-'tom-mee·ah)*
a plastic surgery	**una cirugía plástica** *('oo-nah see-roo-'hee-ah 'plahs-tee-kah)*
a tonsillectomy	**una tonsilectomía** *(oo-nah tohn-see-lehk-toh-'mee-ah)*
a vasectomy	**una vasectomía** *('oo-nah vah-sehk-toh-'mee-ah)*

More action

Más acción *(mahs ahk-see·'ohn)*

The families of patients in surgery have questions, and you need to be as honest and informative as you can. The following list of action words provides you with much of the language that you'll need. Use them with the patterns you are familiar with:

| We need to | **Necesitamos** *(neh-seh-see-'tah-mohs)* |
| We have to | **Tenemos que** *(teh-'neh-mohs keh)* |

We're going to . . .	**Vamos a . . .** *('bah-mohs ah)*
to cover	**tapar** *(tah-'pahr)*
cover you	**. . . taparle** *(tah-'pahr-leh)*
to give	**dar** *(dahr)*
give you the anesthesia	**. . . darle anestesia** *('dahr-leh ah-nehs-'teh- see-ah)*
to operate	**operar** *(oh-peh-'rahr)*
operate on you right now	**. . . operarle ahorita** *(oh-peh-'rahr-leh ah-oh-'ree-tah)*
to prepare	**preparar** *(preh-pah-'rahr)*
prepare you for the operation	**. . . prepararle para la operación** *(preh-pah-'rahr-leh 'pah-rah lah oh-peh-rah-see·'ohn)*
to remove	**sacar** *(sah-'kahr)*
take out your appendix	**. . . sacarle el apéndice** *(sah-'kahr-leh ehl ah-'pehn-dee-seh)*
to repair	**reparar** *(reh-pah-'rahr)*
repair the damage (done to you)	**. . . repararle el daño** *(reh-pah-'rahr-leh ehl 'dah-nyoh)*
to sew	**coser** *(koh-'sehr)*
sew up your wound	**. . . coserle la herida** *(koh-'sehr-leh lah eh-'ree-dah)*
to shave	**afeitar** *(ah-feh-ee-'tahr)*
shave the area (on your body)	**. . . afeitarle el área** *(ah-feh-ee-'tahr-leh ehl 'ah-reh-ah)*
to transplant	**trasplantar** *(trahs-plahn-'tahr)*
transplant the organ	**trasplantar el órgano** *(trahs-plahn-'tahr ehl 'ohr-gah-noh)*

¡No se olvide!

- To remove, **sacar** *(sah-'kahr)* should be practiced with specific body parts. Some of this vocabulary may be new to you.

We are going to remove . . .	**Vamos a sacarle . . .** *('bah-mohs ah sah-'kahr-leh)*
appendix	**el apéndice** *(ehl ah-'pehn-dee-seh)*
cataracts	**las cataratas** *(lah kah-tah-'rah-tahs)*
cyst	**el quiste** *(ehl 'kees-teh)*
gallbladder	**la vesícula biliar** *(lah beh-'see-koo-lah bee-lee-'ahr)*
gallstones	**los cálculos biliares** *(lohs 'kahl-koo-lohs bee-lee-'ah-rehs)*
kidney stones	**los cálculos renales** *(lohs 'kahl-koo-lohs reh-'nah-lehs)*
tonsils	**las amígdalas** *(lahs ah-'meeg-dah-lahs)*

- Keep using **le** *(leh)* after the verb when addressing someone. This personal pronoun means either "him/her/you," or "to him/to her/to you," and therefore switches the sentence from a general to a personal level.

The surgery

La cirugía *(lah see-roo-'hee-ah)*

Keep talking to the Espinozas about the upcoming surgery. Let Miguel and his family know what's going to happen next. Use the forms of **ir a** (to go to) as you discuss future procedures:

He's going to be fine.
Va a estar bien.
(bah ah eh-'stahr bee·ehn)

I'm going to go to the operating room with him.
Voy a ir a la sala de operaciones con él.
('boh·ee ah eer ah lah 'sah-lah deh oh-peh-rah-see·'oh-nehs kohn ehl)

The doctor is going to explain everything.
El doctor le va a explicar todo.
(ehl dohk-'tohr leh bah ah ehks-plee-'kahr 'toh-doh)

The surgery is going to be at . . .
La cirugía va a ser a las . . .
(lah see-roo-'hee-ah bah a sehr ah lahs)

We're going to need your signature.
Vamos a necesitar su firma.
('bah-mohs ah neh-seh-see-'tahr soo 'feer-mah)

Don't forget to talk to Miguel personally. Prior to operating on older children and adults, you may need to exchange information with them directly. Use the various verb forms that you've learned to communicate.

Do you take medication?
¿Toma medicina?
('toh-mah meh-dee-'see-nah)

Do you want another opinion?
¿Quiere otra opinión?
(kee-'eh-reh 'oh-trah oh-pee-nee-'ohn)

Do you want to call someone?
¿Quiere llamar a alguien?
(kee-'eh-reh yah-'mahr ah 'ahl-gee·ehn)

Have you had an operation before?
¿Ha tenido alguna operación antes?
(ah teh-'nee-doh ahl-'goo-nah oh-peh-rah-see·'ohn 'ahn-tehs)

Your family is outside.
Su familia está afuera.
(soo fah-'mee-lee·ah eh-'stah ah-'fweh-rah)

As you prepare Miguel for surgery, it's important that he follows directions carefully. Note that all the following command words are for addressing a child and therefore follow **tú** instead of **usted** rules. (Go to page 119 to review the use of **tú.**

Please . . .	**Por favor . . .** *(pohr fah-'bohr)*
Don't touch.	**No toques.** *(noh 'toh-kehs)*
Drink this.	**Toma esto.** *('toh-mah 'eh-stoh)*
Lie down.	**Acuéstate.** *(ah-'kwehs-tah-teh)*
Look here.	**Mira aquí.** *('mee-rah ah-'kee)*
Turn around.	**Voltéate.** *(bohl-'teh-ah-teh)*

Here are some more words that will help you out in pre-op. Not all of these commands are easy to pronounce, so practice before you direct them at patients. Again, these are in the **tú** (familiar *you*) mode.

bathe	**báñate** *(bah-'nyah-teh)*
drink	**bebe** *('beh-beh)*
keep	**guarda** *('gwarh-dah)*
press	**aprieta** *(ah-pree-'eh-tah)*
put on	**ponte** *('pohn-teh)*
take off	**quítate** *('kee-tah-teh)*
turn off	**apaga** *(ah-'pah-gah)*
turn on	**prende** *('prehn-deh)*
wash	**lávate** *('lah-bah-teh)*
Wash your hands.	**Lávate las manos.** *('lah-bah-teh lahs 'mah-nohs)*

Instruments

Los instrumentos *(lohs eens-troo-'mehn-tohs)*

Here are some words you may need to elaborate on the surgical specifics.

catheter	**el catéter** *(ehl kah-'teh-tehr)*
forceps	**las tenazas** *(lahs teh-'nah-sahs)*
gloves	**los guantes** *(lohs 'gwahn-tehs)*
knife	**el cuchillo** *(ehl koo-'chee-yoh)*
mask	**la máscara** *(lah 'mahs-kah-rah)*
monitor	**el monitor** *(ehl moh-nee-'tohr)*
pincers	**las pinzas** *(lahs 'peen-sahs)*
probe	**la sonda** *(lah 'bohm-bah)*
pump	**la bomba** *(lah 'bohm-bah)*
respirator	**el respirador** *(ehl rehs-pee-rah-'dohr)*
retractor	**el retractor** *(ehl reh-trahk-'tohr)*
scissors	**las tijeras** *(lahs tee-'heh-rahs)*
sponge	**la esponja** *(lah ehs-'pohn-hah)*
stethoscope	**el estetoscopio** *(ehl eh-steh-toh-'skoh-pee·oh)*
suture	**la sutura** *(lah soo-'too-rah)*
thermometer	**el termómetro** *(ehl tehr-'moh-meh-troh)*
tongue depressor	**la pisalengua** *(lah pee-sah-'lehn-gwah)*
tube	**el tubo** *(ehl 'too-boh)*

Clothing

La ropa *(lah 'roh-pah)*

Why not put your new skills into immediate action? In order to prep patients for surgery, you must get them into the proper attire. To do so, apply the commands, **quítese** *('kee-teh-seh)* and **póngase** *('pohn-gah-seh)*, along with the following items of clothing:

Take off . . .	**Quítese . . .** *('kee-teh-seh)*
Put on . . .	**Póngase . . .** *('pohn-gah-seh)*
brassiere	**el sostén** *(ehl sohs-'tehn)*
belt	**el cinturón** *(ehl seen-too-'rohn)*
blouse	**la blusa** *(lah 'bloo-sah)*
boots	**las botas** *(lahs 'boh-tahs)*
dress	**el vestido** *(ehl behs-'tee-doh)*
jacket	**la chaqueta** *(lah chah-'keh-tah)*
pajamas	**los piyamas** *(lohs pee-'yah-mahs)*
panties	**las bragas** *(lahs 'brah-gahs)*
pants	**los pantalones** *(lohs pahn-tah-'loh-nehs)*
robe	**la bata** *(lah 'bah-tah)*
shirt	**la camisa** *(lah kah-'mee-sah)*
shoes	**los zapatos** *(lohs sah-'pah-tohs)*
shorts	**los calzoncillos** *(lohs kahl-sohn-'see-yohs)*
skirt	**la falda** *(lah 'fahl-dah)*
slippers	**las pantuflas** *(lahs pahn-'too-flahs)*
sport jacket	**el saco** *(ehl 'sah-koh)*
socks	**los calcetines** *(lohs kahl-seh-'tee-nehs)*
stockings	**las medias** *(lahs 'meh-dee·ahs)*
suit	**el traje** *(ehl 'trah-heh)*
sweater	**el suéter** *(ehl 'sweh-tehr)*
tie	**la corbata** *(lah kohr-'bah-tah)*
t-shirt	**la camiseta** *(lah kah-mee-'seh-tah)*
underwear	**la ropa interior** *(lah 'roh-pah een-teh-ree-'ohr)*

Clothing isn't the only thing that needs to be set aside. Here are some more personal possessions that you should know. Practice them by saying their names as each one is removed. As you have discovered, the most effective method for learning the names for objects in Spanish is to physically interact with them:

barrettes	**las hebillas** *(lahs eh-'bee-yahs)*
billfold	**la billetera** *(lah bee-yeh-'teh-rah)*
bobby pins	**los ganchos** *(lohs 'gahn-chohs)*

bracelet	**el brazalete** *(ehl brah-sah-'leh-teh)*
cell phone	**el teléfono celular** *(ehl teh-'leh-foh-noh seh-loo-'lahr)*
checkbook	**la chequera** *(lah cheh-'keh-rah)*
contact lenses	**los lentes de contacto** *(lohs 'lehn-tehs deh kohn-'tahk-toh)*
credit card	**la tarjeta de crédito** *(lah tahr-'heh-tah deh 'kreh-dee-toh)*
earrings	**los aretes** *(lohs ah-'reh-tehs)*
glasses	**los anteojos** *(lohs ahn-teh-'oh-hohs)*
gloves	**los guantes** *(lohs 'gwahn-tehs)*
handbag	**la bolsa, la cartera** *(lah 'bohl-sah, lah kahr-'teh-rah)*
hearing aids	**los audífonos** *(lohs ow-'dee-foh-nohs)*
jewelry	**las joyas** *(lahs 'hoh-yahs)*
make-up	**el maquillaje** *(ehl mah-kee-'yah-heh)*
money	**el dinero** *(ehl dee-'neh-roh)*
necklace	**el collar** *(ehl koh-'yahr)*
ring	**el anillo** *(ehl ah-'nee-yoh)*
scarf	**la bufanda** *(lah boo-'fahn-dah)*
watch	**el reloj** *(ehl reh-'loh)*

The anesthesia

La anestesia *(lah ah-nehs-'teh-see·ah)*

Although Miguel is sedated, he still feels pain. It's time to discuss the anesthesia. Bring in his parents and give them the details:

She's the anesthesiologist.
Ella es la anestesista.
('eh-yah ehs lah ah-nehs-teh-'sees-tah)

She's going to give him an injection.
Va a ponerle una inyección.
(bah ah poh-'nehr-leh 'oo-nah een-yehk-see·'ohn)

It hurts a little.
Le duele un poco.
(leh 'dweh-leh oon 'poh-koh)

He will sleep soon.
Va a dormir muy pronto.
(bah ah dohr-'meer moo·ee 'prohn-toh)

¡No se olvide!

- Intravenous—**Intravenoso**—is an important word when talking about surgery. In fact, you'll need that word throughout the hospital: **Vamos a darle un tubo intravenoso.** *('bah-mohs ah 'dahr-leh ehl 'too-boh een-trah-beh-'noh-soh)*

- Notice how many words related to **anestesia** are a lot like English. It should make things easier.

epidural	**epidural** *(eh-pee-doo-'rahl)*
gas	**gas** *(gahs)*
local	**local** *(loh-'kahl)*
general	**general** *(heh-neh-'rahl)*
partial	**parcial** *(pahr-see-'ahl)*
spinal	**espinal** *(ehs-pee-'nahl)*
sodium pentothal	**pentotal de sodio** *(pehn-toh-'tahl deh 'soh-dee·oh)*

Post-op

Después de la operación
(dehs-'pwehs deh lah oh-peh-rah-see·'ohn)

The operation was a success, and there were no **complicaciones** *(kohm-plee-kah-see·'oh-nehs)*. Young Miguel, however, has been through quite an ordeal and is feeling pretty groggy. His parents never left the hospital, and have just been cleared to visit their son in Recovery. Specific instructions and questions cannot be avoided. The Espinozas must be informed immediately of Miguel's situation. Take what you need from the list below.

The operation went well.
La operación salió bien.
(lah oh-peh-rah-see·'ohn sah-lee-'oh bee·ehn)

The tube in his arm is for I.V. fluids.
El tubo en su brazo es para líquidos intravenosos.
(ehl 'too-boh ehn soo 'brah-soh ehs 'pah-rah 'lee-kee-dohs een-trah-beh-'noh-sohs)

The tube in his bladder is for urinating.
El tubo que tiene en su vejiga es para orinar.
(ehl 'too-boh keh tee-'eh-neh ehn soo beh-'hee-gah ehs 'pah-rah oh-ree-'nahr)

The tube in his stomach is for the food.
El tubo que tiene en su estómago es para la comida.
(ehl 'too-boh keh tee-'eh-neh ehn soo ehs-'toh-mah-goh ehs 'pah-rah lah koh-'mee-dah)

The tube in his throat is for breathing.
El tubo que tiene en su garganta es para respirar.
(ehl 'too-boh keh tee-'eh-neh ehn soo gahr-'gahn-tah ehs 'pah-rah rehs-pee-'rahr)

Use this familiar pattern to tell Miguel what's going to happen next:

We're going to . . .	**Vamos a . . .** *('bah-mohs ah)*
change the bandage	**cambiarle el vendaje** *(kahm-bee-'ahr-leh ehl behn-'dah-heh)*
give you a bath	**darle un baño** *('dahr-leh oon 'bah-nyoh)*
take out the I.V.	**sacarle el tubo intravenoso** *(sah-'kahr-leh ehl 'too-boh een-trah-veh-'noh-soh)*
take you to your room	**llevarle a su cuarto** *(yeh-'bahr-leh ah soo 'kwahr-toh)*

¡No se olvide!

- The word "stitches" is **las puntadas** in Spanish, and the word "scar" is **cicatriz.** Most patients seem to ask about them first.

  We're going to remove the stitches.
  Vamos a sacarle las puntadas
  ('bah-mohs ah sah-'kahr-leh lahs poon-'tah-dahs)

  You're going to have a scar.
  Va a tener una cicatriz
  ('bah ah teh-'nehr 'oo-nah see-kah-'trees)

Miguel has been rolled into his room where he'll have to spend the night. A number of standard hospital procedures need to be discussed, along with several important questions and requests. These patterns were presented earlier. Can you translate everything?

Do you want . . .?	**¿Quiere . . .?** *(kee-'eh-reh)*
	sentarse *(sehn-'tahr-seh)*
	dormir *(dohr-'meer)*
	orinar *(oh-ree-'nahr)*
	descansar *(dehs-kahn-'sahr)*

agua *('ah-gwah)*
comida *(koh-'mee-dah)*
medicina *(meh-dee-'see-nah)*
la silla de ruedas *(lah 'see-yah deh roo-'eh-dahs)*
las muletas *(lahs moo-'leh-tahs)*
ayuda *(ah-'yoo-dah)*
un sedante *(oon seh-'dahn-teh)*

It's . . .	**Es . . .** *(ehs)*
codeine	**codeína** *(koh-deh-'ee-nah)*
morphine	**morfina** *(mohr-'fee-nah)*
penicillin	**penicilina** *(peh-nee-see-'lee-nah)*

Controls

Los controles *(lohs kohn-'troh-lehs)*

The room is full of equipment and furniture. Many pieces can be manipulated electrically. Learn their names as you explain their function to Miguel.

It's for controlling the . . .	**Es para controlar . . .** *(ehs 'pah-rah kohn-troh-'lahr)*
bedrails	**las barandas de la cama** *(lahs bah-'rahn-dahs deh lah 'kah-mah)*
bell	**el timbre** *(ehl 'teem-breh)*
the head of the bed	**la cabecera de la cama** *(lah kah-beh-'seh-rah deh lah 'kah-mah)*
light	**la luz** *(lah loos)*
thermostat	**el termostato** *(ehl tehr-moh-'stah-toh)*
TV	**el televisor** *(ehl teh-leh-vee-'sohr)*

In English we say "to check," but in Spanish they use "to verify" (**verificar**) *(beh-ree-fee-'kahr)*. Therefore . . .

We check your . . .	**Verificamos su . . .** *(beh-ree-fee-'kah-mohs soo)*
blood pressure	**presión de sangre** *(preh-see·'ohn deh 'sahn-greh)*
breathing	**respiración** *(rehs-pee-rah-see·'ohn)*
pulse	**pulso** *('pool-soh)*
temperature	**temperatura** *(tehm-peh-rah-'too-rah)*
vital signs	**signos vitales** *('seeg-nohs bee-'tah-lehs)*

Doctor's orders!

¡Las órdenes del doctor!
(lahs 'ohr-deh-nehs dehl dohk-'tohr)

Miguel must follow a few simple instructions. Following are words that you should be using every day. Take time to check up on what you've already learned.

Call the technician.
Llame al técnico. *('yah-meh ahl 'tehk-nee-koh)*

Do not touch the I.V.
No toque el tubo intravenoso.
(noh 'toh-keh ehl 'too-boh een-trah-beh-'noh-soh)

Follow your diet.
Siga su dieta. *('see-gah soo dee-'eh-tah)*

Go to the bathroom.
Vaya al baño. *('bah-yah ahl 'bah-nyoh)*

Stay in bed.
Quédese en la cama. *('keh-deh-seh ehn lah 'kah-mah)*

Tell the nurse.
Dígale a la enfermera. *('dee-gah-leh ah lah ehn-fehr-'meh-rah)*

Try to sleep.
Trate de dormir. *('trah-teh deh dohr-'meer)*

Turn off the T.V.
Apague el televisor. *(ah-'pah-geh el teh-leh-vee-'sohr)*

Bad news

Malas noticias *('mah-lahs noh-'tee-see·ahs)*

Not all surgeries are a complete success. The medical staff is responsible for sharing the bad news as well as the good. Unfortunately, you may need to use the following expressions:

There are complications.
Hay complicaciones. *('ah-ee kohm-plee-kah-see-'oh-nehs)*

He/she is not going to live.
No va a vivir. *(noh bah ah bee-'beer)*

He/she is going to die.
Se va a morir. *(seh bah ah moh-'reer)*

He/she died.
Se murió. *(seh moo-ree-'oh)*

I'm very sorry.
Lo siento mucho. *(loh see-'ehn-toh 'moo-choh)*

It's very serious.
Es muy grave. *(ehs 'moo-ee 'grah-veh)*

(24)   **¿Cuánto aprendió?**

Can you translate these?

¿Quiere . . . ? *(kee-'eh-reh)*
 gloves, shirt, underwear,
 earrings, belt, shoes,
 tube, diet.

Voy a . . . *(boy·ee ah)*
 control the light, have a scar,
 turn on the TV, live,
 call your family, remove your stitches.

Furniture and equipment

Los muebles y el equipo
(lohs 'mweh-blehs ee ehl eh-'kee-poh)

Practice the vocabulary for all the parts of the hospital room by adding them to your commands. You can acquire most of these at home.

Point to . . .	**Señale . . .** *(seh-'nyah-leh)*
Touch . . .	**Toque . . .** *('toh-keh)*
ceiling	**el techo** *(ehl 'teh-choh)*
floor	**el piso** *(ehl 'pee-soh)*
wall	**la pared** *(lah pah-'rehd)*
Open/Close the . . .	**Abra/Cierre . . .** *('ah-brah/see-'eh-reh)*
cabinet	**el gabinete** *(ehl gah-bee-'neh-teh)*
closet	**el ropero** *(ehl roh-'peh-roh)*
curtains	**las cortinas** *(lahs kohr-'tee-nahs)*
door	**la puerta** *(lah 'pwehr-tah)*

drawer	**el cajón** *(ehl kah-'hohn)*
window	**la ventana** *(lah 'behn-tah-nah)*

A few of these words may be new to you. Are you still putting removable labels on everything?

ashtray	**el cenicero** *(ehl seh-nee-'seh-roh)*
bandage	**la venda** *(lah 'vehn-dah)*
bedpan	**la chata** *(lah 'chah-tah)*
blanket	**la frazada** *(lah frah-'sah-dah)*
cup	**la taza** *(lah 'tah-sah)*
flower vase	**el florero** *(ehl floh-'reh-roh)*
fork	**el tenedor** *(ehl teh-neh-'dohr)*
glass	**el vaso** *(ehl 'bah-soh)*
knife	**el cuchillo** *(ehl koo-'chee-yoh)*
mattress	**el colchón** *(ehl kohl-'chohn)*
napkin	**la servilleta** *(lah sehr-bee-'yeh-tah)*
nightstand	**la mesa de noche** *(lah 'meh-sah deh 'noh-cheh)*
pillow	**la almohada** *(lah ahl-moh-'ah-dah)*
pillowcase	**la funda** *(lah 'foon-dah)*
pitcher	**la jarra** *(lah 'har-rah)*
plate	**el plato** *(ehl 'plah toh)*
sheet	**la sábana** *(lah 'sah-bah-nah)*
soap	**el jabón** *(ehl hah-'bohn)*
spoon	**la cuchara** *(lah koo-'chah-rah)*
step	**el escalón** *(ehl ehs-kah-'lohn)*
towel	**la toalla** *(lah toh-'ah-yah)*
trashcan	**el cesto de basura** *(ehl 'sehs-toh deh bah-'soo-rah)*
tray	**la bandeja** *(lah bahn-'deh-hah)*

Here's another one of those phrases that makes learning easier. To ask patients if they like something, use **¿Le gusta . . .?** *(leh 'goos-tah)*

Do you like the bed?	**¿Le gusta la cama?** *(leh 'goos-tah lah 'kah-mah)*
Do you like the food?	**¿Le gusta la comida?** *(leh 'goos-tah lah koh-'mee-dah)*
Do you like the light?	**¿Le gusta la luz?** *(leh 'goos-tah lah loos)*
Do you like the soap?	**¿Le gusta el jabón?** *(leh 'goos-tah ehl hah-'bohn)*

Chances are they'll answer with a "yes." Here's what you'll hear:

¡Sí, me gusta! *(see meh 'goos-tah)*

¿Cuánto aprendió?

How's your pronunciation? Read these sentences aloud:

Press here.	**Apriete aquí.** (ah-pree-'eh-teh ah-'kee)
Turn on the light.	**Prenda la luz.** ('prehn-dah lah loos)
Turn off the TV.	**Apague la televisión.** (ah-'pah-geh lah teh-leh-bee-see-'ohn)
Dial the phone.	**Marque el teléfono.** ('mahr-keh ehl teh-'leh-foh-noh).
Take a nap.	**Tome una siesta.** ('toh-meh 'oo-nah see-'ehs-tah)

The bathroom

El cuarto de baño
(ehl 'kwahr-toh deh 'bah-nyoh)

Miguel has questions about the facility. Prepare yourself for the proper response.

Where is the . . .	**¿Donde está . . .?** ('dohn-deh eh-'stah)
bathtub	**la bañera** (lah bah-'nyeh-rah)
medicine chest	**el botiquín** (ehl boh-tee-'keen)
mirror	**el espejo** (ehl ehs-'peh-hoh)
shower	**la ducha** (lah 'doo-chah)
sink	**el lavamanos** (ehl lah-bah-'mah-nohs)
toilet	**el excusado** (ehl ehs-koo-'sah-doh)
toilet paper	**el papel higiénico** (ehl pah-'pehl ee-hee-'eh-nee-koh)
urinal	**el orinal** (ehl oh-ree-'nahl)
washcloth	**la toallita** (lah toh-ah-'yee-tah)

Special vocabulary

El vocabulario especial
(ehl boh-kah-boo-'lah-ree·oh ehs-peh-see-'ahl)

Miguel should be made aware of everything around him. Use the following pattern along with special hospital vocabulary to familiarize Miguel and others with items found in a hospital room.

Here is (the) . . .	**Aquí está . . .** *(ah-'kee ehs-'tah)*
air conditioning	**el aire acondicionado** *(ehl 'ah·ee-reh ah-kohn-dee-see-oh-'nah-doh)*
alarm	**la alarma** *(lah ah-'lahr-mah)*
computer	**la computadora** *(lah kohm-poo-tah-'doh-rah)*
electric fan	**el ventilador** *(ehl behn-tee-lah-'dohr)*
electricity	**la electricidad** *(lah eh-lehk-tree-see-'dahd)*
heating	**la calefacción** *(lah kah-leh-fahk-see-'ohn)*
light switch	**el interruptor** *(ehl een-teh-rroop-'tohr)*
machine	**la máquina** *(lah 'mah-kee-nah)*
microwave	**el microondas** *(ehl mee-kroh-'ohn-dahs)*
outlet	**el enchufe** *(ehl ehn-'choo-feh)*
refrigerator	**el refrigerador** *(ehl reh-free-heh-rah-'dohr)*
remote control	**el control remoto** *(ehl kohn-'trohl reh-'moh-toh)*
wire	**el cable** *(ehl 'kah-bleh)*

The recovery

La recuperación
(lah reh-koo-peh-rah-see·'ohn)

While Miguel rests in his hospital bed, you will be busy with a number of routine duties. As you treat the recovering patient, make up general comments and questions using the Spanish that you know. Notice that none of these are translated:

Necesita . . . *(neh-seh-'see-tah)*
  un examen. *(oon ehk-'sah-mehn)*
  dormir. *(dohr-'meer)*
  comer. *(koh-'mehr)*

¿Tiene . . . *(tee-'eh-neh)*
  sueño? *('sweh-nyoh)*
  dolores? *(doh-'loh-rehs)*

Voy a . . . *(boh·ee ah)*
  hacer la cama. *(ah-'sehr lah 'kah-mah)*
  tomar el pulso. *(toh-'mahr ehl 'pool-soh)*

¿Está cómodo? *(eh-'stah 'koh-moh-doh)*

Su dieta es muy importante.
(soo dee-'eh-tah ehs moo·ee eem-pohr-'tahn-teh)

Es necesario descansar. *(ehs neh-seh-'sah-ree·oh dehs-kahn-'sahr)*

He terminado. *(eh tehr-mee-'nah-doh)*

It is imperative that Miguel is given all the correct information. He will be released soon and wants to know what the doctors are saying.

Doctor's orders.
Órdenes del médico. *('ohr-deh-nehs dehl 'meh-dee-koh)*

The doctor says no.
El médico dice que no. *(ehl 'meh-dee-koh 'dee-seh keh noh)*

Don't try to do too much.
No trate de hacer demasiado.
(noh 'trah-teh deh ah-'sehr deh-mah-see-'ah-doh)

We have to talk with your doctor first.
Tenemos que hablar con su doctor primero.
(teh-'neh-mohs keh ah-'blahr kohn soo dohk-'tohr pree-'meh-roh)

You are not well enough.
No está completamente bien.
(noh-eh-'stah kohm-pleh-tah-'mehn-teh bee·'ehn)

Miguel is ready to be released to his family. Make a few final comments to him and his family.

You are going to be discharged today.
Le van a dar de alta hoy. *(leh bahn ah dahr deh 'ahl-tah 'oh·ee)*

You have to sign the release.
Tiene que firmar el permiso.
(tee-'eh-neh keh feer-'mahr ehl pehr-'mee-soh)

You need to return in one week.
Necesita regresar en una semana.
(neh-seh-'see-tah reh-greh-'sahr ehn 'oo-nah seh-'mah-nah)

 ¿Cuánto aprendió?

Translate the following sentences:

Mueva . . . *('mweh-bah)*
(the cabinet, the mirror, the tray)

Traiga . . . *('trah·ee-gah)*
(the plate, the fan, the soap, the spoon, the blanket)

Necesita . . . *(neh-seh-'see-tah)*
(shower, nap)

Chapter Eight

Capítulo Ocho
(kah-'pee-too-loh 'oh-choh)

Carlos Espinoza,
Age 65

Carlos has just finished dinner and his favorite cigar when he feels a tightness in his chest and pains down his left arm. He realizes immediately what is happening, and is able to remain calm. Within minutes, the pains subside. He decides to call his son, Juan, to let him know what has happened, but instead of waiting for assistance, he stubbornly climbs into his pickup truck and drives three blocks to the local Medical Center.

Once admitted, a series of test results including an electrocardiogram, **el electrocardiograma** *(ehl eh-lehk-troh-kahr-dee-oh-'grah-mah)*, confirm his fears—he has suffered a heart attack. But that's not all. A routine chest X ray reveals a possible mass at the base of his right lung. More tests are needed, in addition to a variety of treatments and medications. Follow along as we explore the Spanish that is required in various fields of specialized medicine.

First, use the familiar commands to get Carlos to relax. He has begun to panic:

¡Siéntese! *(see-'ehn-teh-seh)*
¡Cálmese! *('kahl-meh-seh)*
¡No se preocupe! *(noh seh preh-oh-'koo-peh)*

Now, help him breathe. These words allow you to be very specific:

Breathe . . .	**Respire . . .** *(rehs-'pee-reh)*
again	**otra vez** *('oh-trah behs)*
deeply	**profundamente** *(proh-foon-dah-'mehn-teh)*
in	**hacia adentro** *('ah-see·ah ah-'dehn-troh)*

normally   **normalmente** *(nohr-mahl-'mehn-teh)*

out   **hacia afuera** *('ah-see·ah ah-'fweh-rah)*

Ask him some questions related to his physical condition.

Was it a sharp or dull pain?	**¿Fue un dolor agudo o sordo?** *(fweh oon doh-'lohr ah-'goo-doh oh 'sohr-doh)*
In what part?	**¿En qué parte?** *(ehn keh 'pahr-teh)*
How long ago?	**¿Hace cuánto tiempo?** *('hah-seh 'kwahn-toh tee-'ehm-poh)*
How often?	**¿Con qué frecuencia?** *(kohn keh freh-'kwehn-see·ah)*
What were you doing at the time?	**¿Qué estaba usted haciendo entonces?** *(keh ehs-'tah-bah oo-'stehd ah-see-'ehn-doh ehn-'tohn-sehs)*

These two questions may help to locate his pain. Don't forget that the word **se** is frequently part of an action word:

to stay	**Quedarse** *(keh-'dahr-seh)*
Does it stay?	**¿Se queda?** *(seh 'keh-dah)*
to spread	**Extenderse** *(ehks-tehn-'dehr-seh)*
Does it spread?	**¿Se extiende?** *(seh ehks-tee'ehn-deh)*

Now ask the patient:

Do you have . . .?	**¿Tiene . . .?** *(tee-'eh-neh)*
burning	**ardor** *(ahr-'dohr)*
chest pains	**dolores en el pecho** *(doh-'loh-rehs ehn ehl 'peh-choh)*
heart murmurs	**murmullos en el corazón** *(moor-'moo-yohs ehn ehl koh-rah-'sohn)*
irregular heartbeats	**latidos de corazón irregulares** *(lah-'tee-dohs deh koh-rah-'sohn ee-rreh-goo-'lah-rehs)*
shortness of breath	**falta de aliento** *('fahl-tah deh ah-lee-'ehn-toh)*
tingling	**hormigueo** *(ohr-mee-'geh-oh)*

Heart attack!

¡El ataque cardíaco!
(ehl ah-'tah-keh kahr-'dee-ah-koh)

You need as much information as possible. Look at all the verb forms that you know!

Do you cough up blood?
¿Escupe sangre?
(ehs-'koo-peh 'sahn-greh)

Do you get short of breath upon exertion?
¿Se queda sin aliento después de hacer un esfucrzo?
(seh 'keh-dah seen ah-lee-'ehn-toh dehs-'pwehs deh ah-'sehr oon ehs-'fwehr-soh)

Do you feel pressure?
¿Siente presión?
(see-'ehn-teh preh-see·'ohn)

Do your legs swell?
¿Se le hinchan las piernas?
(seh leh 'een-chahn lahs pee-'ehr-nahs)

Do you sleep well?
¿Duerme bien?
('dwehr-meh bee·'ehn)

Do you take medication?
¿Toma medicinas?
('toh-mah meh-dee-'see-nahs)

Do you wake up at night with shortness of breath and perspiring?
¿Despierta por la noche con la respiración corta y sudando?
(dehs-pee-'ehr-tah pohr lah 'noh-cheh kohn lah rehs-pee-rah-see·'ohn 'kohr-tah ee soo-'dahn-doh)

Have you ever had a heart attack?
¿Ha tenido alguna vez un ataque cardíaco?
(ah teh-'nee-doh ahl-'goo-nah behs oon ah-'tah-keh kahr-'dee-ah-koh)

How many pillows do you sleep on?
¿Con cuántas almohadas duerme?
(kohn 'kwahn-tahs ahl-moh-'ah-dahs 'dwehr-meh)

When did the problem begin?
¿Cuándo empezó el problema?
('kwahn-doh ehm-peh-'soh ehl proh-'bleh-mah)

Here are some more key words related to heart attacks. These will not only help you form specific questions, but they will help you understand the patient's responses:

aorta	**la aorta** *(lah ah-'ohr-tah)*
atrium	**la cámara** *(lah 'kah-mah-rah)*
blocked artery	**la arteria obstruida** *(lah ahr-'teh-ree·ah ohb-stroo-'ee-dah)*
brain	**el cerebro** *(ehl seh-'reh-broh)*
graft	**el injerto** *(ehl een-'hehr-toh)*
hardening	**el endurecimiento** *(ehl ehn-doo-reh-see mee-'ehn-toh)*
heartbeat	**el ritmo cardíaco** *(ehl 'reet-moh kahr-'dee-ah-koh)*
hypertension	**la hipertensión arterial** *(lah ee-pehr-tehn-see·'ohn ahr-teh-ree-'ahl)*
overweight	**el sobrepeso** *(ehl soh-breh-'peh-soh)*
oxygen level	**el nivel de oxígeno** *(ehl nee-'behl deh ohk-'see-heh-noh)*
pacemaker	**el marcapasos** *(ehl mahr-kah-'pah-sohs)*
rupture	**la ruptura** *(lah roop-'too-rah)*
strained muscle	**el músculo forzado** *(ehl 'moos-koo-loh fohr-'sah-doh)*
stress	**el estrés** *(ehl ehs-'trehs)*
stroke	**el ataque** *(ehl ah-'tah-keh)*
valve	**la válvula** *(lah 'bahl-boo-lah)*
vein	**la vena** *(lah 'beh-nah)*
ventricle	**el ventrículo** *(ehl behn-'tree-koo-loh)*

Now take a few minutes to translate the following. They are so similar to English that you shouldn't have to look them up.

aneurisma *(ah-neh-oo-'rees-mah)*
angina *(ahn-'hee-nah)*
angiografía *(ahn-hee-oh-grah-'fee-ah)*
angioplastia *(ahn-hee-oh-'plahs-tee-ah)*
arritmias *(ah-'rreet-mee-ahs)*
arteriosclerosis *(ahr-teh-ree-oh-skleh-'roh-sees)*
cardiología *(kahr-dee-oh-loh-'hee-ah)*
cardiovascular *(kahr-dee-oh-bahs-koo-'lahr)*
circulación *(seer-koo-lah-see·'ohn)*
coagulación *(koh-ah-goo-lah-see-'ohn)*
colesterol *(koh-leh-steh-'rohl)*

coronaria *(koh-roh-'nah-ree-ah)*
dilatación *(dee-lah-tah-see-'ohn)*
enfisema *(ehn-fee-'seh-mah)*
hematócrito *(eh-mah-toh-'kree-toh)*
hemorragia *(eh-moh-'rrah-hee-ah)*
hipertensión *(ee-pehr-tehn-see·'ohn)*
nitroglicerina *(nee-troh-glee-seh-'ree-nah)*
taquicardia *(tah-kee-'kahr-dee-ah)*
triglicéridos *(tree-glee-'seh-ree-dahs)*

Results

Los resultados *(lohs reh-sool-'tah-dohs)*

After the physical examination and tests, give Carlos all the data that you have. When he and his family ask, "What is happening?" **¿Qué está pasando?** *(keh eh-'stah pah-'sahn-doh)* let him know what is wrong:

Your blood pressure is very high.
Su presión es muy alta.
(soo preh-see·'ohn ehs 'moo·ee 'ahl-tah)

The artery is blocked.
La arteria está obstruida.
(lah ahr-'teh-ree·ah eh-'stah ohb-stroo-'ee-dah)

The heart muscles are strained.
Los músculos del corazón están forzados.
(lohs 'moos-koo-lohs dehl koh-rah-'sohn eh-'stahn fohr-'sah-dohs)

There is some hardening of the coronary arteries.
Tiene algo de endurecimiento de las arterias coronarias.
(tee-'eh-neh 'ahl-goh deh ehn-doo-reh-see-mee-'ehn-toh deh lahs ahr-'teh-ree·ahs koh-roh-'nah-ree·ahs)

You are overweight.
Tiene sobrepeso. *(tee-'eh-neh soh-breh-'peh-soh)*

Your case is (not) serious.
Su caso (no) es grave. *(soo 'kah-soh [noh] ehs 'grah-beh)*

Your pulse is very fast.
Su pulso es muy rápido. *(soo 'pool-soh ehs 'moo·ee 'rah-pee-doh)*

Your color is good.
Tiene buen color. *(tee-'eh-neh boo-'ehn koh-'lohr)*

Therapy and treatment

Terapia y tratamiento
(teh-'rah-pee-ah ee 'trah-tah-mee-ehn-toh)

After telling the patient and his family what is wrong with him, learn some of the following sentences to explain the next step:

I want to explain the equipment in this room.
Quiero explicarle el equipo de este cuarto.
(kee-'eh-roh ehks-plee-'kahr-leh ehl eh-'kee-poh deh 'eh-steh 'kwahr-toh)

We are going to draw a little blood from your vein.
Vamos a sacar un poco de sangre de su vena.
('bah-mohs ah sah-'kahr-leh oon 'poh-koh deh 'sahn-greh deh soo 'beh-nah)

We are going to check the cardiovascular function.
Vamos a verificar el funcionamiento cardiovascular.
('bah-mohs ah beh-ree-fee-'kahr ehl foon-see-oh-nah-mee-'ehn-toh kahr-dee-oh-bahs-koo-'lahr)

We are going to give you medications.
Vamos a darle medicamentos.
('bah-mohs ah 'dahr-leh meh-dee-kah-'mehn-tohs)

You need complete bed rest for now.
Por ahora, necesita completo descanso en cama.
(pohr ah-'oh-rah neh-seh-'see-tah kohm-'pleh-toh dehs-'kahn-soh ehn 'kah-mah)

You need to keep your legs straight.
Necesita tener sus piernas en posición recta.
(neh-seh-'see-tah teh-'nehr soos pee-'ehr-nahs ehn poh-see-see-'ohn 'rehk-tah)

We are going to put the catheter in the artery.
Vamos a poner el catéter en la arteria.
('bah-mohs ah poh-'nehr ehl kah-'teh-tehr ehn lah ahr-'teh-ree-ah)

The balloon will open the blocked artery.
El globito va a abrir la arteria obstruída.
(ehl gloh-'bee-toh vah ah ahb-'reer lah ahr-'teh-ree-ah ohbs-troo-'ee-dah)

Dos culturas

When conversing with Hispanics about foods, stress both the good as well as the bad, and remember that their basic meals may differ from those eaten by most Americans.

The dietician

El dietista *(ehl dee-eh-'tees-tah)*

Because Carlos Espinoza is overweight and has poor eating habits, a dietician is contacted to help counsel him. As a matter of fact, all of the Espinozas could use some sound advice. It's visiting hours and they're all gathered around the patient's bed. Now is a good time to get the background information you need. At this stage of language development, most of these basic survival verb forms and vocabulary have been introduced:

Are you allergic to any food?
¿Tiene alergias a alguna comida?
(tee-'eh-neh ah-'lehr-hee·ahs ah ahl-'goo-nah koh-'mee-dah)

Do you have problems swallowing?
¿Tiene problemas al tragar?
(tee-'eh-neh proh-'bleh-mahs ahl trah-'gahr)

Have you gained or lost weight?
¿Ha ganado o perdido peso?
(ah gah-'nah-doh oh pehr-'dee-doh 'peh-soh)

How is your appetite?
¿Cómo está su apetito?
('koh-moh eh-'stah soo ah-peh-'tee-toh)

Have you had any operation on your digestive system?
¿Ha tenido alguna operación en el sistema digestivo?
(ah teh-'nee-doh ahl-'goo-nah oh-peh-rah-see·'ohn ehn ehl sees-'teh-mah dee-hehs-'tee-boh)

What do you eat?
¿Qué come?
('keh 'koh-meh)

Give Carlos and his family a few practical suggestions:

You have to follow a diet.
Tiene que seguir una dieta.
(tee-'eh-neh keh seh-'geer 'oo-nah dee-'eh-tah)

You need to eat three meals a day.
Necesita comer tres comidas al día.
(neh-seh-'see-tah koh-'mehr trehs koh-'mee-dahs ahl 'dee-ah)

Do not eat between meals.
No coma entre comidas.
(noh 'koh-mah 'ehn-treh koh-'mee-dahs)

When it comes to good health, you can never have enough vocabulary:

You cannot eat . . .	**No puede comer . . .** (noh 'pweh-deh koh-'mehr)
baking soda	**bicarbonato** (bee-kahr-boh-'nah-toh)
dairy products	**productos lácteos** (proh-'dook-tohs 'lahk-teh-ohs)
fried foods	**comida frita** (koh-'mee-dah 'free-tah)
margarine	**margarina** (mahr-gah-'ree-nah)
red meat	**carne roja** ('kahr-neh 'roh-hah)
salt	**sal** (sahl)
seasonings	**condimentos** (kohn-dee-'mehn-tohs)
snacks	**meriendas** (meh-ree-'ehn-dahs)
spices	**especias** (eh-'speh-see·ahs)
sugar	**azúcar** (ah-'soo-kahr)
sweets	**dulces** ('dool-sehs)
raw vegetables	**legumbres crudas** (leh-'goom-brehs 'kroo-dahs)

The diet

La dieta (lah dee-'eh-tah)

Now you need to talk to Carlos and his family. Use this menu to select the items that are to be allowed or forbidden in his diet.

Eat . . .	**Coma . . .** ('koh-mah)
Do not eat . . .	**No coma . . .** (noh 'koh-mah)
breakfast	**el desayuno** (ehl deh-sah-'yoo-noh)
lunch	**el almuerzo** (ehl ahl-moo-'ehr-soh)
dinner	**la cena** (lah 'seh-nah)
apple	**la manzana** (lah mahn-'sah-nah)
avocado	**el aguacate, la palta** (ehl ah-gwah-'kah-teh, lah 'pahl-tah)
banana	**el plátano** (ehl 'plah-tah-noh)
bread	**el pan** (ehl pahn)
butter	**la mantequilla** (lah 'mahn-teh-'kee-yah)
cabbage	**el repollo** (ehl reh-'poh-yoh)
cake	**la torta** (lah 'tohr-tah)
candy	**el dulce** (ehl 'dool-seh)
carrot	**la zanahoria** (lah sah-nah-'oh-ree·ah)

cereal	**el cereal** *(ehl seh-reh-'ahl)*
cheese	**el queso** *(ehl 'keh-soh)*
cherry	**las cerezas** *(lahs seh-'reh-sahs)*
chicken	**el pollo** *(ehl 'poh-yoh)*
cookie	**la galleta** *(lah gah-'yeh-tah)*
corn	**el maíz** *(ehl mah-'ees)*
cream	**la crema** *(lah 'kreh-mah)*
dessert	**el postre** *(ehl poh-'streh)*
egg	**el huevo** *(ehl 'weh-bohs)*
fish	**el pescado** *(ehl pehs-'kah-doh)*
flour	**la harina** *(lah ah-'ree-nah)*
garlic	**el ajo** *(ehl 'ah-hoh)*
grape	**las uvas** *(lahs 'oo-bahs)*
grapefruit	**la toronja** *(lah toh-'rohn-hah)*
green bean	**el ejote** *(ehl eh-'hoh-teh)*
gum	**el chicle** *(ehl 'chee-kleh)*
ice cream	**el helado** *(ehl eh-'lah-doh)*
jelly	**la jalea** *(lah hah-'leh-ah)*
lamb	**el carnero** *(ehl kahr-'neh-roh)*
lard	**la manteca** *(lah mahn-'teh-kah)*
lemon	**el limón** *(ehl lee-'mohn)*
lettuce	**la lechuga** *(lah leh-'choo-gah)*
milk	**la leche** *(lah 'leh-cheh)*
noodles	**los fideos** *(lohs fee-'deh-ohs)*
nuts	**las nueces** *(lahs noo-'eh-sehs)*
oil	**el aceite** *(ehl ah-'seh-ee-teh)*
onion	**la cebolla** *(lah seh-'boh-yah)*
orange	**la naranja** *(lah nah-'rahn-hah)*
peas	**los chícharos** *(lohs 'chi-chah-rrohs)*
pepper	**la pimienta** *(lah pee-mee-'ehn-tah)*
pie	**el pastel** *(ehl pah-'stehl)*
pineapple	**la piña** *(lah 'pee-nyah)*
pork	**el cerdo** *(ehl 'sehr-doh)*
potato	**la papa** *(lah 'pah-pah)*
rice	**el arroz** *(ehl ah-'rrohs)*
salad	**la ensalada** *(lah ehn-sah-'lah-dah)*
salt	**la sal** *(lah sahl)*
sauce	**la salsa** *(lah 'sahl-sah)*
shellfish	**los mariscos** *(lohs mah-'rees-kohs)*
soup	**la sopa** *(lah 'soh-pah)*
steak	**el bistec** *(ehl bees-'tehk)*
strawberry	**las fresas** *(lahs 'freh-sahs)*

sugar	**el azúcar** (*ehl ah-'soo-kahr*)
tomato	**el tomate** (*ehl toh-'mah-teh*)
turkey	**el pavo** (*ehl 'pah-boh*)
yogurt	**el yogur** (*ehl yoh-'goor*)
Drink . . .	**Tome . . .** (*'toh-meh*)
Do not drink . . .	**No tome . . .** (*noh 'toh-meh*)
beer	**la cerveza** (*lah sehr-'beh-sah*)
coffee	**el café** (*ehl 'kah-feh*)
decaffeinated coffee	**el café descafeinado**
	(*ehl kah-'feh dehs-kah-feh·ee-'nah-doh*)
juice	**el jugo** (*ehl 'hoo-goh*)
liquor	**el licor** (*ehl lee-'kohr*)
milk	**la leche** (*lah 'leh-cheh*)
soft drink	**el refresco** (*ehl reh-'frehs-koh*)
tea	**el té** (*ehl teh*)
water	**el agua** (*ehl 'ah-gwah*)
wine	**el vino** (*ehl 'bee-noh*)

By the way, the word for "ice" is **hielo** (*ee-'eh-loh*). **Traiga el hielo.** (*'trah-ee-gah ehl ee-'eh-loh*)

(26) **¿Cuánto aprendió?**

Fill in the following:

- **No coma . . .** (*Noh 'koh-mah*)
  (butter, salt, candy, cheese, steak, cookies)

- **Tome . . .** (*'toh-meh*)
  (tea, milk, juice)

- **Voy a . . .** (*'boh·ee ah*)
  (give you medication)
  (explain the equipment)
  (draw a little blood)
  (listen to your chest)

Now you must give the family some sound advice.

You need . . .	**Necesita . . .** (*neh-seh-'see-tah*)
a bland diet	**una dieta blanda** (*'oo-nah dee-'eh-tah 'blahn-dah*)
a calorie-controlled diet	**una dieta controlada en calorías** (*'oo-nah dee-'eh-tah kohn-troh-'lah-dah ehn kah-loh-'ree-ahs*)
cooked foods	**las comidas cocidas** (*lahs koh-'mee-dahs koh-'see-dahs*)
decaffeinated coffee	**café descafeinado** (*kah-'feh dehs-kah-feh-ee-'nah-doh*)
a diabetic diet	**una dieta para diabéticos** (*'oo-nah dee-'eh-tah 'pah-rah dee-ah-'beh-tee-kohs*)
more fiber	**más fibra** (*mahs 'feeb-rah*)
more fruits and vegetables	**más frutas y legumbres** (*mahs 'froo-tahs ee leh-'goom-brehs*)
iron	**hierro** (*ee-'ehr-roh*)
less sodium and potassium	**menos sodio y potasio** (*'meh-nohs 'soh-dee·oh ee poh-'tah-see·oh*)
to lower your cholesterol level	**bajar su nivel de colesterol** (*bah-'hahr soo nee-'behl deh koh-lehs-teh-'rohl*)
a low-fat diet	**una dieta baja en grasa** (*'oo-nah dee-'eh-tah 'bah-hah ehn 'grah-sah*)
magnesium	**magnesia** (*mahg-'neh-see-ah*)
minerals	**minerales** (*mee-neh-'rah-lehs*)
more calcium	**más calcio** (*mahs 'kahl-see-oh*)
more exercise	**más ejercicio** (*mahs eh-hehr-'see-see·oh*)
more liquids	**más líquidos** (*mahs 'lee-kee-dohs*)
more protein	**más proteínas** (*mahs proh-teh-'ee-nahs*)
more soy	**más soya** (*mahs 'soh-yah*)
nutritional supplement	**un suplemento nutritivo** (*oon soo-pleh-'mehn-toh noo-tree-'tee-boh*)
organic foods	**alimentos orgánicos** (*ah-lee-'mehn-tohs ohr-'gah-nee-kohs*)
a restricted diet	**una dieta limitada** (*'oo-nah dee-'eh-tah lee-mee-'tah-dah*)
vitamins	**vitaminas** (*bee-tah-'mee-nahs*)

You can't!

¡No puede! *(noh 'pweh-deh)*

Carlos needs to be warned about the possible dangers of his heart condition:

Don't overeat.
No coma demasiado.
(noh 'koh-mah deh-mah-see-'ah-doh)

For now, you can't drive a car.
Por ahora, no puede manejar un carro.
('pohr ah-'oh-rah noh 'pweh-deh mah-neh-'hahr oon 'kah-rroh)

You can't do strenuous exercise.
No puede hacer mucho ejercicio físico.
(noh 'pweh-deh ah-'sehr 'moo-choh eh-hehr-'see-see·oh 'fee-see-koh)

You can't have a lot of stress or tension.
No puede tener mucho estrés o tensión.
(noh 'pweh-deh teh-'nehr 'moo-choh ehs-'trehs oh tehn-see-'ohn)

The tests

Las pruebas *(lahs proo-'eh-bahs)*

Cardiac patients like Carlos have to be watched closely, even when they leave the hospital. The following tests are vital for monitoring a patient's progress in the doctor's office or in the hospital as an outpatient:

Holter monitor

La prueba de Holter
(lah proo-'eh-bah deh ohl-'tehr)

This is a heart monitoring test.
Este es un monitor para controlar el corazón.
('eh-steh ehs oon moh-nee-'tohr 'pah-rah kohn-troh-'lahr ehl koh-rah-'sohn)

It lasts 24 hours.
Dura veinticuatro horas.
('doo-rah veh·een-tee-'kwah-troh 'oh-rahs)

You need to wear the monitor at all times.
Necesita llevar el monitor constantemente.
(neh-seh-'see-tah yeh-'bahr ehl moh-nee-'tohr kohn-stahn-teh-'mehn-teh)

During the test, write down what you do and how you feel.
Durante la prueba, anote lo que hace y como se siente.
(doo-'rahn-teh lah proo-'eh-bah, ah-'noh-teh loh keh 'ah-seh ee 'koh-moh seh see-'ehn-teh)

Stress test

La prueba del estrés
(lah proo-'eh-bah dehl eh-'strehs)

You cannot eat anything for twelve hours before the test.
No puede comer nada por doce horas antes de la prueba.
(noh 'pweh-deh koh-'mehr 'nah-dah pohr 'doh-seh 'oh-rahs 'ahn-tehs deh lah proo-'eh-bah)

During the test, you have to stay relaxed.
Durante la prueba, tiene que estar tranquilo.
(doo-'rahn-teh lah proo-'eh-bah, tee-'eh-neh keh eh-'stahr trahn-'kee-loh)

We are going to give you something to increase the heart rate.
Vamos a darle algo para acelerar el ritmo cardíaco.
('bah-mohs ah 'dahr-leh 'ahl-goh 'pah-rah ah-seh-leh-'rahr ehl 'reet-moh kahr-'dee-ah-koh)

You must wear comfortable clothes and sneakers.
Tiene que usar ropa cómoda y zapatillas.
(tee-'eh-neh keh oo-'sahr 'roh-pah 'koh-moh-dah ee sah-pah-'tee-yahs)

We are going to change the speed of the machine.
Vamos a cambiar la velocidad de la máquina.
('bah-mohs ah kahm-'bee-'ahr lah beh-loh-see-'dahd deh lah 'mah-kee-nah)

Pulmonary function test

Prueba de la función pulmonar
(proo-'eh-bah deh lah foon-see·'ohn pool-moo-'nahr)

It is a breathing test.
Es una prueba de respiración.
(ehs 'oo-nah proo-'eh-bah deh rehs-pee-rah-see·'ohn)

I am going to put medicine in your mouth.
Voy a poner medicina en su boca.
('boh·ee ah poh-'nehr meh-dee-'see-nah ehn soo 'boh-kah)

Breathe normally through the mouth.
Respire normalmente por la boca.
(reh-'spee-reh nohr-mahl-'mehn-teh pohr lah 'boh-kah)

You may swallow normally.
Puede tragar normalmente.
('pweh-deh trah-'gahr nohr-mahl-'mehn-teh)

Try to let out all of the air in your lungs.
Trate de sacar todo el aire de los pulmones.
('trah-teh deh sah-'kahr 'toh-doh ehl 'ah·ee-reh deh lohs pool-'moh-nehs)

Breathe deeply.
Respire profundamente.
(reh-'spee-reh proh-foon-dah-'mehn-teh)

Gastrointestinal problems

Los problemas gastrointestinales
(lohs proh-'bleh-mahs gahs-troh-een-tehs-tee-'nah-lehs)

Now learn those lines in Spanish you'll need to discuss gastrointestinal problems. Open with questions about what Carlos likes to drink.

How many alcoholic beverages do you drink a day?
¿Cuántas bebidas alcohólicas toma cada día?
('kwahn-tahs beh-'bee-dahs ahl-koh-'oh-lee-kahs 'toh-mah 'kah-dah 'dee-ah)

How many bottles of soft drink?
¿Cuántas botellas de refresco?
('kwahn-tahs boh-'teh-yahs deh reh-'frehs-koh)

How many cups of coffee do you drink?
¿Cuántas tazas de café toma?
('kwahn-tahs 'tah-sahs deh kah-'feh 'toh-mah)

How many glasses of water?
¿Cuántos vasos de agua?
('kwahn-tohs 'bah-sohs deh 'ah-gwah)

How much milk?
¿Cuánta leche? *('kwahn-tah 'leh-cheh)*

What do you like to drink?
¿Qué le gusta tomar? *(keh leh 'goos-tah toh-'mahr)*

Now ask about food:

Do you eat spicy, fried, or fatty foods?
¿Come comidas picantes, fritas o grasosas?
('koh-meh koh-'mee-dahs pee-'kahn-tehs, 'free-tahs, oh grah-'soh-sahs)

Is there any food you cannot eat?
¿Hay alguna comida que no puede comer?
('ah·ee ahl-'goo-nah koh-'mee-dah keh noh 'pweh-deh koh-'mehr)

Use this formula to find out about the patient's history:

Have you had . . .?	**¿Ha tenido . . . ?** *(ah teh-'nee-doh)*
abdominal pain	**dolor abdominal** *(doh-'lohr ahb-doh-mee-'nahl)*
amoebas	**amebas** *(ah-'meh-bahs)*
a barium enema	**un enema de bario** *(oon eh-'neh-mah deh 'bah-ree·oh)*
blood in the stool	**sangre en los excrementos** *('sahn-greh ehn lohs ehks-kreh-'mehn-tohs)*
a colonoscopy	**una colonoscopía** *('oo-nah koh-loh-nohs-koh-'pee-ah)*
constipation	**estreñimento** *(ehs-treh-nyee-mee-'ehn-toh)*
diarrhea	**diarrea** *(dee-ah-'rreh-ah)*
an endoscopy	**una endoscopía** *('oo-nah ehn-dohs-koh-'pee-ah)*
flatulence	**flatulencia** *(flah-too-'lehn-see·ah)*
a gastrointestinal illness	**alguna enfermedad gastrointestinal** *(ahl-'goo-nah ehn-fehr-meh-'dahd gahs-troh-een-tehs-tee-'nahl)*
heartburn	**ardor en el estómago** *(ahr-'dohr ehn ehl ehs-'toh-mah-goh)*
hemorrhoids	**hemorroides** *(eh-moh-'rroh·ee-dehs)*

hiccups	**hipo** *('ee-poh)*
intestinal surgery	**cirugía intestinal** *(see-roo-'hee-ah een-tehs-tee-'nahl)*
parasites in your stool	**parásitos en el excremento** *(pah-'rah-see-tohs ehn ehl ehks-kreh-'mehn-toh)*
sour regurgitations	**sabor ácido en la boca** *(sah-'bohr 'ah-see-doh ehn lah 'boh-kah)*
a stroke	**un ataque** *(oon ah-'tah-keh)*
tapeworm infection	**infección de lombrices intestinales** *(een-fehk-see-'ohn deh lohm-'bree-sehs een-tehs-tee-'nah-lehs)*
ulcers	**úlceras** *('ool-seh-rahs)*

 # ¿Cuánto aprendió?

- Try to guess at these terms: (They are just like English.)

  Tiene. . . *(tee-'eh-neh)*
  anorexia *(ah-noh-'rehk-see·ah)*
  botulismo *(boh-too-'lees-moh)*
  bulimia *(boo-'lee-mee·ah)*
  colitis *(koh-'lee-tees)*

  Necesita. . . *(neh-seh-'see-tah)*
  leche de magnesia *('leh-cheh deh mahg-'neh-see·ah)*
  supositorios *(soo-poh-see-'toh-ree·ohs)*
  aceite mineral *(ah-'seh·ee-teh mee-neh-'rahl)*

Now fill in the following:

- **¿Ha tenido . . . ?** *(ah teh-'nee-doh)*
  (diarrhea, a barium enema, heartburn, alcoholic beverages)

- **Quiere . . .** *(kee-'eh-reh)*
  (decaffeinated coffee, to lose thirty pounds, to eat breakfast, a fat-restricted diet, a laxative)

Oncology

La oncología *(lah ohn-koh-loh-'hee-ah)*

The doctors are discussing the mass in Carlos' lung. They need to be explicit as they explain the various details to their non-English speaking patient. Results from their tests could indicate a life-threatening situation. Use the new verb **encontrar** (to find) to express yourself:

We found . . .	**Encontramos . . .** *(ehn-kohn-'trah-mohs)*
an abnormality	**una anormalidad** *('oo-nah ah-nohr-mah-lee-'dahd)*
a bump	**una protuberancia** *('oo-nah proh-too-beh-'rahn-see·ah)*
a cyst	**un quiste** *(oon 'kees-teh)*
a lesion	**una llaga** *('oo-nah 'yah-gah)*
a lump	**un bulto** *(oon 'bool-toh)*
a polyp	**un pólipo** *(oon 'poh-lee-poh)*
a spot	**una mancha** *('oo-nah 'mahn-chah)*
a tumor	**un tumor** *(oon too-'mohr)*

The biopsy

La biopsia *(lah bee-'ohp-see·ah)*

So far, all examinations have been preliminary. Obviously, specialists would like to look closely at a piece of the lung tissue. First, create general statements, and then specify in detail with further tests and treatment.

The doctor needs a biopsy from your _____ .
El médico necesita una biopsia de su _____ .
(ehl 'meh-dee-koh neh-seh-'see-tah 'oo-nah bee-'oh-psee·ah de soo)

He's going to give you an injection.
Va a darle una inyección.
(bah ah 'dahr-leh 'oo-nah een-yehk-see-'ohn)

He's going to use a special needle.
Va a usar una aguja especial.
(bah ah oo-'sahr 'oo-nah ah-'goo-hah ehs-peh-see-'ahl)

He has to clean the area first.
Tiene que limpiar el área primero.
(tee-'eh-neh keh leem-pee-'ahr lah 'ah-reh-ah pree-'meh-roh)

He has to send the sample to the laboratory.
Tiene que mandar la muestra al laboratorio.
(tee-'eh-neh keh mahn-'dahr lah 'mwehs-trah ahl lah-boh-rah-'toh-ree·oh)

When we receive the results, we'll know what to do.
Cuando recibamos los resultados, sabremos qué hacer.
('kwahn-doh reh-see-'bah-mohs lohs reh-sool-'tah-dohs, sah-'breh-mohs keh ah-'sehr)

Keep your ears and eyes open for the following terms. They will undoubt-edly surface during conversations with patients such as Carlos. Can you come up with something to say about each one? Write it?

bone marrow	**la médula** *(lah 'meh-doo-lah)*
tissue	**el tejido** *(ehl teh-'hee-doh)*
spinal fluid	**el líquido cefalorraquídeo** *(ehl 'lee-kee-doh seh-fah-loh-rrah-'kee-deh-oh)*
cells	**las células** *(lahs 'seh-loo-lahs)*
blood count	**el recuento de los glóbulos sanguíneos** *(ehl reh-'kwehn-toh deh lohs 'gloh-boo-lohs sahn-'gee-neh-ohs)*
clinical studies	**los estudios clínicos** *(lohs ehs-'too-dee-ohs 'klee-nee-kohs)*
self-examination	**el autoexamen** *(ehl ah-oo-toh-ek-'sah-mehn)*

¡No se olvide!

These procedures demand a command.

Lie on your side.
Acuéstese de lado.
(ah-'kwehs-teh-seh deh 'lah-doh)

Relax and breathe through your mouth.
Relájese y respire por la boca.
(reh-'lah-heh-seh ee rehs-'pee-reh pohr lah 'boh-kah)

Stay very still.
Quédese muy quieto.
('keh-deh-seh moo·ee kee-'eh-toh)

Call the doctor if you cough up blood.
Llame al doctor si tose y escupe sangre.
('yah-meh ahl dohk-'tohr see 'toh-seh ee ehs-'koo-peh 'sahn-greh)

Lumbar puncture

La punción lumbar
(lah poon-see·'ohn loom-'bahr)

Here are some expressions you will need to know in order to explain these procedures:

The doctor needs a sample of your spinal fluid.
El doctor necesita una muestra de su líquido cefalorraquídeo.
(ehl dohk-'tohr neh-seh-'see-tah 'oo-nah 'mwehs-trah deh soo 'lee-kee-doh 'seh-fah-loh-rrah-'kee-deh-oh)

First you'll need local anesthesia.
Primero necesita anestesia local.
(pree-'meh-roh neh-seh-'see-tah ah-nehs-'teh-see·ah loh-'kahl)

He has to put a needle in your spine.
Tiene que poner una aguja en su columna.
(tee-'eh-neh keh poh-'nehr 'oo-nah ah-'goo-hah ehn soo koh-'loom-nah)

Lie on your back for one hour after the procedure.
Acuéstese de espalda por una hora después del procedimiento.
(ah-'kwehs-teh-seh deh ehs-'pahl-dah pohr 'oo-nah 'oh-rah dehs-'pwehs dehl proh-seh-dee-mee-'ehn-toh)

Colonoscopy

Colonoscopía *(koh-loh-nohs-koh-'pee·ah)*

This is a colon examination.
Este es un examen del colon.
('eh-steh ehs oon ehk-'sah-mehn dehl 'koh-lohn)

Take an enema one hour before the procedure.
Hágase un enema una hora antes del procedimiento.
('ah-gah-seh oon eh-'neh-mah oonah 'oh-rah 'ahn-tehs dehl proh-seh-dee-mee-'ehn-toh)

The doctor is inserting the instrument into your rectum.
El médico está introduciendo el instrumento en el recto.
(ehl 'meh-dee-koh eh-'stah een-troh-doo-see-'ehn-doh ehl eens-troo-'mehn-toh ehn ehl 'rehk-toh)

He is removing the instrument.
Está sacando el instrumento.
(eh-'stah sah-'kahn-doh ehl een-stroo-'mehn-toh)

More tests

Más pruebas *('mahs proo·'eh-bahs)*

Some additional tests you should know how to describe are:

MRI (Magnetic Resonance Imaging)
Imagen por resonancia magnética
(ee-'mah-hehn pohr reh-soh-'nahn-see·ah mahg-'neh-tee-kah)

Sonogram
Sonograma
(soh-noh-'grah-mah)

Angiogram
Angiograma
(ahn-hee-oh-'grah-mah)

EEG (Electroencephalogram)
Electroencefalograma
(eh-lehk-troh-ehn-seh-fah-loh-'grah-mah)

(28) # ¡No se olvide!

As you continue to acquire more Spanish, be aware once again of the similarities to English. Match each word below with its translation:

el mamograma *(ehl mah-moh-'grah-mah)*   CT

la tomografía computarizada   cystoscopy
(lah toh-moh-grah-'fee-ah kohm-poo-tah-ree-'sah-dah)

la prueba del sistema gastrointestinal   mammogram
  (lah proo·'eh-bah dehl sees-'teh-mah gahs-troh-een-tehs-tee-'nahl)

la cistoscopía *(lah sees-toh-sko-'pee·ah)*   Upper GI

el electrocardiograma   ECG
(ehl eh-lehk-troh-kahr-dee-oh-'grah-mah)

Cancer

El cáncer *(ehl 'kahn-sehr)*

The examinations are completed, and there were no major communication problems between medical staff and patient. Carlos and his family wait nervously for his test results. They are frightened because they know very little about oncology. Finally, the doctor gives them the news. Here are the phrases that often describe cancer:

The cells . . .	**Las células . . .** *(lahs 'seh-loo-lahs)*
are normal.	**son normales.** *(sohn nohr-'mah-lehs)*
are benign.	**son benignas.** *(sohn beh-'neeg-nahs)*
are malignant.	**son malignas.** *(sohn mah-'leeg-nahs)*
grow very fast.	**crecen rápidamente.** *('kreh-sehn rah-pee-dah-'mehn-teh)*
are abnormal.	**son anormales.** *(sohn ah-nohr-'mah-lehs)*

The family has many questions about cancer treatment.

Chemotherapy

La quimoterapia *(lah kee-moh-teh-'rah-pee·ah)*

He is going to . . .   **Va a . . .** *(bah ah)*

feel tired and weak.
sentirse cansado y débil.
(sehn-'teer-seh kahn-'sah-doh ee 'deh-beel)

have nausea, vomiting, diarrhea, and constipation.
tener náuseas, vómitos, diarrea y estreñimiento.
(teh-'nehr 'now-seh-ahs, 'boh-mee-tohs, dee-ah-'rreh-ah ee ehs-treh-'nyee-mee-'ehn-toh)

have some side effects.
tener algunos efectos secundarios.
(teh-'nehr ahl-'goo-nohs eh-'fehk-tohs seh-koon-'dah-ree·ohs)

lose bone marrow cells.
perder células de la médula de los huesos.
(pehr-'dehr 'seh-loo-lahs deh lah 'meh-doo-lah deh lohs 'weh-sohs)

need radiation treatment.
necesitar radioterapia.
(neh-seh-see-'tahr rah-dee-oh-teh-'rah-pee-ah)

lose his hair and skin color.
perder el pelo y el color de la piel.
(pehr-'der ehl 'peh-loh ee ehl koh-'lohr deh lah pee-'ehl)

Explain to the Espinozas that cancer patients are required to follow strict orders.

Come to the hospital tomorrow.
Venga al hospital mañana.
('behn-gah ahl ohs-pee-'tahl mah-'nyah-nah)

Drink lots of liquids.
Tome muchos líquidos.
('toh-meh 'moo-chohs 'lee-kee-dohs)

If the test results indicate that the cells are benign the doctor will say "All is well!" **¡Todo está bien!** *('toh-doh eh-'stah 'bee·ehn)*

Types of cancer

Tipos de cáncer *('tee-pohs deh 'kahn-sehr)*

Learn the following terms:

bone cancer	**cáncer del hueso** *('kahn-sehr dehl 'weh-soh)*
brain cancer	**cáncer del cerebro** *('kahn-sehr dehl she-'reh-broh)*
breast cancer	**cáncer del seno** *('kahn-sehr dehl 'seh-noh)*
cervical cancer	**cáncer cervical** *('kahn-sehr sehr-bee-'kahl)*
colon cancer	**cáncer del colon** *('kahn-sehr dehl 'koh-lohn)*
Hodgkin's lymphoma	**linfoma de Hodgkin** *(leen-'foh-mah deh Hodgkin)*
kidney cancer	**cáncer del riñón** *('kahn-sehr dehl reen-'yohn)*
leukemia	**leucemia** *(leh-oo-'seh-mee·ah)*
lung cancer	**cáncer del pulmón** *('kahn-sehr dehl pool-'mohn)*
pancreatic cancer	**cáncer pancreático** *('kahn-sehr pahn-kreh-'ah-tee-koh)*
prostate cancer	**cáncer de la próstata** *('kahn-sehr deh lah 'proh-stah tah)*
skin cancer	**cáncer de la piel** *('kahn-sehr deh lah pee-'ehl)*
stomach cancer	**cáncer del estómago** *('kahn-sehr dehl ehs-'toh-mah-goh)*
thyroid cancer	**cáncer de la tiroides** *('kahn-sehr deh lah tee-'roh-ee-dehs)*
uterine cancer	**cáncer uterino** *('kahn-sehr oo-teh-'ree-noh)*

¡No se olvide!

- Work on these invaluable expressions:

  You need to come.
  Necesita venir. *(neh-seh-'see-tah beh-'neer)*

  His condition is worse.
  Su condición está peor. *(soo kohn-dee-see-'ohn eh-'stah peh-'ohr)*

  He is asking for you.
  Está preguntando por usted.
  (eh-'stah preh-goon-'tahn-doh pohr oo-'stehd)

Chapter Nine

Capítulo Nueve

(kah-'pee-too-loh 'nweh-beh)

The Elderly

Los Ancianos

(lohs ahn-see-'ah-nohs)

Due to the need for constant medical attention, Guadalupe Lourdes Velásquez de Espinoza, age 90, was recently admitted to a skilled nursing home. Family and friends visit frequently, but her condition has worsened.

Throughout the hospital, senior patients are requiring the services of numerous specialists. Let's focus on those other major areas where Spanish is needed the most.

First of all, become familiar with these terms:

ambulatory care	**cuidado ambulatorio**
	(kwee-'dah-doh ahm-boo-lah-'toh-ree·oh)
intermediate care	**cuidado intermedio**
	(kwee-'dah-doh een-tehr-'meh-dee·oh)
nursing care	**cuidado con enfermera**
	(kwee-'dah-doh kohn ehn-fehr-'meh-roh)
total care	**cuidado total** *(kwee-'dah-doh toh-'tahl)*

Orthopedics

Ortopedia *(ohr-toh-'peh-dee-ah)*

Brittle bones abound in the nursing home, so orthopedic treatment and physical therapy are frequently in demand. If you work with the elderly, here are some of the terms you may need:

He/She needs (the) . . .	**Necesita . . .** *(neh-seh-'see-tah)*
cane	**el bastón** *(ehl bahs-'tohn)*
continuous passive motion machine	**la máquina de movimiento continuo** *(lah 'máh-kee-nah deh moh-vee-mee-'ehn-toh kohn-'tee-noo-oh)*
exercises	**ejercicios** *(eh-hehr-'see-see·ohs)*
girdle	**la faja** *(lah 'fah-hah)*
physical therapy	**la terapia física** *(lah teh-'rah-pee-ah 'fee-see-kah)*
sling	**el cabestrillo** *(ehl kah-behs-'tree-yoh)*
traction	**la tracción** *(lah trahk-see-'ohn)*
trapeze	**el trapecio** *(ehl trah-'peh-see-oh)*
ultrasound	**el ultrasonido** *(ool-trah-soh-'nee-doh)*
walker	**la caminadora** *(lah kah-mee-nah-'doh-rah)*
whirlpool bath	**el baño con agua circulante** *(ehl 'bah-nyoh kohn 'ah-gwah seer-koo-'lahn-teh)*

Bones

Los huesos *(lohs 'weh-sohs)*

The Espinozas are obviously concerned, and would like to know more specifics about **abuelita's** physical condition. She has been complaining of pain. To understand what she's saying, first review the parts of the skeleton—**esqueleto.**

I feel pain in . . .	**Me duele . . .** *(meh-'dweh-leh)*
breastbone	**el esternón** *(ehl ehs-tehr-'nohn)*
cranium	**el cráneo** *(ehl 'krah-neh-oh)*
hip	**la cadera** *(lah kah-'deh-rah)*
joint	**la coyuntura** *(lah koh-yoon-'too-rah)*
rib	**la costilla** *(lah kohs-'tee-yah)*
spine	**la columna vertebral** *(lah koh-'loohm-nah behr-teh-'brahl)*

Now, can you identify these?

la escápula *(lah ehs-'kah-poo-lah)*
el radio *(ehl 'rah-dee·oh)*
la ulna *(lah 'ool-nah)*
el fémur *(ehl 'feh-moor)*
la tibia *(lah 'tee-bee·ah)*
la fíbula *(lah 'fee-boo-lah)*
la clavícula *(lah klah-'bee-koo-lah)*
la vértebra *(lah 'fehr-teh·brah)*

Hip surgery

Cirugía de la cadera
(see-roo-'hee-ah deh lah kah-'deh-rah)

Do not cross your legs or ankles.
No cruce sus piernas ni sus tobillos.
(noh 'kroo-seh soos pee-'ehr-nahs nee soos toh-'bee-yohs)

Do not turn your hips.
No voltee sus caderas.
(noh bohl-'teh-eh soos kah-'deh-rahs)

This helps prevent a hip dislocation.
Esto ayuda a prevenir una dislocación de las caderas.
('ehs-toh ah-'yoo-dah ah preh-beh-'neer 'oo-nah dees-loh-kah-see-'ohn deh lahs kah-'deh-rahs)

Muscles

Los músculos *(lohs 'moos-koo-lohs)*

After discussing her bones—**huesos** *('weh-sohs)*—mention the muscles—**músculos** *('moos-koo-lohs)*. They are easy to remember:

biceps	**bíceps** *('bee-sehps)*
external oblique	**oblicuo mayor** *(oh-'blee-koo-oh mah-'yohr)*
peroneus	**peroneo largo** *(peh-roh-'neh-oh 'lahr-goh)*
pectoris major	**pectoral mayor** *(pehk-toh-'rahl mah-'yohr)*
rectus abdominis	**rector del abdomen**
	(rehk-'tohr dehl ahb-'doh-mehn)

sartorius	**sartorio** *(sahr-'toh-ree·oh)*
trapezius	**trapecio** *(trah-'peh-see·oh)*
triceps	**tríceps** *('tree-sehps)*

Genitourinary

Genitourinario *(heh-nee-toh-oo-ree-'nah-ree·oh)*

In addition to structural damage, Mrs. Lupe shows signs of internal problems. In elderly patients, the genitourinary system often shows signs of functional change. Lupe has been having problems in this area for several years. She once met with specialists, and a number of sensitive topics were discussed. First, we'll discuss a few female concerns and then address typical male problems. All of these questions contain vocabulary that you should become familiar with:

Did you have a hysterectomy?
¿Tuvo una histerectomía?
('too-boh 'oo-nah ees-teh-rehk-toh-'mee-ah)

Did you have menstrual problems when young?
¿Ha tenido problemas menstruales cuando joven?
(ah teh-'nee-doh proh-'bleh-mahs mehn-stroo-'ah-lehs 'kwahn-doh 'hoh-behn)

Did they remove your tubes?
¿Le sacaron los tubos?
(leh sah-'kah-rohn lohs 'too-bohs)

Do you ever lose your urine?
¿Se orina sin querer a veces?
(seh oh-'ree-nah seen keh-'rehr ah 'beh-sehs)

Do your ovaries or vagina hurt?
¿Le duelen los ovarios o la vagina?
(leh 'dweh-lehn lohs oh-'bah-ree·ohs oh lah bah-'hee-nah)

Have you used contraceptive methods in the past?
¿Ha usado métodos anticonceptivos en el pasado?
(ah oo-'sah-doh 'meh-toh-dohs ahn-tee-kohn-sehp-'tee-bohs ehn ehl pah-'sah-doh)

How many pregnancies have you had?
¿Cuántas veces quedó embarazada?
('kwahn-tahs 'beh-sehs keh-'doh ehm-bah-rah-'sah-dah)

When did your periods stop?
¿Cuándo se terminó su regla?
('kwahn-doh seh tehr-mee-'noh soo 'reh-glah)

Now learn some terms for discussing these problems with men—**los hombres** *(lohs 'ohm-brehs)*. This time, use the same pattern to pick up on any new vocabulary:

Have you had . . . ?	**¿Ha tenido . . . ?** *(ah teh-'nee-doh)*
operations on your penis	**operaciones en su pene** *(oh-per-rah-see·oh-nehs ehn soo 'peh-neh)*
pain in your scrotum	**dolor en su escroto** *(doh-'lohr ehn soo ehs-'kroh-toh)*
problems with your foreskin	**problemas con su prepucio** *(proh-'bleh-mahs kohn soo preh-'poo-see·oh)*
problems with the testicles	**problemas con los testículos** *(proh-'bleh-mahs kohn lohs tehs-'tee-koo-lohs)*
problems during urination	**problemas al orinar** *(proh-'bleh-mahs ahl oh-ree-'nahr)*
a semen examination	**un examen del semen** *(oon ehk-'sah-mehn dehl 'seh-mehn)*
sores on your penis	**llagas en su pene** *('yah-gahs ehn soo 'peh-neh)*

Now here are some questions that work with both sexes:

Have you ever had . . .?	**¿Ha tenido alguna vez . . . ?** *(ah teh-'nee-doh ahl-'goo-nah behs)*
bleeding when urinating	**sangramiento al orinar** *(sahn-grah-mee-'ehn-toh ahl oh-ree-'nahr)*
a burning sensation	**una sensación de ardor** *('oo-nah sehn-sah-see·'ohn deh ahr-'dohr)*
a discharge	**un desecho** *(oon dehs-'eh-choh)*
itching	**picazón** *(pee-kah-'sohn)*
pain while urinating	**dolor al orinar** *(doh-'lohr ahl oh-ree-'nahr)*
pain during sexual relations	**dolor durante las relaciones sexuales** *(doh-'lohr doo-'rahn-teh lahs reh-lah-see·'oh-nehs sehk-soo-'ah-lehs)*
pus	**pus** *(poos)*
rashes	**sarpullidos** *(sahr-poo-'yee-dohs)*
sores	**llagas** *('yah-gahs)*
swelling	**hinchazón** *(een-chah-'sohn)*
urinary infection	**infección urinaria** *(een-fehk-see·'ohn oo-ree-'nah-ree·ah)*
venereal disease	**una enfermedad venérea** *('oo-nah ehn-fehr-meh-'dahd beh-'neh-reh-ah)*

Proctology

Proctología *(prohk-toh-loh-'hee-ah)*

As long as you are discussing bodily functions with Guadalupe, why not practice a few lines from **el examen proctológico** *(ehl ehk-'sah-mehn prohk-toh-'loh-hee-koh)*. Mix in phrases that you know along with any new vocabulary:

Have you had . . . ?	**¿Ha tenido . . . ?** *(ah teh-'nee-doh)*
blood in the stool	**sangre en el excremento** *('sahn-greh ehn ehl ehks-kreh-'mehn-toh)*
constipation	**estreñimiento** *(ehs-treh-'nyee-mee-'ehn-toh)*
diarrhea	**diarrea** *(dee-ah-'rreh-ah)*
an enema	**un enema** *(oon eh-'neh-mah)*
hemorrhoids	**hemorroides** *(eh-moh-'rroh-ee-dehs)*
pain when defecating	**dolor al defecar** *(doh-'lohr ahl deh-feh-'kahr)*
parasites	**parásitos** *(pah-'rah-see-tohs)*
rectal trouble	**problemas en el recto** *(proh-'bleh-mahs ehn ehl 'rehk-toh)*
swollen glands	**glándulas hinchadas** *('glahn-doo-lahs een-'chah-dahs)*

How are your translation skills? Say each of the following with the proper Spanish pronunciation:

impotencia *(eem-poh-'tehn-see·ah)*
esterilidad *(ehs-teh-ree-lee-'dahd)*
masturbación *(mahs-toor-bah-see·'ohn)*
secreción *(seh-kreh-see·'ohn)*
prostatitis *(proh-stah-'tee-tees)*
menopausia *(meh-noh-'pow-see·ah)*
menstruación *(mehn-stroo-ah-see·'ohn)*
inflamación *(een-flah-mah-see·'ohn)*
infección por HIV *(een-fehk-see·'ohn pohr 'ah-cheh ee 'beh 'chee-kah)*
estrógeno *(ehs-'troh-heh-noh)*
testosterona *(tehs-tohs-teh-'roh-nah)*

Continue to guess:

cirrosis *(seer-'roh-sees)*
esclerosis *(ehs-kleh-'roh-sees)*
hernia *('ehr-nee-ah)*
reumatismo *(reh-oo-mah-'tees-moh)*
vaginitis *(bah-gee-'nee-tees)*

(29)   **¿Cuánto aprendió?**

Try to make sentences out of the following terms:

- **Necesita . . .** *(neh-seh-'see-tah)*
  (ambulatory care, whirlpool bath, exercises)

- **Me duele...** *(meh 'dweh-leh)*
  (spine, joint, penis)

- **¿Ha tenido...?** *(ah teh-'nee-doh)*
  (menstrual problems, a semen exam, venereal disease, swollen glands,
  problems with your ovaries)

The nervous system

El sistema nervioso
(ehl sees-'teh-mah nehr-bee-'oh-soh)

In addition to all of her other problems, Guadalupe has recently shown signs of
a nervous disorder. Look at the following questions and mix any previously
learned vocabulary with these words you are unfamiliar with:

Have you had . . . ?	**¿Ha tenido . . .?** *(ah teh-'nee-doh)*
any paralysis	**algún tipo de parálisis** *(ahl-'goon 'tee-poh deh pah-'rah-lee-sees)*
convulsions	**convulsiones** *(kohn-'bool-see·'oh-nehs)*
discharge from your ears	**desecho de los oídos** *(dehs-'eh-choh deh lohs oh-'ee-dohs)*
dizziness	**mareos** *(mah-'reh-ohs)*
emotional problems	**problemas emocionales** *(proh-bleh-mahs eh-moh-see-oh-'nah-lehs)*

fainting spells	**desmayos** *(dehs-'mah-yohs)*
headaches	**dolores de cabeza** *(doh-'loh-rehs deh kah-'beh-sah)*
problems with your balance	**problemas con su equilibrio** *(proh-'bleh-mahs kohn soo eh-kee-'lee-bree·oh)*
problems with your sight	**problemas con la vista** *(proh-'bleh-mahs kohn lah 'bees-tah)*

Ask a variety of questions in Spanish. Now create your own sentences using the vocabulary below:

Do you have . . .?	**¿Tiene . . .?** *(tee-'eh-neh)*
blurred vision	**visión borrosa** *(bee-see·'ohn boh-'rroh-sah)*
double vision	**doble visión** *('doh-bleh bee-see·'ohn)*
excessive snoring	**ronquidos excesivos** *(rohn-'kee-dohs ehk-seh-'see-vohs)*
migraines	**migrañas** *(mee-'grahn-yahs)*
numbness	**adormecimiento** *(ah-dohr-meh-see-'mee-'ehn-toh)*
ringing in the ears	**silbido en el oído** *(seel-'bee-doh ehn ehl oh-'ee-doh)*
sensitivity	**sensibilidad** *(sehn-see-bee-lee-'dahd)*
tingling	**hormigueo** *(ohr-mee-'geh-oh)*
weakness	**debilidad** *(deh-bee-lee-'dahd)*

The neuropsychiatric unit

La unidad neurosiquiátrica
(lah oo-nee-'dahd neh-oo-roh-see-kee-'ah-tree-kah)

When abnormal behaviors are evident, it may be a good idea to check on the patient's mental or emotional condition. In Guadalupe's case, senility—**la senilidad** *(lah seh-nee-lee-'dahd)*—has set in, and lots of questions need to be answered, either by the mental health professional or her family, to get to the source. Study the key terms below, and then develop phrases you can use:

Feelings

<h2 style="text-align:center">Los sentimientos (lohs sehn-tee-mee-'ehn-tohs)</h2>

Do you feel . . .?	**¿Se siente . . .?** *(seh see-'ehn-teh)*
abused	**abusado/a** *(ah-boo-'sah-doh/dah)*
ashamed	**avergonzado/a** *(ah-behr-gohn-'sah-doh/dah)*
confused	**confundido/a** *(kohn-foon-'dee-doh/dah)*
depressed	**deprimido/a** *(deh-pree-'mee-doh/dah)*
desperate	**desesperado/a** *(deh-sehs-peh-'rah-doh/dah)*
frustrated	**frustrado/a** *(froos-'trah-doh/dah)*
guilty	**culpable** *(kool-'pah-bleh)*
insecure	**inseguro/a** *(een-seh-'goo-roh/rah)*
jealous	**celoso/a** *(seh-'loh-soh/sah)*
lost	**perdido/a** *(pehr-'dee-doh/dah)*
overwhelmed	**abrumado/a** *(ah-broo-'mah-doh/dah)*
persecuted	**perseguido/a** *(perhr-seh-'ghee-doh/dah)*
restless	**inquieto/a** *(een-kee-'eh-toh/tah)*
sensitive	**sensible** *(sehn-'see-bleh)*
strange	**raro/a** *('rah-roh/rah)*
suicidal	**con tendencias suicidas** *(kohn tehn-'dehn-see-ahs soo-ee-'see-dahs)*
trapped	**atrapado/a** *(ah-trah-'pah-doh/dah)*

Introduce yourself

<h2 style="text-align:center">Preséntese (preh-'sehn-teh-seh)</h2>

I'm (a) . . .	**Soy (un/una) . . .** *('soh-ee oon/'oo-nah)*
counselor	**consejero/a** *(kohn-seh-'heh-roh/ah)*
mental health professional	**especialista en salud mental** *(ehs-peh-see-ah-lees-tah ehn sah-'lood mehn-'tahl)*
neurologist	**neurólogo/a** *(neh-oo-'roh-loh-goh/ah)*
provider	**proveedor/a** *(proh-veh-eh-'dohr/ah)*
psychiatrist	**psiquiatra** *(see-kee-'ah-trah)*
psychologist	**psicólogo/a** *(see-'koh-loh-goh)*
social worker	**trabajador/a social** *(trah-bah-hah-'dohr/ah soh-see-'ahl)*
therapist	**terapeuta** *(teh-rah-'peh-oo-tah)*

Do you have . . . ?	**¿Tiene usted . . . ?** *(tee-'eh-neh oos-'tehd)*
a lot of stress	**mucho estrés** *('moo-choh ehs-'trehs)*
addictions	**adicciones** *(ah-deek-see-'oh-nehs)*
blurred vision	**visión borrosa** *(vee-see-'ohn boh-'rroh-sah)*
delusions	**ilusiones falsas** *(ee-loo-see-'oh-nehs 'fahl-sahs)*
depression	**depresión** *(deh-preh-see-'ohn)*
difficulty in concentrating	**dificultad para concentrarse** *(dee-fee-kool-'tahd 'pah-rah kohn-sehn-'trahr-seh)*
disability	**incapacidad** *(een-kah-pah-see-'dahd)*
dizziness	**mareos** *(mah-'reh-ohs)*
drowsiness	**somnolencia** *(sohm-noh-'lehn-see-ah)*
dry mouth	**sequedad en la boca** *(she-keh-'dahd ehn lah 'boh-kah)*
good appetite	**buen apetito** *(boo-'ehn ah-peh-'tee-toh)*
hallucinations	**alucinaciones** *(ah-loo-see-nah-see-'oh-nehs)*
hostility	**hostilidad** *(ohs-tee-lee-'dahd)*
hypersensitivity	**hipersensibilidad** *(ee-pehr-sehn-see-bee-lee-'dahd)*
hysteria attacks	**ataques de histeria** *(ah'tah-kehs deh ees-'teh-ree-ah)*
impulsive behaviors	**comportamientos impulsivos** *(kohm-pohr-tah-mee-'ehn-tohs eem-pool-'see-vohs)*
increased energy	**aumento de energía** *(ah-oo-'mehn-toh deh eh-nehr-'hee-ah)*
insomnia	**insomnio** *(een-'sohm-nee-oh)*
lack of energy	**falta de energía** *('fahl-tah deh eh-nehr-'hee-ah)*
memory loss	**pérdida de memoria** *('pehr-dee-dah deh meh-'moh-ree-ah)*
migraines	**migrañas** *(mee-'grahn-yahs)*
much fear	**mucho miedo** *('moo-choh mee-'eh-doh)*
nightmares	**pesadillas** *(peh-sah-'dee-yahs)*
panic attacks	**ataques de pánico** *(ah-'tah-kehs deh 'pah-nee-koh)*
rage and anger	**ira y cólera** *('ee-rah ee 'koh-leh-rah)*
ravings	**delirios** *(deh-'lee-ree-ohs)*
reduced libido	**disminución del líbido** *(dees-mee-noo-see-'ohn dehl 'lee-bee-doh)*
relapses	**recaídas** *(reh-kah-'ee-dahs)*

relationship problems	**dificultades en las relaciones** *(dee-fee-kool-'tah-dehs ehn lahs reh-lah-see-'oh-nehs)*
seizures	**ataques** *(ah-'tah-kehs)*
strange behaviors	**comportamientos extraños** *(kohm-pohr-tah-mee-'ehn-tohs eks-'tran-yohs)*
ticks	**movimientos incontrolables** *(moh-vee-mee-'ehn-tohs een-kohn-troh-'lah-blehs)*
ups and downs	**altibajos emocionales** *(ahl-tee-'bah-hohs eh-moh-see-oh-'nah-lehs)*
visions	**visiones** *(vee-see-'oh-nehs)*
weight gain	**aumento de peso** *(ah-oo-'mehn-toh deh 'peh-soh)*
weight loss	**pérdida de peso** *('pehr-dee-dah deh 'peh-soh)*
Do you feel _____?	**¿Se siente _____?** *(seh see-'ehn-teh)*
alienation	**alienado(a)** *(ah-lee-eh-'nah-doh/dah)*
anguish	**angustiado(a)** *(ahn-good-tee-'ah-doh/dah)*
apathy	**apático(a)** *(ah-'pah-tee-koh/kah)*
confusion	**confuso(a)** *(kohn-'foo-soh/sah)*
loneliness	**solo(a)** *('soh-loh/lah)*
sadness	**triste** *('trees-teh)*
worry	**preocupado(a)** *(preh-oh-koo-'pah-doh/dah)*
Was there _____ abuse?	**¿Hubo abuso _____?** *('oo-boh ah-'boo-soh)*
alcohol	**de alcohol** *(deh ahl-koh-'ohl)*
drugs	**de drogas** *(deh 'droh-gahs)*
emotional	**emocional** *(eh-moh-see-oh-'nahl)*
physical	**físico** *('fee-see-koh)*
sexual	**sexual** *(sehk-soo-'ahl)*
You need...	**Necesita...** *(neh-seh-'see-tah)*
to contact the AA	**contactar a Alcohólicos Anónimos** *(kohn-tahk-'tahr ah ahl-koh-'oh-lee-kohs ah-'noh-nee-mohs)*
continuous care	**cuidado continuo** *('kwee-dah-doh kohn-'tee-nwoh)*
counseling	**consejería** *(kohn-seh-heh-'ree-ah)*
a diagnosis	**un diagnóstico** *(oon dee-ahg-'nohs-tee-koh)*
an exam	**un examen** *(oon ehk-'sah-mehn)*

financial help	**ayuda financiera** *(ah-'yoo-dah fee-nahn-see-'eh-rah)*
food	**comida** *(koh-'mee-dah)*
help	**ayuda** *(ah-'yoo-dah)*
housing	**asistencia de vivienda** *(ah-sees-'tehn-see-ah deh vee-vee-'ehn-dah)*
intensive therapy	**terapia intensiva** *(teh-'rah-pee-ah een-tehn-'see-vah)*
a job	**un empleo** *(oon ehm-'pleh-oh)*
medical assistance	**asistencia médica** *(ah-sees-'tehn-see-ah 'meh-dee-kah)*
medical supervision	**supervisión médica** *(soo-pehr-vee-see-'ohn 'meh-dee-kah)*
psychiatric treatment	**tratamiento psiquiátrico** *(trah-tah-mee-'ehn-toh see-kee-'ah-tree-koh)*
rehabilitation	**rehabilitación** *(reh-ah-bee-lee-tah-see-'ohn)*
a support group	**un grupo de apoyo** *(oon 'groo-poh deh ah-'poh-yoh)*
a test	**una prueba** *('oo-nah proo-'eh-bah)*
transportation	**transporte** *(trahns-'pohr-teh)*
treatment	**tratamiento** *(trah-tah-mee-'ehn-toh)*

Notice how opposites with negative meanings can be formed in Spanish:

real	**real** *(re-'ahl)*
unreal	**irreal** *(ee-rreh-'ahl)*
appropriate	**propio** *('proh-pee-oh)*
inappropriate	**impropio** *(eem-'proh-pee-oh)*
acceptable	**aceptable** *(ah-sehp-'tah-bleh)*
unacceptable	**inaceptable** *(ee-nah-sehp-'tah-bleh)*
normal	**normal** *(nohr-'mahl)*
abnormal	**anormal** *(ah-nohr-'mahl)*
balance	**equilibrio** *(eh-kee-'lee-bree-oh)*
imbalance	**desequilibrio** *(dehs-eh-kee-'lee-bree-oh)*

Guess what these mental health words mean in English:

patóloga *(pah-'toh-loh-gah)* _____

comatosis *(koh-mah-'toh-sees)* _____

inteligencia *(een-teh-lee-'hehn-see-ah)* _____

farmacéutico *(fahr-mah-'seh-oo-tee-koh)* _____

carácter *(kah-'rahk-tehr)* _____

psicosocial *(see-koh-soh-see-'ahl)* _____

neurosis *(neh-oo-'roh-sees)* _____

parálisis *(pah-'rah-lee-sees)* _____

More action

Más acción *(mahs ahk-see·'ohn)*

Don't be content with simple patterns and vocabulary lists. As you develop more advanced skills in Spanish, it will become evident that you are always going to need more action words. Just keep in mind that the best way to memorize verbs is through regular practice in everyday situations. Here are a few that will help you to communicate better with Mrs. Lupe or other elderly patients:

to apply	**aplicar** *(ah-plee-'kahr)*
I have to apply traction to you.	**Tengo que aplicarle tracción.** *('tehn-goh keh ah-plee-'kahr-leh trahk-see·'ohn)*
to avoid	**evitar** *(eh-bee-'tahr)*
You must avoid coffee.	**Necesita evitar el café.** *(neh-seh-'see-tah eh-bee-'tahr ehl kah-'feh)*
to hear	**oír** *(oh-'eer)*
We don't hear anything.	**No oímos nada.** *(noh oh-'ee-mohs 'nah-dah)*
to pray	**rezar** *(reh-'sahr)*
They pray a lot.	**Ellos rezan mucho.** *('eh-yohs 'reh-sahn 'moo-choh)*
to relieve	**aliviar** *(ah-lee-bee-'ahr)*
I am going to relieve your pain.	**Voy a aliviarle el dolor.** *('boh·ee ah ah-lee-bee-'ahr-leh ehl doh-'lohr)*
to see	**ver** *(behr)*
I like to see the sky.	**Me gusta ver el cielo.** *(meh 'goos-tah behr ehl see-'eh-loh)*

to smell	**oler** *(oh-lehr)*
He can't smell the medicine.	**No puede oler la medicina.** *(noh 'pweh-deh oh-'lehr lah meh-dee-'see-nah)*
to spit	**escupir** *(ehs-koo-'peer)*
He spits in the bath.	**El escupe en el baño.** *(ehl ehs-'koo-peh ehn ehl 'bah-nyoh)*
to taste	**saborear** *(sah-boh-reh-'ahr)*
Do you want to taste the fruit?	**¿Quiere saborear la fruta?** *(kee-'eh-reh sah-boh-reh-'ahr lah 'froo-tah)*
to think	**pensar** *(pehn-'sahr)*
What are you thinking about?	**¿En qué piensa usted?** *(ehn keh pee-'ehn-sah oo-'stehd)*

More verb infinitives

Más infinitivos verbales
(mahs een-fee-nee-'tee-bohs behr-'bah-lehs)

to accumulate	**acumular** *(ah-koo-moo-'lahr)*
to assist	**atender** *(ah-tehn-'dehr)*
to avoid	**evitar** *(eh-bee-'tahr)*
to breast-feed	**lactar** *(lahk-'tahr)*
to burn	**quemar** *(keh-'mahr)*
to burp	**eructar** *(eh-rook-'tahr)*
to cause	**causar** *(kow-'sahr)*
to certify	**certificar** *(sehr-tee-fee-'kahr)*
to check	**verificar** *(beh-ree-fee-'kahr)*
to chew	**mascar** *('mahs-kahr)*
to cross	**cruzar** *(kroo-'sahr)*
to detect	**detectar** *(deh-tehk-'tahr)*
to improve	**mejorar** *(meh-hoh-'rahr)*
to itch	**picar** *(pee-'kahr)*
to lack	**faltar** *(fahl-'tahr)*
to last	**durar** *(doo-'rahr)*
to perspire	**sudar** *(soo-'dahr)*
to prevent	**prevenir** *(preh-beh-'neer)*
to proceed	**proceder** *(proh-seh-'dehr)*
to prohibit	**prohibir** *(proh-hee-'beer)*
to protect	**proteger** *(proh-teh-'hehr)*
to pull	**jalar** *(hah-'lahr)*

to pump	**bombear** *(bohm-beh-'ahr)*
to purify	**purificar** *(poo-ree-fee-'kahr)*
to push	**empujar** *(ehm-poo-'hahr)*
to readmit	**readmitir** *(reh-ahd-mee-'teer)*
to replace	**remplazar** *(rehm-plah-'sahr)*
to research	**investigar** *(een-behs-tee-'gahr)*
to resist	**resistir** *(reh-sees-'teer)*
to rinse	**enjuagar** *(ehn-hwah-'gahr)*
to scratch	**rascar** *('rahs-kahr)*
to shave	**afeitarse** *(ah-feh-ee-'tahr-seh)*
to shower	**ducharse** *(doo-'chahr-seh)*
to sneeze	**estornudar** *(ehs-tohr-noo-'dahr)*
to spit	**escupir** *(ehs-koo-'peer)*
to squeeze	**apretar** *(ah-preh-'tahr)*
to sterilize	**esterilizar** *(ehs-teh-ree-lee-'sahr)*
to swallow	**tragar** *(trah-'gahr)*
to try	**tratar** *(trah-'tahr)*
to turn oneself over	**voltearse** *(bohl-teh-'ahr-seh)*
to vaccinate	**vacunar** *(bah-koo-'nahr)*
to weigh	**pesar** *(peh-'sahr)*
to worsen	**empeorar** *(ehm-peh-oh-'rahr)*

(30) ## ¿Cuánto aprendió?

- Have you had...? **¿Ha tenido...?** *(ah teh-'nee-doh)*

  fainting spells _____

  double vision _____

  loss of memory _____

  divorce _____

  visions _____

  fear _____

  money problems _____

- **Tiene...** *(tee-'eh-neh)*
  (insomnia, depression, fits)

Chapter Ten

Capítulo Diez

(kah-'pee-too-loh dee-'ehs)

Additional Health Care Services

Servicios de Salud Adicionales

(sehr-'bee-se·ohs deh sah-'lood ah-dee-see-oh-'nah-lehs)

The social worker

El trabajador social
(ehl trah-bah-hah-'dohr soh-see-'ahl)

Guadalupe is under the care of several fine physicians, and life for her today is much more bearable. She is grateful to all of them, and especially to the person who has been there from the beginning—the social worker.

When she was first brought to the nursing home, a social worker was involved. Before any decisions were made, trust had to be established between patient and medical facility. In the Hispanic culture, it is imperative that such professionals work closely with family members in order to do what's best for an ailing relative. Social workers handle a variety of cases. This is an overview of the kinds of questions they might ask the patient or family. Many of these terms were previously mentioned, so practicing should be no problem at all:

Do you need . . .?	**¿Necesita . . .?** *(neh-seh-'see-tah)*
advice	**consejo** *(kohn-'seh-hoh)*
an agency	**una agencia** *('oo-nah ah-'hehn-see·ah)*
an appointment	**una cita** *('oo-nah 'see-tah)*
assistance	**ayuda** *(ah-'yoo-dah)*
employment	**empleo** *(ehm-'pleh-oh)*
an exam	**una prueba** *('oo-nah proo-'eh-bah)*
food stamps	**cupones de alimentos** *(koo-'poh-nehs deh ah-lee-'mehn-tohs)*
health department	**el departamento de salud pública** *(ehl deh-pahr-tah-'mehn-toh deh sa-'lood 'poo-blee-kah)*
insurance	**seguro** *(seh-'goo-roh)*
an interpreter	**un intérprete** *(oon een-'tehr-preh-teh)*
medication	**medicinas** *(meh-dee-'see-nahs)*
a priest	**un sacerdote** *(oon sah-sehr-'doh-teh)*
a private nurse	**una enfermera privada** *('oo-nah ehn-fehr-'meh-rah pree-'bah-dah)*
security	**la seguridad** *(lah seh-goo-ree-'dahd)*
services	**servicios** *(sehr-'bee-see·ohs)*
social security	**seguro social** *(seh-'goo-roh soh-see-'ahl)*
therapy	**terapia** *(teh-'rah-pee·ah)*
transportation	**transporte** *(trahns-'pohr-teh)*
vaccinations	**vacunas** *(bah-'koo-nahs)*
welfare	**ayuda del bienestar social** *(ah-'you-dah dehl bee-ehn-eh-'stahr soh-see-'ahl)*

If you are closely involved with a patient's well-being, these topics are designed for you. The Espinoza family was interviewed recently and this is what they wanted to talk about to the social worker:

I want to talk about . . .	**Quiero hablar de . . .** *(kee-'eh-roh ah-'blahr deh)*
child abuse	**el abuso de los niños** *(ehl ah-'boo-soh deh lohs 'nee-nyohs)*
child care	**el cuidado del niño** *(ehl 'kwee-dah-doh dehl 'nee-nyoh*
drug abuse	**el abuso de las drogas** *(ehl ah-'boo-soh deh lahs 'droh-gahs)*
family problems	**los problemas familiares** *(lohs proh-'bleh-mahs fah-mee-lee-'ah-rehs)*
financial problems	**los problemas económicos** *(lohs proh-'bleh-mahs eh-koh-'noh-mee-kohs)*
the law	**la ley** *(lah leh·ee)*

marriage	**el matrimonio** *(ehl mah-tree-'moh-nee·oh)*
sanitary conditions	**las condiciones sanitarias**
	(lahs kohn-dee-see·'oh-nehs sah-nee-'tah-ree·ahs)

(31) ## ¿Cuánto aprendió?

Finish the following sentences:

- **Necesita . . .** *(neh-seh-'see-tah)*
  (welfare, child care, food stamps)

- **Quiero hablar de . . .** *(kee-'eh-roh ah-'blahr deh)*
  (marriage, child abuse, family problems)

The dentist

El dentista *(ehl dehn-'tees-tah)*

Elderly patients often wear dentures and Mrs. Lupe is no exception. As a matter of fact, all of the Espinozas have had problems with their teeth and gums. Let's check up on some of the words and phrases that dentists need to use when communicating with their Spanish-speaking patients. Listen in as each family member shares a different concern:

I have a cavity.	**Tengo una carie.**
	('tehn-goh 'oo-nah 'kah-ree·eh)
I have a toothache.	**Tengo dolor de muelas.**
	('tehn-goh doh-'lohr deh 'mweh-lahs)
I need a filling.	**Necesito un empaste.**
	(neh-seh-'see-toh oon ehm-'pah-steh)
I want a cleaning.	**Quiero una limpieza.**
	(kee-'eh-roh 'oo-nah leem-pee-'eh-sah)
I would like a checkup.	**Quisiera un examen.**
	(kee-see-'eh-rah oon ehk-'sah-mehn)
My denture is bothering me.	**Mi dentadura postiza me molesta.**
	(mee dehn-'tah-'doo-rah pohs-'tee-sah meh moh-'lehs-tah)
My gums are bleeding.	**Mis encías están sangrando.**
	(mees ehn-'see-ahs eh-'stahn sahn-'grahn-doh)
This tooth hurts.	**Este diente me duele.**
	('ehn-steh dee-'ehn-teh meh 'dweh-leh)

Use all the expressions you know in Spanish to ask the patient about his or her problem. None of these words should be foreign to you:

Does it hurt to chew?
¿Le duele al masticar?
(leh 'dweh-leh ahl mah-stee-'kahr)

Does it hurt in the front or in the back?
¿Le duele enfrente o detrás?
(leh 'dweh-leh ehn-'frehn-teh oh deh-'trahs)

Does it hurt more in the day or at night?
¿Le duele más en el día o en la noche?
(leh 'dweh-leh mahs ehn ehl 'dee-ah oh ehn lah 'noh-cheh)

Does it hurt in the upper or lower part?
¿Le duele en la parte de arriba o de abajo?
(leh 'dweh-leh ehn lah 'pahr-teh deh ah-'rree-bah oh deh ah-'bah-hoh)

Does it hurt when you drink or eat something cold or hot?
¿Le duele cuando toma o come algo frío o caliente?
(leh 'dweh-leh 'kwahn-doh 'toh-mah oh 'koh-meh 'ahl-goh 'free-oh oh kah-lee-'ehn-teh)

To the right or to the left?
¿A la derecha o a la izquierda?
(ah lah deh-'reh-chah oh ah lah ees-kee-'ehr-dah)

Is it loose?
¿Está flojo?
(eh-'stah 'floh-hoh)

Now discuss your findings with the patient:

You have . . .	**Tiene . . .** *(tee-'eh-neh)*
an abscess	**un absceso** *(oon ahb-'seh-soh)*
bad breath	**mal aliento** *(mahl ah-lee-'ehn-toh)*
a badly decayed tooth	**un diente muy cariado** *(oon dee-'ehn-teh 'moo·ee kah-ree-'ah-doh)*
a cavity	**una carie** *('oo-nah 'kah-ree·eh)*
gingivitis	**gingivitis** *(heen-hee-'bee-tees)*
an impaction	**una impacción** *('oo-nah eem-pahk-see·'ohn)*
an infection	**una infección** *('oo-nah een-fehk-see·'ohn)*
inflammation	**inflamación** *(een-flah-mah-see·'ohn)*
plaque	**placa** *('plah-kah)*
pyorrhea	**piorrea** *(pee-oh-'rreh-ah)*
a sore	**una ulceración** *('oo-nah ool-seh-rah-see·'ohn)*
a lot of tartar	**mucho sarro** *('moo-choh 'sah-rroh)*

And, don't forget to isolate the pain. Use **tiene problemas** *(tee-'eh-neh proh-'bleh-mahs)* for these:

You have problems with . . .	**Tiene problemas con . . .** *(tee-'eh-neh proh-'bleh-mahs kohn)*
the baby tooth	**el diente de leche** *(ehl dee-'ehn-teh de 'leh-cheh)*
the canine tooth	**el diente canino** *(ehl dee-'ehn-teh kah-'nee-noh)*
your denture	**su dentadura postiza** *(soo dehn-tah-'doo-rah poh-'stee-sah)*
the gums	**las encías** *(lahs ehn-'see-ahs)*
the jaw	**la mandíbula** *(lah mahn-'dee-boo-lah)*
the molar	**la muela** *(lah 'mweh-lah)*
the nerve	**el nervio** *(ehl 'nehr-vee-oh)*
the palate	**el paladar** *(ehl pah-lah-'dahr)*
the root	**la raíz** *(lah rah-'ees)*
the wisdom tooth	**la muela del juicio** *(lah 'mweh-lah dehl hoo·'ee-see·oh)*

Now look at what you can do with these important words! Combine them with the phrases you've mastered to communicate a variety of messages.

Discuss your recommendations with the family:

You need . . .	**Necesita . . .** *(neh-seh-'see-tah)*
anesthesia	**anestesia** *(ah-nehs-'teh-see·ah)*
another visit	**otra visita** *('oh-trah bee-'see-tah)*
braces	**frenillos** *(freh-'nee-yohs)*
a bridge	**un puente** *(oon 'pwehn-teh)*
a checkup	**un reconocimiento dental** *(oon reh-koh-noh-see-mee-'ehn-toh dehn-'tahl)*
cosmetic surgery	**cirugía cosmética** *(see-roo-'hee-ah kohs-'meh-tee-kah)*
a crown	**una corona** *('oo-nah koh-'roh-nah)*
dentures	**dentaduras postizas** *(dehn-tah-'doo-rahs pohs-'tee-sahs)*
an extraction	**una extracción** *('oo-nah ehks-trahk-see·'ohn)*
a filling	**un empaste** *(oon ehm-'pahs-teh)*
fluoride	**fluoruro** *(floo-oh-'roo-roh)*
implants	**implantes** *(eem-'plahn-tehs)*
an inlay	**una incrustación** *('oo-nah een-kroos-tah-see·'ohn)*
a mouthguard	**un protector dental** *(oon proh-tehk-'tohr dehn-'tahl)*

mouthwash	**un enjuague bucal**
	(oon ehn-'hwah-geh boo-'kahl)
periodontal surgery	**cirugía periodontal**
	(see-roo-'hee-ah peh-ree·oh-dohn-'tahl)
a plate	**una plancha** *('oo-nah 'plahn-chah)*
root canal work	**un tratamiento del nervio**
	(oon trah-tah-mee-'ehn-toh dehl 'nehr-bee·oh)
treatment	**tratamiento** *(trah-tah-mee-'ehn-toh)*
X rays	**rayos equis** *(rah-'yohs 'eh-kees)*

X rays indicate that there is plenty of work to be done. Tell the patient about the following dental procedures. Start with:

I'm going to . . .	**Voy a . . .** *('boh·ee ah)*
clean it	**limpiarlo** *(leem-pee-'ahr-loh)*
change it	**cambiarlo** *(kahm-bee-'ahr-loh)*
cure it	**curarlo** *(koo-'rahr-loh)*
fill it	**empastarlo** *(ehm-pahs-'tahr-loh)*
remove it	**sacarlo** *(sah-'kahr-loh)*

This selection of verbs describes the job in full detail:

I need . . .	**Necesito . . .** *(neh-seh-'see-toh)*
to cut	**cortar** *(kohr-'tahr)*
to drill	**perforar** *(pehr-foh-'rahr)*
to extract	**extraer** *(ehks-trah-'ehr)*
to file	**limar** *(lee-'mahr)*
to fill	**empastar** *(ehm-pah-'stahr)*
to make an impression	**hacer una impresión**
	(ah-'sehr 'oo-nah eem-preh-see·'ohn)
to numb	**adormecer** *(ah-dohr-meh-'sehr)*
to scrape	**raspar** *(rahs-'pahr)*
to straighten	**enderezar** *(ehn-deh-reh-'sahr)*
to use gas	**usar gas** *(oo-'sahr gahs)*
to use novocaine	**usar novocaína** *(oo-'sahr noh-boh-kah-'ee-nah)*
to wire	**poner alambre** *(poh-'nehr ah-'lahm-breh)*

If you need any assistance, call on the following specialists:

I'm going to speak with a(n) . . .	**Voy a hablar con . . .** *('boh·ee ah ah-'blahr kohn)*
endodontist	**el endodontista** *(ehl ehn-doh-dohn-'tees-tah)*
hygienist	**el higienista** *(ehl ee-hee-eh-'nees-tah)*
orthodontist	**el ortodoncista** *(ehl ohr-toh-dohn-'sees-tah)*

periodontist	**el periodontista**
	(ehl peh-ree-oh-dohn-'tees-tah)
surgeon	**el cirujano** *(ehl see-roo-'hah-noh)*

Here are some special commands you should become familiar with:

Bite.	**Muerda.** *('mwehr-dah)*
Brush.	**Cepíllese.** *(seh-'pee-yeh-seh)*
Gargle.	**Haga gárgaras.** *('ah-gah 'gahr-gah-rahs)*
Open your mouth.	**Abra la boca.** *('ah-brah lah 'boh-kah)*
Rinse.	**Enjuáguese.** *(ehn-'hwah-geh-seh)*
Spit.	**Escupa.** *(ehs-'koo-pah)*

Additional vocabulary may be required, so use this command technique to practice Spanish with coworkers. First review the names for each item. Then, instead of using English, ask for each one in your new language!

Bring . . .	**Traiga . . .** *('trah·ee-gah)*
clasp	**el gancho** *(ehl 'gahn-choh)*
cuspidor	**la escupidera** *(lah ehs-koo-pee-'deh-rah)*
dental floss	**el hilo dental** *(ehl 'ee-loh dehn-'tahl)*
drill	**el taladro** *(ehl tah-'lah-droh)*
file	**la lima** *(lah 'lee-mah)*
forceps	**las tenazas** *(lahs teh-'nah-sahs)*
headrest	**el apoyo** *(ehl ah-'poh-yoh)*
mirror	**el espejo** *(ehl ehs-'peh-hoh)*
mold	**el molde** *(ehl 'mohl-deh)*
toothbrush	**el cepillo de dientes**
	(ehl seh-'pee-yoh deh dee-'ehn-tehs)
toothpaste	**la pasta de dientes**
	(lah 'pah-stah deh dee-'ehn-tehs)
tweezers	**las pinzas** *(lahs 'peen-sahs)*
water pick	**el limpiador** *(ehl leem-pee-ah-'dohr)*

When the dental work is complete and you need to describe the dentures or fillings, use **es:**

It's . . .	**Es . . .** *(ehs)*
artificial	**artificial** *(ahr-tee-fee-see-'ahl)*
cement	**cemento** *(seh-'mehn-toh)*
enamel	**esmalte** *(ehs-'mahl-teh)*
false	**postiza** *(poh-'stee-sah)*
fixed	**fija** *('fee-hah)*
full	**completa** *(kohm-'pleh-tah)*

gold	**oro** *('oh-roh)*
partial	**parcial** *(pahr-see-'ahl)*
porcelain	**porcelana** *(pohr-seh-'lah-nah)*
removable	**sacable** *(sah-'kah-bleh)*
silver	**plata** *('plah-tah)*

The optometrist

El optometrista *(ehl ohp-toh-meh-'trees-tah)*

Many patients require the services of an optometrist. Since qualified medical treatment includes the continuous exchange of valuable information, take a moment to focus on what's going on here. These are extremely helpful because they only require a **sí** or **no** answer. And, you should recognize all the vocabulary:

Are your glasses broken?
¿Están rotos los anteojos?
(eh-'stahn 'roh-tohs lohs ahn-teh-'oh-hohs)

Can you read this?
¿Puede leer esto?
('pweh-deh leh-'ehr 'eh-stoh)

Can you see very well?
¿Puede ver bien?
('pweh-deh behr 'bee·ehn)

Do you have blurred vision?
¿Tiene visión borrosa?
(tee-'eh-neh bee-see·'ohn boh-'rroh-sah)

Do you have difficulty reading?
¿Tiene dificultad al leer?
(tee-'eh-neh dee-fee-kool-'tahd ahl leh-'ehr)

Do you have lots of headaches?
¿Tiene muchos dolores de cabeza?
(tee-'eh-neh 'moo-chohs doh-'loh-rehs deh kah-'beh-sah)

Do you have something in your eye?
¿Tiene algo en el ojo?
(tee-'eh-neh 'ahl-goh ehn ehl 'oh-hoh)

Do you see double?
¿Ve doble?
(beh 'doh-bleh)

Do you wear glasses or contact lenses?
¿Usa anteojos o lentes de contacto?
(*'oo-sah ahn-teh-'oh-hohs oh 'lehn-tehs deh kohn-'tahk-toh*)

Who is your ophthalmologist?
¿Quién es su oftalmólogo?
(*kee-'ehn ehs soo ohf-tahl-'moh-loh-goh*)

Mrs. Lupe is losing her sight rapidly, and she needs frequent examinations. The following expressions will help you communicate with her. Open with a few commands and then use familiar patterns to discuss your patient's unique needs. There's lots of new vocabulary, so choose only a few key phrases at a time:

Cover your eye.	**Tape el ojo.** (*'tah-peh ehl 'oh-hoh*)
Look here.	**Mire aquí.** (*'mee-reh ah-'kee*)
Look up and down.	**Mire hacia arriba y abajo.**
	(*'mee-reh 'ah-see·ah ah-'rree-bah ee ah-'bah-hoh*)
Read this.	**Lea esto.** (*'leh-ah 'eh-stoh*)

As you carry out the examination, these questions will be helpful:

Is it . . . ?	**¿Está . . . ?** (*eh-'stah*)
better	**mejor** (*meh-'hohr*)
clear	**claro** (*'klah-roh*)
cloudy	**borroso** (*boh-'rroh-soh*)
dark	**oscuro** (*oh-'skoo-roh*)
double	**doble** (*'doh-bleh*)
worse	**peor** (*peh-'ohr*)

To discuss her vision problems with her and her family, say:

She needs . . .	**Necesita . . .** (*neh-seh-'see-tah*)
bifocals	**bifocales** (*bee-foh-'kah-lehs*)
a cataract operation	**una operación de cataratas**
	(*'oo-nah oh-peh-rah-see·'ohn deh kah-tah-'rah-tahs*)
disinfectant	**desinfectante** (*deh-seen-fehk-'tahn-teh*)
eye drops	**gotas para los ojos**
	(*'goh-tahs 'pah-rah lohs 'oh-hohs*)
laser surgery	**cirugía con láser** (*see-roo-'hee-ah kohn 'lah-sehr*)
new frames	**marcos nuevos** (*'mahr-kohs noo-'eh-bohs*)
new lenses	**lentes nuevos** (*'lehn-tehs noo-'eh-bohs*)
a prescription	**una receta** (*'oo-nah reh-'seh-tah*)
progressive glasses	**lentes progresivos** (*'lehn-tehs proh-greh-'see-vohs*)
reading glasses	**lentes para leer** (*'lehn-tehs 'pah-rah leh-'ehr*)
saline solution	**solución salina** (*soh-loo-see-'ohn sah-'lee-nah*)

| sunglasses | **lentes de sol** *('lehn-tehs deh sohl)* |
| two pair | **dos pares** *(dohs 'pah-rehs)* |

She has . . .	**Tiene . . .** *(tee-'eh-neh)*
astigmatism	**astigmatismo** *(ahs-teeg-mah-'tees-moh)*
cataracts	**cataratas** *(kah-tah-'rah-tahs)*
conjunctivitis	**conjuntivitis** *(kohn-hoon-tee-'vee-tees)*
Daltonism	**daltonismo** *(dahl-toh-'nees-moh)*
double vision	**doble visión** *('doh-bleh bee-see-'ohn)*
dyslexia	**dislexia** *(dees-'lehk-see-ah)*
glaucoma	**glaucoma** *(glow-'koh-mah)*
an infection	**una infección** *('oo-nah een-fehk-see-'ohn)*
redness	**enrojecimiento** *(ehn-roh-heh-see-mee-'ehn-toh)*
a scratch	**un rasguño** *(oon rahs-'goon-yoh)*
a sty	**un orzuelo** *(oon ohr-'sweh-loh)*
a virus	**un virus** *(oon 'vee-roos)*

She is . . .	**Es . . .** *(ehs)*
blind	**ciega** *(see-'eh-gah)*
color-blind	**daltónica** *(dahl-'toh-nee-kah)*
farsighted	**présbita** *('prehs-bee-tah)*
nearsighted	**miope** *(mee-'oh-peh)*

(32) # ¿Cuánto aprendió?

- Fill in the following:

  Necesita . . . *(neh-seh-'see-tah)*
  (a crown, dentures, braces)

  Tiene . . . *(tee-'eh-neh)*
  (bad breath, tartar, cavities, gum problems)

  Voy a . . . *('boh·ee ah)*
  (remove the root, drill, straighten the molars)

  Es . . . *(ehs)*
  (false, made of gold, removable, enamel)

  Translate: Rinse and spit!
                    Look here.

- Fill in the following:

  Necesita . . . *(neh-seh-'see-tah)*
  (new frames, an optometrist, contact lenses)

  Translate: Lupe is farsighted and has astigmatism.

Holistic health

La salud holística *(lah sah-'lood oh-'lees-tee-kah)*

Use the following words and expressions if you practice holistic health or work in the field of alternative medicine:

We use...	**Usamos...** *(oo-'sah-mohs)*
acupressure	**la acupresión** *(lah ah-koo-preh-see-'ohn)*
acupuncture	**la acupuntura** *(lah ah-koo-pun-'too-rah)*
alternative methods	**los métodos alternativos** *(los 'meh-toh-dohs ahl-tehr-nah-'tee-vohs)*
aromatherapy	**la aromaterapia** *(lah ah-roh-mah-teh-'rah-pee-ah)*
art therapy	**la terapia artística** *(lah teh-'rah-pee-ah ahr-'tees-tee-kah)*
chiropractics	**la quiropráctica** *(lah kee-roh-'prahk-tee-kah)*
deep cleansing	**la limpieza profunda** *(lah leem-pee-'eh-sah proh-'foon-dah)*
exercise	**el ejercicio** *(ehl eh-her-'see-see-oh)*
holistic techniques	**las técnicas holísticas** *(lahs 'tehk-nee-kahs oh-'lees-tee-kahs)*
homeopathy	**la homeopatía** *(lah oh-meh-oh-pah-'tee-ah)*
hormonal therapy	**la terapia hormonal** *(lah teh-'rah-pee-ah ohr-moh-'nahl)*
immune therapy	**la inmunoterapia** *(lah een-moo-noh-teh-'rah-pee-ah)*
massage	**el masaje** *(ehl mah-'sah-heh)*
meditation	**la meditación** *(lah meh-dee-tah-see-'ohn)*
natural herbs	**las hierbas naturales** *(lahs ee-'ehr-bahs nah-too-'rah-lehs)*
non-traditional remedies	**los remedios no tradicionales** *(lohs reh-'meh-dee-ohs noh trah-dee-see-oh-'nah-lehs)*
nutritional treatment	**el tratamiento nutricional** *(ehl trah-tah-mee-'ehn-toh noo-tree-see-oh-'nahl)*
organic foods	**los alimentos orgánicos** *(lohs ah-lee-'mehn-tohs ohr-'gah-nee-kohs)*
relaxation	**la relajación** *(lah reh-lah-hah-see-'ohn)*
religion	**la religión** *(lah reh-lee-hee-'ohn)*
self-help	**la autoayuda** *(lah ah-oo-toh-ah-'yoo-dah)*
Tai Chi	**el tai chi** *(ehl 'tah-ee chee)*
vitamins	**las vitaminas** *(lahs vee-tah-'mee-nahs)*
yoga	**el yoga** *(ehl 'yoh-gah)*

Do you understand the...?	**¿Entiende ...?** *(ehn-tee-'ehn-deh)*
approach	**el enfoque** *(ehl ehn-'foh-keh)*
concept	**el concepto** *(ehl kohn-'sehp-toh)*
idea	**la idea** *(lah ee-'deh-ah)*
method	**el método** *(ehl 'meh-toh-doh)*
plan	**el plan** *(ehl plahn)*
procedure	**el procedimiento** *(ehl proh-seh-dee-mee-'ehn-toh)*
system	**el sistema** *(ehl sees-'teh-mah)*
This is a (an) .... treatment	**Este es un tratamiento ...** *('ehs-teh ehs oon trah-tah-mee-'ehn-toh)*
alternative	**alternativo** *(ahl-tehr-nah-'tee-voh)*
biological	**biológico** *(bee-oh-'loh-hee-koh)*
comprehensive	**comprensivo** *(kohm-prehn-'see-voh)*
Eastern	**oriental** *(oh-ree-ehn-'tahl)*
environmental	**ambiental** *(ahm-bee-ehn-'tahl)*
existencial	**existencial** *(ehk-sees-tehn-see-'ahl)*
holistic	**holístico** *(oh-'lees-tee-koh)*
home-made	**casero** *(kah-'seh-roh)*
homeopathic	**homeopático** *(oh-meh-oh-'pah-tee-koh)*
natural	**natural** *(nah-too-'rahl)*
organic	**orgánico** *(ohr-'gah-nee-koh)*
spiritual	**espiritual** *(ehs-pee-ree-'twahl)*
unconventional	**no convencional** *(noh kohn-vehn-see-oh-'nahl)*
universal	**universal** *(oo-nee-vehr-'sahl)*
Vegan	**vegetariano estricto** *(veh-heh-tah-ree-'ah-noh ehs-'treek-toh)*
vegetarian	**vegetariano** *(veh-heh-tah-ree-'ah-noh)*
Try (the)...	**Pruebe...** *(proo-'eh-beh)*
aloe	**el áloe** *(ehl 'ah-loh-eh)*
anise	**el anís** *(ehl ah-'nees)*
chamomile	**la manzanilla** *(lah mahn-sah-'nee-yah)*
coriander	**el cilantro** *(ehl see-'lahn-troh)*
garlic	**el ajo** *(ehl 'ah-hoh)*
mint	**la menta** *(lah 'mehn-tah)*
olive oil	**el aceite de oliva** *(ehl ah-'seh-ee-teh deh oh-'lee-vah)*
sage	**la salvia** *(lah 'sahl-vee-ah)*

Chapter Eleven

Capítulo Once

(kah-'pee-too-loh 'ohn-seh)

Patient Discharge

Dar de Alta al Paciente

(dahr deh 'ahl-tah ahl pah-see-'ehn-teh)

At the time of being discharged from the hospital, all members of the Espinoza family must follow similar procedures. The following expressions should help you with some of them.

Before leaving you must go to Administration.
Antes de irse debe ir a la Administración.
('ahn-tehs deh 'eer-teh 'deh-beh eer ah lah ahd-mee-nee-strah-see·'ohn)

You must pay what the insurance does not cover.
Usted debe pagar lo que el seguro no cubre.
(oo-'stehd 'deh-beh pah-'gahr loh keh ehl seh-'goo-roh noh 'koo-breh)

They will send the bill to your home.
Le enviarán la cuenta a su casa.
(leh ehn-bee-ah-'rahn lah 'kwehn-tah ah soo 'kah-sah)

The telephone and TV rental must be paid at once.
El arriendo del teléfono y televisor debe ser pagado de inmediato.
(ehl ah-rree-'ehn-doh dehl teh-'leh-foh-noh ee teh-leh-bee-'sohr 'deh-beh sehr pah-'gah-doh deh een-meh-dee-'ah-toh)

You must talk to the social worker.
Debe hablar con el trabajador social.
('deh-beh ah-blahr kohn ehl trah-bah-hah-'dohr soh-see-'ahl)

You should talk to the priest.
Debiera hablar con el sacerdote.
('deh-bee-'eh-rah ah-'blahr kohn ehl sah-sehr-'doh-teh)

Take these medicines with you.
Tome estas medicinas con usted.
('toh-meh 'ehs-tahs meh-dee-'see-nahs kohn oo-'stehd)

Here is the prescription to buy more medication.
Aquí tiene la receta para comprar más medicamentos.
(ah-'kee tee-'eh-neh lah reh-'seh-tah 'pah-rah kohm-'prahr mahs meh-dee-kah-'mehn-tohs)

A nurse will come every _____ days to your home.
Una enfermera vendrá cada _____ días a su casa.
('oo-nah ehn-fehr-'meh-rah vehn-'drah 'kah-dah _____ 'dee-ahs ah soo 'kah-sah)

Do not forget to return every _____ weeks (_____ days).
No olvide volver cada _____ semanas (_____ días).
(noh ohl-'bee-deh bohl-'behr 'kah-dah _____ seh-'mah-nahs (_____ 'dee-ahs)

Here are the names and telephone numbers of the physicians who took care of you.

Aquí están los nombres y teléfonos de los médicos que lo atendieron.
(ah-'kee eh-'stahn lohs 'nohm-brehs ee teh-'leh-foh-nohs deh lohs 'meh-dee-kohs keh loh ah-tehn-dee-'eh-rohn)

Back to the city

De vuelta en la ciudad
(de 'bwehl-tah ehn lah see-oo-'dahd)

Aside from strict health care vocabulary, there are urban and rural words that you must know in order to communicate. Learn the following nouns and verify your progress by creating sentences with them.

ambulance	**la ambulancia** *(lah ahm-boo-'lahn-see-ah)*
bicycle	**la bicicleta** *(lah bee-see-'kleh-tah)*
boat	**el barco** *(ehl 'bahr-koh)*
bridge	**el puente** *(ehl 'pwehn-teh)*
bus	**el autobús** *(ehl ow-toh-'boos)*
car	**el carro** *(ehl 'kah-rroh)*
city block	**la cuadra** *(lah 'kwah-drah)*
corner	**la esquina** *(lah ehs-'kee-nah)*
curb	**la orilla** *(lah oh-'ree-yah)*
grass	**el césped** *(ehl 'sehs-pehd)*
helicopter	**el helicóptero** *(ehl eh-lee-'kohp-teh-roh)*

highway	**la carretera** *(lah kah-rreh-'teh-rah)*
lane	**el carril** *(ehl kah-'rreel)*
motorcycle	**la motocicleta** *(lah moh-toh-see-'kleh-tah)*
plane	**el avión** *(ehl ah-bee-'ohn)*
road	**el camino** *(ehl kah-'mee-noh)*
sidewalk	**la acera** *(lah ah-'seh-rah)*
street	**la calle** *(lah 'kah-yeh)*
subway	**el metro** *(ehl 'meh-troh)*
train	**el tren** *(ehl trehn)*
truck	**el camión** *(ehl kah-mee-'ohn)*

Outside the city

Fuera de la ciudad
('fweh-rah deh lah see-oo-'dahd)

For those incidents outside city limits, you may need these terms:

beach	**la playa** *(lah 'plah-yah)*
countryside	**el campo** *(ehl 'kahm-poh)*
desert	**el desierto** *(ehl deh-see-'ehr-toh)*
dirt	**la tierra** *(lah tee-'eh-rrah)*
dust	**el polvo** *(ehl 'pohl-boh)*
forest	**el bosque** *(ehl 'bohs-keh)*
jungle	**la selva** *(lah 'sehl-bah)*
lake	**el lago** *(ehl 'lah-goh)*
mountains	**las montañas** *(lahs mohn-'tah-nyahs)*
mud	**el lodo** *(ehl 'loh-doh)*
park	**el parque** *(ehl 'pahr-keh)*
river	**el río** *(ehl 'ree-oh)*
rock	**la piedra** *(lah pee-'eh-drah)*
sand	**la arena** *(lah ah-'reh-nah)*
sea	**el mar** *(ehl mahr)*

Good-bye everyone!

¡Adiós a todos! *(ah-dee-'ohs ah 'toh-dohs)*

All of the Espinozas have been treated and released. Thanks to the hospital employees who tried out their new Spanish skills, everyone in the family is delighted with the facility. Juan and María have already told their friends about the care they received, and have praised the physicians, nurses, and other staff members.

The administration—**la administración**—is pleased. The use of a few Spanish words and phrases by hospital staff members has increased hospital admissions. The Hispanic community feels comfortable here. They have found a facility where they can truly communicate their health care needs:

Are you satisfied?　　　　**¿Está satisfecho?** *(eh-'stah sah-tees-'feh-choh)*

Several of the administrators are determined to learn Spanish too, so they have decided to give the Espinozas a follow-up phone call. Follow along as one of the CEOs give his new skills a try. No doubt all of the answers to these questions will be **"sí."**

Are the employees good?
¿Son buenos los empleados?
(sohn boo-'eh-nohs lohs ehm-pleh-'ah-dohs)

Are you satisfied with the care given?
¿Está satisfecho con el cuidado recibido?
(eh-'stah sah-tees'feh-choh kohn ehl kwee-'dah-doh reh-see-'bee-doh)

Did you have any suggestions or criticism?
¿Tiene cualquier sugerencia o crítica?
(tee-'eh-neh kwahl-kee-'ehr soo-heh-'rehn-see·ah oh 'kree-tee-kah)

Did you like the food?
¿Le gustó la comida?
(leh goo-'stoh lah koh-'mee-dah)

If necessary, would you return to this hospital?
Si fuese necesario, ¿volvería a este hospital?
(see 'fweh-seh neh-seh-'sah-ree·oh, bohl-beh-'ree-ah ah 'eh-steh ohs-pee-'tahl)

Was everything very clean?
¿Fue todo muy limpio?
(foo-'eh 'toh-doh 'moo·ee 'leem-pee·oh)

(33) **¿Cuánto aprendió?**

Read aloud and translate these final comments.

Soy de la administración del hospital.
(*'soh·ee deh lah ahd-mee-nees-trah-see·'ohn dehl ohs-pee-'tahl*)

Llame a la oficina si tiene algún problema.
(*'yah-meh ah lah oh-fee-'see-nah see tee-'eh-neh ahl-'goon proh-'bleh-mah*)

Muchas gracias, buena suerte y adiós.
(*'moo-chahs 'grah-see·ahs, 'bweh-nah 'swehr-teh ee ah-dee-'ohs*)

Now that you've finished reading this book, are you ready to put all your skills into practice? Why don't you start today? Good-bye and good luck! **¡Adiós y buena suerte!**

Answers to ¿Cuánto Aprendió?

1   **Muy bien.** *('moo-ee bee-'ehn)*
    ¡De nada! *(deh 'nah-dah)*
    ¡Pase! *('pah-seh)*

2   **doscientos cuartos** *(dohs-see-'ehn-tohs 'kwahr-tohs)*
    ochenta mesas *(oh-'chehn-tah 'meh-sahs)*
    tres enfermeros *(trehs ehn-fehr-'meh-rohs)*
    setenta y cinco libros *(seh-'tehn-tah ee 'seen-koh 'lee-brohs)*
    diez pisos *(dee-'ehs 'pee-sohs)*
    trescientos sesenta y un bebés
    (trehs-see-'ehn-tohs seh-'sehn-tah ee oon beh-'behs)

3   A lot of pain
    Three forms
    Injury and sickness
    Two appointments
    More help

4   **¿Qué pasa? Nada.**
    ¿Cómo está? Muy bien.
    ¿Quién es la enfermera? Kathy.
    ¿Cuál color? Verde.
    ¿Cuántos visitantes? Seis.
    ¿Cuánta medicina? Mucha.

5   **¿Quiénes son? Somos enfermeros.**
    ¿Dónde está? Estoy en el cuarto.
    ¿Qué medicinas son blancas? Las aspirinas.
    ¿Cuánta agua hay el baño? Mucha.
    ¿Qué comida es buena? Pizza.
    ¿Cuántas camas hay en el hospital? Doscientas cincuenta.

6   I am Robert. I am in the hospital. I have a pain in my stomach. There is a nurse in the room. She has the white medicine.

7   My head hurts.   They are arms.

      Do your feet hurt?   The nose is on the face.

      What hurts you?   There are many teeth in the mouth.

      My eyes don't hurt.   He doesn't have ten fingers.

8   **su** *(soo)*

      su *(soo)*

      nuestro *(noo-'ehs-troh)*

9   She is tall and he is short.

      The children are asleep.

      We are not very rich.

      The doctor is old and thin.

      Where is the hot water?

      tan enferma como su hermano
      (tahn ehn-'fehr-mah 'koh-moh soo ehr-'mah-noh)

      enferma *(ehn-'fehr-mah)*

      más enferma *(mahs ehn-'fehr-mah)*

      gordo *('gohr-doh)*

      débil *('deh-beel)*

      joven *('hoh-behn)*

      mayores *(mah-'yoh-rehs)*

      bonitas *(boh-'nee-tahs)*

      delgadas *(dehl-'gah-dahs)*

10   I need an appointment.

      Do you need medicine?

      Margaret and I need beds.

11   **primer nombre** *(pree-'mehr 'nohm-breh)*, **apellido paterno**
      (ah-peh-'yee-doh pah-'tehr-noh), **dirección** *(dee-rehk-see-'ohn)*

      es el doctor *(ehs ehl dohk-'tohr)*, **está enfermo** *(eh-'stah ehn-'fehr-moh)*

      seguro médico *(seh-'goo-roh 'meh-dee-koh)*, **el recibo** *(ehl reh-'see-boh)*

12   What kind of insurance do you have?
     What is your employer's address?
     You need accident insurance.

13   **en frente del salón** *(ehn 'frehn-teh dehl sah-'lohn)*
     allí *(ah-'yee)*
     afuera *(ah-foo-'eh-rah)*
     adelante *(ah-deh-'lahn-teh)*

     Go up the elevator and turn right.

14   **miércoles**
     sábado
     abril
     agosto

15   **la fuente de agua** *(lah foo-'ehn-teh deh 'ah-gwah)*
     el buzón *(ehl boo-'sohn)*
     las escaleras *(lahs ehs-kah-'leh-rahs)*
     la sala de emergencia *(lah 'sah-lah deh eh-mehr-'hehn-see-ah)*
     el pediatra *(ehl peh-dee-'ah-trah)*
     el ginecólogo *(ehl hee-neh-'koh-loh-goh)*
     el terapeuta *(ehl teh-rah-'peh-oo-tah)*

16   convulsions
     nausea
     vomiting
     dilated pupils
     reduced pupils
     temperature
     nervousness
     depression
     tension
     paranoid illusions
     hallucinations
     aggressiveness
     confusion

respiratory difficulty

irritability

insomnia

17 a week ago

between three and four

the following day

last year

next month

until tomorrow

within two hours

18 What did you eat?

Did you take medicine?

Did you smoke?

Did you get sick?

Did you have problems?

19 **ampollas** *(ahm-'poh-yahs)*, **hipo** *('ee-poh)*, **flema** *('fleh-mah)*

la enfermera *(lah ehn-fehr-'meh-rah)*, **levantarse** *(leh-bahn-'tahr-seh)*, **sentarse** *(sehn-'tahr-seh)*

¿Duerme ella?

¿Llora ella?

¿Camina ella?

20 **paperas** *(pah-'peh-rahs)*

enfermedad del corazón *(ehn-fehr-meh-'dahd dehl koh-rah-'sohn)*

enfermedades graves *(ehn-fehr-meh-'dah-dehs 'grah-behs)*

tosferina *(tohs-feh-'ree-nah)*

21 • **tomó la medicina** *(toh-'moh lah meh-dee-'see-nah)*, **tuvo un accidente** *('too-boh oon ahk-see-'dehn-teh)*, **habló con el doctor** *(ah-'bloh kohn ehl dohk-'tohr)*

• **el polen** *(ehl 'poh-lehn)*, **las picaduras de insectos** *(lahs pee-kah-'doo-rahs deh een-'sehk-tohs)*, **gatos** *('gah-tohs)*

• **un dolor de cabeza** *(oon doh-'lohr deh kah-'beh-sah)*, **un resfrío** *(oon rehs-'free-oh)*, **problemas con este tiempo** *(proh-'bleh-mahs kohn 'eh-steh tee-'ehm-poh)*

- **tomar su presión arterial** *(toh-'mahr soo preh-see-'ohn ahr-teh-ree-'ahl)*, **mover su cabeza** *(moh-'behr soo kah-'beh-sah)*

- **Está nublado.** *(eh-'stah noo-'blah-doh)*
  Hace sol. *('ah-seh sohl)*
  Está nevando. *(es-'stah neh-'bahn-doh)*

- **¡Tome la medicina!** *('toh-meh lah meh-dee-'see-nah)*
  ¡Estire su pierna! *(ehs-'tee-reh soo pee-'ehr-nah)*
  ¡Escriba su nombre! *(ehs-'kree-bah soo 'nohm-breh)*
  ¡Describa el dolor! *(dehs-'kree-bah ehl doh-'lohr)*
  ¡Siéntese en la cama! *(see-'ehn-teh-seh ehn lah 'kah-mah)*

22 **la aspirina** *(lah ahs-pee-'ree-nah)*
    las tijeras *(lahs tee-'heh-rahs)*
    las flores *(lahs 'floh-rehs)*
    las tarjetas de saludo *(lahs tahr-'heh-tahs deh sah-'loo-doh)*
    un peine *(oon 'peh-ee-neh)*

23 - **una muestra de sangre** *(oo-nah moo-'ehs-trah deh 'sahn-greh)*,
      un examen *(oon ehk-'sah-mehn)*, **más líquidos** *(mahs 'lee-kee-dohs)*

    - **leer la etiqueta** *(leh-'ehr lah eh-tee-'keh-tah)*, **tomar la mitad**
      (toh-'mahr lah mee-'tahd)

    - **Tome las píldoras con agua.**
      ('toh-meh lahs 'peel-doh-rahs kohn 'ah-gwah)
      Tome dos cucharadas tres veces cada día.
      ('toh-meh dohs koo-chah-'rah-dahs trehs 'beh-sehs 'kah-dah 'dee-ah)
      Necesita bañarse en agua caliente.
      (neh-seh-'see-tah bahn-'yahr-seh ehn 'ag-wah kah-lee-'ehn-teh)
      Vamos a bajar la dosis.
      ('bah-mohs ah bah-'hahr lah 'doh-sees)

24 **los guantes** *(lohs 'gwahn-tehs)*, **la camisa** *(lah kah-'mee-sah)*, **la ropa
    interior** *(lah 'roh-pah een-teh-ree-'ohr)*, **los aretes** *(lohs ah-'reh-tehs)*,
    el cinturón *(ehl seen-too-'rohn)*, **los zapatos** *(lohs sah-'pah-tohs)*,
    el tubo *(ehl 'too-boh)*, **la dieta** *(lah dee-'eh-tah)*

    controlar la luz *(kohn-troh-'lahr lah loos)*, **tener una cicatriz**
    (teh-'nehr 'oo-nah see-kah-'trees), **prender la televisión**
    (prehn-'dehr lah teh-leh-bee-see-'ohn), **vivir** *(bee-'beer)*,
    llamar a su familia *(yah-'mahr ah soo fah-'mee-lee-ah)*,
    sacarle las puntadas *(sah-'kahr-leh lahs poon-'tah-dahs)*

25   • **el gabinete** *(ehl gah-bee-'neh-teh),* **el espejo** *(ehl ehs-'peh-hoh),*
     la bandeja *(lah bahn-'deh-hah)*

     • **el plato** *(ehl 'plah-toh),* **el ventilador** *(ehl behn-tee-lah-'dohr),*
     el jabón *(ehl hah-'bohn),* **la cuchara** *(lah koo-'chah-rah),*
     la frazada *(lah frah-'sah-dah)*

     • **una ducha** *('oo-nah 'doo-chah),* **una siesta** *('oo-nah see-'ehs-tah)*

26   • **la mantequilla** *(lah mahn-teh-'kee-yah),* **la sal** *(lah sahl),* **el dulce**
     (ehl 'dool-seh), **el queso** *(ehl 'keh-soh),* **el bistec** *(ehl bees-'tehk),*
     las galletas *(lahs gah-'yeh-tahs)*

     • **el té** *(ehl teh),* **la leche** *(lah 'leh-cheh),* **el jugo** *(ehl 'hoo-goh)*

     • **darle medicamentos** *('dahr-leh meh-dee-kah-'mehn-tohs)*
     explicar el equipo *(ehks-plee-'kahr ehl eh-'kee-poh)*
     sacar un poco de sangre *(sah-'kahr oon 'poh-koh deh 'sahn-greh)*
     escuchar su pecho *(ehs-koo-'chahr soo 'peh-choh)*

27   • anorexia, botulism, bulimia, colitis
     milk of magnesia, suppositories, mineral oil

     • **diarrea** *(dee-ahr-'reh-ah),* **un enema de bario** *(oon eh-'neh-mah deh*
     'bah-ree-oh), **ardor en el estómago** *(ahr-'dohr ehn ehl ehs-'toh-mah-*
     goh), **bebidas alcohólicas** *(beh-'bee-dahs ahl-koh-'oh-lee-kahs)*

     • **café descafeinado** *(kah-'feh dehs-kah-feh-ee-'nah-doh),* **perder**
     treinta libras *(pehr-'dehr 'treh-een-tah 'leeb-rahs),* **comer desayuno**
     (koh-'mehr deh-sah-'yoo-noh), **una dieta limitada** *('oo-nah dee-'eh-tah*
     lee-mee-'tah-dah) **un laxante** *(oon lahk-'sahn-teh)*

28   **el mamograma**—mammogram

     la tomografía computarizada—CT

     la prueba del sistema gastrointestinal—upper GI

     la cistoscopía—cistoscopy

     el electrocardiograma—ECG

29   • **cuidado ambulatorio** *(kwee-'dah-doh ahm-boo-lah-'toh-ree-oh),*
     el baño con agua circulante *(ehl 'bahn-yoh kohn 'ah-gwah*
     seer-koo-'lahn-teh), **ejercicios** *(eh-hehr-'see-see-ohs)*

     • **la columna vertebral** *(lah koh-'loom-nah behr-teh-'brahl),*
     la coyuntura *(lah koh-yoon-'too-rah),* **el pene** *(ehl 'peh-neh)*

     • **problemas menstruales** *(proh-'bleh-mahs mehns-troo-'ah-lehs),* **un**
     examen del semen *(oon ehk-'sah-mehn dehl 'seh-mehn),* **una**
     enfermedad venérea *('oo-nah ehn-fehr-meh-'dahd beh-'neh-reh-ah),*

glándulas hinchadas *('glahn-doo-lahs een-'chah-dahs)*, **problemas con sus ovarios** *(proh-'bleh-mahs kohn soos oh-'bah-ree-ohs)*

30 • **desmayos** *(dehs-'mah-yohs)*
doble visión *('doh-bleh bee-see-'ohn)*
falta de memoria *('fahl-tah deh meh-'moh-ree-ah)*
divorcio *(dee-'bohr-see-oh)*
visiones *(bee-see-'oh-nehs)*
miedo *(mee-'eh-doh)*
problemas económicos *(proh-'bleh-mahs eh-koh-'noh-mee-kohs)*

• **insomnio** *(een-'sohm-nee-oh)*, **depresión** *(deh-preh-see-'ohn)*, **ataques** *(ah-'tah-kehs)*

31 • **ayuda del bienestar social** *(ah-'yoo-dah dehl bee-eh-nehs-'tahr soh-see-'ahl)*, **el cuidado del niño** *(ehl 'kwee-dah-doh dehl 'neen-yoh)*, **cupones de alimentos** *(koo-'poh-nehs deh ah-lee-'mehn-tohs)*

• **el matrimonio** *(ehl mah-tree-'moh-nee-oh)*, **el abuso de menores** *(ehl ah-'boo-soh deh meh-'noh-rehs)*, **los problemas familiares** *(lohs proh-'bleh-mahs fah-mee-lee-'ah-rehs)*

32 • **una corona** *('oo-nah koh-'roh-nah)*, **dentaduras postizas** *(dehn-tah-'doo-rahs pohs-'tee-sahs)*, **frenillos** *(freh-'nee-yohs)*

• **mal aliento** *(mahl ah-lee-'ehn-toh)*, **sarro** *('sahr-roh)*, **caries** *('kah-ree-ehs)*, **problemas con las encías** *(proh-'bleh-mahs kohn lahs ehn-'see-ahs)*

• **sacar la raíz** *(sah-'kahr lah rah-'ees)*, **perforar** *(pehr-foh-'rahr)*, **enderezar las muelas** *(ehn-deh-reh-'sahr lahs moo-'eh-lahs)*

• **falso** *(fahl-soh)*, **hecho de oro** *('eh-choh deh 'oh-roh)*, **sacable** *(sah-'kah-bleh)*, **esmalte** *(ehs-'mahl-teh)*

• **¡Enjuáguese y escupa!** *(ehn-'hwah-geh-seh ee ehs-'koo-pah)* **Mire aquí.** *('mee-reh ah-'kee)*

• **marcos nuevos** *('mahr-kohs noo-'eh-bohs)*, **un optometrista** *(oon ohp-toh-meh-'trees-tah)*, **lentes de contacto** *('lehn-tehs deh kohn-'tahk-toh)*

• **Lupe es présbita y tiene astigmatismo.** *('loo-peh ehs 'prehs-bee-tah ee tee-'eh-neh ahs-teeg-mah-'tees-moh)*

33 I'm from the hospital administration.
Call the office if you have a problem.
Thanks a lot, good luck, and good-bye.

Cognate Words

Thousands of health care vocabulary words are similar in their forms and meanings in both Spanish and English. Notice these common patterns:

appendicitis	**apendicitis** (*ah-pehn-dee-'see-tees*)
arthritis	**artritis** (*ahr-'tree-tees*)
bronchitis	**bronquitis** (*brohn-'kee-tees*)
laryngitis	**laringitis** (*lah-reen-'hee-tees*)
hepatitis	**hepatitis** (*eh-pah-'tee-tees*)
analysis	**análisis** (*ah-'nah-lee-sees*)
syphilis	**sífilis** (*'see-fee-lees*)
psychosis	**psicosis** (*see-'koh-sees*)
sclerosis	**esclerosis** (*ehs-kleh-'roh-sees*)
tuberculosis	**tuberculosis** (*too-behr-koo-'loh-sees*)
flexibility	**flexibilidad** (*flehk-see-bee-lee-'dahd*)
mobility	**movilidad** (*moh-bee-lee-'dahd*)
maternity	**maternidad** (*mah-tehr-nee-'dahd*)
sterility	**esterilidad** (*ehs-teh-ree-lee-'dahd*)
abnormality	**anormalidad** (*ah-nohr-mah-lee-'dahd*)
possible	**posible** (*poh-'seeb-leh*)
controllable	**controlable** (*kohn-troh-'lahb-leh*)
unstable	**inestable** (*een-ehs-'tahb-leh*)
responsible	**responsable** (*rehs-pohn-'sahb-leh*)
operable	**operable** (*oh-peh-'rahb-leh*)
genetic	**genético** (*heh-'neh-tee-koh*)
antiseptic	**antiséptico** (*ahn-tee-'sehp-tee-koh*)
diabetic	**diabético** (*dee-ah-'beh-tee-koh*)
diagnostic	**diagnóstico** (*dee-ah-'gnohs-tee-koh*)
accident	**accidente** (*ahk-see-'dehn-teh*)
transparent	**transparente** (*trahns-pah-'rehn-teh*)
persistent	**persitente** (*pehr-sees-'tehn-teh*)
urgent	**urgente** (*oor-'hehn-teh*)
patient	**paciente** (*pah-see-'ehn-teh*)

cancerous	**canceroso** *(kahn-seh-'roh-soh)*
contagious	**contagioso** *(kohn-tah-gee-'oh-soh)*
intravenous	**intravenoso** *(een-trah-beh-'noh-soh)*
nervous	**nervioso** *(nehr-bee-'oh-soh)*
mucous	**mucoso** *(moo-'koh-soh)*
alcoholism	**alcoholismo** *(ahl-koh-oh-'lees-moh)*
aneurysm	**aneurismo** *(ah-neh-oo-'rees-moh)*
astigmatism	**astigmatismo** *(ahs-teeg-mah-'tees-moh)*
metabolism	**metabolismo** *(meh-tah-boh-'lees-moh)*
rheumatism	**reumatismo** *(reh-oo-mah-'tees-moh)*
radiologist	**radiólogo** *(rah-dee-'oh-loh-goh)*
dermatologist	**dermatólogo** *(dehr-mah-'toh-loh-goh)*
gynecologist	**ginecólogo** *(hee-neh-'koh-loh-goh)*
ophthalmologist	**oftalmólogo** *(ohf-tahl-'moh-loh-goh)*
proctologist	**proctólogo** *(prohk-'toh-loh-goh)*
allergy	**alergia** *(ah-'lehr-hee-ah)*
atrophy	**atrofia** *(ah-'troh-fee-ah)*
autopsy	**autopsia** *(ow-'tohp-see-ah)*
biopsy	**biopsia** *(bee-'ohp-see-ah)*
epilepsy	**epilepsia** *(eh-pee-'lehp-see-ah)*
respiratory	**respiratorio** *(rehs-pee-rah-'toh-ree-oh)*
ambulatory	**ambulatorio** *(ahm-boo-lah-'toh-ree-oh)*
laboratory	**laboratorio** *(lah-boh-rah-'toh-ree-oh)*
ovary	**ovario** *(oh-'bah-ree-oh)*
sanitary	**sanitario** *(sah-nee-'tah-ree-oh)*
medicine	**medicina** *(meh-dee-'see-nah)*
toxin	**toxina** *(tohk-'see-nah)*
penicillin	**penicilina** *(peh-nee-see-'lee-nah)*
urine	**orina** *(oh-'ree-nah)*
aspirin	**aspirina** *(ahs-pee-'ree-nah)*
biology	**biología** *(bee-oh-loh-'hee-ah)*
radiology	**radiología** *(rah-dee-oh-loh-'hee-ah)*
psychology	**psicología** *(see-koh-loh-'hee-ah)*
cardiology	**cardiología** *(kahr-dee-oh-loh-'hee-ah)*
urology	**urología** *(oo-roh-loh-'hee-ah)*

coagulation	**coagulación** *(koh-ah-goo-lah-see-'ohn)*
rehabilitation	**rehabilitación** *(reh-ah-bee-lee-tah-see-'ohn)*
hospitalization	**hospitalización** *(ohs-pee-tah-lee-sah-see-'ohn)*
evacuation	**evacuación** *(eh-bah-kwah-see-'ohn)*
condition	**condición** *(kohn-dee-see-'ohn)*
detection	**detección** *(deh-tehk-see-'ohn)*
infection	**infección** *(een-fehk-see-'ohn)*
amputation	**amputación** *(ahm-poo-tah-see-'ohn)*
inflammation	**inflamación** *(een-flah-mah-see-'ohn)*
hypertension	**hipertensión** *(ee-pehr-tehn-see-'ohn)*
contraction	**contracción** *(kohn-trahk-see-'ohn)*
sensation	**sensación** *(sehn-sah-see-'ohn)*
complication	**complicación** *(kohm-plee-kah-see-'ohn)*
decision	**decisión** *(deh-see-see-'ohn)*
depression	**depresión** *(deh-preh-see-'ohn)*
circulation	**circulación** *(seer-koo-lah-see-'ohn)*
nutrition	**nutrición** *(noo-tree-see-'ohn)*
transfusion	**transfusión** *(trahns-foo-see-'ohn)*
reconstruction	**reconstrucción** *(reh-kohns-trook-see-'ohn)*
solution	**solución** *(soh-loo-see-'ohn)*
palpitation	**palpitación** *(pahl-pee-tah-see-'ohn)*
prevention	**prevención** *(preh-behn-see-'ohn)*
respiration	**respiración** *(rehs-pee-rah-see-'ohn)*
resuscitation	**resucitación** *(reh-soo-see-tah-see-'ohn)*
ulceration	**ulceración** *(ool-seh-rah-see-'ohn)*

Cognate Verbs

to absorb	**absorber** *(ahb-sohr-'behr)*
to accept	**aceptar** *(ah-sehp-'tahr)*
to adjust	**ajustar** *(ah-hoos-'tahr)*
to alter	**alterar** *(ahl-teh-'rahr)*
to amputate	**amputar** *(ahm-poo-'tahr)*
to analyze	**analizar** *(ah-nah-lee-'sahr)*
to authorize	**autorizar** *(ow-toh-ree-'sahr)*
to balance	**balancear** *(bah-lahn-seh-'ahr)*
to calm	**calmar** *(kahl-'mahr)*
to cause	**causar** *(cow-'sahr)*
to circulate	**circular** *(seer-koo-'lahr)*
to coagulate	**coagular** *(koh-ah-goo-'lahr)*
to communicate	**comunicar** *(koh-moo-nee-'kahr)*
to concentrate	**concentrar** *(kohn-sehn-'trahr)*
to consider	**considerar** *(kohn-see-deh-'rahr)*
to consist	**consistir** *(kohn-sees-'teer)*
to constipate	**constipar** *(kohns-tee-'pahr)*
to consult	**consultar** *(kohn-sool-'tahr)*
to contaminate	**contaminar** *(kohn-tah-mee-'nahr)*
to contain	**contener** *(kohn-teh-'nehr)*
to control	**controlar** *(kohn-troh-'lahr)*
to converse	**conversar** *(kohn-behr-'sahr)*
to convert	**convertir** *(kohn-behr-'teer)*
to cost	**costar** *(kohs-'tahr)*
to cure	**curar** *(koo-'rahr)*
to cut	**cortar** *(kohr-'tahr)*
to debilitate	**debilitar** *(deh-bee-lee-'tahr)*
to decide	**decidir** *(deh-see-'deer)*
to declare	**declarar** *(deh-klah-'rahr)*
to depend	**depender** *(deh-pehn-'dehr)*
to describe	**describir** *(dehs-kree-'beehr)*
to discover	**descubrir** *(dehs-koob-'reer)*
to disinfect	**desinfectar** *(dehs-een-fehk-'tahr)*
to destroy	**destruir** *(dehs-troo-'eer)*
to determine	**determinar** *(deh-tehr-mee-'nahr)*
to diagnose	**diagnosticar** *(dee-ahg-nohs-tee-'kahr)*
to dilate	**dilatar** *(dee-lah-'tahr)*
to discuss	**discutir** *(dees-koo-'teer)*
to dissolve	**disolver** *(dee-sohl-'behr)*
to distribute	**distribuir** *(dees-tree-boo-'eer)*

to divide	**dividir** *(dee-bee-'deer)*
to eliminate	**eliminar** *(eh-lee-mee-'nahr)*
to evacuate	**evacuar** *(eh-bah-koo-'ahr)*
to evaluate	**evaluar** *(eh-bah-loo-'ahr)*
to examine	**examinar** *(ehk-sah-mee-'nahr)*
to exist	**existir** *(ehk-sees-'teer)*
to explore	**explorar** *(ehks-ploh-'rahr)*
to facilitate	**facilitar** *(fah-see-lee-'tahr)*
to form	**formar** *(fohr-'mahr)*
to fracture	**fracturar** *(frahk-too-'rahr)*
to function	**funcionar** *(foon-see-oh-'nahr)*
to include	**incluir** *(een-kloo-'eer)*
to indicate	**indicar** *(een-dee-'kahr)*
to infect	**infectar** *(een-fehk-'tahr)*
to inform	**informar** *(een-fohr-'mahr)*
to immunize	**inmunizar** *(een-moo-nee-'sahr)*
to inoculate	**inocular** *(ee-noh-koo'lahr)*
to inspect	**inspeccionar** *(eens-pehk-see-oh-'nahr)*
to interpret	**interpretar** *(een-tehr-preh-'tahr)*
to maintain	**mantener** *(mahn-teh-'nehr)*
to note	**notar** *(noh-'tahr)*
to observe	**observar** *(ohb-sehr-'bahr)*
to obstruct	**obstruir** *(ohbs-troo-'eer)*
to occur	**ocurrir** *(oh-koor-'reer)*
to operate on	**operar** *(oh-peh-'rahr)*
to penetrate	**penetrar** *(peh-neht-'rahr)*
to permit	**permitir** *(pehr-mee-'teer)*
to practice	**practicar** *(prahk-tee-'kahr)*
to prepare	**preparar** *(preh-pah-'rahr)*
to prevent	**prevenir** *(preh-beh-'neer)*
to proceed	**proceder** *(proh-seh-'dehr)*
to progress	**progresar** *(prohg-reh-'sahr)*
to prohibit	**prohibir** *(proh-ee-'beer)*
to prolong	**prolongar** *(proh-lohn-'gahr)*
to protect	**proteger** *(proh-teh-'hehr)*
to propose	**proponer** *(proh-poh-'nehr)*
to purify	**purificar** *(poo-ree-fee-'kahr)*
to recommend	**recomendar** *(reh-koh-mehn-'dahr)*
to recognize	**reconocer** *(reh-koh-noh-'sehr)*
to recuperate	**recuperar** *(reh-koo-peh-'rahr)*
to reduce	**reducir** *(reh-doo-'seer)*
to refer	**referir** *(reh-feh-'reer)*
to relate	**relatar** *(reh-lah-'tahr)*
to remedy	**remediar** *(reh-meh-dee-'ahr)*
to renovate	**renovar** *(reh-noh-'bahr)*

to repair	**reparar** *(reh-pah-'rahr)*
to repeat	**repetir** *(reh-peh-'teer)*
to resolve	**resolver** *(reh-sohl-'behr)*
to respect	**respetar** *(rehs-peh-'tahr)*
to restore	**restaurar** *(rehs-tah-oo-'rahr)*
to resuscitate	**resucitar** *(reh-soo-see-'tahr)*
to result	**resultar** *(reh-sool-'tahr)*
to resume	**resumir** *(reh-soo-'meer)*
to select	**seleccionar** *(seh-lehk-see-oh-'nahr)*
to separate	**separar** *(seh-pah-'rahr)*
to sterilize	**esterilizar** *(ehs-teh-ree-lee-'sahr)*
to suffer	**sufrir** *(soof-'reer)*
to transmit	**transmitir** *(trahns-mee-'teer)*
to ulcerate	**ulcerar** *(ool-seh-'rahr)*
to urinate	**orinar** *(oh-ree-'nahr)*
to use	**usar** *(oo-'sahr)*
to utilize	**utilizar** *(oo-tee-lee-'sahr)*
to ventilate	**ventilar** *(behn-tee-'lahr)*
to visit	**visitar** *(bee-see-'tahr)*
to vomit	**vomitar** *(boh-mee-'tahr)*

Word and Expression Finder

Do you need a translation in a hurry? Main entries, subentries, and useful questions and expressions are alphabetically listed in the English-Spanish Word and Expression Finder.

Feminine nouns are followed by the feminine article "the" (*la*) in parentheses, and the masculine nouns are followed by the masculine article "the" (*el*). The same happens with the plurals *las* and *los*. The gender of pronouns and adjectives is indicated by (m.) or (f.). Terms related to the main entry are indented once. Expressions and phrases related to the main entry are indented twice.

Does your Spanish patient wish to tell you something, but does not know the word? Show him or her the Spanish-English Word Finder, and let the patient point at the Spanish word. The English equivalent will appear in the right column.

English-Spanish Word Finder

a	un (m.); una (f.) (*oon, 'oo-nah*)
a.m.	de la mañana (*deh lah mah-'nyah-nah*)
abandonment	abandono (*el*) (*ehl ah-bahn-'doh-noh*)
abdominal pain	dolor abdominal (*el*) (*ehl doh-'lohr ahb-doh-mee-'nahl*)
abnormal	anormal (*ah-nohr-'mahl*)
abortion	aborto (*el*) (*ehl ah-'bohr-toh*)

Did you have an abortion?
¿Tuvo usted un aborto?
(*too-boh oo-'stehd oon ah-'bohr-toh*)

Do you want an abortion?
¿Desea usted un aborto?
(*deh-'seh-ah oo-'stehd oon ah-'bohr-toh*)

How many abortions have you had?
¿Cuántos abortos hatenido?
(*'kwahn-tohs ah-'bohr-tohs ah teh-'nee-doh*)

about	sobre (*'soh-breh*)
above	encima de (*ehn-'see-mah deh*)
abscess	absceso (*el*) (*ehl ahb-'seh-soh*)

abuse	abuso *(el)* *(ehl ah-'boo-soh)*
child abuse	abuso de los niños *(el)* *(ehl ah-'boo-soh deh lohs nee-'nyohs)*
drug abuse	abuso de las drogas *(el)* *(ehl ah-'boo-soh deh lahs 'droh-gahs)*

This boy has been abused.
Este niño ha sido abusado.
('ehs-teh 'nee-nyoh ah 'see-doh ah-boo-'sah-doh)

Who abused this girl?
¿Quién abusó a esta niña? *(kee-'ehn ah-boo-'soh ah 'ehs-tah 'nee-nyah)*

accident	accidente *(el)* *(ehl ahk-see-'dehn-teh)*
accumulate (to)	acumular *(ah-koo-moo-'lahr)*
acid	ácido *(el)* *(ehl 'ah-see-doh)*
acrylic	acrílico *(el)* *(ehl ah-'kree-lee-koh)*
action	acción *(la)* *(lah ahk-see·'ohn)*
addict	adicto *(el)*, adicta *(la)* *(ehl ah-'deek-toh, lah ah-'deek-tah)*
address	dirección *(la)* *(lah dee-rehk-see·'ohn)*

Give me your address.
Deme su dirección. *(deh-meh soo dee-rehk-see·'ohn)*

This is my address.
Esta es mi dirección.
(ehs-'tah ehs mee dee-rehk-see·'ohn)

adhesive tape	cinta adhesiva *(la)* *(lah 'seen-tah ah-deh-'see-bah)*
administration	administración *(la)* *(lah ahd-mee-nee-stra-see·'ohn)*

Go to the administration office.
Vaya a la oficina de la administración.
('bah-yah ah lah oh-fee-'see-nah deh lah ahd-mee-nees-trah-see·'ohn)

adopted child	niño adoptado *(el)* *(ehl 'neen-yoh ah-dohp-'tah-doh)*
adoption	adopción *(la)* *(lah ah-dohp-see·'ohn)*

You need adoption papers.
Necesita papeles de adopción.
(neh-seh-'see-tah pah-'peh-lehs deh ah-dohp-see·'ohn)

Do you wish to adopt a child?
¿Desea adoptar un niño?
(deh-'seh-ah ah-dohp-'tahr oon 'nee-nyoh)

after	después *(dehs-'pwehs)*

age	edad *(la)* *(lah eh-'dahd)*
	How old are you?
	¿Qué edad tiene usted?
	(keh eh-'dahd tee-'eh-neh oo-'stehd)
	What is his/her age?
	¿Cuál es su edad?
	('kwahl ehs soo eh-'dahd)
agency	agencia *(la)* *(lah ah-'hehn-see·ah)*
AIDS	SIDA *(el)* *(ehl 'see-dah)*
	You don't have AIDS.
	Usted no tiene el SIDA.
	(oo-'stehd noh tee-'eh-neh ehl 'see-dah)
	You have AIDS.
	Usted tiene SIDA.
	(oo-'stehd tee-'eh-neh 'see-dah)
air conditioning	aire acondicionado *(el)*
	(ehl 'ah·ee-reh ah-kohn-dee-see-oh-'nah-doh)
airport	aeropuerto *(el)* *(ehl ah·ee-roh-'pwehr-toh)*
alarm	alarma *(la)* *(lah ah-'lahr-mah)*
alcoholic	alcohólico *(el)*, alcohólica *(la)*
	(ehl ahl-koh-'oh-lee-koh, lah ahl-koh-'oh-lee-kah)
alive	vivo (m.); viva (f.) *('bee-boh, 'bee-bah)*
	He is alive.
	El está vivo. *(ehl ehs-'tah 'bee-boh)*
all	todo *('toh-doh)*
allergies	alergias *(las)* *(lahs ah-'lehr-hee·ahs)*
	Are you allergic to any food?
	¿Tiene alergias a alguna comida?
	(tee-'eh-neh ah-'lehr-hee·ahs ah ahl-'goo-nah koh-'mee-dah)
almost	casi *('kah-see)*
alone	solo (m.); sola (f.) *('soh-loh, 'soh-lah)*
already	ya *(yah)*
also	también *(tahm-'bee·ehn)*
always	siempre *(see-'ehm-preh)*
ambulance	ambulancia *(la)* *(lah ahm-boo-'lahn-see-ah)*
ambulatory care	cuidado ambulatorio *(el)*
	(ehl kwee-'dah-doh ahm-boo-lah-'toh-ree·oh)
ammonia	amoníaco *(el)* *(ehl ah-moh-'nee-ah-koh)*

amniotic sac	bolsa amniótica *(la)* *(lah 'bohl-sah ahm-nee-'oh-tee-kah)*
amoebas	amebas *(las)* *(lahs ah-'meh-bahs)*
amphetamines	anfetaminas *(las)* *(lahs ahn-feh-tah-'mee-nahs)*
amputate (to)	amputar *(ahm-poo-'tahr)*
amputation	amputación *(la)* *(lah ahm-poo-tah-see 'ohn)*
and	y *(ee)*
anemia	anemia *(la)* *(lah ah-'neh-mee·ah)*
anesthesia	anestesia *(la)* *(lah ah-nehs-'teh-see·ah)*
anger	cólera *(la)* *(lah 'koh-leh-rah)*
angry	enojado (m.); enojada (f.) *(eh-noh-'hah-doh, eh-noh-'hah-dah)*
angiogram	angiograma *(el)* *(ehl ahn-gee-oh-'grah-mah)*
animal	animal *(el)* *(ehl ah-nee-'mahl)*
	stuffed animals animales de peluche *(los)* *(lohs ah-nee-'mah-lehs deh peh-'loo-cheh)*
ankle	tobillo *(el)* *(ehl toh-'bee-yoh)*
	sprained ankle tobillo torcido *(el)* *(ehl toh-'bee-yoh tohr-'see-doh)*
answer (to)	contestar *(kohn-tehs-'tahr)*
	Answer all the questions. Conteste a todas las preguntas. *(kohn-'tehs-teh ah 'toh-dahs lahs preh-'goon-tahs)*
antibiotic	antibiótico *(el)* *(ehl ahn-tee-bee-'oh-tee-koh)*
anus	ano *(el)* *(ehl 'ah-noh)*
anxiety	ansiedad *(la)* *(lah ahn-see-eh-'dahd)*
anxiety attack	ataque de ansiedad *(el)* *(ehl ah-'tah-keh deh ahn-see-eh-'dahd)*
aorta	aorta *(la)* *(lah ah-'ohr-tah)*
appendectomy	apendectomía *(la)* *(lah ah-pehn-dehk-toh-'mee-ah)*
appendix	apéndice *(el)* *(ehl ah-'pehn-dee-seh)*
	Did they remove your appendix? ¿Le han sacado el apéndice? *(leh ahn sah-'kah-doh ehl ah-'pehn-dee-seh)*
appetite	apetito *(el)* *(ehl ah-peh-'tee-toh)*
	How is your appetite? ¿Cómo está su apetito? *('koh-moh ehs-'tah soo ah-peh-'tee-toh)*

apple	manzana *(la)* *(lah mahn-'sah-nah)*
apply (to)	aplicar *(ah-plee-'kahr)*
appointment	cita *(la)* *(lah 'see-tah)*
April	abril *(ah-'breel)*
area	área *(el)* *(ehl 'ah-reh-ah)*
arm	brazo *(el)* *(ehl 'brah-soh)*
armpit	axila *(la)* *(lah ahk-'see-lah)*
artery	arteria *(la)* *(lah ahr-'teh-ree·ah)*
arthritis	artritis *(la)* *(lah ahr-'tree-tees)*
artificial	artificial *(ahr-tee-fee-see-'ahl)*
ash tray	cenicero *(el)* *(ehl seh-nee-'seh-roh)*
ask (to)	preguntar *(preh-goon-'tahr)*
asleep	dormido (m.); dormida (f.) *(dohr-'mee-doh)*, *(dohr-'mee-dah)*
assist (to)	atender *(ah-tehn-'dehr)*
assistant	ayudante *(el)* *(ehl ah-yoo-'dahn-teh)*
asthma	asma *(el)* *(ehl 'ahs-mah)*
astigmatism	astigmatismo *(el)* *(ehl ahs-teeg mah 'tees-moh)*
at	en *(ehn)*
August	agosto *(ah-'gohs-toh)*
aunt	tía *(la)* *(lah 'tee-ah)*
auricle	aurícula *(la)* *(lah ow-'ree-koo-lah)*
automobile	automóvil *(el)* *(ehl ow-toh-moh-'beel)*
available	disponible *(dees-poh-'neeb-leh)*
avocado	aguacate *(el)* *(ehl ah-gwah-'kah-teh)*
avoid (to)	evitar *(eh-bee-'tahr)*
	Avoid eating nuts. Evite comer nueces. *(eh-'bee-teh koh-'mehr noo·'eh-sehs)*
awake	despierto (m.); despierta (f.) *(dehs-pee-'ehr-toh, dehs-pee-'ehr-tah)*
baby	bebé *(el)* *(ehl beh-'beh)*
back	espalda *(la)* *(lah ehs-'pahl-dah)*
	backaches dolores de espalda *(los)* *(lohs doh-'loh-rehs deh ehs-'pahl-dah)*
backbone	espinazo *(el)* *(ehl ehs-pee-'nah-soh)*
bacteriologist	bacteriólogo *(el)* *(ehl bahk-teh-ree-'oh-loh-goh)*

bad (n.)	mal (m. & f.) *(mahl)*
bad (adj.)	malo *('mah-loh)*
	This is bad.
	Esto está malo. *(ehs-'toh eh-'stah 'mah-loh)*
bad weather	mal tiempo *(el) (ehl mahl tee-'ehm-poh)*
baking soda	bicarbonato *(el) (ehl bee-kahr-boh-'nah-toh)*
balance	equilibrio *(el) (ehl eh-kee-'lee-bree·oh)*
	Do you lose your balance?
	¿Pierde el equilibrio?
	(pee-'ehr-deh ehl eh-kee-'lee-bree·oh)
bald	calvo *('kahl-boh)*
ball	pelota *(la) (lah peh-'loh-tah)*
balloons	globos *(los) (lohs 'gloh-bohs)*
banana	plátano *(el) (ehl 'plah-tah-noh)*
bandage	vendaje *(el) (ehl behn-'dah-heh)*
Band-Aid®	curita *(la) (lah koo-'ree-tah)*
bank	banco *(el) (ehl 'bahn-koh)*
baptism	bautismo *(el) (ehl bow-'tees-moh)*
barbiturates	barbitúricos *(los) (lohs bahr-bee-'too-ree-kohs)*
barrette	hebilla *(la) (lah eh-'bee-yah)*
basement	sótano *(el) (ehl 'soh-tah-noh)*
bassinet	bacinete *(el) (ehl bah-see-'neh-teh)*
bathe (to)	bañarse *(bah-'nyahr-seh)*
	Bathe *(request to)* Báñese. *('bah-nyeh-seh)*
	Do you need help to bathe?
	¿Necesita ayuda para bañarse?
	(neh-seh-'see-tah ah-'yoo-dah 'pah-rahbah-'nyahr-seh)
	Do you prefer a sponge bath?
	¿Prefiere un baño de esponja?
	(preh-fee-'eh-reh oon 'bah-nyoh dehehs-'pohn-hah)
bathroom	baño *(el) (ehl 'bah-nyoh)*
	Do you need help to go to the bathroom?
	¿Necesita ayuda para ir al baño?
	(neh-seh-'see-tah ah-'yoo-dah 'pah-rah eer ahl 'bah-nyoh)
bathtub	bañera *(la) (lah bah-'nyeh-rah)*
battery	pila *(la) (lah 'pee-lah)*

be able (to)   poder *(poh-'dehr)*

Are you able to stand?
¿Puede pararse? *('pweh-deh pah-'rahr-seh)*

be born (to)   nacer *(nah-'sehr)*

She was born on April 5.
Ella nació el cinco de abril.
('eh-yah nah-see-'oh ehl 'seen-koh de hah-'breel)

The baby will be born in May.
El bebé nacerá en mayo.
(ehl beh-'beh nah-seh-'rah ehn 'mah-yoh)

be (to)   estar, ser *(ehs-'tahr, sehr)*

beach   playa *(la) (lah 'plah-yah)*

beat (to)   golpear *(gohl-peh-'ahr)*

because   porque *('pohr-keh)*

bed   cama *(la) (lah 'kah-mah)*

bedpan   chata *(la) (lah 'chah-tah)*

Do you need a bedpan?
¿Necesita una chata?
(neh-seh-'see-tah 'oo-nah 'chah-tah)

bedrails   barandas de la cama *(las)*
(lahs bah-'rahn-dahs deh lah 'kah-mah)

bee   abeja *(la) (lah ah-'beh-hah)*

bee sting   picadura de abeja *(la)*
(lah pee-kah-'doo-rah deh ah 'beh hah)

beer   cerveza *(la) (lah sehr-'beh-sah)*

before   antes *('ahn-tehs)*

begin (to)   comenzar *(koh-mehn-'sahr)*

behind   detrás de *(deh-'trahs deh)*

bell   timbre *(el) (ehl 'teem-breh)*

belt   cinturón *(el) (ehl seen-too-'rohn)*

bend (to)   doblar *(doh-'blahr)*

Bend *(request to)*
Doble. *('doh-bleh)*

Bend your arm. Doble el brazo.
('doh-bleh ehl 'brah-soh)

benefits   beneficios *(los) (lohs beh-neh-'fee-see-ohs)*

benign   benigno *(beh-'neeg-noh)*

bent   doblado (m.); doblada (f.)
(doh-'blah-doh, doh-'blah-dah)

better	mejor *(meh-'hohr)*
between	entre *('ehn-treh)*
	between meals
	entre comidas *('ehn-treh koh-'mee-dahs)*
beverage	bebida *(la) (lah beh-'bee-dah)*
bicarbonate	bicarbonato *(el) (ehl bee-kahr-boh-'nah-toh)*
bicycle	bicicleta *(la) (lah bee-see-'kleh-tah)*
bifocals	bifocales *(los) (lohs bee-foh-'kah-lehs)*
big	grande *('grahn-deh)*
billfold	billetera *(la) (lah bee-yeh-'teh-rah)*
biopsy	biopsia *(la) (lah bee-'ohp-see·ah)*
bird	pájaro *(el) (ehl 'pah-hah-roh)*
bird flu	influenza aviar *(la) (lah een-floo-'ehn-sah ah-vee-'ahr)*
birth	nacimiento *(el) (ehl nah-see-mee-'ehn-toh)*
	birth control
	anticoncepción *(la) (lah ahn-tee-kohn-sehp-see·'ohn)*
	birth control pills
	píldoras anticonceptivas *(las)*
	(lahs 'peel-doh-rahs ahn-tee-kohn-sehp-'tee-vahs)
	birth defect
	defecto de nacimiento *(el)*
	(ehl deh-'fehk-toh deh nah-see-mee-'ehn-toh)
birthdate	fecha de nacimiento *(la)*
	(lah 'feh-chah deh nah-see-mee-'ehn-toh)
bite (to)	morder *(mohr-'dehr)*
	Bite *(request to)*
	Muerda. *('mwehr-dah)*
black	negro *(el)*; negra *(la) (ehl 'neh-groh, lah 'neh-grah)*
black boy	niño negro *(el) (ehl 'nee-nyoh 'neh-groh)*
black girl	niña negra *(la) (lah 'nee-nyah 'neh-grah)*
black man	hombre negro *(el) (ehl 'ohm-breh 'neh-groh)*
black woman	mujer negra *(la) (lah moo-'hehr 'neh-grah)*
blackout	pérdida de conocimiento *(la)*
	(lah 'pehr-dee-dah deh koh-noh-see-mee-'ehn-toh)
bladder	vejiga *(la) (lah beh-'hee-gah)*
	bladder infection
	infección de la vejiga *(la)*
	(lah een-fehk-see·'ohn deh lah beh-'hee-gah)

blanket	cobija *(la)*, frazada *(la)* *(lah koh-'bee-hah, lah frah-'sah-dah)*
bleeding	hemorragia *(la)* *(lah eh-moh-'rrah-hee·ah)*
Bless you!	¡Salud! *(sah-'lood)*
blind	ciego *(el)*, ciega *(la)* *(ehl see-'eh-goh, lah see-'eh-gah)*
blister	ampolla *(la)* *(lah ahm-'poh-yah)*
blisters	ampollas *(las)* *(lahs ahm-'poh-yahs)*
blond	rubio *(el)*; rubia *(la)* *(ehl 'rroo-bee·oh, lah 'rroo-bee·ah)*
blood	sangre *(la)* *(lah 'sahn-greh)*
	blood count recuento de la sangre *(el)* *(eh reh-'kwehn-toh deh lah 'sahn-greh)*
	blood pressure presión de la sangre *(la)* *(lah preh-see·'ohn deh lah 'sahn-greh)*
	blood transfusion transfusión de sangre *(la)* *(lah trahns-foo-see·'ohn deh 'sahn-greh)*
	blood type tipo de sangre *(el)* *(ehl 'tee-poh deh 'sahn-greh)*
	blood in the stool sangre en los excrementos *(la)* *(lah 'sahn-greh ehn lohs ehks-kreh-'mehn-tohs)*
blouse	blusa *(la)* *(lah 'bloo-sah)*
blue	azul *(ah-'sool)*
Blue Cross	Cruz Azul *(la)* *(lah kroos ah-'sool)*
Blue Shield	Escudo Azul *(el)* *(ehl ehs-'koo-doh ah-'sool)*
bobby pin	horquilla *(la)* *(lah ohr-'kee-yah)*
body	cuerpo *(el)* *(ehl 'kwehr-poh)*
bone	hueso *(el)* *(ehl 'weh-soh)*
	bone marrow médula *(la)* *(lah 'meh-doo-lah)*
	broken bone hueso roto *(el)* *(ehl 'weh-soh 'roh-toh)*
book	libro *(el)* *(ehl 'lee-broh)*
boots	botas *(las)* *(lahs 'boh-tahs)*
bored	aburrido (m.); aburrida (f.) *(ah-boor-'ree-doh, ah-boor-'ree-dah)*

bottle	botella *(la)* *(lah boh-'teh-yah)*
	bottle nipple
	chupete *(el)* *(ehl choo-'peh-teh)*
botulism	botulismo *(el)* *(ehl boh-too-'lees-moh)*
boyfriend	novio *(el)* *(ehl 'noh-bee·oh)*
bracelet	brazalete *(el)* *(ehl brah-sah-'leh-teh)*
braces	frenillos *(los)* *(lohs freh-'nee-yohs)*
brain	cerebro *(el)* *(ehl seh-'reh-broh)*
brain cancer	cáncer del cerebro *(el)*
	(ehl 'kahn-sehr dehl seh-'reh-broh)
brassiere	sostén *(el)* *(ehl sohs-'tehn)*
bread	pan *(el)* *(ehl pahn)*
breakfast	desayuno *(el)* *(ehl deh-sah-'yoo-noh)*
breast-feed (to)	lactar *(lahk-'tahr)*
breast feeding	amamantamiento *(el)*
	(ehl ah-mah-mahn-tah-mee-'ehn-toh)
breasts	senos *(los)*, pechos *(los)*
	(lohs 'seh-nohs; lohs 'peh-chohs)
breath	aliento *(el)* *(ehl ah-lee-'ehn-toh)*
breathe (to)	respirar *(rehs-pee-'rahr)*
	Breathe *(request to)*
	Respire. *(rehs-'pee-reh)*
breathing	respiración *(la)* *(lah rehs-pee-rah-see·'ohn)*
bridge	puente *(el)* *(ehl 'pwehn-teh)*
bring (to)	traer *('trah-ehr)*
	Bring a sample in this cup.
	Traiga una muestra en este vaso.
	('trah·ee-gah 'oo-nah 'mwehs-trah ehn 'eh-steh 'bah-soh)
	Bring *(request to)*
	Traiga. *('trah·ee-gah)*
bronchitis	bronquitis *(la)* *(lah brohn-'kee-tees)*
brother	hermano *(el)* *(ehl ehr-'mah-noh)*
brother-in-law	cuñado *(el)* *(ehl koo-'nyah-doh)*
brown	café *(kah-'feh)*
brunette	morena *(moh-'reh-nah)*
brush	cepillo *(el)* *(ehl seh-'pee-yoh)*
	Brush *(request to)*
	Cepíllese. *(seh-'pee-yeh-seh)*

buddy	compañero (m.); compañera (f.) (*kohm-pah-nee-'eh-roh, kohm-pah-nee-'eh-rah*)
building	edificio (*el*) (*ehl eh-dee-'fee-se·oh*)
bump	protuberancia (*la*) (*lah proh-too-beh-'rahn-see·ah*)
bumps	protuberancias (*las*) (*lahs proh-too-beh-'rahn-see-ahs*)
bunion	juanete (*el*) (*ehl wah-'neh-teh*)
burn (to)	quemar (*keh-'mahr*)
burning (n.)	ardor (*el*) (*ehl ahr-'dohr*)
burning (adj.)	quemante (*keh-'mahn-teh*)
burp (to)	eructar (*eh-rook-'tahr*)
bus	autobús (*el*) (*ehl ow-toh-'boos*)
bush	arbusto (*el*) (*ehl ahr-'boos-toh*)
business	negocio (*el*) (*ehl neh-goh-'see·oh*)
busy	ocupado (m.); ocupada (f.) (*oh-koo-'pah-doh, oh-koo-'pah-dah*)
but	pero (*'peh-roh*)
butter	mantequilla (*la*) (*lah mahn-teh-'kee-yah*)
buttock	nalga (*la*) (*lah 'nahl-gah*)
cabbage	repollo (*el*) (*ehl reh-'poh-yoh*)
cabinet	gabinete (*el*) (*ehl gah-bee-'neh-teh*)
cafeteria	cafetería (*la*) (*lah kah-feh-teh-'ree-ah*)
cake	torta (*la*), bizcocho (*el*) (*lah 'tohr-tah; ehl bees-'koh-choh*)
calendar	calendario (*el*) (*ehl kah-lehn-'dah-ree·oh*)
calf	pantorrilla (*la*) (*lah pahn-toh-'rree-yah*)
call (to)	llamar (*yah-'mahr*)
	Call me. Llámeme. (*'yah-meh-meh*)
	Call _____ . (*request to*) Llame a _____ . (*'yah-meh ah ___ .*)
	Call the doctor. Llame al doctor. (*'yah-meh ahl dohk-'tohr*)
calluses	callos (*los*) (*lohs 'kah-yohs*)
calm	calmado (m.); calmada (f.) (*kahl-'mah-doh, kahl-'mah-dah*)
	Be at ease. Esté tranquilo. (*ehs-'teh trahn-'kee-loh*)
can (container)	lata (*la*) (*lah 'lah-tah*)

cancel (to)	cancelar *(kahn-seh-'lahr)*
cancer	cáncer *(el) (ehl 'kahn-sehr)*
candy	dulce *(el) (ehl 'dool-seh)*
cane	bastón *(el) (ehl bahs-'tohn)*
canker sore	úlcera en la boca *(la)* *(lah 'ool-seh-rah ehn lah 'boh-kah)*
CAP test	prueba de CAP *(la) (lah 'proo-eh-bah deh KAHP)*
capsule	cápsula *(la) (lah 'kahp-soo-lah)*
	Don't take the capsules. No tome las cápsulas. *(noh 'toh-meh lahs 'kah-psoo-lahs)*
car	carro *(el) (ehl 'kah-rroh)*
carbon monoxide	monóxido de carbono *(el)* *(ehl moh-'nohk-see-doh deh kahr-'boh-noh)*
cardiologist	cardiólogo *(el) (ehl kahr-dee-'oh-loh-goh)*
care	cuidado *(el) (ehl kwee-'dah-doh)*
carpenter	carpintero *(el) (ehl kahr-peen-'teh-roh)*
carrot	zanahoria *(la) (lah sah-nah-'oh-ree·ah)*
carry (to)	llevar *(yeh-'bahr)*
	Carry *(request to)* Lleve. *('yeh-beh)*
cartilage	cartílago *(el) (ehl kahr-'tee-lah-goh)*
cash	efectivo *(el) (ehl eh-'fehk-'tee-boh)*
cashier	cajero *(el)*, cajera *(la)* *(ehl kah-'heh-roh, lah kah-'heh-rah)*
cast	armadura de yeso *(la)* *(lah ahr-mah-'doo-rah deh 'yes-oh)*
cat	gato *(el)*, gata *(la) (ehl 'gah-toh, lah 'gah-tah)*
cataract	catarata *(la) (lah kah-tah-'rah-tah)*
catheter	catéter *(el) (ehl kah-'teh-tehr)*
cause (to)	causar *(kow-'sahr)*
cavity	carie *(la) (lah 'kah-ree·eh)*
CD	disco compacto *(el) (ehl 'dees-koh kohm-'pahk-toh)*
ceiling	cielo raso *(el) (ehl see-'eh-loh 'rrah-soh)*
cell	célula *(la) (lah 'seh-loo-lah)*
cell phone	teléfono cellular *(el)* *(ehl teh-'leh-foh-noh seh-loo-'lahr)*
cement	cemento *(el) (ehl seh-'mehn-toh)*

cereal	cereal (*el*) (*ehl seh-reh-'ahl*)
cerebral palsy	parálisis cerebral (*la*) (*lah pah-'rah-lee-sees seh-reh-'brahl*)
Certificate of Live Birth	partida de nacimiento vivo (*la*) (*lah pahr-'tee-dah deh nah-see-mee-'ehn toh 'bee-boh*)
certify (to)	certificar (*sehr-tee-fee-'kahr*)
cervical canal	canal cervical (*el*) (*ehl kah-'nahl sehr-bee-'kahl*)
cervix	cuello uterino (*el*) (*ehl 'kweh-yoh oo-teh-'ree-noh*)
cesarean section	operación cesárea (*la*) (*lah oh-peh-rah-see·'ohn ceh-'sah-ree-ah*)
CF	fibrosis cística (*la*) (*lah fee-'broh-sees 'sees-tee-kah*)
chair	silla (*la*) (*lah 'see-yah*)
change (to)	cambiar (*kahm-bee-'ahr*)
	Change the baby. Cambie al bebé. (*'kahm-bee·eh ahl beh-'beh*)
chapel	capilla (*la*) (*lah kah-'pee-yah*)
charge	cargo (*el*) (*ehl 'kahr-goh*)
chart	gráfico (*el*) (*ehl 'grah-fee-koh*)
check	cheque (*el*) (*ehl 'cheh-keh*)
check (to)	verificar (*beh-ree-fee-'kahr*)
checkup	reconocimiento (*el*) (*ehl reh-koh-noh-see-mee-'ehn-toh*)
	Did you have a checkup? ¿Le hicieron un reconocimiento? (*leh ee-see-'eh-rohn oon reh-koh-noh-see-mee-'ehn-toh*)
	You need a checkup. Necesita un reconocimiento. (*neh-seh-'see-tah oon reh-koh-noh-see-mee-'ehn-toh*)
cheek	mejilla (*la*) (*lah meh-'hee-yah*)
cheekbone	pómulo (*el*) (*ehl 'poh-moo-loh*)
cheese	queso (*el*) (*ehl 'keh-soh*)
chemical	producto químico (*el*) (*ehl proh-'dook-toh 'kee-mee-koh*)
cherry	cereza (*la*) (*lah seh-'reh-sah*)
chest	pecho (*el*) (*ehl 'peh-choh*)
chest pain	dolor de pecho (*el*) (*ehl doh-'lohr deh 'peh-choh*)
chew (to)	mascar, masticar (*mahs-'kahr, mahs-tee-'kahr*)
	Chew (*request to*) Mastique. (*mahs-'tee-keh*)

chicken	pollo *(el)* *(ehl 'poh-yoh)*
chicken pox	varicela *(la)* *(lah bah-ree-'seh-lah)*
child	niño *(el)*, niña *(la)* *(ehl 'neen-yoh, lah 'neen-yah)*
	Is it your first child?
	¿Es su primer niño? *(ehs soo pree-'mehr 'nee-nyoh)*
childbirth	parto *(el)* *(ehl 'pahr-toh)*
	natural childbirth
	parto natural *(el)* *(ehl 'pahr-toh nah-too-'rahl)*
childcare	cuidado del niño *(el)*
	(ehl kwee-'dah-doh dehl 'neen-yoh)
chills	escalofríos *(los)* *(lohs ehs-kah-loh-'free-ohs)*
chin	barbilla *(la)* *(lah bahr-'bee-yah)*
chiropractor	quiropráctico *(el)* *(ehl kee-roh-'prahk-tee-koh)*
chocolate	chocolate *(el)* *(ehl choh-koh-'lah-teh)*
cholera	cólera *(el)* *(ehl 'koh-leh-rah)*
church	iglesia *(la)* *(lah ee-'gleh-see·ah)*
cigar	puro *(el)* *(ehl 'poo-roh)*
cigarette	cigarrillo *(el)* *(ehl see-gah-'rree-yoh)*
circumcision	circuncisión *(la)* *(lah seer-koon-see-see·'ohn)*
city	ciudad *(la)* *(lah see-oo-'dahd)*
	city block
	cuadra *(la)* *(lah 'kwah-drah)*
clasp	broche *(el)* *(ehl 'broh-cheh)*
class	clase *(la)* *(lah 'klah-seh)*
clean	limpio (m.); limpia (f.) *('leem-pee·oh, 'leem-pee-ah)*
clean (to)	limpiar *(leem-pee-'ahr)*
	Is everything clean?
	¿Está todo muy limpio?
	(eh-'stah 'toh-doh 'moo·ee 'leem-pee·oh)
	Clean *(request to)*
	Limpie. *('leem-pee·eh)*
cleaning	limpieza *(la)* *(lah leem-pee-'eh-sah)*
cleanliness	limpieza *(la)* *(lah leem-pee-'eh-sah)*
clear	despejado *(dehs-peh-'hah-doh)*
cleft lip	labio leporino *(el)* *(ehl 'lah-bee-oh leh-poh-'ree-noh)*
clinical study	estudio clínico *(el)* *(ehl ehs-'too-dee-oh 'klee-nee-koh)*
close (to)	cerrar *(seh-'rrahr)*

Close *(request to)*
Cierre *(see-'eh-rreh)*

Close your mouth.
Cierre la boca. *(see-'eh-rreh lah 'boh-kah)*

closed	cerrado (m.); cerrada (f.) *(seh-'rrah-doh, seh-'rrah-dah)*
closer	más cerca *(mahs 'sehr-kah)*
closet	ropero *(el) (ehl roh-'peh-roh)*
clothing	ropa *(la) (lah 'roh-pah)*
cloudy	nublado *(noo-'blah-doh)*
cocaine	cocaína *(la) (lah koh-kah-'ee-nah)*
codeine	codeína *(la) (lah koh-deh-'ee-nah)*
coffee	café *(el) (ehl 'kah-feh)*
cold	frío *(el) (ehl 'free-oh)*

Are you cold?
¿Tiene frío? *(tee-'eh-neh 'free-oh)*

cold (illness)	resfrío *(el) (ehl rehs-'free-oh)*

Does he/she have a cold?
¿Tiene un resfrío?
(ehl rehs-'free-oh tee-'eh-neh oon rehs-'free-oh)

colic	cólico *(el) (ehl 'koh-lee-koh)*
collarbone	clavícula *(la) (lah klah-'bee-koo-lah)*
colon	colon *(el) (ehl 'koh-lohn)*
colonoscopy	colonoscopía *(la) (lah koh-loh-nohs-koh-'pee-ah)*
color	color *(el) (ehl koh-'lohr)*
color-blind	daltónico *(dahl-'toh-nee-koh)*
comb	peine *(el) (ehl 'peh·ee-neh)*
come (to)	venir *(beh-'neer)*

Come *(request to)*
Venga. *('behn-gah)*

comfortable	cómodo *('koh-moh-doh)*
common	común *(koh-'moon)*
company	compañía *(la) (lah kohm-pah-'nyee-ah)*
complex	complejo *(kohm-'pleh-hoh)*
compress	compresa *(la) (lah kohm-'preh-sah)*
computer	computadora *(la) (lah kohm-poo-tah-'doh-rah)*
concussion	concusión *(la) (lah kohn-koo-see-'ohn)*
condition	estado *(el) (ehl ehs-'tah-doh)*

She is in bad condition.
Ella está en mal estado.
('eh-yah eh-'stah ehn mahl eh-'stah-doh)

He is in good condition.
El está en buen estado.
(ehl eh-'stah ehn bwehn ehs-'tah-doh)

condom
condón *(el) (ehl kohn-'dohn)*

Always use condoms.
Siempre use condones.
(see-'ehm-preh 'oo-seh kohn-'doh-nehs)

conference room
sala de conferencias *(la)*
(lah 'sah-lah deh kohn-feh-'rehn-see-ahs)

confused
confuso (m.); confusa (f.) *(kohn-'foo-soh, koh-'foo-sah)*

confusion
confusión *(la) (lah kohn-foo-see-'ohn)*

conjunctivitis
conjuntivitis *(la) (lah kohn-hoon-tee-'vee-tees)*

conscious
consciente (m. & f.) *(kohn-see-'ehn-teh)*

consent form
formulario de consentimiento *(el)*
(ehl fohr-moo-'lah-ree-oh deh kohn-sehn-tee-mee-'ehn-toh)

constant
constante *(kohn-'stahn-teh)*

constipated
estreñido *(ehs-treh-'nyee-doh)*

Are you constipated?
¿Está estreñido? *(eh-'stah ehs-treh-'nyee-doh)*

constipation
estreñimiento *(el) (ehl ehs-treh-nyee-mee-'ehn-toh)*

consult (to)
consultar *(kohn-sool-'tahr)*

Consult with your doctor.
Consulte a su médico.
(kohn-'sool-teh ah soo 'meh-dee-koh)

contact lenses
lentes de contacto *(los)*
(lohs 'lehn-tehs deh kohn-'tahk-toh)

Do you wear contact lenses?
¿Usa lentes de contacto?
('oo-sah 'lehn-tehs deh kohn-'tahk-toh)

When were they prescribed?
¿Cuándo se los recetaron?
('kwahn-doh se lohs reh-seh-'tah-rohn)

continuous passive motion machine
máquina de movimiento continuo *(la)*
(lah 'mah-kee-nah deh moh-bee-mee-'ehn-toh kohn-'tee-noo-oh)

contractions	contracciones (*las*) (*lahs kohn-trahk-see·'oh-nehs*)
	How often are the contractions?
	¿Cuán rápido vienen las contracciones? (*kwahn 'rah-pee-doh bee-'eh-nehn lahs kohn-trahk-see·'oh-nehs*)
control (to)	controlar (*kohn-troh-'lahr*)
	Control the child.
	Controle al niño. (*kohn-'troh-leh ahl 'nee-nyoh*)
convulsion	convulsión (*la*) (*lah kohn-bool-see·'ohn*)
cook	cocinero (m.); cocinera (f.) (*koh-see-'neh-roh, koh-see-'neh-rah*)
cook (to)	cocinar (*koh-see-'nahr*)
	Cook without salt.
	Cocine sin sal. (*koh-'see-neh seen sahl*)
cookie	galleta (*la*) (*lah gah-'yeh-tah*)
co-pay amount	co-pago (*el*) (*ehl koh-'pah-goh*)
corn	callo (*el*) (*ehl 'kah-yoh*)
corn (food)	maíz (*el*) (*ehl mah-'ees*)
corner	esquina (*la*) (*lah ehs-'kee-nah*)
correct	correcto (*koh-'rrehk-toh*)
cosmetics	cosméticos (*los*) (*lohs kohs-'meh-tee-kohs*)
cosmetic surgery	cirugía cosmética (*la*) (*lah see-roo-'hee-ah kohs-'meh-tee-kah*)
cost	costo (*el*) (*ehl 'kohs-toh*)
cough	tos (*la*) (*lah tohs*)
cough (to)	toser (*toh-'sehr*)
	painful cough
	tos dolorosa (*la*) (*lah tohs doh-loh-'roh-sah*)
	Do you cough often?
	¿Tose a menudo? (*'toh-seh ah meh-'noo-doh*)
	Cough (*request to*)
	Tosa. (*'toh-sah*)
cough syrup	jarabe para la tos (*el*) (*ehl hah-'rah-beh 'pah-rah lah tohs*)
counsel	consejo (*el*) (*ehl kohn-'seh-hoh*)
counseling	consejería (*la*) (*lah kohn-seh-heh-'ree-ah*)
counselor	consejero (*el*), consejera (*la*) (*ehl kohn-seh-'heh-roh; lah kohn-seh'heh-rah*)
	Go to the counselor.
	Vaya al consejero. (*'bah-yah ahl kohn-seh-'heh-roh*)

count	recuento *(el)* *(ehl reh-'kwehn-toh)*
countryside	campo *(el)* *(ehl 'kahm-poh)*
couple	pareja *(la)* *(lah pah-'reh-hah)*
cousin	primo (m.); prima (f.) *('pree-moh, 'pree-mah)*
cover (to)	tapar *(tah-'pahr)*
	Cover the baby.
	Tape al bebé. *('tah-peh ahl beh-'beh)*
	Cover yourself.
	Tápese. *('tah-peh-seh)*
coverage	cobertura *(la)* *(lah koh-behr-'too-rah)*
CPR	resucitación cardiopulmonar *(la)* *(lah reh-soo-see-tah-see-'ohn kahr-dee-oh-pool-moh-'nahr)*
crack (drug)	crack *(krahk)*
cramps	calambres *(los)* *(lohs kah-'lahm-brehs)*
	Do you have cramps often?
	¿Tiene calambres a menudo? *(tee-'eh-neh kah-'lahm-brehs ah meh-'noo-doh)*
cranium, skull	cráneo *(el)* *(ehl 'krah-neh-oh)*
crash (to)	chocar *(choh-'kahr)*
crawl (to)	gatear *(gah-teh-'ahr)*
crazy	loco (m.); loca (f.) *('loh-koh, 'loh-kah)*
cream	crema *(la)* *(lah 'kreh-mah)*
credit card	tarjeta de crédito *(la)* *(lah tahr-'heh-tah deh 'kreh-dee-toh)*
	Do you have a credit card?
	¿Tiene tarjeta de crédito? *(tee-'eh-neh tahr-'heh-tah deh 'kreh-dee-toh)*
crib	cuna *(la)* *(lah 'koo-nah)*
criminal	criminal (m. & f.) *(ehl (lah) kree-mee-'nahl)*
cross (to)	cruzar *('kroo-sahr)*
	Cross *(request to)*
	Cruce. *('kroo-seh)*
	Cross your arms.
	Cruce los brazos. *('kroo-seh lohs 'brah-sohs)*
cross-eyed	bizco (m.); bizca (f.) *('bees-koh; 'bees-kah)*
crown	corona *(la)* *(lah koh-'roh-nah)*

cry (to)	llorar (*yoh-'rahr*)
	Does the baby cry a lot?
	¿Llora mucho el bebé?
	(*'yoh-rah 'moo-choh ehl beh-'beh*)
CT scan	tomografía computarizada (*la*)
	(*lah toh-moh-grah-'fee-ah kom-poo-tah-ree-'zah-dah*)
cup	copa (*la*) (*lah 'koh-pah*)
curb	orilla (*la*) (*lah oh-'ree-yah*)
cure (to)	curar (*koo-'rahr*)
	You are cured.
	Está usted curado. (*eh-'stah oo-'stehd koo-'rah-doh*)
curtains	cortinas (*las*) (*lahs kohr-'tee-nahs*)
cut	corte (*el*) (*ehl 'kohr-teh*)
	Are you cut?
	¿Está cortado? (*eh-'stah kohr-'tah-doh*)
	He is cut.
	El está cortado. (*ehl eh-'stah kohr-'tah-doh*)
	She cut herself.
	Ella se cortó. (*'eh-yah seh kohr-'toh*)
cute	simpático (*seem-'pah-tee-koh*)
	How cute!
	¡Qué simpático! (*keh seem-'pah-tee-koh*)
cyanide	cianuro (*el*) (*ehl see-ah-'noo-roh*)
cyst	quiste (*el*) (*ehl 'kees-teh*)
cystic fibrosis	fibrosis cística (*la*) (*lah fee-'broh-sees 'sees-tee-kah*)
cystoscopy	cistoscopía (*la*) (*lah sees-toh-skoh-'pee-ah*)
dairy products	productos lácteos (*los*)
	(*lohs proh-'dook-toh 'lack-teh-ohs*)
Daltonism	daltonismo (*el*) (*ehl dahl-toh-'nees-moh*)
dangerous	peligroso (*peh-lee-'groh-soh*)
	It is dangerous.
	Es peligroso. (*ehs peh-lee-'groh-soh*)
	It is not dangerous.
	No es peligroso. (*noh ehs peh-lee-'groh-soh*)
dark-skinned	prieto (*coll.*) (*pree-'eh-toh*)
daughter	hija (*la*) (*lah 'ee-hah*)
daughter-in-law	nuera (*la*) (*lah 'noo-eh-rah*)
day	día (*el*) (*ehl 'dee-ah*)

dead	muerto (m.); muerta (f.) (*'mwehr-toh, 'mwehr-tah*)
	He is dead.
	El está muerto. (*ehl eh-'stah 'mwehr-toh*)
	She is not dead.
	Ella no está muerta.
	(*'eh-yah noh eh-'stah 'mwehr-tah*)
deaf	sordo (m.); sorda (f.) (*'sohr-doh, 'sohr-dah*)
death	muerte (*la*) (*lah 'mwehr-teh*)
decaffeinated	descafeinado (*dehs-kah-feh·ee-'nah-doh*)
December	diciembre (*dee-see-'ehm-breh*)
decongestant	descongestionante (*el*)
	(*ehl dehs-kohn-hehs-tee-oh-'nahn-teh*)
deductible	deducible (*el*) (*ehl deh-doo-'seeb-leh*)
deep	profundo (m.); profunda (f.)
	(*proh-'foon-doh, proh-'foon-dah*)
defecate (to)	defecar (*deh-feh-'kahr*)
dehydration	deshidratación (*la*) (*lah dehs-ee-drah-tah-see-'ohn*)
delivery room	sala de partos (*la*) (*lah 'sah-lah deh 'pahr-tohs*)
dental care	cuidado dental (*el*) (*ehl koo-ee-'dah-doh dehn-'tahl*)
dental floss	hilo dental (*el*) (*ehl 'ee-loh dehn-'tahl*)
denture	dentadura postiza (*la*)
	(*lah dehn-tah-'doo-rah pohs-'tee-sah*)
	Do the dentures fit well?
	¿Le calzan bien las dentaduras postizas?
	(*leh 'kahl-sahn 'bee·ehn lahs dehn-tah-doo-rahs pohs-'tee-sahs*)
	Do you have denture pain?
	¿Tiene dolor de las dentaduras postizas?
	(*tee-'eh-neh doh-'lohr deh lahs dehn-tah-'doo-rahs pohs-'tee-sahs*)
	Do you wear dentures?
	¿Tiene dentaduras postizas?
	(*tee-'eh-neh dehn-tah-'doo-rahs pohs'tee-sahs*)
	You need dentures.
	Usted necesita dentaduras postizas.
	(*oo-'stehd neh-seh-'see-tah dehn-tah-'doo-rahs pohs-'tee-sahs*)
deodorant	desodorante (*el*) (*ehl dehs-oh-doh-'rahn-teh*)
department	departamento (*el*) (*ehl deh-pahr-tah-'mehn-toh*)

dependent	dependiente *(el)* *(ehl deh-pehn-dee-'ehn-teh)*
deposit	depósito *(el)* *(ehl deh-'poh-see-toh)*
depressants	sedantes *(los)* *(lohs seh-'dahn-tehs)*
depression	depresión *(la)* *(lah deh-preh-see-'ohn)*
	Do you feel depressed?
	¿Se siente deprimido?
	(seh see-'ehn-teh deh-pree-'mee-doh)
dermatologist	dermatólogo *(el)* *(ehl dehr-mah-'toh-loh-goh)*
description	descripción *(la)* *(lah dehs-'kreep-see-on)*
	Describe *(request to)*
	Describa. *(dehs-'kree-bah)*
desert	desierto *(el)* *(ehl deh-see-'ehr-toh)*
desire	deseo *(el)* *(ehl deh-'seh-oh)*
desk	escritorio *(el)* *(ehl ehs-kree-'toh-ree·oh)*
desperate	desesperado (m.); desesperada (f.)
	(deh-sehs-peh-'rah-doh; deh-sehs-peh-'rah-dah)
dessert	postre *(el)* *(ehl 'pohs-treh)*
detect (to)	detectar *(deh-tehk-'tahr)*
detergent	detergente *(el)* *(ehl deh-tehr-'hehn-teh)*
diabetes	diabetes *(la)* *(lah dee-ah-'beh-tehs)*
diagnosis	diagnóstico *(el)* *(ehl dee-ahg-'nohs-tee-koh)*
dial (to)	marcar *('mahr-kahr)*
	Dial *(request to)*
	Marque. *('mahr-keh)*
diaper	pañal *(el)* *(ehl pah-'nyahl)*
diaphragm	diafragma *(el)* *(ehl dee-ah-'frahg-mah)*
	Do you wear a diaphragm?
	¿Tiene puesto un diafragma?
	(tee-'eh-neh 'pwehs-toh oon dee-ah-'frahg-mah)
diarrhea	diarrea *(la)* *(lah dee-ah-'rreh-ah)*
	Do you have diarrhea?
	¿Tiene diarrea?
	(tee-'eh-neh dee-ah-'rreh-ah)
die (to)	morir *(moh-'reer)*
	What did he/she die of?
	¿De qué se murió?
	(deh keh seh moo-ree-'oh)
	He/she is going to die.
	Se va a morir. *(seh bah ah moh-'reer)*

diet   dieta *(la)* *(lah dee-'eh-tah)*
bland diet
dieta blanda *(una)* *('oo-nah dee-'eh-tah 'blahn-dah)*
diabetic diet
dieta para diabéticos *(una)*
('oo-nah dee-'eh-tah 'pah-rah dee-ah-'beh-tee-kohs)
restricted diet
dieta limitada *(una)*
('oo-nah dee-'eh-tah lee-mee-'tah-dah)
You have to follow the diet.
Tiene que seguir la dieta.
(tee-'eh-neh keh seh-'geer lah dee-'eh-tah)

dietician   dietista *(el)*, dietista *(la)*
(ehl dee-eh-'tees-tah, lah dee-eh-'tees-tah)

different   diferente *(dee-feh-'rehn-teh)*

difficult   difícil *(dee-'fee-seel)*

dinner   cena *(la)* *(lah 'seh-nah)*

diphteria   difteria *(la)* *(lah deef-'teh-ree·ah)*

directions   instrucciones *(las)* *(lahs een-strook-see-'oh-nehs)*

direct pressure   presión directa *(la)* *(lah preh-see-'ohn dee-'rehk-tah)*

dirt   tierra *(la)* *(lah tee-'eh-rrah)*

dirty   sucio (m.); sucia (f.) *('soo-see·oh, 'soo-see·ah)*

disability   incapacidad *(la)* *(lah een-kah-pah-see-'dahd)*

discharge   flujo *(el)* *(ehl 'floo-hoh)*

discharge (to)   dar de alta *(dahr deh 'ahl-tah)*
You will be discharged tomorrow.
Mañana lo darán de alta.
(mah-'nyah-nah loh dah-'rahn deh 'ahl-tah)

discount   descuento *(el)* *(ehl dehs-kwehn-toh)*

disease   enfermedad *(la)* *(lah ehn-fehr-meh-'dahd)*

disinfect (to)   desinfectar *(dehs-een-fehk-'tahr)*

disinfectant   desinfectante *(el)* *(ehl deh-seen-fehk-'tahn-teh)*

disorder   trastorno *(el)* *(ehl trahs-'tohr-noh)*

disturbance   disturbio *(el)* *(ehl dees-'toor-bee·oh)*

divorce   divorcio *(el)* *(ehl dee-'bohr-see·oh)*

dizziness   mareos *(los)* *(lohs mah-'reh-ohs)*

dizzy   mareado (m.); mareada (f.)
(mah-reh-'ah-doh, mah-reh-'ah-dah)

do (to)	hacer (*ah-'sehr*)
	Did you feel . . .?
	¿Sintió usted. . . ? (*seen-tee-'oh oo-'stehd*)
	Did you have. . .?
	¿Tuvo usted . . .? (*'too-boh oo-'stehd*)
	Did you want . . .?
	¿Deseó usted . . .? (*deh-seh-'oh oo-'stehd*)
	Do you feel . . .?
	¿Siente usted . . .? (*see-'ehn-teh oo-'stehd*)
	Do you have. . .?
	¿Tiene usted . . .? (*tee-'eh-neh oo-'stehd*)
	Do you want . . .?
	¿Desea usted. . . ? (*deh-'seh-ah oo-'stehd*)
doctor	doctor (*el*), doctora (*la*) or médico (*el*); médica (*la*) (*ehl dohk-tohr, lah dohk-'toh-rah* or *ehl 'meh-dee-koh, lah 'meh-dee-kah*)
dog	perro (*el*) (*ehl 'peh-rroh*)
	dog bite
	mordedura de perro (*la*) (*lah mohr-deh-'doo-rah deh 'peh-rroh*)
doll	muñeca (*la*) (*lah moo-'nyeh-kah*)
door	puerta (*la*) (*lah 'pwehr-tah*)
dosage	dosis (*la*) (*lah 'doh-sees*)
	high dosage
	dosis alta (*la*) (*lah 'doh-sees 'ahl-tah*)
	low dosage
	dosis baja (*la*) (*lah 'doh-sees 'bah-hah*)
	Let's lower the dosage.
	Vamos a bajar la dosis. (*'bah-mohs ah bah-'hahr lah 'doh-sees*)
double	doble (*el*) (*ehl 'doh-bleh*)
down	abajo de (*ah-'bah-hoh deh*)
drawer	cajón (*el*) (*ehl kah-'hohn*)
dreams	sueños (*los*) (*lohs 'sweh-nyohs*)
dress	vestido (*el*) (*ehl behs-'tee-doh*)
drill	taladro (*el*) (*ehl tah-'lah-droh*)
drill (to)	perforar (*pehr-foh-'rahr*)

drink (to)	beber *(beh-'behr)*
	Don't drink alcohol with this.
	No beba alcohol con esto.
	(noh 'beh-bah ahl-koh-'ohl kohn 'eh-stoh)
	Drink *(request to)*
	Beba. *('beh-bah)*
drive (to)	manejar *(mah-neh-'hahr)*
driver's license	licencia de manejar *(la)*
	(lah lee-'sehn-see·ah deh mah-neh-'hahr)
drops	gotas *(las) (lahs 'goh-tahs)*
drought	sequía *(la) (lah seh-'kee-ah)*
drown oneself (to)	ahogarse *(ah-oh-'gahr-seh)*
	He/she drowned.
	Se ahogó. *(seh ah-oh-'goh)*
drugs	drogas *(las) (lahs 'droh-gahs)*
drugs (legal)	remedios *(los) (lohs reh-'meh-dee·ohs)*
	drug addict
	drogadicto *(el)*,drogadicta *(la)*
	(ehl droh-ah-'deek-toh, lah drohg-ah-'deek-tah)
	drug addiction
	drogadicción *(la) (lah drohg-ah-deek-see·'ohn)*
	drug dealer
	droguero *(el)*, traficante de drogas *(el)*
	(ehl droh-'geh-roh, ehl trah-fee-'kahn-teh deh 'droh-gahs)
	drug traffic
	narcotráfico *(nahr-koh-'trah-fee-koh*
	drug use
	uso de drogas *(el) (ehl 'oo-soh deh 'droh-gahs)*
	drug-related
	relacionado con drogas
	(reh-lah-see·oh-'nah-doh kohn 'droh-gahs)
	Have you been drinking or taking drugs?
	¿Ha tomado licor o drogas?
	(ah toh-'mah-doh lee-'kohr oh 'droh-gahs)
drunk	borracho *(el)*, borracha *(la)*
	(ehl boh-'rrah-choh, lah boh-'rrah chah)
dry	seco (m.); seca (f.) *('seh-koh, 'seh-kah)*
dull (edge)	romo *('roh-moh)*

dull (sound)	sordo ('sohr-doh)
dust	polvo (el) (ehl 'pohl-boh)
ear	oído (el) (ehl oh-'ee-doh)
earache	dolor de oído (doh-'lohr deh oh-'ee-doh)

Are you exposed to loud noise?
¿Está expuesto a ruidos fuertes?
(eh-'stah ehks-'pwehs-toh ah roo-'ee-dohs 'fwehr-tehs)

Are you losing your hearing?
¿Está poniéndose sordo?
(eh-'stah poh-nee-'ehn-doh-seh 'sohr-doh)

Did you have an ear injury?
¿Tuvo una lesión en el oído?
(too-boh 'oo-nah leh-see-'ohn ehn ehl oh-'ee-doh)

Do you hear ringing or buzzing?
¿Oye un campanilleo o un zumbido?
('oh-yeh oon kahm-pah-nee-'yeh-oh oh oon soom-'bee-doh)

Do you lose your balance easily?
¿Pierde el equilibrio fácilmente?
(pee-'ehr-deh ehl eh-kee-'lee-bree-oh fah-seel-'mehn-teh)

Do your ears itch?
¿Le pican los oídos? (leh 'pee-kahn lohs oh-'ee-dohs)

Does your ear suppurate?
¿Le sale líquido del oído?
(leh 'sah-leh 'lee-kee-doh dehl oh-'ee-doh)

early	temprano (tehm-prah-noh)
earrings	aretes (los) (lohs ah-'reh-tehs)
earthquake	terremoto (el) (ehl teh-rreh-'moh-toh)
easy	fácil ('fah-seel)
eat (to)	comer (koh-'mehr)

Eat (request to)
Coma. ('koh-mah)

ECG	electrocardiograma (el) (ehl eh-lehk-troh-kahr-dee-oh-'grah-mah)
ecstasy	éxtasis (la) (lah 'eks-tah-sees)
EEG	electroencefalograma (el) (ehl eh-lehk-troh-ehn-seh-fah-loh-'grah-mah)
egg	huevo (el) (ehl 'weh-boh)

eight	ocho *('oh-choh)*
eighth	octavo *(ohk-'tah-boh)*
elbow	codo *(el)* *(ehl 'koh-doh)*
elderly	ancianos *(los)* *(lohs ahn-see-'ah-nohs)*
elderly person	anciano (m.); anciana (f.) *(ahn-see-'ah-noh, ahn-see-'ah-nah)*
electric fan	ventilador *(el)* *(ehl behn-tee-lah-'dohr)*
electric wires	cables eléctricos *(los)* *(lohs 'kah-blehs eh-'lehk-tree-kohs)*
electricity	electricidad *(la)* *(lah eh-lehk-tree-see-'dahd)*
elevator	ascensor *(el)* *(ehl ah-sehn-'sohr)*
eleven	once *('ohn-seh)*
embryo	embrión *(el)* *(ehl ehm-bree-'ohn)*
emergency	emergencia *(la)* *(lah eh-mehr-'hehn-see·ah)*
	emergency operation operación de emergencia *(la)* *(lah oh-peh-rah-see·'ohn deh eh-mehr-'hehn-see·ah)*
	Emergency Room sala de emergencia *(la)* *(lah 'sah-lah deh eh-mehr-'hehn-see·ah)*
emotional problems	problemas emocionales *(los)* *(lohs proh-'bleh-mahs eh-moh-see·oh-'nah-lehs)*
emphysema	enfisema *(la)* *(lah ehn-fee-'seh-mah)*
employee	empleado *(el)*, empleada *(la)* *(ehl ehm-pleh-'ah-doh, lah ehm-pleh-'ah-dah)*
employer	empresario *(el)*, patrón *(el)*, jefe *(el)* *(ehl ehm-preh-'sah-ree·oh, ehl pah-'trohn, ehl 'heh-feh)*
	Who is your employer? ¿Quién es su patrón (jefe)? *(kee-'ehn ehs soo pah-'trohn 'heh-feh)*
employment	empleo *(el)* *(ehl ehm-'pleh-oh)*
	Are you employed now? ¿Tiene empleo ahora? *(tee-'eh-neh ehm-'pleh-oh ah-'oh-rah)*
	When did you stop working? ¿Cuándo dejó de trabajar? *('kwahn-doh deh-'hoh deh trah-bah-'hahr)*
empty	vacío *(bah-'see-oh)*
enamel	esmalte *(el)* *(ehl ehs-'mahl-teh)*

end (to)	terminar *(tehr-mee-'nahr)*
endoscopy	endoscopía *(la) (lah ehn-dohs-koh-'pee-ah)*
enema	enema *(el) (ehl eh-'neh-mah)*
enough	bastante *(bahs-'tahn-teh)*
enroll (to)	matricularse *(mah-tree-koo-'lahr-seh)*
entrance	entrada *(la) (lah ehn-'trah-dah)*
envelope	sobre *(el) (ehl 'soh-breh)*
epidemic	epidemia *(la) (lah eh-pee-'deh-mee·ah)*
epidural	epidural *(m. & f.) (eh-pee-'doo-rahl)*
epilepsy	epilepsia *(la) (lah eh-pee-'lehp-see·ah)*
epileptic	epiléptico *(el)*, epiléptica *(la)* *(ehl-eh-pee-'lehp-tee-koh, lah-eh-pee-'lehp-tee-kah)*
epsom salt	sal de epsom *(la) (lah sahl deh ehp-'sohm)*
equipment	equipo *(el) (ehl eh-'kee-poh)*
erectile dysfunction	disfunción eréctil *(la)* *(lah dees-foon-see-'ohn eh-'rehk-teel)*
esophagus	esófago *(el) (ehl eh-'soh-fah-goh)*
evaluate (to)	evaluar *(eh-bah-loo-'ahr)*
exam	examen *(el) (ehl ehk-'sah-mehn)*
	The exam will take two hours.
	El examen tomará dos horas.
	(ehl ehk-'sah-mehn toh-mah-'rah dohs 'oh-rahs)
examine (to)	examinar *(ehk-sah-mee-'nahr)*
	I'm going to examine your leg.
	Voy a examinar su pierna.
	('boh·ee ah ehk-sah-mee-'nahr soo pee-'ehr-nah)
excessive	excesivo *(m.)*; excesiva *(f.)* *(eks-seh-'see-voh; eks-seh-'see-vah)*
excited	emocionado *(m.)*; emocionada *(f.)* *(eh-moh-see-oh-'nah-doh, eh-moh-see-oh-'nah-dah)*
exercise	ejercicio *(el) (ehl eh-hehr-'see-see·oh)*
	Do you exercise often?
	¿Hace ejercicios a menudo?
	('ah-seh eh-hehr-'see-see·ohs ah meh-'noo-doh)
exhale (to)	exhalar *(ehks-ah-'lahr)*
	Exhale *(request to)*
	Exhale. *(ehks-'ah-leh)*
	Exhale slowly.
	Exhale lentamente. *(ehks-'ah-leh lehn-tah-'mehn-teh)*

exhausted	agotado (m.); agotada (f.) *(ah-goh-'tah-doh, ah-goh-'tah-dah)*
	Are you exhausted?
	¿Está agotado? *(eh-'stah ah-goh-'tah-doh)*
exhaustion	cansancio *(el) (ehl kahn-'sahn-see·oh)*
exit	salida *(la) (lah sah-'lee-dah)*
expenses	gastos *(los) (lohs 'gahs-tohs)*
explain (to)	explicar *(ehks-plee-'kahr)*
extend	estirar *(ehs-'tee-rahr)*
	Extend (*request to*)
	Estire. *(ehs-'tee-reh)*
extract (to)	extraer *(ehks-trah-'ehr)*
	Do you want me to extract the tooth?
	¿Desea que yo extraiga el diente? *(deh-'seh-ah keh yoh ehks-'trah·ee-gah ehl dee-'ehn-teh)*
	I will extract the tooth.
	Voy a extraer el diente. *('boh·ee ah ehks-trah-'ehr ehl dee-'ehn-teh)*
extraction	extracción *(la) (lah ehks-trahk-see·'ohn)*
eye	ojo *(el) (ehl 'oh-hoh)*
	Are you color blind?
	¿No ve usted los colores? *(noh beh oo-'stehd lohs koh-'loh-rehs)*
	Are you farsighted?
	¿Tiene usted presbicia? *(tee-'eh-neh oo-'stehd prehs-'bee-see·ah)*
	Are you nearsighted?
	¿Tiene usted miopía? *(tee-'eh-neh oo-'stehd mee-oh-'pee-ah)*
	Close your eyes.
	Cierre los ojos. *(see-'eh-rreh los 'oh-hohs)*
	Do you have pain in the eyes?
	¿Le duelen los ojos? *(leh 'dweh-lehn lohs 'oh-hohs)*
	Do you have something in your eye?
	¿Tiene algo en el ojo? *(tee-'eh-neh 'ahl-goh ehn ehl 'oh-hoh)*
	Do you see double?
	¿Lo ve todo doble? *(loh beh 'toh-doh 'doh-bleh)*

Do you see spots?
¿Ve puntos delante de los ojos?
(beh 'poon-tohs deh-'lahn-teh deh lohs 'oh-hohs)

Do you wear glasses?
¿Usa usted anteojos?
('oo-sah oo-'stehd ahn-teh-'oh-hohs)

Do your eyes water?
¿Le lloran los ojos?
(leh 'yoh-rahn lohs 'oh-hohs)

Open your eyes.
Abra los ojos.
('ah-brah lohs 'oh-hohs)

eye drops	gotas para los ojos (las) (lahs 'goh-tahs 'pah-rah lohs 'oh-hohs)
eyebrow	ceja (la) (lah 'seh-hah)
eyelash	pestaña (la) (lah pehs-'tah-nyah)
eyelid	párpado (el) (ehl 'pahr-pah-doh)
face	cara (la) (lah 'kah-rah)
factory	fábrica or factoría (la) (lah 'fah-bree-kah, fahk-toh-'ree-ah)
failure	fracaso (el) (ehl frah-'kah-soh)
faint (to)	desmayarse (dehs-mah-'yahr-seh)
fainting spell	desmayo (el) (ehl dehs-'mah-yoh)
fall	otoño (el) (ehl oh-'tohn-yoh)
Fallopian tubes	trompas de Falopio (las) (lahs 'trohm-pahs deh fah-'loh-pee·oh)
false	postizo (pohs-'tee-soh)
family	familia (la) (lah fah-'mee-lee-ah)
farmer	campesino (el) (ehl kahm-peh-'see-noh)
fast	rápido ('rah-pee-doh)
fat (food)	grasa (la) (lah 'grah-sah)
fat (person)	gordo ('gohr-doh)
father	padre (el) (ehl 'pah-dreh)
father-in-law	suegro (el) (ehl 'sweh-groh)
fatigue	fatiga (la) (lah fah-'tee-gah)
fear	miedo (el) (ehl mee-'eh-doh)
February	febrero (feh-'breh-roh)
feed (to)	alimentar (ah-lee-mehn-'tahr)

feel (to)	sentir *(sehn-'teer)*
feminine napkin	paño higiénico *(el)* *(ehl 'pah-nyoh ee-hee-'eh-nee-koh)*
fertilization	fertilización *(la)* *(lah fehr-tee-lee-sah-see·'ohn)*
fetal alcohol syndrome	síndrome del alcohol fetal *(el)* *(ehl 'seen-droh-meh dehl ahl-koh-'ohl)* *(feh-'tahl)*
fetus	feto *(el)* *(ehl 'feh-toh)*
fever	fiebre *(la)* *(lah fee-'eh-breh)*
few	pocos *('poh-kohs)*
fiber	fibra *(la)* *(lah 'feeb-rah)*
fifth	quinto *('keen-toh)*
fight (to)	pelear *(peh-leh-'ahr)*
file (nailfile)	lima *(la)* *(lah 'lee-mah)*
file (to)	limar *(lee-'mahr)*
fill out (to)	llenar *(yeh-'nahr)*
fill (teeth) (to)	empastar *(ehm-pahs-'tahr)*
filling (dental)	empaste *(el)* *(ehl ehm-'pahs-teh)*
find (to)	encontrar *(ehn-kohn-'trahr)*
finger	dedo *(el)* *(ehl 'deh-doh)*
fire	fuego *(el)*, incendio *(el)* *(ehl 'fweh-goh, ehl een-'sehn-dee·oh)*
fireman	bombero *(el)* *(ehl bohm-'beh-roh)*
fireworks	fuegos artificiales *(los)* *(lohs 'fweh-gohs ahr-tee-fee-see-'ah-lehs)*
first	primero *(pree-'meh-roh)*
first aid	primeros auxilios *(los)* *(lohs pree-'meh-rohs owk-'see-lee-ohs)*
first floor	primer piso *(el)* *(ehl pree-'mehr 'pee-soh)*
fish	pescado *(el)* *(ehl pehs-'kah-doh)*
fits	ataques *(los)* *(lohs ah-'tah-kehs)*
fixed	fijo *('fee-hoh)*
flames	llamas *(las)* *(lahs 'yah-mahs)*
flatulence	flatulencia *(la)* *(lah flah-too-'lehn-see·ah)*
flea	pulga *(la)* *(lah 'pool-gah)*
flood	inundación *(la)* *(lah een-oon-dah-see·'ohn)*
floor	piso *(el)* *(ehl 'pee-soh)*
flour	harina *(la)* *(lah ah-'ree-nah)*
fluoride	fluoruro *(el)* *(ehl floo-oh-'roo-roh)*

flower	flor *(la) (lah flohr)*
flower vase	florero *(el) (ehl floh-'reh-roh)*
flu shot	vacuna contra la influenza *(la)* *(lah vah-'koo-nah 'kohn-trah lah een-floo-'ehn-sah)*
foam	espuma *(la) (lah ehs-'poo-mah)*
fog	neblina *(la) (lah neh-'blee-nah)*
follow (to)	seguir *(seh-'geer)*
	Follow *(request to)*
	Siga. *('see-gah)*
	Follow the diet.
	Siga la dieta. *('see-gah lah dee-'eh-tah)*
	Follow the instructions.
	Siga las instrucciones. *('see-gah lahs een-strook-see-'oh-nehs)*
food	comida *(la) (lah koh-'mee-dah)*
food poisoning	intoxicación alimentaria *(la)* *(lah een-tohk-see-kah-see-'ohn ah-lee-mehn-'tah-ree-ah)*
foot	pie *(el) (ehl pee-'eh)*
for	por, para *(pohr, 'pah-rah)*
forceps	tenazas *(las) (lahs teh-'nah-sahs)*
forearm	antebrazo *(el) (ehl ahn-teh-'brah-soh)*
forehead	frente *(la) (lah 'frehn-teh)*
forest	bosque *(el) (ehl 'bohs-keh)*
forest fire	incendio de bosque *(el)* *(ehl een-'sehn-dee-oh deh 'bohs-keh)*
fork	tenedor *(el) (ehl teh-neh-'dohr)*
form	formulario *(el) (ehl fohr-moo-'lah-ree·oh)*
	Fill out this form.
	Llene este formulario. *('yeh-neh 'ehs-teh fohr-moo-'lah-ree·oh)*
formula	fórmula *(la) (lah 'fohr-moo-lah)*
foster child	ahijado (el)/ahijada (la) *(ehl ah-ee-'hah-doh/lah ah-ee-'hah-dah)*
fourth	cuarto *('kwahr-toh)*
free	gratis *('grah-tees)*
frequency	frecuencia *(la) (lah freh-'kwen-see-ah)*
frequently	con frecuencia *(kohn freh-'kwehn-see-ah)*
Friday	viernes *(bee-'ehr-nehs)*

frigidity	frigidez *(la)* *(lah free-hee-'dehs)*
front of	frente de *('frehn-teh deh)*
frost	escarcha *(la)* *(lah ehs-'kahr-chah)*
frostbite	congelamiento *(el)* *(ehl kohn-heh-lah-mee-'ehn-toh)*
fruit	fruta *(la)* *(lah 'froo-tah)*
full	lleno *('yeh-noh)*
function (to)	funcionar *(foon-see-oh-'nahr)*
furniture	muebles *(los)* *(lohs 'mweh-blehs)*
gain (weight) (to)	engordar *(ehn-gohr-'dahr)*

They are gaining weight.
Están engordando.
(Eh-'stahn ehn-gohr-'dahn-doh)

gallstones	cálculos en la vesícula *(los)* *(lohs 'kahl-koo-lohs ehn lah beh-'see-koo-lah)*
game	juego *(el)* *(ehl 'hweh-goh)*
gardener	jardinero *(el)* *(ehl hahr-dee-'neh-roh)*
gargle (to)	hacer gárgaras *(ah-'sehr 'gahr-gah-rahs)*
garlic	ajo *(el)* *(ehl 'ah-hoh)*
gas	gas *(el)* *(ehl gahs)*
gastroenterologist	gastroenterólogo *(el)* *(ehl gahs-troh-ehn-teh-'roh-loh-goh)*
gastroenterology	gastroenterología *(la)* *(lah gahs-troh-ehn-teh-roh-loh-'gee-ah)*
gastrointestinal	gastrointestinal *(lo)* *(loh gahs-troh-een-tehs-tee-'nahl)*

Are your stools black?
¿Son de color negro sus excrementos?
(sohn deh koh-'lohr 'neh-groh soos ehks-kreh-'mehn-tohs)

Are your stools bloody?
¿Tienen sangre sus excrementos?
(tee-'eh-nehn 'sahn-greh soos ehks-kreh-'mehn-tohs)

Do you ever vomit blood?
¿Vomita sangre a veces?
(boh-'mee-tah 'sahn-greh ah 'beh-sehs)

Do you feel itching, pain, or burning in the rectum?
¿Siente picazón, dolor o quemazón en el recto?
(see-'ehn-teh pee-kah-'sohn, doh-'lohr oh keh-mah-'sohn ehn ehl 'rehk-toh)

Do you have a good appetite?
¿Tiene buen apetito?
(tee-'eh-neh bwehn ah-peh-'tee-toh)

Do you have frequent stomachaches?
¿Le duele el estómago a menudo?
(leh 'dweh-leh ehl ehs-'toh-mah-goh ah meh-'noo-doh)

Do you have indigestion and heartburn often?
¿Tiene indigestión y ardor de estómago a menudo?
(tee-'eh-neh een-dee-hehs-tee·'ohn ee ahr-'dohr deh ehs-'toh-mah-goh ah meh-'noo-doh)

Do you have nausea often?
¿Tiene náuseas con frecuencia?
(tee-'eh-neh 'now-seh-ahs kohn freh-'kwehn-see·ah)

gastritis	gastritis *(la) (lah gahs-'tree-tees)*
gauze	gasa *(la) (lah 'gah-sah)*
genes	genes *(los) (lohs 'heh-nehs)*
genitals	genitales *(los) (lohs heh-nee-'tah-lehs)*
genital warts	verrugas genitales *(las)* *(lahs veh-'rroo-gahs heh-nee-'tah-lehs)*
genitourinary	genitourinario *(heh-nee-toh-oo-ree-'nah-ree·oh)*
German measles	rubéola *(la) (lah roo-'beh-oh-lah)*
gestation	gestación *(la) (lah hehs-tah-see-'ohn)*
get dressed (to)	vestirse *(behs-'teer-seh)*
get sick (to)	enfermarse *(ehn-fehr-'mahr-seh)*
gift	regalo *(el) (ehl reh-'gah-loh)*
gift shop	tienda de regalos *(la)* *(lah tee-'ehn-dah deh reh-'gah-lohs)*
girdle	faja *(la) (lah 'fah-hah)*
girlfriend	novia *(la) (lah 'noh-bee·ah)*
give (to)	dar *(dahr)*
glands	glándulas *(las) (lahs 'glahn-doo-lahs)*
glass (drinking)	vaso *(el) (ehl 'bah-soh)*
glasses (eyewear)	anteojos *(los) (lohs ahn-teh-'oh-hohs)*

Do you wear glasses or contact lenses?
¿Usa anteojos o lentes de contacto?
('oo-sah ahn-teh-'oh-hohs oh 'lehn-tehs deh kohn-'tahk-toh)

glaucoma	glaucoma *(el) (ehl glaw-'koh-mah)*
gloves	guantes *(los) (lohs 'gwahn-tehs)*

glue	goma *(la) (lah 'goh-mah)*
go to (to)	ir *(eer)*
go up (to)	subir *(soo-'beer)*
gold	oro *(el) (ehl 'oh-roh)*
gonorrhea	gonorrea *(la) (lah goh-noh-'rreh-ah)*
good	bueno *('bweh-noh)*
gout	gota *(la) (lah 'goh-tah)*
grab (to)	agarrar *(ah-gah-'rrahr)*
	Grab my hand.
	Agarre mi mano. *(ah-'gah-rreh mee 'mah-noh)*
graft	injerto *(el) (ehl een-'hehr-toh)*
grams	gramos *(los) (lohs 'grah-mohs)*
granddaughter	nieta *(la) (lah nee-'eh-tah)*
grandfather	abuelo *(el) (ehl ah-'bweh-loh)*
grandmother	abuela *(la) (lah ah-'bweh-lah)*
grandson	nieto *(el) (ehl nee-'eh-toh)*
grape	uva *(la) (lah 'oo-bah)*
grapefruit	toronja *(la) (lah toh-'rohn-hah)*
grass	hierba *(la) (lah 'yehr-bah)*
gray	gris *(grees)*
grease	grasa *(la) (lah 'grah-sah)*
green	verde *('behr-deh)*
green bean	ejote *(el) (ehl eh-'hoh-teh)*
greeting card	tarjeta de saludo *(la)*
	(lah tahr-'heh-tah deh sah-'loo-doh)
grief	tristeza *(la) (lah trees-'teh-sah)*
groin	ingle *(la) (lah 'een-gleh)*
group	grupo *(el) (ehl 'groo-poh)*
grow (to)	crecer *(kreh-'sehr)*
guardian	guardián *(el/la) (ehl/lah goo-ahr-dee-'ahn)*
gum	chicle *(el) (ehl 'chee-kleh)*
gums	encías *(las) (lahs ehn-'see-ahs)*
gunshot wound	herida de bala *(la) (lah eh-'ree-dah deh 'bah-lah)*
gynecologist	ginecólogo *(el) (ehl hee-neh-'koh-loh-goh)*
hair	cabello *(el) (ehl kah-'beh-yoh)*
haircut	corte de pelo *(el) (ehl 'kohr-teh deh 'peh-loh)*
half	mitad *(la) (lah mee-'tahd)*
hallway	corredor *(el) (ehl koh-rreh-'dohr)*

hand	mano *(la)* *(lah 'mah-noh)*
handbag	bolsa *(la)* *(lah 'bohl-sah)*
hangnail	padrastro *(el)* *(ehl pah-'drahs-troh)*
happy	feliz (m. & f.) *(feh-'lees)*
hard	duro (m.); dura (f.) *('doo-roh, 'doo-rah)*
hardening	endurecimiento *(el)* *(ehl ehn-doo-reh-see-mee-'ehn-toh)*
have (to)	tener *(teh-'nehr)*

Do you have problems with . . .?
¿Tiene problemas con . . .?
(tee-'eh-neh proh-'bleh-mahs kohn)

Have you had problems?
¿Ha tenido problemas?
(ah teh-'nee-doh proh-'bleh-mahs)

I have a lot of pain.
Tengo mucho dolor. *('tehn-goh 'moo-choh doh-'lohr)*

hay fever	rinitis alérgica *(la)* *(lah ree-'nee-tees ah-'lehr-hee-kah)*
he	él *(ehl)*
head	cabeza *(la)* *(lah kah-'beh-sah)*
headache	dolor de cabeza *(el)* *(ehl doh-'lohr deh kah-'beh-sah)*
headrest	apoyo *(el)* *(ehl ah-'poh-yoh)*
health	salud *(la)* *(lah sah-'lood)*

health care
servicios de salud *(los)*
(lohs sehr-'bee-see ohs deh sah-'lood)

health department
departamento de salud pública *(el)*
(ehl deh-pahr-tah-'mehn-toh deh sah-'lood 'poo-blee-kah)

hear (to)	oír *(oh-'eer)*
hearing aids	audífonos *(los)* *(lohs ow-'dee-foh-nohs)*
heart	corazón *(el)* *(ehl koh-rah-'sohn)*

heart attack
ataque cardíaco *(el)* *(ehl ah-'tah-keh kahr-'dee-ah-koh)*

heart disease
enfermedad cardíaca *(la)* *(lah ehn-fehr-meh-'dahd kahr-'dee-ah-kah)*

heart murmurs
murmullos en el corazón *(los)*
(lohs moor-'moo-yohs ehn ehl koh-rah-'sohn)

	heartbeat
	ritmo cardíaco *(el)* *(ehl 'reet-moh kahr-'dee-ah-koh)*
heat	calor *(el)* *(ehl kah-'lohr)*
	heat stroke
	postración *(la)* *(lah pohs-trah-see-'ohn)*
heating	calefacción *(la)* *(lah kah-leh-fahk-see·'ohn)*
heel	talón *(el)* *(ehl tah-'lohn)*
height	altura *(la)* *(lah ahl-'too-rah)*
helicopter	helicóptero *(el)* *(ehl eh-lee-'kohp-teh-roh)*
help	ayuda *(la)* *(lah ah-'yoo-dah)*
help (to)	ayudar *(ah-yoo-'dahr)*
	We're going to help the patient.
	Vamos a ayudar al paciente.
	('bah-mohs ah ah-yoo-'dahr ahl pah-see-'ehn-teh)
hemorrhage	hemorragia *(la)* *(lah eh-mohr-'rah-hee-ah)*
hemorrhoids	hemorroides *(los)* *(lohs eh-moh-'rroh·ee-dehs)*
hepatitis	hepatitis *(la)* *(lah ehp-ah-'tee-tees)*
her	su *(soo)*
here	aquí *(ah-'kee)*
hereditary	hereditario *(eh-reh-dee-'tah-ree·oh)*
hernia	hernia *(la)* *(lah 'ehr-nee-ah)*
heroin	heroína *(la)* *(lah eh-roh-'ee-nah)*
hiccups	hipo *(el)* *(ehl 'ee-poh)*
high cholesterol	colesterol alto *(el)* *(ehl koh-lehs-teh-'rohl 'ahl-toh)*
highway	carretera *(la)* *(lah kah-rreh-'teh-rah)*
hip	cadera *(la)* *(lah kah-'deh-rah)*
his	su *(soo)*
HIV	VIH *(el)* *(ehl beh-ee-'ah-cheh)*
hives	urticaria *(la)* *(lah oor-tee-'kah-ree·ah)*
Hodgkin's lymphoma	linfoma de Hodgkin (el) *(ehl leen-'foh-mah deh Hodgkin)*
hold (to)	mantener *(mahn-teh-'nehr)*
	Hold *(request to)*
	Mantenga. *(mahn-'tehn-gah)*
Holter scan	prueba de Holter *(la)* *(lah proo·'eh-bah deh ohl-'tehr)*
honey	miel *(la)* *(lah mee-e'ehl)*
hormone therapy	terapia hormonal *(la)* *(lah teh-'rah-pee-ah ohr-moh-'nahl)*

hormones	hormonas *(las)* *(lahs ohr-'moh-nahs)*
hospital	hospital *(el)* *(ehl ohs-pee-'tahl)*
hot	caliente *(kah-lee-'ehn-teh)*
	hot flashes
	bochornos *(los)* *(lohs boh-'chohr-nohs)*
hours	horas *(las)* *(lahs 'oh-rahs)*
	visiting hours
	horas de visita *(las)* *(lahs 'oh-rahs deh bee-'see-tah)*
how?	¿cómo? *('koh-moh)*
how many?	¿cuántos? *('kwahn-tohs)*
how much?	¿cuánto? *('kwahn-toh)*
however	sin embargo *(seen ehm-'bahr-goh)*
humidity	humedad *(la)* *(lah oo-meh-'dahd)*
hunger	hambre *(el)* *(ehl 'ahm-breh)*
hungry	hambriento (m.); hambrienta (f.) *(ahm-bree-'ehn-toh, ahm-bree-'ehn-tah)*
hurricane	huracán *(el)* *(ehl oo-rah-'kahn)*
husband	esposo *(el)* *(ehl ehs-'poh-soh)*
hydrogen peroxide	agua oxigenada *(el)* *(ehl 'ah-gwah ohk-see-heh-'nah-dah)*
hygienist	higienista (m. & f.) *(ehl (lah) ee-hee·eh-'nees-tah)*
hypertension	hipertensión *(la)* *(lah ee-per-ten-see·'ohn)*
hypoglycemia	hipoglicemia *(la)* *(lah ee-poh-glee-'seh-mee-ah)*
hysterectomy	histerectomía *(la)* *(lah ees-teh-rehk-toh-'mee-ah)*
hysteria	histerismo *(el)* *(ehl ees-teh-'rees-moh)*
I	yo *(yoh)*
I.V.	intravenoso *(een-trah-beh-'noh-soh)*
ice	hielo *(el)* *(ehl 'yeh-loh)*
ice cream	helado *(el)* *(ehl eh-'lah-doh)*
ice pack	bolsa de hielo *(la)* *(lah 'bohl-sah deh ee-'eh-loh)*
identification	identificación *(la)* *(lah ee-dehn-tee-fee-kah-see·'ohn)*
illness	enfermedad *(la)* *(lah ehn-fehr-meh-'dahd)*
	mental illness
	enfermedad mental *(la)* *(lah ehn-fehr-meh-'dahd mehn-'tahl)*
immediately	inmediatamente *(eeh-meh-dee-ah-tah-'mehn-teh)*
immunotherapy	inmunoterapia *(la)* *(lah een-moo-noh-teh-'rah-pee·ah)*
immune system	sistema inmune *(el)* *(ehl sees-'teh-mah een-'moo-neh)*

impaction	impacción *(la) (lah eem-pahk-see·'ohn)*
	impacted tooth
	diente impactado *(el)*
	(ehl dee-'ehn-teh eem-pahk-'tah-doh)
implants	implantes *(los) (lohs eem-'plahn-tehs)*
impotence	impotencia *(la) (lah eem-poh-'tehn-see-ah)*
improve (to)	mejorar *(meh-hoh-'rahr)*
in, on	en *(ehn)*
in-patient	paciente interno *(el)*
	(ehl pah-see-'ehn-teh een-'tehr-noh
inch	pulgada *(la) (lah pool-'gah-dah)*
income	ingreso *(el) (ehl een-'greh-soh)*
incubator	incubadora *(la) (lah een-koo-bah-'doh-rah)*
indigestion	indigestión *(la) (lah een-dee-hehs-tee-'ohn)*
induced abortion	aborto inducido *(el) (ehl ah-'bohr-toh een-doo-'see-doh)*
infant	infante *(el) (ehl een-'fahn-teh)*
	infant car seat
	asiento para infantes *(el)*
	(ehl ah-see-'ehn-toh 'pah-rah een-'fahn-tehs)
infected	infectado (m.); infectada (f.)
	(een-fehk-'tah-doh, een-fehk-'tah-dah)
infection	infección *(la) (lah een-fehk-see·'ohn)*
infertility	infertilidad *(la) (lah een-fehr-tee-lee-'dahd)*
inflamed	inflamado (m.); inflamada (f.)
	(een-flah-'mah-doh, een-flah-'mah-dah)
inflammation	inflamación *(la) (lah een-flah-mah-see·'ohn)*
information	información *(la) (lah een-fohr-mah-see·'ohn)*
ingrown toenail	uña encarnada *(la) (lah 'oo-nyah ehn-kahr-'nah-dah)*
inhale (to)	aspirar *(ahs-'pee-rahr)*
	Inhale *(request to)*
	Aspire. *(ahs-'pee-reh)*
inhalants	inhaladores *(los) (lohs een-ah-lah-'doh-rehs)*
injection	inyección *(la) (lah een-yehk-see·'ohn)*
injury	herida *(la) (lah eh-'ree-dah)*
	injured
	herido (m.); herida (f.) *(eh-'ree-doh, eh-'ree-dah)*
	Are you injured?
	¿Está herido? *(eh-'stah eh-'ree-doh)*
inlay	incrustación *(la) (lah een-kroos-tah-see·'ohn)*

insanity	locura *(la)* *(lah loh-'koo-rah)*
insect bite	mordedura de insecto *(la)* *(lah mohr-deh-'doo-rah deh een-'sehk-toh)*
insecticide	insecticida *(el)* *(ehl een-sehk-tee-'se-dah)*
inside	adentro de *(ah-'dehn-troh deh)*
insomnia	insomnio *(el)* *(ehl een-'sohm-nee·oh)*
instrument	instrumento *(el)* *(ehl een-stroo-'mehn-toh)*
insulin	insulina *(la)* *(lah een-soo-'lee-nah)*
insurance	seguro *(el)* *(ehl seh-'goo-roh)*

accident insurance
seguro de accidente *(el)*
(ehl seh-'goo-roh deh ahk-see-'dehn-teh)

health insurance
seguro de salud *(el)* *(ehl seh-'goo-roh deh sah-'lood)*

insurance card
tarjeta de seguro *(la)* *(lah tahr-'heh-tah deh seh-'goo-roh)*

insurance company
compañía de seguros *(la)*
(lah kohm-pah-'nyee-ah deh seh-'goo-rohs)

life insurance
seguro de vida *(el)* *(ehl seh-'goo-roh deh 'bee-dah)*

Do you have insurance?
¿Tiene seguro? *(tee-'eh-neh seh-'goo-roh)*

Intensive Care	sala de cuidados intensivos *(la)* *(lah 'sah-lah deh kwee-'dah-dohs een-tehn-'see-bohs)*
intermediate care	cuidado intermedio *(el)* *(ehl kwee-'dah-doh een-tehr-'meh-dee·oh)*
intermittent	intermitente *(een-tehr-mee-'tehn-teh)*
interpreter	intérprete (m. & f.) *(ehl (lah) een-'tehr-preh-teh)*
intestinal surgery	cirugía intestinal *(la)* *(lah see-roo-'hee-ah een-tehs-tee-'nahl)*
intoxication	intoxicación *(la)* *(lah een-tohk-see-kah-see·'ohn)*
intravenous fluids	líquidos intravenosos *(los)* *(lohs 'lee-kee-dohs in-trah-veh-'noh-sohs)*
iron	hierro *(el)* *(ehl ee-'ehr-roh)*
irritated	irritado (m.); irritada (f.) *(eer-ree-'tah-doh, eer-ree-'tah-dah)*
itch (to)	picar *(pee-'kahr)*
itching	picazón *(la)* *(lah pee-kah-'sohn)*

jacket	chaqueta (la) (lah chah-'keh-tah)
January	enero (eh-'neh-roh)
jaundice	ictericia (la) (lah eek-teh-'ree-see·ah)
jaw	mandíbula (la) (lah mahn-'dee-boo-lah)
jelly	jalea (la) (lah hah-'leh-ah)
jewelry	joyas (las) (lahs 'hoh-yahs)
joints	articulaciones (las) (lahs ahr-tee-koo-lah-see-'oh-nehs)
juice	jugo (el) (ehl 'hoo-goh)
July	julio ('hoo-lee·oh)
June	junio ('hoo-nee·oh)
jungle	selva (la) (lah 'sehl-bah)
keep (to)	guardar ('gwahr-dahr)
	Keep (*request to*)
	Guarde. ('gwahr-deh)
kick (to)	patear (pah-teh-'ahr)
kidney	riñón (el) (ehl reen-'yohn)
	kidney cancer
	cáncer del riñón (el) (ehl 'kahn-sehr dehl reen-'yohn)
	kidney stones
	cálculos en los riñones (los)
	(lohs 'kahl-koo-lohs ehn lohs reen-'yohn-ehs)
knee	rodilla (la) (lah roh-'dee-yah)
kneecap	rótula (la) (lah 'roh-too-lah)
knife	cuchillo (el) (ehl koo-'chee-yoh)
knife gash	cuchillada (la) (lah koo-chee-'yah-dah)
label	etiqueta (la) (lah eh-tee-'keh-tah)
labor pains	dolores de parto (los) (doh-'loh-rehs deh 'pahr-toh)
laboratory	laboratorio (el) (ehl lah-boh-rah-'toh-ree-oh)
laborer	obrero (el) (ehl oh-'breh-roh)
lack (to)	faltar (fahl-'tahr)
lake	lago (el) (ehl 'lah-goh)
landlord	propietario (el) (ehl proh-pee-eh-'tah-ree-oh)
landslide	avalancha (la) (lah ah-vah-'lahn-chah)
lane	pista (la) (lah 'pees-tah)
language	lenguaje (el) (ehl lehn-'gwah-heh)
laparoscopy	laparoscopia (la) (lah lah-pah-roh-'skoh-pee·ah)
lard	manteca (la) (lah mahn-'teh-kah)
last	último ('ool-tee-moh)

last (to)	durar *(doo-'rahr)*
late	tarde *('tahr-deh)*
later	más tarde *(mahs 'tahr-deh)*
law	ley *(la) (lah 'leh·ee)*
lawyer	abogado (m.); abogada (f.) *(ehl ah-boh-'gah-doh, lah ah-boh-'gah-dah)*
laxative	laxante *(el) (ehl lahk-'sahn-teh)*
learn (to)	aprender *(ah-prehn-'dehr)*
leave (to)	salir *(sah-'leer)*
left	izquierdo (m.); izquierda (f.) *(ees-kee-'ehr-doh, ees-kee-'ehr-dah)*
	to the left a la izquierda *(ah lah ees-kee-'ehr-dah)*
leg	pierna *(la) (lah pee-'ehr-nah)*
lemon	limón *(el) (ehl lee-'mohn)*
lesions	lesiones *(las) (lahs leh-see-'oh-nehs)*
less	menos *('meh-nohs)*
lettuce	lechuga *(la) (lah leh-'choo-gah)*
leukemia	leucemia *(la) (lah leh-oo-'seh-mee·ah)*
liability	responsabilidad legal *(la)* *(lah rehs-pohn-sah-bee-lee-'dahd leh-'gahl)*
lice	piojo *(el) (ehl pee-'oh-hoh)*
lie down (to)	acostarse *(ah-cost-'ahr-se)*
	Lie down *(request to)* Acuéstese. *(ah-'kweh-steh-se)*
	Lie on your back. Acuéstese de espalda. *(ah-'kwehs-teh-seh deh ehs-'pahl-dah)*
	Lie on your side. Acuéstese de lado. *(ah-'kweh-steh-seh deh 'lah-doh)*
life	vida *(la) (lah 'bee-dah)*
ligament	ligamento *(el) (ehl lee-gah-'mehn-toh)*
light	luz *(la) (lah loos)*
	light switch interruptor de la luz *(el)* *(ehl een-tehr-roop-'tohr deh lah loos)*
like (to)	gustar *(goos-'tahr)*
	Do you like the bed? ¿Le gusta la cama? *(leh 'goos-tah lah 'kah-mah)*

liniment	linimento *(el)* *(ehl lee-nee-'mehn-toh)*
lip	labio *(el)* *(ehl 'lah-bee·oh)*
liquid	líquido *(el)* *(ehl 'lee-kee-doh)*
liquor	licor *(el)* *(ehl lee-'kohr)*
listen (to)	escuchar *(ehs-koo-'chahr)*
	Listen *(request to)*
	Escuche. *(ehs-'koo-cheh)*
liters	litros *(los)* *(lohs 'leet-rohs)*
live (to)	vivir *(bee-'beer)*
	He/she is not going to live.
	No va a vivir. *(noh bah ah bee-'beer)*
liver	hígado *(el)* *(ehl 'ee-gah-doh)*
loan	préstamo *(el)* *(ehl 'prehs-tah-moh)*
lobby	salón *(el)* *(ehl sah-'lohn)*
lobe	lóbulo *(el)* *(ehl 'loh-boo-loh)*
look (to)	mirar *(mee-'rahr)*
	Look *(request to)*
	Mire. *('mee-reh)*
look for (to)	buscar *(boos-'kahr)*
loose	flojo (m.); floja (f.) *('floh-hoh, 'floh-hah)*
lose (to)	perder *(pehr-'dehr)*
lost	perdido (m.); perdida (f.) *(pehr-'dee-doh; pehr-'dee-dah)*
lotion	loción *(la)* *(lah loh-see·'ohn)*
lots of times	muchas veces *('moo-chahs 'beh-sehs)*
lower (to)	bajar *(bah-'hahr)*
	Lower *(request to)*
	Baje. *('bah-heh)*
lozenge	pastilla *(la)* *(lah pahs-'tee-yah)*
LSD	ácido *(el)* *(ehl 'ah-see-doh)*
lump	bulto *(el)* *(ehl 'bool-toh)*
lungs	pulmones *(los)* *(lohs pool-'moh-nehs)*
lunch	almuerzo *(el)* *(ehl ahl-moo·'ehr-soh)*
machine	máquina *(la)* *(lah 'mah-kee-nah)*
Mad Cow Disease	enfecalopatía espongiforme bovina *(la)* *(lah ehn-seh-fah-loh-pah-'tee-ah ehs-pohn-gee-'fohr-meh boh-'vee-nah)*
magazine	revista *(la)* *(lah reh-'bees-tah)*

magnesium	magnesia *(la)* *(lah mahg-'neh-see-ah)*
mailbox	buzón *(el)* *(ehl boo-'sohn)*
main lobby	salón principal *(el)* *(ehl sah-'lohn preen-see-'pahl)*
make-up	maquillaje *(el)* *(ehl mah-kee-'yah-heh)*
malaria	malaria *(la)* *(lah mah-'lah-ree·ah)*
malignant	maligno *(mah-'leeg-noh)*
malnutrition	desnutrición *(la)* *(lah dehs-noo-tree-see-'ohn)*
mammogram	mamograma *(el)* *(ehl mah-moh-'grah-mah)*
man	hombre *(el)* *(ehl 'ohm-breh)*
manager	gerente *(m. & f.)* *(ehl (lah) heh-'rehn-teh)*
maniac	maniático *(m.);* maniática *(f.)* *(mah-nee-'ah-tee-koh, mah-nee-'ah-tee-kah)*
many	muchos *(m.);* muchas *(f.)* *('moo-chohs, 'moo-chahs)*
map	mapa *(el)* *(ehl 'mah-pah)*
March	marzo *('mahr-soh)*
margarine	margarina *(la)* *(lah mahr-gah-'ree-nah)*
marijuana	marijuana *(la)* *(lah mah-ree-'wah-nah)*
marital status	estado civil *(el)* *(ehl ehs-'tah-doh see-'beel)*
marriage	matrimonio *(el)* *(ehl mah-tree-'moh-nee·oh)*
married	casado *(m.);* casada *(f.)* *(kah-'sah-doh, kah-'sah-dah)*
mask	máscara *(la)* *(lah 'mahs-kah-rah)*
mastectomy	mastectomía *(la)* *(lah mahs-tehk-toh-'mee-ah)*
matches	fósforos *(los)* *(lohs 'fohs-foh-rohs)*
Maternity Ward	sala de maternidad *(la)* *(lah 'sah-lah deh mah-tehr-nee-'dahd)*
mattress	colchón *(el)* *(ehl kohl-'chohn)*
May	mayo *('mah-yoh)*
MD	distrofia muscular *(la)* *(lah dees-'troh-fee-ah moos-koo-'lahr)*
measles	sarampión *(el)* *(ehl sah-rahm-pee·'ohn)*
measure (to)	medir *(meh-'deer)*
meat	carne *(la)* *(lah 'kar-neh)*
mechanic	mecánico *(el)* *(ehl meh-'kah-nee-koh)*
medicine	medicina *(la)* *(lah meh-dee-'see-nah)*
medicine chest	botiquín *(el)* *(ehl boh-tee-'keen)*
meditation room	sala de meditación *(la)* *(lah 'sah-lah deh meh-dee-tah-see-'ohn)*
member	miembro *(m. & f.)* *(mee-'ehm-broh)*

memory	memoria *(la) (lah meh-'moh-ree·ah)*
meningitis	meningitis *(la) (lah meh-neen-'hee-tees)*
menstrual cycle	ciclo menstrual *(el) (ehl 'seek-loh mehn-stroo-'ahl)*
menstruate (to)	menstruar *(mens-troo-'ahr)*
mental health	salud mental *(la) (lah sah-'lood mehn-'tahl)*
mescaline	mescalina *(la) (lah mehs-kah-'lee-nah)*
meters	metros *(los) (lohs 'meht-rohs)*
microwave	microondas *(el) (ehl mee-kroh-'ohn-dahs)*
migraine	migraña *(la) (lah mee-'grahn-yah)*
mild	moderado *(moh-deh-'rah-doh)*
milk	leche *(la) (lah 'leh-cheh)*
minerals	minerales *(los) (lohs mee-neh-'rah-lehs)*
minor	menor de edad *(el) (ehl meh-'nohr deh eh-'dahd)*
mirror	espejo *(el) (ehl ehs-'peh-hoh)*
miscarriage	pérdida *(la) (lah 'pehr-dee-dah)*
mixture	mezcla *(la) (lah 'mehs-klah)*
molar	muela *(la) (lah 'mweh-lahv)*
mold	molde *(el) (ehl mohl-deh)*
molestation	vejación sexual *(la),*molestia sexual *(la)* *(lah beh-hah-see·'ohn sehk-soo-'ahl, lah moh-'lehs-tee·ah sehk-soo-'ahl)*
Monday	lunes *('loo-nehs)*
money	dinero *(el) (ehl dee-'neh-roh)*
monitor	monitor *(el) (ehl moh-nee-'tohr)*
mononucleosis	mononucleosis *(la) (lah moh-noh-noo-kleh-'oh-sees)*
month	mes *(el) (ehl mehs)*
monthly	mensual *(mehn-soo-'ahl)*
more	más *(mahs)*
morphine	morfina *(la) (lah mohr-'fee-nah)*
mosquito	zancudo *(el) (ehl sahn-'koo-doh)*
mother	madre *(la) (lah 'mah-dreh)*
mother-in-law	suegra *(la) (lah 'sweh-grah)*
motorcycle	motocicleta *(la) (lah moh-toh-see-'cleh-tah)*
mountain	montaña *(la) (lah mohn-'tah-nyah)*
mouse	ratón *(el) (ehl rah-'tohn)*
mouth	boca *(la) (lah 'boh-kah)*
	Do you have a sore mouth?
	¿Le duele la boca? *(leh 'dweh-leh lah 'boh-kah)*

Do you have a sore tongue?
¿Le duele la lengua? *(leh 'dweh-leh lah 'lehn-gwah)*

Do your gums bleed often?
¿Le sangran las encías con frecuencia?
(leh 'sahn-grahn lahs ehn-'see-ahs kohn freh-'kwehn-see·ah)

Has your mouth felt swollen?
¿Siente hinchada la boca?
(see-'ehn-teh een-'chah-dah lah 'boh-kah)

Has your sense of taste changed?
¿Tiene problemas con su sentido del gusto?
(tee-'eh-neh proh-'bleh-mahs kohn soo sehn-'tee-doh dehl 'goos-toh)

mouthguard	protector dental *(el)* *(ehl proh-tehk-'tohr dehn-'tahl)*
mouthwash	enjuague bucal *(el)* *(ehl ehn-'hwah-geh boo-'kahl)*
move (to)	mover *(moh-'vehr)*
	Move *(request to)*
	Mueva. *('mweh-bah)*
movie theater	cine *(el)* *(ehl 'see-neh)*
MRI	imagen por resonancia magnética *(la)* *(lah ee-'mah-hen pohr reh-soh-'nahn-see-ah mag-'neh-tee-kah)*
MS	esclerosis múltiple *(la)* *(lah ehs-kleh-'roh-sees 'mool-tee-pleh)*
mucous	mucoso (m.); mucosa (f.) *(moo-'koh-soh, moo-'koh-sah)*
mucus	moco *(el)* *(ehl 'moh-koh)*
mucus	mucosidad *(la)* *(lah moo-koh-see-'dahd)*
mud	lodo *(el)* *(ehl 'loh-doh)*
multiple sclerosis	esclerosis múltiple *(la)* *(lah ehs-kleh-'roh-sees 'mool-tee-pleh)*
mumps	paperas *(las)* *(lahs pah-'peh-rahs)*
murder (to)	matar *(mah-'tahr)*
muscle	músculo *(el)* *(ehl 'moos-koo-loh)*
	pulled muscle
	músculo rasgado *(el)* *('moos-koo-loh rahs-'gah-doh)*
muscular dystrophy	distrofia muscular *(la)* *(lah dees-'troh-fee-ah moos-koo-'lahr)*
mushroom	hongo *(el)* *(ehl 'ohn-goh)*

my	mi *(mee)*
nail	uña *(la) (lah 'oon-yah)*
name	nombre *(el) (ehl 'nohm-breh)*
	father's last name
	apellido paterno *(el)*
	(ehl ah-peh-'yee-doh pah-'tehr-noh)
	first name
	primer nombre *(el) (ehl pree-'mehr 'nohm-breh)*
	mother's last name apellido materno *(el)*
	(ehl ah-peh-'yee-doh mah-'tehr-noh)
nap	siesta *(la) (lah see-'ehs-'tah)*
napkin	servilleta *(la) (lah sehr-bee-'yeh-tah)*
nationality	nacionalidad *(la) (lah nah-see-oh-nah-lee-'dahd)*
natural childbirth	parto natural *(el) (ehl 'pahr-toh nah-too-'rahl)*
nausea	náusea *(la) (lah 'now-seh-ah)*
navel	ombligo *(el) (ehl ohm-'blee-geh)*
near	cerca de *('sehr-kah deh)*
near-sighted	miope *(mee-'oh-peh)*
necessary	necesario *(neh-seh-'sah-ree·oh)*
neck	cuello *(el) (ehl 'kweh-yoh)*
neck brace	collar de soporte *(el) (ehl koh-'yahr deh soh-'pohr-teh)*
necklace	collar *(el) (ehl koh-'yahr)*
need (to)	necesitar *(neh-seh-see-'tahr)*
needle	aguja *(la) (lah ah-'goo-hah)*
nephew	sobrino *(el) (ehl soh-'bree-noh)*
nerve	nervio *(el) (ehl 'nehr-bee·oh)*
nervous	nervioso (m.); nerviosa (f.)
	(nehr-bee-'oh-soh, nehr-bee-'oh-sah)
	nervous breakdown
	postración nerviosa *(la)*
	(lah pohs-trah-see·'ohn nehr-bee-'oh-sah)
	nervous system
	sistema nervioso *(el)*
	(ehl sees-'teh-mah nehr-bee-'oh-soh)
neuro-psychiatric unit	unidad neurosiquiátrica *(la)*
	(lah oo-nee-'dahd neh·oo-roh-see-kee-'ah-tree-kah)
neurologist	neurólogo *(el) (ehl neh·oo-'roh-loh-goh)*
neurosis	neurosis *(la) (lah neh oo-'roh-sees)*
never	nunca *('noon-kah)*

new	nuevo *('noo·eh-boh)*
newborn	recién nacido (m.); recién nacida (f.) *(reh-see-'ehn nah-'see-doh, reh-see-'ehn nah-'see-dah)*
newspaper	periódico *(el) (ehl peh-ree-'oh-dee-koh)*
next	siguiente *(see-gee-'ehn-teh)*
next of kin	pariente más cercano *(el) (ehl pah-ree-'ehn-teh mahs sehr-'kah-noh)*
next to	al lado de *(ahl 'lah-doh deh)*
niece	sobrina *(la) (lah soh-'bree-nah)*
night	noche *(la) (lah 'noh-cheh)*
	last night
	anoche *(ah-'noh-cheh)*
nightstand	mesa de noche *(la) (lah 'meh-sah de 'noh-cheh)*
nipple	pezón *(el) (ehl peh-'sohn)*
none	ninguno (m.); ninguna (f.) *(neen-'goo-noh, neen-'goo-nah)*
noodle	fideo *(el) (ehl fee-'deh-oh)*
normal	normal *(nohr-'mahl)*
normally	normalmente *(nohr-mahl-'mehn-teh)*
nose	nariz *(la) (lah nah-'rees)*

Do you feel pain in your nose?
¿Siente dolor en la nariz?
(see-'ehn-teh doh-'lohr ehn lah nah-'rees)

Do you feel stuffiness often, and when?
¿Siente la nariz taponada a menudo y cuándo?
(see-'ehn-teh lah nah-'rees tah-poh-'nah-dah ah meh-'noo-doh ee 'kwahn-doh)

Do you get nosebleeds often?
¿Le sangra la nariz a menudo?
(leh 'sahn-grah lah nah-'rees ah meh-'noo-doh)

Do you sneeze all the time?
¿Estornuda todo el tiempo?
(ehs-tohr-'noo-dah 'toh-doh ehl tee-'ehm-poh)

Have you ever injured your nose?
¿Se ha lesionado la nariz alguna vez?
(seh ah leh-see-oh-'nah-doh lah nah-'rees ahl-'goo-nah behs)

Is the nose constantly runny?
¿Le gotea la nariz continuamente?
(leh goh-'teh-ah lah nah-'rees kohn-tee-noo-ah-'mehn-teh)

nostril	fosa nasal *(la) (lah 'foh-sah nah-'sahl)*
nothing	nada *('nah-dah)*
November	noviembre *(noh-bee-'ehm-breh)*
now	ahora *(ah-'oh-rah)*
nowadays	ahora *(ah-'oh-rah)*
numb (to)	adormecer *(ah-dohr-meh-'sehr)*
numbness	adormecimiento *(el)* *(ehl ah-dohr-meh-see-mee-'ehn-toh)*
nurse	enfermero (m.); enfermera (f.) *(ehn-fehr-'meh-roh, ehn-fehr-'meh-rah)*
nurse (to)	lactar *(lahk-'tahr)*
nursery	guardería *(la) (lah gwahr-deh-'ree-ah)*
nursing bottle	biberón *(el) (ehl bee-beh-'rohn)*
nursing care	cuidado con enfermera *(el)* *(el kwee-'dah-doh kohn ehn-fehr-'meh-rah)*
nut	nuez *(la) (lah noo-'ehs)*
obesity	obesidad *(la) (lah oh-beh-see-'dahd)*
observe (to)	observar *(ohb-sehr-'bahr)*
obstetrician	obstetriz (m. & f.) *(ehl (lah) ohb-steh-'trees)*
October	octubre *(ohk-'too-breh)*
of	de *(deh)*
office	oficina *(la) (lah oh-fee-'see-nah)*
oil	aceite *(el) (ehl ah-'seh·ee-teh)*
ointment	ungüento *(el) (ehl oon-'gwehn-toh)*
old	viejo *(bee-'eh-hoh)*
older	mayor *(mah-'yohr)*
on	en *(ehn)*
once	una vez *('oo-nah behs)*
oncology	oncología *(la) (lah ohn-koh-loh-'hee-ah)*
onion	cebolla *(la) (lah seh-'boh-yah)*
open (to)	abrir *(ah-'breer)*
	Open *(request to)* Abra. *('ah-brah)*
	Open your hand. Abra la mano. *('ah-brah lah 'mah-noh)*
operate (to)	operar *(oh-peh-'rahr)*
Operating Room	sala de operaciones *(la)* *(lah 'sah-lah deh oh-peh-'rah-see·'oh-nehs)*

operation	operación *(la)* *(lah oh-peh-rah-see·'ohn)*
	To prepare you for the operation.
	Prepararle para la operación.
	(preh-pah-'rahr-leh 'pah-rah lah oh-peh-rah-see·'ohn)
ophthalmologist	oftalmólogo *(el)* *(ehl ohf-tahl-'moh-loh-goh)*
opinion	opinión *(la)* *(lah oh-pee-nee·'ohn)*
ophthalmologist	oftalmólogo *(el)* *(ehl ohf-tahl-'moh-loh-goh)*
optometrist	optometrista *(el)* *(ehl ohp-toh-meh-'trees-tah)*
or	o *(oh)*
orange (color)	anaranjado (m.); anaranjada (f.)
	(ah-nah-rahn-'hah-doh, ah-nah-rahn-'hah-dah)
orderly	practicante *(el)* *(ehl prahk-tee-'kahn-teh)*
organ	órgano *(el)* *(ehl 'ohr-gah-noh)*
organic foods	alimentos orgánicos *(los)*
	(lohs ah-lee-mehn-tohs ohr-'gah-nee-kohs)
orthodontist	ortodoncista (m. & f.)
	(ehl (lah) ohr-toh-dohn-'sees-tah)
orthopedic surgeon	cirujano ortopédico *(el)*, cirujana ortopédica *(la)*
	(ehl see-roo-'hah-noh ohr-toh-'peh-dee-koh, lah see-roo-'hah-nah ohr-toh-'peh-dee-kah)
orthopedics	ortopedia *(la)* *(lah ohr-toh-'peh-dee·ah)*
ounces	onzas *(las)* *(lahs 'ohn-sahs)*
our	nuestro (m.); nuestra (f.) *('nwehs-troh, nwes-trah)*
outlet	enchufe *(el)* *(ehl ehn-'choo-feh)*
ovary	ovario *(el)* *(ehl oh-'bah-ree·oh)*
overdose	dosis excesiva *(la)* *(lah 'doh-sees ehk-seh-'see-bah)*
overwhelmed	abrumado (m.); abrumada (f.)
	(ah-broo-'mah-doh; ah-broo-'mah-dah)
ovum	óvulo *(el)* *(ehl 'oh-boo-loh)*
oxygen	oxígeno *(el)* *(ehl ohk-'see-heh-noh)*
P.M.	de la tarde *(deh lah 'tahr-deh)*
pacemaker	marcapasos *(el)* *(ehl mahr-kah-'pah-sohs)*
pacifier	chupete *(el)* *(ehl choo-'peh-teh)*
pain	dolor *(el)* *(ehl doh-'lohr)*
	constant pain
	dolor constante *(el)* *(ehl doh-'lohr kohn-'stahn-teh)*
	pain in the chest
	dolor en el pecho *(el)* *(ehl doh-'lohr ehn ehl 'peh-choh)*

Have you had this pain before?
¿Ha tenido este dolor antes?
(ah teh-'nee-doh 'eh-steh doh-'lohr 'ahn-tehs)

I have a lot of pain.
Tengo mucho dolor. *('tehn-goh 'moo-choh doh-'lohr)*

This is for the pain.
Esto es para el dolor. *('eh-stoh ehs 'pah-rah ehl doh-'lohr)*

Was it a sharp or dull pain?
¿Fue un dolor agudo o sordo?
(fweh oon doh-'lohr ah-'goo-doh oh 'sohr-doh)

paint	pintura *(la)* *(lah peen-'too-rah)*
painter	pintor (m.); pintora (f.) *(ehl peen-'tohr, lah peen-'toh-rah)*
pajamas	pijamas *(las)* *(lahs pee-'hah-mahs)*
palate	paladar *(el)* *(ehl pah-lah-'dahr)*
palm	palma de la mano *(la)* *(lah 'pahl-mah deh lah 'mah-noh)*
palpitations	palpitaciones *(las)* *(lahs pahl-pee-tah-see·'oh-nehs)*
pan	bacín *(el)* *(ehl bah-'seen)*
pancreas	páncreas *(el)* *(ehl pahn-kreh-ahs)*
panties	bragas *(las)* *(lahs 'brah-gahs)*
pants	pantalones *(los)* *(lohs pahn-tah-'loh-nehs)*
pap smear	examen de Papanicolao *(el)* *(ehl ehk-'sah-mehn deh pah-pah-nee-koh-'lah-oh)*
paper	papel *(el)* *(ehl pah-'pehl)*
paralysis	parálisis *(la)* *(lah pah-'rah-lee-sees)*
paramedic	paramédico (el) *(ehl pah-rah-'meh-dee-koh)*
parasites	parásitos *(los)* *(lohs pah-'rah-see-tohs)*
park	parque *(el)* *(ehl 'pahr-keh)*
parking lot	estacionamiento *(el)* *(ehl ehs-tah-see·oh-nah-mee-'ehn-toh)*
part	parte *(la)* *(lah 'pahr-teh)*
partner	socio *(el)* *(ehl 'soh-see-oh)*
pathologist	patólogo *(el)* *(ehl pah-'toh-loh-goh)*
patient	paciente (m. & f.) *(ehl (lah) pah-see-'ehn-teh)*
pay (to)	pagar *(pah-'gahr)*
payment	pago *(el)* *(ehl 'pah-goh)*
pea	chícharo *(el)* *(ehl 'chee-chah-roh)*

pediatrician	pediatra *(m. & f.)* *(ehl (lah) peh-dee-'ah-trah)*
pelvis	pelvis *(la)* *(lah 'pehl-bees)*
pen	lapicero *(el)* *(ehl lah-pee-'seh-roh)*
pencil	lápiz *(el)* *(ehl 'lah-pees)*
penicillin	penicilina *(la)* *(lah peh-nee-see-'lee-nah)*
penis	pene *(el)* *(ehl 'peh-neh)*
people	gente *(la)* *(lah 'hehn-teh)*
pepper	pimienta *(la)* *(lah pee-mee-'ehn-tah)*
percent	porcentaje *(el)* *(ehl pohr-sehn-'tah-heh)*
period (menstrual)	regla *(la)*; período *(el)*
	(lah 'reh-glah; ehl peh-'ree-oh-doh)
	When was your last period?
	¿Cuándo fue su última regla?
	('kwahn-doh fweh soo 'ool-tee-mah 'reh-glah)
permission	permiso *(el)* *(ehl pehr-'mee-soh)*
persecuted	perseguido *(m.)*; perseguida *(f.)*
	(pehr-seh-'ghee-doh; pehr-seh-'ghee-dah)
person	persona *(la)* *(lah pehr-'soh-nah)*
perspire (to)	sudar *(soo-'dahr)*
pharmacist	farmacéutico *(el)* *(ehl fahr-mah-'seh-oo-tee-koh)*
pharmacy	farmacia *(la)* *(lah fahr-'mah-see·ah)*
phlegm	flema *(la)* *(lah 'fleh-mah)*
physical exam	examen físico *(el)* *(ehl ehk-'sah-mehn 'fee-see-koh)*
physical therapy	terapia física *(la)* *(lah the-'rah-pee-ah 'fee-see-kah)*
pic	pastel *(el)* *(ehl pahs-'tehl)*
pill	píldora *(la)* *(lah 'peel-doh-rah)*
pillow	almohada *(la)* *(lah ahl-moh-'ah-dah)*
pillowcase	funda *(la)* *(lah 'foon-dah)*
pimple	grano *(el)* *(ehl 'grah-noh)*
pin	alfiler *(el)* *(ehl ahl-fee-'lehr)*
pineapple	piña *(la)* *(lah 'pee-nyah)*
pink	rosado *(m.)*; rosada *(f.)* *(roh-'sah-doh, roh-'sah-dah)*
pitcher	jarra *(la)* *(lah 'har-rah)*
placenta	placenta *(la)* *(lah plah-'sehn-tah)*
plague	plaga *(la)* *(lah 'plah-gah)*
plan	plan *(el)* *(ehl plahn)*
planning	planificación *(la)* *(lah plah-nee-fee-kah-see-'ohn)*

plaque	placa (la) (lah 'plah-kah)
plate	plato (el) (ehl 'plah-toh)
plumber	plomero (el) (ehl plo-'meh-roh)
pneumonia	pulmonía (la) (lah pool-moh-'nee-ah)
podiatrist	podiatra (m. & f.) (ehl (lah) poh-dee-'ah-trah)
point (to)	señalar (seh-nyah-'lahr)
	Point (request to)
	Señale. (seh-'nyah-leh)
poison	veneno (el) (ehl beh-'neh-noh)
poison ivy	hiedra venenosa (la) (lah 'yeh-drah beh-neh-'noh-sah)
poison oak	encina venenosa (la) (lah ehn-'see-nah beh-neh-'noh-sah)
police	policía (la) (lah poh-lee-'see-ah)
police officer	policía (m. & f.) (ehl (lah) poh-lee-'see-ah)
policy	póliza (la) (lah 'poh-lee-sah)
polio	polio (el) (ehl 'poh-lee·oh)
pollen	polen (el) (ehl 'poh-lehn)
polyp	pólipo (el) (ehl 'poh-lee-poh)
poor	pobre ('poh-breh)
porcelain	porcelana (la) (lah pohr-seh-'lah-nah)
post-op	después de la operación (dehs-'pwehs deh lah oh-peh-rah-see-'ohn)
postcard	tarjeta postal (la) (lah tahr-'heh-tah pohs-'tahl)
potassium	potasio (el) (ehl poh-'tah-see·oh)
potato	papa (la) (lah 'pah-pah)
pound	libra (la) (lah 'lee-brah)
pray (to)	rezar (reh-'sahr)
pre-approval	aprobación previa (la) (lah ah-proh-bah-see-'ohn 'preh-vee-ah)
pregnant	embarazada (ehm-bah-rah-'sah-dah)
	You are pregnant.
	Está embarazada. (eh-'stah ehm-bah-rah-'sah-dah)
premature	prematuro (m.); prematura (f.) (preh-mah-'too-roh, preh-mah-'too-rah)
premature ejaculation	eyaculación precoz (la) (lah eh-yah-koo-lah-see-'ohn preh-kohs)
prenatal care	atención prenatal (la) (lah ah-tehn-see-'ohn preh-nah-'tahl)

prepare (to)	preparar *(preh-pah-'rahr)*
pretty	bonito (m.); bonita (f.) *(boh-'nee-toh, boh-'nee-tah)*
prescription	receta médica *(la) (lah reh-'seh-tah 'meh-dee-kah)*
	Take this prescription.
	Tome esta receta. *('toh-meh 'eh-stah reh-'seh-tah)*
press (to)	apretar *(ah-preh-'tahr)*
	Press *(request to)*
	Apriete. *(ah-pree-'eh-teh)*
prevent (to)	prevenir *(preh-beh-'neer)*
price	precio *(el) (ehl 'preh-see-oh)*
priest	sacerdote *(el) (ehl sah-sehr-'doh-teh)*
private	privado (m.); privada (f.) *(pree-'bah-doh, pree-'bah-dah)*
private care	cuidado privado *(el) (ehl kwee-'dah-doh pree-'bah-doh)*
probe	sonda *(la) (lah 'sohn-dah)*
procedure	procedimiento *(el) (ehl proh-seh-dee-me-'ehn-toh)*
proceed (to)	proceder *(proh-seh-'dehr)*
proctologist	proctólogo *(el) (ehl prohk-'toh-loh-goh)*
proctology	proctología *(la) (lah prohk-toh-loh-'hee-ah)*
proctoscopy	proctoscopía *(la) (lah prohk-toh-skoh-'pee-ah)*
progressive sunglasses	lentes progresivos *(los) (lohs 'lehn-tehs proh-greh-'see-vohs)*
prohibit (to)	prohibir *(proh-hee-'beer)*
prohibited	prohibido *(proh-ee-'bee-doh)*
protect (to)	proteger *(proh-teh-'hehr)*
protein	proteína *(la) (lah proh-teh-'ee-nah)*
provider	proveedor (m.); proveedora (f.) *(proh-beh-eh-'dohr, proh-beh-eh-'doh-rah)*
psychiatric hospital	hospital psiquiátrico *(el) (ehl ohs-pee-'tahl see-kee-'aht-ree-koh)*
psychiatrist	psiquiatra (m. & f.) *(ehl (lah) see-kee-'ah-trah)*
	The psychiatrist will help you.
	El psiquiatra le ayudará.(m. & f.) *(ehl (lah) (see-kee-'ah-trah leh ah-yoo-dah-'rah)*
psychiatry	psiquiatría *(la) (lah see-kee-ah-'tree-ah)*
psychologist	psicólogo (m.); psicóloga (f.) *(see-'koh-loh-goh, see-'koh-loh-gah)*

psychology	psicología *(la) (lah see-koh-loh-'hee-ah)*
psychotherapy	psicoterapia *(la) (lah see-koh-teh-'rah-pee-ah)*
pull (to)	jalar *(hah-'lahr)*
	Pull *(request to)*
	Jale. *('hah-leh)*
pulled muscle	distensión *(la) (lah dees-tehn-see-'ohn)*
pulse	pulso *(el) (ehl 'pool-soh)*
	Your pulse is very fast.
	Su pulso es muy rápido.
	(soo 'pool-soh ehs 'moo·ee 'rah-pee-doh)
	Your pulse is very slow.
	Su pulso es muy lento.
	(soo 'pool-soh ehs 'moo·ee 'lehn-toh)
pump	bomba *(la) (lah 'bohm-bah)*
pump (to)	bombear *(bohm-beh-'ahr)*
purify (to)	purificar *(poo-ree-fee-'kahr)*
purple	morado (m.); morada (f.)
	(moh-'rah-doh, moh-'rah-dah)
pus	pus *(el) (ehl poos)*
push (to)	empujar *(ehm-poo-'har)*
	Push *(request to)*
	Empuje. *(ehm-'poo-heh)*
put (to)	poner *(poh-'nehr)*
	Put on *(request to)*
	Póngase. *('pohn-gah-seh)*
	Put *(request to)*
	Ponga. *('pohn-gah)*
pyorrhea	piorrea *(la) (lah pee-oh-'rreh-ah)*
question	pregunta *(la) (lah preh-'goon-tah)*
	Do you have a question?
	¿Tiene una pregunta?
	(tee-'eh-neh 'oo-nah preh-'goon-tah)
quickly	rápidamente *('rah-pee-dah-mehn-teh)*
rabbit	conejo *(el) (ehl koh-'neh-hoh)*
race	raza *(la) (lah 'rah-sah)*
radiation	irradiación *(la) (lah eer-rah-dee-ah-see-'ohn)*
radiation therapy	radioterapia *(la) (lah rah-dee-oh-teh-'rah-pee-ah)*
radiologist	radiólogo (m.); radióloga (f.)
	(rah-dee-'oh-loh-goh, rah-dee-'oh-loh-gah)

radiology	radiología *(la)* *(lah rah-dee-oh-loh-'hee-ah)*
radiotherapy	radioterapia *(la)* *(lah rah-dee-oh-teh-'rah-pee·ah)*
rain	lluvia *(la)* *(lah 'yoo-bee·ah)*
raise (to)	levantar *(leh-bahn-'tahr)*
	Raise *(request to)*
	Levante. *(leh-'bahn-teh)*
rape	violación *(la)* *(lah bee-oh-lah-see-'ohn)*
rape (to)	violar *(bee-oh-'lahr)*
rashes	sarpullidos *(los)* *(lohs sahr-poo-'yee-dohs)*
rat	rata *(la)* *(lah 'rah-tah)*
razor blade	hoja de afeitar *(la)* *(lah 'oh-hah de ah-feh·ee-'tahr)*
read (to)	leer *(leh-'ehr)*
readmit (to)	readmitir *(reh-ahd-mee-'teer)*
receipt	recibo *(el)* *(ehl reh-'see-boh)*
receive (to)	recibir *(reh-see-'beer)*
recommend (to)	recomendar *(reh-koh-mehn-'dahr)*
Recovery Room	sala de recuperación *(la)*
	(lah 'sah-lah deh reh-koo-peh-rah-see-'ohn)
rectum	recto *(el)* *(ehl 'rehk-toh)*
recuperate (to)	recuperar *(reh-koo-peh-'rahr)*
recuperation	recuperación *(la)* *(lah recuperación)*
red	rojo (m.); roja (f.) *('roh-hoh, 'roh-hah)*
redhead	pelirrojo (m.); pelirroja (f.)
	(peh-lee-'rroh-hoh, peh-lee-'rroh-hah)
refrigerator	refrigerador *(el)* *(ehl reh-free-heh-rah-'dohr)*
register (to)	registrar *(reh-hees-'trahr)*
redness	enrojecimiento *(el)*
	(ehl ehn-roh-heh-see-mee-'ehn-toh)
referral	referencia *(la)* *(lah reh-feh-'rehn-see-ah)*
relationship (family)	parentezco *(el)* *(ehl pah-rehn-'tehs-koh)*
relaxed	relajado (m.); relajada (f.)
	(reh-lah-'hah-doh, reh-lah-'hah-dah)
release (to)	dar de alta *(dahr deh 'ahl-tah)*
relieve (to)	aliviar *(ah-lee-bee-'ahr)*
religion	religión *(la)* *(lah reh-lee-hee-'ohn)*
remedy	remedio *(el)* *(ehl reh-'meh-dee·oh)*
remember (to)	recordar *(reh-kohr-'dahr)*

remove (to)	sacar *(sah-'kahr)*
	We're going to remove the stitches.
	Vamos a sacarle los puntos.
	('bah-mohs ah sah-'kahr-leh lohs 'poon-tohs)
repair (to)	reparar *(reh-pah-'rahr)*
replace (to)	remplazar *(rehm-plah-'sahr)*
research (to)	investigar *(een-behs-tee-'gahr)*
resist (to)	resistir *(reh-sees-'teer)*
resources	recursos *(los)* *(lohs reh-'koor-sohs)*
respirator	respirador *(el)* *(ehl rehs-pee-rah-'dohr)*
rest (to)	descansar *(dehs-kahn-'sahr)*
restaurant	restaurante *(el)* *(ehl rehs-tow-'rahn-teh)*
restless	inquieto (m.); inquieta (f.)
	(een-kee-'eh-toh, een-kee-'eh-tah)
restrictions	restricciones *(las)* *(lahs rehs-treek-see-'oh-nehs)*
return (to)	regresar, volver *(reh-greh-'sahr, bohl-'behr)*
	Are you going to return?
	¿Va a regresar? *(bah ah reh-greh-'sahr)*
rheumatic fever	fiebre reumática *(la)*
	(lah fee-'eh-breh reh-oo-'mah-tee-kah)
rib	costilla *(la)* *(lah kos-'tee-yah)*
rice	arroz *(el)* *(ehl ah-'rrohs)*
rich	rico (m.); rica (f.) *('rree-koh, 'rree-kah)*
right	derecho (m.); derecha (f.)
	(deh-'reh-choh, deh-'reh-chah)
	to the right
	a la derecha *(ah lah deh-'reh-chah)*
rights	derechos *(los)* *(lohs deh-'reh-chohs)*
ring	anillo *(el)* *(ehl ah-'nee-yoh)*
ringing in the ear	silbido en el oído *(el)*
	(ehl seel-'bee-doh ehn ehl oh-'ee-doh)
rinse (to)	enjuagar *(ehn-hwah-'gahr)*
	Rinse *(request to)*
	Enjuáguese. *(ehn-'hwah-geh-seh)*
risky	arriesgado (m.); arriesgada (f.)
	(ahr-ree-ehs-'gah-doh, ahr-ree-ehs-'gah-dah)
river	río *(el)* *(ehl 'ree-oh)*
road	camino *(el)* *(ehl kah-'mee-noh)*

robe	bata *(la)* *(lah 'bah-tah)*
rock	piedra *(la)* *(lah pee-'eh-drah)*
room	cuarto *(el)* *(ehl 'kwahr-toh)*
root	raíz *(la)* *(la rah-'ees)*
	root canal
	tratamiento del nervio dental
	(ehl trah-tah-mee-'ehn-toh dehl 'nehr-bee·oh dehn-'tahl)
run (to)	correr *(koh-'rrehr)*
runny nose	goteo nasal *(el)* *(ehl goh-'teh-oh nah-'sahl)*
rupture	ruptura *(la)* *(lah roop-'too-rah)*
sad	triste (m. & f.) *('trees-teh)*
safe	seguro *(seh-'goo-roh)*
salad	ensalada *(la)* *(lah ehn-sah-lah-dah)*
salesperson	vendedor (m.); vendedora (f.)
	(ehl behn-deh-'dohr, lah behn-deh-'doh-rah)
saliva	saliva *(la)* *(lah sah-'lee-bah)*
salt	sal *(la)* *(lah sahl)*
same	mismo (m.); misma (f.) *('mees-moh, 'mees-mah)*
sample	muestra *(la)* *(lah 'mwehs-trah)*
sand	arena *(la)* *(lah ah-'reh-nah)*
sane	cuerdo (m.); cuerda (f.) *('kwehr-doh, 'kwehr-dah)*
satisfied	satisfecho (m.); satisfecha (f.)
	(sah-tees-'feh-choh, sah-fees-'feh-chah)
Saturday	sábado *(el)* *(ehl 'sah-bah-doh)*
sauce	salsa *(la)* *(lah 'sahl-sah)*
say (to)	decir *(deh-'seer)*
	Say (*request to*)
	Diga. *('dee-gah)*
scab	costra *(la)* *(lah 'kos-trah)*
scale (of skin)	costra *(la)* *(lah 'kohs-trah)*
scale (on teeth)	sarro *(el)* *(ehl 'sah-rroh)*
scale (weighing)	báscula *(la)* *(lah 'bahs-koo-lah)*
scar	cicatriz *(la)* *(lah see-kah-'trees)*
scared	espantado (m.); espantada (f.)
	(ehs-pahn-'tah-doh, ehs-pahn-'tah-dah)
scarf	bufanda *(la)* *(lah boo-'fahn-dah)*
scarlet fever	escarlatina *(la)* *(lah ehs-kahr-lah-'tee-nah)*
schedule	horario *(el)* *(ehl oh-'rah-ree·oh)*

schizophrenic	esquizofrénico (m.); esquizofrénica (f.) *(ehl ehs-kee-soh-'freh-nee-koh, lah ehs-kee-soh-'freh-nee-kah)*
school	escuela *(la) (lah ehs-'kweh-lah)*
scissors	tijeras *(las) (lahs tee-'heh-rahs)*
scorpion	escorpión *(el) (ehl ehs-kohr-pee·'ohn)*
scratch	rasguño *(el) (ehl rahs-'goon-yoh)*
scratch (to)	rascar *(rahs-'kahr)*
scrotum	escroto *(el) (ehl ehs-'kroh-toh)*
sea	mar *(el) (ehl mahr)*
second	segundo *(el) (ehl seh-'goon-doh)*
second opinion	segunda opinión *(la) (lah seh-'goon-dah oh-pee-nee-'ohn)*
secretary	secretario (m.); secretaria (f.) *(seh-kreh-'tah-ree·oh, seh-kreh-'tah-ree·ah)*
security	seguridad *(la) (lah seh-goo-ree-'dahd)*
sedative	sedante *(el) (ehl seh-'dahn-teh)*
see (to)	ver *(behr)*
seizures	ataques *(los) (lohs ah-'tah-kehs)*
self-examination	autoexamen *(el) (ehl ah-oo-toh-ehk-'sah-mehn)*
semen	semen *(el) (ehl 'seh-mehn)*
send (to)	mandar *(mahn-'dahr)*
senile	senil *(seh-'neel)*
senile dementia	demencia senil *(la) (lah deh-'mehn-see·ah seh-'neel)*
senility	senilidad *(la) (lah seh-nee-lee-'dahd)*
sensitivity	sensibilidad *(la) (lah sehn-see-bee-lee-'dahd)*
September	septiembre *(sehp-tee-'ehm-breh)*
serious	grave *('grah-beh)*
servant	criado *(el)*, criada *(la) (ehl kree-ah-doh, lah kree-ah-dah)*
service	servicio *(el) (ehl sehr-'bee-see·oh)*
seventh	séptimo *(sehp-tee-moh)*
severe	muy fuerte *('moo·ee 'fwehr-teh)*
severe	severo (m.); severa (f.) *(seh-'beh-roh, seh-'beh-rah)*
sew (to)	coser *(koh-'sehr)*
sex	sexo *(el) (ehl 'sehk-soh)*
sexual relations	relaciones sexuales *(las) (lahs reh-lah-see·'oh-nehs sehk-soo-'ah-lehs)*

shallow (person)	superficial *(soo-pehr-fee-see-'ahl)*
sharp	agudo *(ah-'goo-doh)*
sharp (edge)	afilado *(ah-fee-'lah-doh)*
sharp (sound)	agudo *(ah-'goo-doh)*
shave (to)	afeitar *(ah-feh-ee-'tahr)*
she	ella *('eh-yah)*
sheet	sábana *(la) (lah 'sah-bah-nah)*
shellfish	mariscos *(los) (lohs mah-'rees-kohs)*
ship	barco *(el) (ehl 'bahr-koh)*
shirt	camisa *(la) (lah kah-'mee-sah)*
shoe	zapato *(el) (ehl sah-'pah-toh)*
shoot (to)	disparar *(dees-pah-'rahr)*
shortness of breath	falta de aliento *(la) (lah 'fahl-tah deh ah-lee-'ehn-toh)*
shorts	calzoncillos *(los) (lohs kahl-sohn-'see-yohs)*
shoulder	hombro *(el) (ehl 'ohm-broh)*
	dislocated shoulder
	hombro dislocado *(el) (ehl 'ohm-broh dees-loh-'kah-doh)*
shower	ducha *(la) (lah 'doo-chah)*
shower (to)	ducharse *(doo-'chahr-seh)*
sick	enfermo (m.); enferma (f.) *(ehn-'fehr-moh, ehn-'fehr-mah)*
	When did he/she get sick?
	¿Cuándo se enfermó? *('kwahn-doh seh ehn-fehr-'moh)*
sickness	enfermedad *(la) (lah ehn-fehr-meh-'dad)*
sidewalk	acera *(la) (lah ah-'seh-rah)*
SIDS	síndrome de muerte infantil súbita *(el)* *(ehl 'seen-droh-meh deh 'mwehr-teh een-fahn-'teel 'soo-bee-tah)*
sight	vista *(la) (lah 'bees-tah)*
sign (to)	firmar *(feer-'mahr)*
	Sign *(request to)*
	Firme. *('feer-meh)*
	Sign your name.
	Firme su nombre. *('feer-meh soo 'nohm-breh)*
signature	firma *(la) (lah 'feer-mah)*
silver	plata *(la) (lah 'plah-tah)*
simple	sencillo *(sehn-'see-yoh)*
single (person)	soltero (m.); soltera (f.) *(sohl-'teh-roh, sohl-'teh-rah)*

sink	lavamanos *(el)* *(ehl lah-bah-'mah-nohs)*
sister	hermana *(la)* *(lah ehr-'mah-nah)*
sister-in-law	cuñada *(la)* *(lah koo-'nyah-dah)*
sit down (to)	sentarse *(sehn-'tahr-seh)*
	Have a seat. Siéntese. *(see-'ehn-teh-sah)*
sixth	sexto *('sehks-toh)*
size	tamaño *(el)* *(ehl tah-'mahn-yoh)*
skeleton	esqueleto *(el)* *(ehl ehs-keh-'leh-toh)*
skin	piel *(la)* *(lah pee-'ehl)*
	skin cancer
	cáncer de la piel *(el)* *(ehl 'kahn-sehr deh lah pee-'ehl)*
	skin disease
	enfermedad de la piel *(la)*
	(lah ehn-fehr-meh-'dahd deh lah pee-'ehl)
	skin rash
	erupción en la piel *(la)*
	(lah eh-roop-see·'ohn ehn lah pee-'ehl)
skirt	falda *(la)* *(lah 'fahl-dah)*
sleep (to)	dormir *(dohr-'meer)*
sleeping pill	somnífero *(el)* *(ehl sohm-'nee-feh-roh)*
sleepy	soñoliento (m.); soñolienta (f.)
	(soh-nyoh-lee-'ehn-toh, soh-nyoh-lee-'ehn-tah)
	Are you sleepy?
	¿Tiene sueño? *(tee-'eh-neh 'sweh-nyoh?)*
sleeve	manga *(la)* *(lah 'mahn-gah)*
sling	cabestrillo *(el)* *(ehl kah-behs-'tree-yoh)*
slippers	pantuflas *(las)* *(lahs pahn-'too-flahs)*
slow	lento (m.); lenta (f.) *('lehn-toh, 'lehn-tah)*
slowly	lentamente, despacio
	(lehn-tah-'mehn-teh, dehs-'pah-see·oh)
small	chico (m.); chica (f.) *('chee-koh, 'chee-kah)*
smallpox	viruela *(la)* *(lah bee-roo-'eh-lah)*
smear	frotis *(el)* *(ehl 'froh-tees)*
smell (to)	oler *(oh-'lehr)*
smile	sonrisa *(la)* *(lah sohn-'ree-sah)*
smoke	humo *(el)* *(ehl 'oo-moh)*
smoke (to)	fumar *(foo-'mahr)*
snack	merienda *(la)* *(lah meh-ree-'ehn-dah)*

snake	culebra *(la)* *(lah 'koo-'leh-brah)*
	poisonous snake
	víbora venenosa *(la)*
	(lah 'bee-boh-rah beh-neh-'no-sah)
	snake bite
	mordedura de culebra *(la)*
	(lah mohr-deh-'doo-rah deh koo-leh-brah)
sneeze (to)	estornudar *(ehs-tohr-noo-'dahr)*
snoring	ronquido *(el)* *(ehl rohn-'kee-doh)*
snow	nieve *(la)* *(lah nee-'eh-beh)*
so	así que *(ah-'see keh)*
soap	jabón *(el)* *(ehl hah-'bohn)*
Social Security number	número de seguro social *(el)*
	(ehl 'noo-meh-roh deh seh-'goo-roh soh-see-'ahl)
social worker	trabajador social *(el)*, trabajadora social *(la)*
	(ehl trah-bah-hah-'dohr soh-see-'ahl, lah trah-bah-hah-'doh-rah soh-see-'ahl)
socks	calcetines *(los)* *(lohs kahl-seh-'tee-nehs)*
sodium	sodio *(el)* *(ehl 'soh-dee·oh)*
soft	blando (m.); blanda (f.) *('blahn-doh, 'blahn-dah)*
soft drink	refresco *(el)* *(ehl reh-'frehs-koh)*
sole	planta del pie *(la)* *(lah 'plahn-tah dehl pee-'eh)*
solution	solución *(la)* *(lah soh-loo-see-'ohn)*
some	unos (m.); unas (f.) *('oo-nohs, 'oo-nahs)*
something	algo *('ahl-goh)*
sometimes	a veces *(ah 'beh-sehs)*
son	hijo *(el)* *(ehl 'ee-hoh)*
son-in-law	yerno *(el)* *(ehl 'yehr-noh)*
sonogram	sonograma *(el)* *(ehl soh-noh-'grah-mah)*
soon	pronto *('prohn-toh)*
sore (person)	dolorido (m.); dolorida (f.) *(doh-loh-'ree-doh, doh-loh-'ree-dah)*
sore (wound)	llaga *(la)* *(lah 'yah-gah)*
sound	sonido *(el)* *(ehl soh-'nee-doh)*
soup	sopa *(la)* *(lah 'soh-pah)*
spasm	espasmo *(el)* *(ehl ehs-'pahs-moh)*
speak (to)	hablar *(ah-'blahr)*
	Do you speak English?
	¿Habla inglés? *(ah-'blah een-'glehs)*

I speak a little Spanish.
Hablo un poquito de español.
(*'ah-bloh oon poh-'kee-toh deh ehs-pah-'nyohl*)

special	especial (*ehs-peh-see-'ahl*)
specialist	especialista (m. & f.) (*ehl (lah) ehs-peh-see-ah-'lees-tah*)
speed (amphetamine)	anfetamina (*la*) (*lah ahn-feh-tah-'mee-nah*)
sperm	esperma (*la*) (*lah ehs-'pehr-mah*)
spicy	picante (*pee-'kahn-teh*)
	spicy food comida picante (*la*) (*lah koh-'me-dah pee-'kahn-teh*)
spinal fluid	líquido cefaloraquídeo (*el*) (*ehl 'lee-kee-doh seh-fah-loh-rah-'kee-deh-oh*)
spice	especia (*la*) (*lah ehs-'peh-see·ah*)
spider	araña (*la*) (*lah ah-'rah-nyah*)
spinal column	columna vertebral (*la*) (*lah koh-'loom-nah behr-teh-'brahl*)
spinal tap	punción lumbar (*la*) (*lah poon-see·'ohn loom-'bahr*)
spit (to)	escupir (*ehs-koo-'peer*)
spleen	bazo (*el*) (*ehl 'bah-soh*)
splint	tablilla (*la*) (*lah tah-'blee-yah*)
splinter	astilla (*la*) (*lah ahs-'tee-yah*)
sponge	esponja (*la*) (*lah ehs-'pohn-hah*)
spoon	cuchara (*la*) (*lah koo-'chah-rah*)
spot	mancha (*la*) (*lah 'mahn-chah*)
spring	primavera (*la*) (*lah pree-mah-'beh-rah*)
sputum	esputo (*el*) (*ehl ehs-'poo-toh*)
squeeze (to)	apretar (*ah-preh-'tahr*)
stab (to)	apuñalar (*ah-poo-nyah-'lahr*)
stable	estable (m. & f.) (*ehs-'tahb-leh*)
stairs	escaleras (*las*) (*lahs ehs-kah-'leh-rahs*)
stamps	estampillas (*las*) (*lahs ehs-tahm-'pee-yahs*)
stand (to)	pararse (*pah-'rahr-seh*)
stand up (to)	levantarse (*leh-bahn-'tahr-seh*)
start (to)	empezar (*ehm-peh-'sahr*)
station	estación (*la*) (*lah ehs-tah-see·'ohn*)
stay (to)	quedarse (*keh-'dahr-seh*)
steak	bistec (*el*) (*ehl bees-'tehk*)

steam	vapor *(el)* *(ehl vah-'pohr)*
step	escalón *(el)* *(ehl ehs-kah-'lohn)*
stepdaughter	hijastra *(la)* *(lah ee-'hahs-trah)*
stepfather	padrastro *(el)* *(ehl pah-'drahs-troh)*
stepmother	madrastra *(la)* *(lah mah-'drahs-trah)*
stepson	hijastro *(el)* *(ehl ee-'hahs-troh)*
STD	enfermedad venérea *(la)* *(lah ehn-fehr-meh-'dahd veh-'neh-reh-ah)*
sterilize (to)	esterilizar *(ehs-teh-ree-lee-'sahr)*
stethoscope	estetoscopio *(el)* *(ehl ehs-teh-toh-'skoh-pee·oh)*
stillborn	nacido muerto *(nah-'see-doh 'mwehr-toh)*
stimulants	estimulantes *(los)* *(lohs ehs-tee-moo-'lahn-tehs)*
stitches	puntos *(los)* *(lohs 'poon-tohs)*
stockings	medias *(las)* *(lahs 'meh-dee·ahs)*
stomach	estómago *(el)* *(ehl ehs-'toh-mah-goh)*
stomachache	dolor de estómago *(el)* *(ehl doh-'lohr deh ehs-'toh-mah-goh)*
stones	cálculos *(los)* *(lohs 'kahl-koo-lohs)*
store	tienda *(la)* *(lah tee-'ehn-dah)*
straight ahead	adelante *(ah-deh-'lahn-teh)*
straight jacket	camisa de fuerza *(la)* *(lah kah-'mee-sah deh 'fwehr-sah)*
straighten (to)	enderezar *(ehn-deh-reh-'sahr)*
strangulation	estrangulamiento *(el)* *(ehl ehs-trahn-goo-lah-mee-'ehn-toh)*
strawberry	fresa *(la)* *(lah 'freh-sah)*
street	calle *(la)* *(lah 'kah-yeh)*
stretcher	camilla *(la)* *(lah kah-'mee-yah)*
stress	estrés *(el)* *(ehl ehs-'trehs)*
stroke	ataque *(el)* *(ehl ah-'tah-keh)*
stroller	cochecillo *(el)* *(ehl koh-cheh-'see-yoh)*
strong	fuerte *('fwehr-teh)*
student	estudiante *(m. & f.)* *(ehl (lah) ehs-too-dee-'ahn-teh)*
study (to)	estudiar *(ehs-too-dee-'ahr)*
stuffy nose	nariz tapada *(la)* *(lah nah-'rees tah-'pah-dah)*
sty	orzuelo *(el)* *(ehl ohr-'sweh-loh)*

subway	metro *(el)* *(ehl 'meh-troh)*
suck (to)	chupar *(choo-'pahr)*
suffer (to)	sufrir *(soo-'freer)*
suffocation	sofocación *(la)* *(lah soh-foh-kah-see·'ohn)*
sugar	azúcar *(el)* *(ehl ah-'soo-kahr)*
suicide	suicidio *(el)* *(ehl soo-ee-'see-dee·oh)*
	He committed suicide.
	Se suicidó. *(seh soo-ee-see-'doh)*
suit	traje *(el)* *(ehl 'trah-heh)*
summer	verano *(el)* *(ehl beh-'rah-noh)*
sun	sol *(el)* *(ehl sohl)*
Sunday	domingo *(doh-'meen-goh)*
sunglasses	lentes de sol *(los)* *(lohs 'lehn-tehs deh sohl)*
sunstroke	insolación *(la)* *(lah een-soh-lah-see·'ohn)*
suppositories	supositorios *(los)* *(lohs soo-poh-see-'toh-ree·ohs)*
Sure!	¡Claro! *('klah-roh)*
surgeon	cirujano *(el)*, cirujana *(la)* *(ehl see-roo-'hah-noh, lah see-roo-'hah-nah)*
surgery	cirugía *(la)* *(lah see-roo-'hee-ah)*
surprised	sorprendido (m.); sorprendida (f.) *(sohr-prehn-'dee-doh, sohr-prehn-'dee-dah)*
suture	sutura *(la)* *(lah soo-'too-rah)*
swallow (to)	tragar *(trah-'gahr)*
sweat	sudor *(el)* *(ehl soo-'dohr)*
sweater	suéter *(el)* *(ehl 'sweh-tehr)*
sweating	sudor *(el)* *(ehl soo-'dohr)*
sweaty	sudoroso (m.); sudorosa (f.) *(soo-doh-'roh-soh, soo-doh-'roh-sah)*
sweet	dulce *(el)* *('dool-seh)*
swelling	hinchazón *(la)* *(lah een-chah-'sohn)*
swollen glands	glándulas hinchadas *(las)* *(lahs 'glahn-doo-lahs een-'chah-dahs)*
symptom	síntoma *(el)* *(ehl 'seen-toh-mah)*
syndrome	síndrome *(el)* *(ehl 'seen-droh-meh)*
syphilis	sífilis *(la)* *(lah 'see-fee-lees)*
syringe	jeringa *(la)* *(lah heh-'reen-gah)*
syrup	jarabe *(el)* *(ehl hah-'rah-beh)*
table	mesa *(la)* *(lah 'meh-sah)*

tablespoon	cucharada *(la)* *(lah koo-chah-'rah-dah)*
tablet	tableta *(la)* *(lah tah-'bleh-tah)*
take (to)	tomar *(toh-'mahr)*
	Take *(request to)*
	Tome. *('toh-meh)*
take off (clothes) (to)	quitarse *(kee-'tahr-seh)*
	Take off *(request to)*
	Quítese. *('kee-teh-seh)*
talcum powder	talco *(el)* *(ehl 'tahl-koh)*
tape	cinta *(la)* *(lah 'seen-tah)*
tapeworm infection	infección de lombrices intestinales *(la)* *(lah een-fehk-see-'ohn deh lohm-'bree-sehs een-tehs-tee-'nah-lehs)*
tartar	sarro *(el)* *(ehl 'sah-rroh)*
taste (to)	saborear *(sah-boh-reh-'ahr)*
tea	té *(el)* *(ehl teh)*
teacher	maestro *(el)*, maestra *(la)* *(ehl mah-'ehs-troh, lah mah-'ehs-trah)*
teacup	taza *(la)* *(lah 'tah-sah)*
teaspoon	cucharadita *(la)* *(lah koo-chah-rah-'dee-tah)*
technician	técnico (m. & f.) *(ehl (lah) 'tehk-nee-koh)*
telephone	teléfono *(el)* *(ehl teh-'leh-foh-noh)*
	telephone number
	número de teléfono *(el)* *(ehl 'noo-meh-roh deh teh-'leh-foh-noh)*
television	televisión *(la)* *(lah teh-leh-bee-see·ohn)*
tell (to)	decir *(deh-'sihr)*
	Tell *(request to)*
	Diga. *('dee-gah)*
	Tell me.
	Dígame. *('dee-gah-meh)*
	Tell the nurse.
	Diga a la enfermera. *('dee-gah ah lah ehn-fehr-'meh-rah)*
temperature	temperatura *(la)* *(lah tehm-peh-rah-'too-rah)*
temple	sien *(la)* *(lah 'see·ehn)*
tendon	tendón *(el)* *(ehl tehn-'dohn)*
tendonitis	tendonitis *(la)* *(lah tehn-doh-'nee-tees)*
term (insurance)	condición *(la)* *(lah kohn-dee-see-'ohn)*

test	examen *(el)* *(ehl ehk-'sah-mehn)*
testicles	testículos *(los)* *(lohs tehs-'tee-koo-lohs)*
tests	pruebas *(las)* *(lahs proo·'eh-bahs)*
tetanus	tétano *(el)* *(ehl 'teh-tah-noh)*
that	ese (m.); esa (f.) *('eh-seh, 'eh-sah)*
then	entonces *(ehn-'tohn-sehs)*
therapist	terapeuta (m. & f.) *(ehl (lah) teh-rah-'peh-oo-tah)*
therapy	terapia *(la)* *(lah teh-'rah-pee·ah)*
there	allí *(ah-'yee)*
therefore	por eso *(pohr 'eh-soh)*
there is/ there are	hay *('ah·ee)*
thermometer	termómetro *(el)* *(ehl tehr-'moh-meh-troh)*
thermostat	termostato *(el)* *(ehl tehr-moh-'stah-toh)*
these	estos (m.); estas (f.) *('ehs-tohs, 'ehs-tahs)*
they	ellos (m.); ellas (f.) *('eh-yohs, 'eh-yahs)*
thick	grueso (m.); gruesa (f.) *(groo'eh-soh, groo-'eh-sah)*
thigh	muslo *(el)* *(ehl 'moos-loh)*
thin	delgado (m.); delgada (f.) *(dehl-'gah-doh, dehl-'gah-dah)*
thing	cosa *(la)* *(lah 'koh-sah)*
think (to)	pensar *(pehn-'sahr)*
third	tercero *(tehr-'seh-roh)*
thirsty	sediento (m.); sedienta (f.) *(seh-dee-'ehn-toh, seh-dee-'ehn-tah)*
this	este (m.); esta (f.) *('ehs-teh, 'ehs-tah)*
those	esos (m.); esas (f.) *('eh-sohs, 'eh-sahs)*
thread	hilo *(el)* *(ehl 'ee-loh)*
throat	garganta *(la)* *(lah gahr-'gahn-tah)*

sore throat
dolor de garganta *(el)*
(ehl doh-'lohr de gahr-'gahn-tah)

Do you feel a choking sensation when not eating?
¿Tiene sensación de ahogo cuando no está comiendo?
(tee-'eh-neh sehn-sah-see·'ohn deh ah-'oh-goh 'kwahn-doh noh eh-'stah koh-mee-'ehn-doh)

Do you have a sore throat often?
¿Le duele la garganta con frecuencia?
(leh 'dweh-leh lah gahr-'gahn-tah kohn freh-'kwehn-see·ah)

	Is it difficult to swallow food?
	¿Le es difícil tragar comida?
	(leh ehs dee-'fee-seel trah-'gahr koh-'mee-dah)
	Is it hard to swallow liquids?
	¿Le es difícil tragar líquido?
	(leh ehs dee-'fee-seel trah-'gahr 'lee-kee-doh)
throbbing	pulsante *(pool-'sahn-teh)*
Thursday	jueves *('hweh-behs)*
thyroid	tiroides *(la) (lah tee-'roh·ee-dehs)*
	thyroid disease
	enfermedad de la glándula tiroides *(la)*
	(lah ehn-fehr-meh-'dahd deh lah 'glahn-doo-lah tee-'roh·ee-dehs)
ticks	garrapatas *(las) (lahs gahr-rah-'pah-tahs)*
time	tiempo *(el) (ehl tee-'ehm-poh)*
tingling	hormigueo *(el) (ehl ohr-mee-'geh-oh)*
tie	corbata *(la) (lah kohr-'bah-tah)*
tingling	hormigueo *(el) (ehl ohr-mee-'geh-oh)*
tired	cansado (m.); cansada (f.)
	(kahn-'sah-doh, kahn-'sah-dah)
tissue	tejido *(el) (ehl teh-'hee-doh)*
to	a *(ah)*
today	hoy *('oh·ee)*
toe	dedo del pie *(el) (ehl 'deh-doh dehl 'pee-eh)*
toilet	excusado *(el) (ehl ehks-koo-'sah-doh)*
toilet (personal hygiene, grooming)	aseo personal *(el)* *(ehl ah-'seh-oh pehr-soh-'nahl)*
toilet paper	papel higiénico *(el) (ehl pah-'pehl ee-hee-'eh-nee-koh)*
tomato	tomate *(el) (ehl toh-'mah-teh)*
tomorrow	mañana *(mah-'nyah-nah)*
tongue	lengua *(la) (lah 'lehn-gwah)*
tongue depressor	pisalengua *(la) (lah pee-sah-'lehn-gwah)*
tonight	esta noche *('eh-stah 'noh-cheh)*
tonsillitis	amigdalitis *(la) (lah ah-meeg-dah-'lee-tees)*
tonsillitis	tonsilitis *(la) (lah tohn-see-'lee-tees)*
tonsils	amígdalas *(las) (lahs ah-'meeg-dah-lahs)*
too much	demasiado *(deh-mah-see-'ah-doh)*

tooth	diente *(el)* *(ehl dee-'ehn-teh)*
toothache	dolor de muela *(ehl doh-lohr deh 'mweh-lah)*
toothbrush	cepillo de dientes *(el)* *(ehl seh-'pee-yoh deh dee-'ehn-tehs)*
toothpaste	pasta de dientes *(la)* *(lah 'pahs-tah deh dee-'ehn-tehs)*
tornado	tornado *(el)* *(ehl tohr-'nah-doh)*
tourniquet	torniquete *(el)* *(ehl tohr-nee-'keh-teh)*
towel	toalla *(la)* *(lah toh-'ah-yah)*
toy	juguete *(el)* *(ehl hoo-'geh-teh)*
traction	tracción *(la)* *(lah trahk-see·'ohn)*
train	tren *(el)* *(ehl trehn)*
tranquil	tranquilo (m.); tranquila (f.) *(trahn-'kee-loh, trahn-'kee-lah)*
transplant (to)	trasplantar *(trahs-plahn-'tahr)*
transportation	transporte *(el)* *(ehl trahns-'pohr-teh)*
trapeze	trapecio *(el)* *(ehl trah-'peh-see·oh)*
trash	basura *(la)* *(lah bah-'soo-rah)*
trash can	cesto de basura *(el)* *(ehl 'cehs-toh deh bah-'soo-rah)*
trauma	trauma *(el)* *(ehl 'trah·oo-mah)*
tray	bandeja *(la)* *(lah bahn-'deh-hah)*
treatment	tratamiento *(el)* *(ehl trah-tah-mee-'ehn-toh)*
tree	árbol *(el)* *(ehl 'ahr-bohl)*
truck	camión *(el)* *(ehl kah-mee-'ohn)*
	truck driver camionero *(el)* *(ehl kah-mee-oh-'neh-roh)*
try (to)	tratar *(trah-'tahr)*
	Try to (request to) Trate de. *('trah-teh deh)*
t-shirt	camiseta *(la)* *(lah kah-mee-'seh-tah)*
tsunami	sunami *(el)* *(ehl soo-'nah-mee)*
tubal ligation	ligadura de las trompas *(la)* *(lah lee-gah-'doo-rah deh lahs 'trohm-pahs)*
tube	tubo *(el)* *(ehl 'too-boh)*
tuberculosis	tuberculosis *(la)* *(lah too-behr-koo-'loh-sees)*
Tuesday	martes *(ehl 'mahr-tehs)*
turkey	pavo *(el)* *(ehl 'pah-boh)*
turn (to)	voltear *(bohl-teh-'ahr)*
	Turn around (request to) Voltéese. *(bohl-'teh-eh-seh)*

Turn off *(request to)*
Apague. *(ah-'pah-gue)*

Turn on *(request to)*
Prenda. *('prehn-dah)*

Turn *(request to)*
Dé vuelta. *(deh 'bwehl-tah)*

turn oneself over (to)   voltearse *(bohl-teh-'ahr-seh)*

tweezers   pinzas *(las) (lahs 'peen-sahs)*

twin   gemelo (m.); gemela (f.) *(heh-'meh-loh, heh-'meh-lah)*

typhoid   fiebre tifoidea *(la) (lah fee-'eh-breh tee-foh-ee-'deh-ah)*

ugly   feo (m.); fea (f.) *('feh-oh, 'feh-ah)*

ulcer   úlcera *(la) (lah 'ool-seh-rah)*

ultrasound   ultrasonido *(el) (ehl ool-trah-soh-'nee-doh)*

umbilical cord   cordón umbilical *(el)* *(ehl kohr-'dohn oom-bee-lee-'kahl)*

uncle   tío *(el) (ehl 'tee-oh)*

uncomfortable   incómodo (m.); incómoda (f.) *(een-'koh-moh-doh, een-'koh-moh-dah)*

unconscious   inconsciente (m. & f.) *(een-kohn-see-'ehn-teh)*

under   debajo de *(deh-'bah-hoh deh)*

understand (to)   entender *(ehn-tehn-'dehr)*

I don't understand!
¡No entiendo! *(noh ehn-tee-'ehn-doh)*

Do you understand?
¿Entiende? *(ehn-tee-'ehn-deh)*

underwear   ropa interior *(la) (lah 'roh-pah een-teh-ree-'ohr)*

up   arriba de *(ah-'rree-bah deh)*

urethra   uretra *(la) (lah oo-'reh-trah)*

urinal   orinal *(el) (ehl oh-ree-'nahl)*

urinate (to)   orinar *(oh-ree-'nahr)*

urologist   urólogo *(el)*, uróloga *(la)* *(ehl oo-'roh-loh-goh, lah oo-'roh-loh-gah)*

use (to)   usar *(oo-'sahr)*

uterus   útero *(el) (ehl 'oo-teh-roh)*

vaccinate (to)   vacunar *(bah-koo-'nahr)*

vaccination   vacuna *(la) (lah bah-'koo-nah)*

vagina   vagina *(la) (lah bah-'hee-nah)*

valve	válvula *(la)* *(lah 'bahl-boo-lah)*
varicose veins	venas varicosas *(las)* *(lahs 'beh-nahs bah-ree-'koh-sahs)*
vasectomy	vasectomía *(la)* *(lah bah-sehk-toh-'mee-ah)*
vaseline	vaselina *(la)* *(lah bah-seh-'lee-nah)*
vegetable	legumbre *(la)* *(lah leh-'goom-breh)*
vein	vena *(la)* *(lah 'beh-nah)*
venereal disease	enfermedad venérea *(la)* *(lah ehn-fehr-meh-'dahd beh-'neh-reh-ah)*
ventricle	ventrículo *(el)* *(ehl behn-'tree-koo-loh)*
verify (to)	verificar *(beh-ree-fee-'kahr)*
very	muy *('moo·ee)*
virus	virus *(el)* *(ehl 'vee-roos)*
vision	visión *(la)* *(lah bee-see·'ohn)*
	double vision
	doble visión *(la)* *(lah 'doh-bleh bee-see·'ohn)*
vision care	cuidado de la visión *(el)* *(ehl koo-ee-'dah-doh deh lah vee-see-'ohn)*
visit	visita *(la)* *(lah bee-'see-tah)*
visit (to)	visitar *(bee-see-'tahr)*
	When was the doctor's last visit?
	¿Cuándo fue la última visita del doctor? *('kwahn-doh fweh lah 'ool-tee-mah bee-'see-tah dehl dohk-'tohr)*
visitor	visitante (m. & f.) *(ehl (lah) bee-see-'tahn-teh)*
vital signs	signos vitales *(los)* *(lohs 'seeg-nohs bee-'tah-lehs)*
vitamin	vitamina *(la)* *(lah bee-tah-'mee-nah)*
voice	voz *(la)* *(lah bohs)*
vomit (to)	vomitar *(boh-mee-'tahr)*
vulva	vulva *(la)* *(lah 'bool-bah)*
waist	cintura *(la)* *(lah seen-'too-rah)*
wait (to)	esperar *(ehs-peh-'rahr)*
	Wait (request to)
	Espere. *(ehs-'peh-reh)*
waiter	mesero *(el)* *(ehl meh-'seh-roh)*
waiting room	sala de espera *(la)* *(lah 'sah-lah deh ehs-'peh-rah)*
wake up (to)	despertar *(dehs-pehr-'tahr)*
	Wake up (request to)
	Despiértese. *(dehs-pee-'ehr-teh-seh)*

walk (to)	caminar *(kah-mee-'nahr)*
walker	caminadora *(la)* *(lah kah-mee-nah-'doh-rah)*
wall	pared *(la)* *(lah pah-'rehd)*
want (to)	querer *(keh-'rehr)*
	Do you want something else?
	¿Quiere algo más? *(kee-'eh-reh 'ahl-goh mahs)*
warehouse	almacén *(el)* *(ehl ahl-mah-'sehn)*
wart	verruga *(la)* *(lah beh-'rroo-gah)*
washcloth	toallita *(la)* *(lah toh-ah-'yee-tah)*
wash oneself (to)	lavarse *(lah-'bahr-seh)*
	Wash *(request to)*
	Lávese. *('lah-beh-seh)*
watch	reloj de pulsera *(el)* *(ehl reh-'loh deh pool-'seh-rah)*
water	agua *(el)* *(ehl 'ah-gwah)*
water fountain	fuente de agua *(la)* *(lah 'fwehn-teh deh 'ah-gwah)*
watery	aguado (m.); aguada (f.) *(ah-'gwah-doh, ah-'gwah-dah)*
watery eyes	ojos llorosos *(los)* *(lohs 'oh-hohs yoh-'roh-sohs)*
we	nosotros *(noh-'soh-trohs)*
weak	débil (m. & f.) *('deh-beel)*
weakness	debilidad *(la)* *(lah deh-bee-lee-'dahd)*
weather	clima *(el)*, tiempo *(el)* *(ehl 'klee-mah, ehl tee-'ehm-poh)*
Wednesday	miércoles *(mee-'ehr-koh-lehs)*
week	semana *(la)* *(lah seh-'mah-nah)*
weigh (to)	pesar *(peh-'sahr)*
	How much do you weigh?
	¿Cuánto pesa? *('kwahn-toh 'peh-sah)*
weight	peso *(el)* *(ehl 'peh-soh)*
welfare	bienestar social *(el)* *(ehl bee-'ehn-ehs-'tahr soh-see-'ahl)*
well	bien *('bee-ehn)*
West Nile virus	virus del Nilo Occidental *(el)* *(ehl 'vee-roos dehl 'nee-loh ohk-see-dehn-'tahl)*
wet	mojado (m.); mojada (f.) *(moh-'hah-doh, moh-'hah-dah)*
What?	¿Qué? *(keh)*
When?	¿Cuándo? *('kwahn-doh)*
Where?	¿Dónde? *('dohn-deh)*
Which?	¿Cuál? *('kwahl)*

white	blanco (m.); blanca (f.) *('blahn-koh, 'blahn-kah)*
Who?	¿Quién? *(kee-'ehn)*
whooping cough	tos ferina, tos convulsiva *(la)* *(lah tohs feh-'ree-nah, tohs kohn-bool-'see-bah)*
Whose?	¿De quién? *(deh kee-'ehn)*
Why?	¿Por qué? *(pohr keh)*
widow	viuda *(vee-'oo-dah)*
widower	viudo *(vee-'oo-doh)*
wife	esposa *(la)* *(lah ehs-'poh-sah)*
wind	viento *(el)* *(ehl bee-'ehn-toh)*
window	ventana *(la)* *(lah behn-'tah-nah)*
wine	vino *(el)* *(ehl 'bee-noh)*
winter	invierno *(el)* *(ehl een-bee-'ehr-noh)*
with	con *(kohn)*
without	sin *(seen)*
woman	mujer *(la)* *(lah moo-'hehr)*
word	palabra *(la)* *(lah pah-'lah-brah)*
	Another word, please.
	Otra palabra, por favor.
	('oh-trah pah-'lah-brah pohr fah-'bohr)
	Word by word.
	Palabra por palabra.
	(pah-'lah-brah pohr pah-'lah-brah)
work (to)	trabajar *(trah-bah-'hahr)*
workman's compensation	compensación de obrero *(la)* *(lah kohm-pehn-sah-see·'ohn deh oh-'breh-roh)*
worm	gusano *(el)* *(ehl goo-'sah-noh)*
worried	preocupado (m.); preocupada (f.) *(preh-oh-koo-'pah-doh, preh-oh-koo-'pah-dah)*
worse	peor (m. & f.) *(peh-'ohr)*
worsen (to)	empeorar *(ehm-peh-oh-'rahr)*
Wow!	¡Caramba! *(kah-'rahm-bah)*
wrist	muñeca *(la)* *(lah moo-'nyeh-kah)*
write (to)	escribir *(ehs-kree-'beer)*
wrong	equivocado (m.); equivocada (f.) *(eh-kee-boh-'kah-doh, eh-kee-boh-'kah-dah)*
X ray	radiografía *(la)* *(lah rah-dee-oh-grah-'fee-ah)*
X rays	rayos equis *(los)* *(lohs 'rah-yohs 'eh-kees)*

yard	patio *(el)* *(ehl 'pah-tee·oh)*
year	año *(el)* *(ehl 'ah-nyoh)*
yellow	amarillo (m.); amarilla (f.) *(ah-mah-'ree-yoh, ah-mah-'ree-yah)*
yes	sí *(see)*
yesterday	ayer *(ah-'yehr)*
yet	todavía *(toh-dah-'bee-ah)*
yogurt	yogur *(el)* *(ehl yoh-'goor)*
you	usted (respectful), tú (familiar) *(oo-'stehd, too)*
you (plural)	ustedes *(oo-'steh-dehs)*
young	joven *('hoh-behn)*
	young person muchacho *(el)*, muchacha *(la)* *(ehl moo-'chah-choh, lah moo-'chah-chah)*
younger	menor *(meh-'nohr)*
your	su (respectful), tu (familiar) *(soo, too)*
youth	joven (m. & f.) *('hoh-behn)*
zip code	zona postal *(la)* *(lah 'soh-nah pohs-'tahl)*

English-Spanish Expression Finder

Bless you!	¡Salud! *(sah-'lood)*
Calm down!	¡Cálmese! *('kahl-meh-seh)*
May I come in?	¿Se puede? *(seh 'pweh-deh)*
May I help you?	¿Puedo ayudarle? *('pweh-doh ah-yoo-'dahr-leh)*
Congratulations!	¡Felicitaciones! *(feh-lee-see-tah-see·'oh-nehs)*
Danger!	¡Peligro! *(peh-'lee-groh)*
Don't worry!	¡No se preocupe! *(noh seh preh-oh-'koo-peh)*
Excuse me!	¡Perdón! or ¡Disculpe! or ¡Con permiso! *(pehr-'dohn, dees-'kool-peh, kohn pehr-'mee-soh)*
Get well soon!	¡Qué se alivie pronto! *(keh seh ah-'leee-bee-eh 'prohn-toh)*
Go ahead!	¡Pase! *('pah-seh)*
Go with God!	¡Vaya con Dios! *('bah-yah kohn 'dee-ohs)*
Good afternoon.	Buenas tardes *('bweh-nahs 'tahr-dehs)*
Good evening or Good night.	Buenas noches. *('bweh-nahs 'noh-chehs)*
Good luck!	¡Buena suerte! *('bweh-nah 'swehr-teh)*
Good morning.	Buenos días. *('bweh-nohs 'dee-ahs)*
Good-bye.	Adiós. *(ah-dee·'ohs)*
Happy Birthday!	¡Feliz cumpleaños! *(feh-'lees kool-pleh-'ah-nyohs)*
Have a nice day!	¡Que le vaya bien! *(keh leh 'bah-yah 'bee·ehn)*
Hi!	¡Hola! *('oh-lah)*
How are you?	¿Cómo está? *('koh-moh eh-'stah)*
How do you feel?	¿Cómo se siente? *('koh-moh seh see-'ehn-teh)*
How do you say it?	¿Cómo se dice? *('koh-moh seh 'dee-seh)*
How do you write it?	¿Cómo se escribe? *('koh-moh seh ehs-'kree-beh)*
How do you spell it?	¿Cómo se deletrea? *('koh-moh seh deh-leh-'treh-ah)*
How much does it cost?	¿Cuánto cuesta? *('kwahn-toh 'kwehs-tah)*

How old are you?	¿Cuántos años tiene? (*'kwahn-tohs 'ah-nyohs tee-'eh-neh*)
How's it going?	¿Qué tal? (*keh tahl*)
Hurry up!	¡Apúrese! (*ah-'poo-reh-seh*)
I appreciate it!	¡Muy amable! (*'moo·eh ah-'mah-bleh*)
I'm sorry!	¡Lo siento! (*loh see-'ehn-toh*)
More slowly.	Más despacio. (*mahs dehs-'pah-see·oh*)
Nice to meet you.	Mucho gusto. (*'moo-choh 'goos-toh*)
Please.	Por favor. (*pohr fah-'bohr*)
See you tomorrow.	Hasta mañana. (*'ahs-tah mah-'nyah-nah*)
Take it easy!	¡Cúidese bien! (*'kwee-deh-seh 'bee·ehn*)
Thank you.	Gracias. (*'grah-see·ahs*)
That's great!	¡Qué bueno! (*keh 'bweh-noh*)
Very good!	¡Muy bien! (*'moo·ee 'bee·ehn*)
We'll see you!	¡Nos vemos! (*nohs 'beh-mohs*)
Welcome!	¡Bienvenido! (*bee-ehn-beh-'nee-doh*)
What does it mean?	¿Qué significa? (*keh seeg-nee-'fee-kah*)
What time is it?	¿Qué hora es? (*keh 'oh-rah ehs*)
What's happening?	¿Qué pasa? (*keh 'pah-sah*)
What's the date?	¿Cuál es la fecha? (*kwahl ehs lah 'feh-chah*)
What's wrong?	¿Qué pasó? (*keh pah-'soh*)
What's your name?	¿Cuál es su nombre? (*kwahl ehs soo 'nohm-breh*)
Where are you from?	¿De dónde es? (*deh 'dohn-deh ehs*)
You're welcome!	¡De nada! (*deh 'nah-dah*)

Spanish-English Word Finder

a   to
a veces   sometimes
abajo de   down
abandono   abandonment
abeja   bee
abogado, abogada   lawyer
aborto   abortion
aborto inducido   induced abortion
abril   April
abrir   open (to)
abrumado   overwhelmed
absceso   abscess
abuela   grandmother
abuelo   grandfather
aburrido, aburrida   bored
abuso   abuse
  abuso de las drogas   drug abuse
  abuso de los niños   child abuse
accidente   accident
acción   action
aceite   oil
acera   sidewalk
ácido   acid
ácido   LSD
acrílico   acrylic
acostarse   lie down (to)
acumular   accumulate (to)
adelante   straight ahead
adentro de   inside
adicto, adicta   addict
administración   administration
adopción   adoption
adoptar   to adopt
adormecer   numb (to)
adormecimiento   numbness
aeropuerto   airport
afeitar   shave (to)

afilado   sharp (edge)
agarrar   grab (to)
agencia   agency
agosto   August
agotado, agotada   exhausted
agua   water
agua oxigenada   hydrogen peroxide
aguacate   avocado
aguado, aguada   watery
agudo   sharp (sound)
aguja   needle
ahijado(a)   foster child
ahogarse   drown (to)
ahora   now
aire acondicionado   air conditioning
ajo   garlic
al lado de   next to
alarma   alarm
alcohólico, alcohólica   alcoholic
alergias   allergies
alfiler   pin
algo   something
aliento   breath
  falta de aliento   shortness of breath
alimentar   feed (to)
alimentos orgánicos   organic foods
aliviar   relieve (to)
almacén   warehouse
almohada   pillow
almuerzo   lunch
altura   height
allí   there
amamantamiento   breast feeding
amamantar   breast feed (to)
amarillo   yellow
ambulancia   ambulance
amebas   amoebas

amígdalas   tonsils
amigdalitis   tonsillitis
amoníaco   ammonia
ampolla(s)   blister(s)
amputación   amputation
amputar   amputate (to)
anaranjado   orange
anciano, anciana   elderly person
ancianos   elderly
anemia   anemia
anestesia   anesthesia
anfetamina   speed (amphetamine)
angiograma   angiogram
anillo   ring
animal   animal
  animales de peluche   stuffed animals
ano   anus
anoche   last night
anormal   abnormal
ansiedad   anxiety
antebrazo   forearm
anteojos   glasses
antes   before
antibiótico   antibiotic
anticoncepción   birth control
año   year
aorta   aorta
apellido materno   mother's last name
apellido paterno   father's last name
apendectomía   appendectomy
apéndice   appendix
apetito   appetite
aplicar   apply (to)
apoyo   headrest
aprender   learn (to)
apretar   squeeze (to)
aprobación pevia   pre-approval
apuñalar   stab (to)
aquí   here
araña   spider

árbol   tree
arbusto   bush
ardor   burning
área   area
arena   sand
aretes   earrings
armadura de yeso   cast
arriba   up
arriesgado, arriesgada   risky
arroz   rice
arteria   artery
articulaciones   joints
artificial   artificial
artritis   arthritis
ascensor   elevator
aseo personal   toilet (personal hygiene, grooming)
así que   so
asiento para infantes   infant car seat
asma   asthma
astigmatismo   astigmatism
astilla   splinter
ataque   stroke
ataque cardíaco   heart attack
ataque de ansiedad   anxiety attack
ataques   fits, seizures
atención prenatal   prenatal care
atender   assist (to)
audífonos   hearing aids
aurícula   auricle
autobús   bus
autoexamen   self-examination
automóvil   automobile
avalancha   landslide
axila   armpit
ayer   yesterday
ayuda   help
ayudante   assistant
ayudar   help (to)
azúcar   sugar

azul   blue
bacín   pan
bacinete   bassinet
bacteriólogo   bacteriologist
bañarse   bathe (to)
bañera   bathtub
baño   bathroom
banco   bank
bandeja   tray
barandas de la cama   bedrails
barbilla   chin
barbitúricos   barbiturates
barco   boat
báscula   scale (weighing)
bastante   enough
bastón   cane
basura   trash
bata   robe
bautismo   baptism
bazo   spleen
bebé   baby
beber   drink (to)
bebida   beverage
beneficios   benefits
benigno   benign
biberón   nursing bottle
bicarbonato   baking soda
bicarbonato   bicarbonate
bicicleta   bicycle
bien   well
bienestar social   welfare
bifocales   bifocals
billetera   billfold
biopsia   biopsy
bistec   steak
bizco   cross-eyed
blanco   white
blando   soft
blusa   blouse
boca   mouth

bochornos   hot flashes
bolsa   handbag
bolsa amniótica   amniotic sac
bolsa de hielo   ice pack
bomba   pump
bombear   pump (to)
bombero   fireman
bonito   pretty
borracho, borracha   drunk
bosque   forest
botas   boots
botella   bottle
botiquín   medicine chest
botulismo   botulism
bragas   panties
brazalete   bracelet
brazo   arm
broche   clasp
bronquitis   bronchitis
bueno   good
bufanda   scarf
bulto   lump
buscar   look for (to)
buzón   mailbox
cabello   hair
cabestrillo   sling
cabeza   head
cable   wire
cables eléctricos   electric wires
cadera   hip
café (bebida)   coffee
café (color)   brown
cafetería   cafeteria
cajero, cajera   cashier
cajón   drawer
calambres   cramps
calcetines   socks
cálculos   stones
  cálculos en la vesícula   gallstones
  cálculos en los riñones   kidney stones

calefacción   heating
calendario   calendar
caliente   hot
calle   street
callo   corn
callos   calluses
calmado, calmada   calm
calor   heat
calvo   bald
calzoncillos   shorts
cama   bed
cambiar   change (to)
camilla   stretcher
caminadora   walker
caminar   walk (to)
camino   road
camión   truck
  camionero   truck driver
camisa   shirt
  camisa de fuerza   straight jacket
camiseta   t-shirt
campesino, campesina   farmer
campo   countryside
canal cervical   cervical canal
cancelar   to cancel
cáncer   cancer
cáncer del cerebro   brain cancer
cáncer del riñón   kidney cancer
cansado   tired
cansancio   exhaustion
capilla   chapel
cápsula   capsule
cara   face
¡Caramba!   Wow!
cardiólogo   cardiologist
cargo   charge
carie   cavity
carne   meat
carpintero   carpenter
carretera   highway

carro   car
cartílago   cartilage
casi   almost
casado, casada   married
catarata   cataract
catéter   catheter
causar   cause (to)
cebolla   onion
ceja   eyebrow
célula   cell
cemento   cement
cena   dinner
cenicero   ash tray
cepillo de dientes   toothbrush
cerca   near
  más cerca   closer
cereal   cereal
cerebro   brain
cereza   cherry
cerrado   closed
cerrar   close (to)
certificar   certify (to)
cerveza   beer
cesto de basura   trash can
chaqueta   jacket
chata   bedpan
cheque   check
chícharo   pea
chicle   gum
chico, chica   small
chocar   crash (to)
chocolate   chocolate
chupar   suck (to)
chupete   bottle nipple
cianuro   cyanide
cicatriz   scar
ciclo menstrual   menstrual cycle
ciego   blind
cielo raso   ceiling
cigarrillo   cigarette

cine   movie theater

cinta   tape

cinta adhesiva   adhesive tape

cintura   waist

cinturón   belt

circuncisión   circumcision

cirugía   surgery

cirugía cosmética   cosmetic surgery

cirugía intestinal   intestinal surgery

cirujano, cirujana   surgeon

  cirujano ortopédico   orthopedic
    surgeon

cistoscopía   cystoscopy

cita   appointment

ciudad   city

¡Claro!   Sure!

clase   class

clavícula   collarbone

clima, tiempo   weather

cobertura   coverage

cobija   blanket

cocaína   cocaine

cocinar   cook (to)

cocinero, cocinera   cook

cochecillo   stroller

codeína   codeine

codo   elbow

colchón   mattress

cólera   anger

cólera   cholera

colesterol alto   high cholesterol

cólico   colic

colon   colon

colonoscopía   colonoscopy

color   color

columna vertebral   spinal column

collar   necklace

collar de soporte   neck brace

comenzar   begin (to)

comer   eat (to)

comida   food

  entre comidas   between meals

¿Cómo?   how?

cómodo   comfortable

compañero, compañera   buddy

compañía   company

compañía de seguros   insurance
    company

compensación de obrero   workman's
    compensation

complejo   complex

compresa   compress

computadora   computer

común   common

con   with

concusión   concussion

con frecuencia   frequently

condición (seguros)   term

condón   condom

conejo   rabbit

confundido   confused

confusión   confusion

confuso, confusa   confused

congelamiento   frostbite

conjuntivitis   conjunctivitis

consciente   conscious

consejería   counseling

consejero, consejera   counselor

consejos   counseling

constante   constant

consultar   consult (to)

contestar   answer (to)

contracciones   contractions

controlar   control (to)

convulsión   convulsion

copa   cup

co-pago   co-pay amount

corazón   heart

corbata   tie

cordón umbilical   umbilical cord

corona crown
correcto correct
corredor hallway
correr run (to)
cortar cut (to)
corte cut
corte de pelo haircut
cortinas curtains
cosa thing
coser sew (to)
cosméticos cosmetics
costilla rib
costo cost
costra scab
crack (drug) crack
cráneo cranium, skull
crecer grow (to)
crema cream
criado, criada servant
criminal criminal
Cruz Azul Blue Cross
cruzar cross (to)
cuadra city block
¿Cuál? Which?
¿Cuándo? When?
¿Cuánto? How much?
¿Cuántos? How many?
cuarto (cuarta parte) fourth
cuarto (pieza) room
cuchara spoon
cucharada tablespoon
cucharadita teaspoon
cuchillada knife gash
cuchillo knife
cuello neck
   cuello uterino cervix
cuerdo, cuerda sane
cuerpo body
cuidado care
   cuidado ambulatorio ambulatory care

cuidado con enfermera nursing care
cuidado de la visión vision care
cuidado del niño childcare
cuidado dental dental care
cuidado intermedio intermediate care
cuidado privado private care
culebra snake
cuñada sister-in-law
cuñado brother-in-law
cuna crib
curar cure (to)
curita Band-Aid®
daltónico color-blind
daltonismo Daltonism
dar give (to)
   dar de alta discharge (to)
de of
¿De quién? Whose?
debajo de under
débil weak
debilidad weakness
decir say (to)
dedo finger
   dedo del pie toe
deducible deductible
defecar defecate (to)
defecto de nacimiento birth defect
delgado thin
demasiado too much
demencia senil senile dementia
dentaduras postizas false teeth
departamento department
departamento de salud pública health department
dependiente dependent
depósito deposit
depresión depression
derecho, derecha right
   a la derecha to the right

derechos rights
dermatólogo dermatologist
desayuno breakfast
descafeinado decaffeinated
descansar rest (to)
descongestionante decongestant
descuento discount
desear to want
deseo desire
desesperado desperate
deshidratación dehydration
desierto desert
desinfectante disinfectant
desinfectar disinfect (to)
desmayarse faint (to)
desmayo fainting spell
desnutrición malnutrition
desodorante deodorant
despejado clear
despierto awake
después after
detectar detect (to)
detergente detergent
detrás de behind
día day
diabetes diabetes
diafragma diaphragm
diagnóstico diagnosis
diarrea diarrhea
diciembre December
diente tooth
  diente impactado impacted tooth
dieta diet
  dieta blanda bland diet
  dieta limitada restricted diet
  dieta para diabéticos diabetic diet
dietista dietician
diferente different
difícil difficult
difteria diphteria

dinero money
dirección address
disco compacto CD
disfunción eréctil erectile dysfunction
disparar shoot (to)
disponible available
distensión pulled muscle
distrofia muscular MD
disturbio disturbance
divorcio divorce
doblado, doblada bent
doblar bend (to)
doble double
doctor, doctora doctor
dolor pain
  dolor abdominal abdominal pain
  dolor agudo sharp pain
  dolor constante constant pain
  dolor de cabeza headache
  dolor de estómago stomachache
  dolor de garganta sore throat
  dolor de muela toothache
  dolor de oído earache
  dolor de pecho chest pain
  dolor en el pecho pain in the chest
  dolor sordo dull pain
  dolores de espalda backaches
  dolores de parto labor pains
dolorido sore (person)
domingo Sunday
¿Dónde? Where?
dormido, dormida asleep
dormir sleep (to)
dosis dosage
  dosis alta high dosage
  dosis baja low dosage
  dosis excesiva overdose
drogas drugs
  drogadicción drug addiction
  drogadicto, drogadicta drug addict

droguero, traficante de drogas drug dealer

relacionado con drogas drug-related

ducha shower

ducharse shower (to)

dulce (sabor) sweet

dulce (golosina) candy

durar last (to)

duro hard

edad age

edificio building

efectivo cash

ejercicio exercise

ejote green bean

él he

electricidad electricity

electrocardiograma ECG

electrocncefalograma EEG

ella she

ellos, ellas they

embarazada pregnant

embrión embryo

emergencia emergency

emocionado, emocionada excited

empastar fill (teeth) (to)

empaste dental filling

empaste tooth filling

empezar start (to)

empleado, empleada employee

empleo job, employment

empeorar worsen (to)

empresario, patrón, jefe employer

empujar push (to)

en at, in, on

encefalopatía espongiforme bovina Mad Cow Disease

encías gums

encima de above

encina venenosa poison oak

encontrar find (to)

enchufe outlet

enderezar straighten (to)

endoscopía endoscopy

endurecimiento hardening

enema enema

enero January

enfermarse get sick (to)

enfermedad sickness

enfermedad cardíaca heart disease

enfermedad de la glándula tiroides thyroid disease

enfermedad de la piel skin disease

enfermedad mental mental illness

enfermedad venérea STD

enfermero, enfermera nurse

enfermo, enferma sick

enfisema emphysema

engordar gain (weight) (to)

enjuagar to rinse

enjuague bucal mouthwash

enojado, enojada angry

enrojecimiento redness

ensalada salad

entender understand (to)

entonces then

entrada entrance

entre between

epidemia epidemic

epidural epidural

epilepsia epilepsy

epiléptico, epiléptica epileptic

equilibrio balance

equipo equipment

equivocado wrong

eructar burp (to)

erupción rash

erupción en la piel skin rash

escaleras stairs

escalofríos chills

escalón step

escarcha   frost
escarlatina   scarlet fever
esclerosis múltiple   MS
escorpión   scorpion
escribir   write (to)
escritorio   desk
escroto   scrotum
Escudo Azul   Blue Shield
escuela   school
escupir   spit (to)
ese, esa   that
esmalte   enamel
esófago   esophagus
esos, esas   those
espalda   back
espantado, espantada   scared
espasmo   spasm
especia   spice
especial   special
especialista   specialist
espejo   mirror
esperma   sperm
espinazo   backbone
esponja   sponge
esposa   wife
esposo   husband
espuma   foam
esputo   sputum
esqueleto   skeleton
esquina   corner
esquizofrénico, esquizofrénica
   schizophrenic
estable   stable
estación   station
estacionamiento   parking lot
estado   condition
 estado civil   marital status
estampillas   stamps
estar, ser   be (to)
este, esta   this

esterilizar   sterilize (to)
estetoscopio   stethoscope
estilete   probe
estimulantes   stimulants
estómago   stomach
estornudar   sneeze (to)
estos, estas   these
estrangulamiento   strangulation
estreñimiento   constipation
estrés   stress
estudiante   student
estudiar   study (to)
etiqueta   label
evaluar   evaluate (to)
evitar   avoid (to)
examen   exam
  examen de Papanicolao   pap smear
  examen físico   physical exam
examinar   examine (to)
excesivo   excessive
excusado   toilet
exhalar   exhale (to)
explicar   explain (to)
éxtasis   ecstasy
extracción   extraction
extraer   extract (to)
eyaculación precoz   premature
   ejaculation
fábrica o factoría   factory
fácil   easy
faja   girdle
falda   skirt
faltar   lack (to)
familia   family
farmacéutico   pharmacist
farmacia   pharmacy
fatiga   fatigue
febrero   February
fecha   date
  fecha de nacimiento   birthdate

feliz happy
feo ugly
fertilización fertilization
feto fetus
fibra fiber
fibrosis cística CF
fideo noodle
fiebre fever
  fiebre del heno hay fever
  fiebre reumática rheumatic fever
  fiebre tifoidea typhoid
fijo fixed
firma signature
fisioterapia physical therapy
flatulencia flatulence
flema phlegm
flojo, floja loose
flor flower
florero flower vase
flujo discharge
fluoruro fluoride
fórmula formula
formulario form
formulario de consentimiento consent
  form
fosa nasal nostril
fósforos matches
fracaso failure
frazada blanket
frecuencia frequency
frenillos braces
frente forehead
frente de front of
fresa strawberry
frigidez frigidity
frío cold
frotis smear
fruta fruit
fuego, incendio fire
fuegos artificiales fireworks

fuente de agua water fountain
fuerte strong
fumar smoke (to)
funcionar function (to)
funda pillowcase
gabinete cabinet
galleta cookie
garganta throat
garrapatas ticks
gas gas
gasa gauze
gastos expenses
gastroenterología gastroenterology
gastroenterólogo gastroenterologist
gastrointestinal gastrointestinal
gastritis gastritis
gatear crawl (to)
gato cat
gemelo, gemela twin
genes genes
genitales genitals
genitourinario genitourinary
gente people
gerente manager
gestación gestation
ginecólogo gynecologist
glándulas glands
glándulas hinchadas swollen glands
glaucoma glaucoma
globos balloons
golpear beat (to)
goma glue
gonorrea gonorrhea
gordo fat (person)
gota (enfermedad) gout
gotas drops
gotas para los ojos eye drops
goteo nasal runny nose
gráfico chart
gramos grams

grande   big
grano   pimple
grasa   fat (food)
gratis   free
grave   serious
gris   gray
grueso, gruesa   thick
grupo   group
guantes   gloves
guardería   nursery
guardián   guardian
gusano   worm
gustar   like (to)
hablar   speak (to)
hacer   do (to)
  hacer gárgaras   gargle (to)
hambre   hunger
hambriento   hungry
harina   flour
hay   there is/there are
hebilla   barrette
helado   frozen, ice cream
helicóptero   helicopter
hemorragia   hemorrhage
hemorroides   hemorrhoids
hepatitis   hepatitis
hereditario   hereditary
herida   injury
  herida de bala   gunshot wound
herido, herida   injured
hermana   sister
hermano   brother
hernia   hernia
heroína   heroin
hiedra venenosa   poison ivy
hielo   ice
hierba   grass
hierro   iron
hígado   liver
higienista   hygienist

hija   daughter
hijastra   stepdaughter
hijastro   stepson
hijo   son
hilo   thread
  hilo dental   dental floss
hinchazón   swelling
hipertensión   hypertension
hipo   hiccups
hipoglicemia   hypoglycemia
histerectomía   hysterectomy
histerismo   hysteria
hoja de afeitar   razor blade
hombre   man
hombro   shoulder
  hombro dislocado   dislocated shoulder
hongo   mushroom
horario   schedule
horas   hours
  horas de visita   visiting hours
hormigueo   tingling
hormona   hormone
horquilla   bobby-pin
hospital   hospital
hoy   today
hueso   bone
  hueso roto   broken bone
huevo   egg
humedad   humidity
humo   smoke
huracán   hurricane
ictericia   jaundice
identificación   identification
iglesia   church
imagen por resonancia magnética
   MRI
impacción   impaction
implante   implant
impotencia   impotence
incapacidad   disability

incendio de bosque   forest fire
incómodo, incómoda   uncomfortable
inconsciente   unconscious
incrustación   inlay
incubadora   incubator
indigestión   indigestion
infante   infant
infección   infection
infección de lombrices intestinales
  tapeworm infection
infectado, infectada   infected
infertilidad   infertility
inflamación   inflammation
inflamado, inflamada   inflamed
influenza aviar   bird flu
información   information
ingle   groin
ingreso   income
inhalar   to inhale
inhaladores   inhalants
injerto   graft
inmediatamente   immediately
inmunoterapia   immunotherapy
inquieto, inquieta   restless
insecticida   insecticide
insolación   sunstroke
insomnio   insomnia
instrucciones   directions
instrumento   instrument
insulina   insulin
intermitente   intermittent
intérprete   interpreter
interruptor de la luz   light switch
intoxicación   intoxication
intoxicación alimentaria   food
  poisoning
intravenoso   I.V.
  líquidos intravenosos   I.V. fluids
inundación   flood
investigar   research (to)

invierno   winter
inyección   shot
ir   go (to)
irradiación   radiation
irritado, irritada   irritated
izquierdo, izquierda   left
  a la izquierda   to the left
jabón   soap
jalar   pull (to)
jalea   jelly
jarabe   syrup
jarabe para la tos   cough syrup
jardinero   gardener
jarra   pitcher
jeringa   syringe
joven   young
joven   youth
joyas   jewelry
juanete   bunion
juego   game
jueves   Thursday
jugo   juice
juguete   toy
julio   July
junio   June
labio   lip
labio leporino   cleft lip
laboratorio   laboratory
lactar   breast-feed (to)
lago   lake
laparoscopia   laparoscopy
lapicero   pen
lápiz   pencil
lata   can (container)
lavamanos   sink
lavarse   wash oneself (to)
laxante   laxative
leche   milk
lechuga   lettuce
leer   read (to)

legumbre vegetable
lengua tongue
lenguaje language
lentamente, despacio slowly
lentes de contacto contact lenses
lentes de sol sunglasses
lentes progresivos progressive glasses
lento slow
lesiones lesions
leucemia leukemia
levantarse stand up (to)
ley law
libra pound
libro book
licencia de manejar driver's license
licor liquor
ligadura de las trompas tubal ligation
ligamento ligament
lima file (nailfile)
limar file (to)
limón lemon
limpiar clean (to)
linfoma de Hodgkin Hodgkin's
  lymphoma
linimento liniment
líquido liquid
 líquido cefaloraquídeo spinal fluid
litros liters
llaga sore (wound)
llamar call (to)
llamas flames
llenar fill out (to)
lleno full
llevar carry (to)
llorar cry (to)
lluvia rain
lóbulo lobe
loción lotion
loco, loca crazy
locura insanity

lodo mud
lunes Monday
luz light
madrastra stepmother
madre mother
maestro, maestra teacher
magnesia magnesium
maíz corn (food)
mal bad
malaria malaria
maligno malignant
malo bad
mal tiempo bad weather
mamograma mammogram
mañana tomorrow
 por la mañana A.M.
mancha spot
mandar send (to)
mandíbula jaw
manejar drive (to)
manga sleeve
maniática, maniático maniac
manicomio psychiatric hospital
mano hand
manteca lard
mantequilla butter
manzana apple
mapa map
maquillaje make-up
máquina machine
máquina de movimiento continuo
  continuous passive motion machine
mar sea
marcapasos pacemaker
mareado, mareada dizzy
mareos dizziness
margarina margarine
marijuana marijuana
mariscos shellfish
martes Tuesday

marzo March
más more
 más tarde later
máscara mask
mastectomía mastectomy
masticar chew (to)
matar murder (to)
matricularse to enroll
matrimonio marriage
mayo May
mayor older
mecánico mechanic
medias stockings
medicina medicine
médico, médica physician
medir measure (to)
médula bone marrow
mejilla cheek
mejor better
mejorar improve (to)
memoria memory
meningitis meningitis
menor younger
menor de edad minor
menos less
menstruar menstruate (to)
mensual monthly
merienda snack
mes month
mesa table
mesa de noche nightstand
mescalina mescaline
mesero waiter
metro subway
metros meters
mezcla mixture
mi my
microondas microwave
miedo fear
miel honey

miembro member
miércoles Wednesday
migraña migraine
minerales minerals
ministro minister
miope near-sighted
mismo same
mitad half
moco mucus
moderado mild
mojado, mojada wet
molde mold
monitor monitor
mononucleosis mononucleosis
monóxido de carbono carbon monoxide
montaña mountain
morado purple
mordedura bite
  mordedura de culebra snake bite
  mordedura de insecto insect bite
  mordedura de perro dog bite
morder bite (to)
morena brunette
morfina morphine
morir to die
motocicleta motorcycle
muchacho, muchacha young person
muchas veces lots of times
muchos many
mucoso mucous
muebles furniture
muela molar
muerte death
muerto, muerta dead
muestra sample
mujer woman
muñeca (cuerpo) wrist
muñeca (juguete) doll
murmullos en el corazón heart
  murmurs

músculo   muscle
  músculo rasgado   pulled muscle
muslo   thigh
muy   very
muy fuerte   severe, very strong
nacer   be born (to)
  nacido muerto   stillborn
nacimiento   birth
nacionalidad   nationality
nada   nothing
nalga   buttock
narcotráfico   drug traffic
nariz   nose
  dolor de nariz   nose pain
  goteo de nariz   nose drip
  sange de nariz   nosebleed
  nariz tapada   stuffy nose
náusea   nausea
neblina   fog
necesario   necessary
necesitar   need (to)
negocio   business
negro, negra   black
  hombre negro   black man
  mujer negra   black woman
  niña negra   black girl
  niño negro   black boy
nervio   nerve
nervioso, nerviosa   nervous
neurólogo   neurologist
neurosis   neurosis
nieta   granddaughter
nieto   grandson
nieve   snow
ninguno   none
niño adoptado   adopted child
niño, niña   child
noche   night
  esta noche   tonight
nombre   name

normal   normal
normalmente   normally
nosotros   we
novia   girlfriend
noviembre   November
novio   boyfriend
nublado   cloudy
nuera   daughter-in-law
nuestro   our
nuevo   new
nuez   nut
número   number
  número de seguro social   Social
    Security number
  número de teléfono   telephone
    number
nunca   never
o   or
obesidad   obesity
obrero   laborer
observar   observe (to)
obstetriz   obstetrician
octavo   eighth
octubre   October
ocupado, ocupada   busy
ocho   eight
oficina   office
oftalmólogo   ophthalmologist
oído   ear
  dolor de oído   earache
  sangre del oído   earbleed
  sordera   deafness
oír   hear (to)
ojo   eye
  dolor de ojo   eyepain
  ojos llorosos   crying eyes
  ojos llorosos   watery eyes
  ver puntos   to see spots
  ver borroso   blurred vision
  vision doble   double vision

oler   smell (to)
ombligo   navel
once   eleven
oncología   oncology
onzas   ounces
operación   operation
  antes de la operación   pre-op
  después de la operación   post-op
  operación cesárea   cesarean section
  operación de emergencia   emergency operation
  preparar para la operación   to prepare for the operation
operar   operate (to)
opinión   opinion
optometrista   optometrist
órgano   organ
orilla   curb
orinal   urinal
orinar   urinate (to)
oro   gold
ortodoncista   orthodontist
ortopedia   orthopedics
orzuelo   sty
otoño   fall
ovario   ovary
óvulo   ovum
oxígeno   oxygen
paciente   patient
  paciente externo   outpatient
  paciente interno   in-patient
padrastro (familia)   stepfather
padrastro (uña)   hangnail
padre   father
pagar   pay (to)
pago   payment
pájaro   bird
palabra   word
paladar   palate

palma de la mano   palm
palpitaciones   palpitations
pan   bread
pañal   diaper
paño higiénico   feminine napkin
páncreas   pancreas
pantalones   pants
pantorrilla   calf
pantuflas   slippers
papa   potato
papel   paper
papel higiénico   toilet paper
paperas   mumps
parálisis   paralysis
parálisis cerebral   cerebral palsy
paramédico   paramedic
pararse   stand (to)
parásitos   parasites
pared   wall
pareja   couple
parentezco   relationship
pariente más cercano   next of kin
párpado   eyelid
parque   park
parte   part
partida de nacimiento vivo   Certificate of Live Birth
parto   childbirth
  parto natural   natural childbirth
pasta de dientes   toothpaste
pastel   pie
pastilla   lozenge
patear   kick (to)
patio   yard
patólogo   pathologist
patrón   employer
pavo   turkey
pecho   chest
pediatra   pediatrician
peine   comb

pelear   fight (to)
peligroso   dangerous
pelirrojo, pelirroja   redhead
pelota   ball
pelvis   pelvis
pene   penis
penicilina   penicillin
pensar   think (to)
peor   worse
perder   lose (to)
pérdida   miscarriage, loss
perdido   lost
pérdida de conocimiento   blackout
perforar   drill (to)
periódico   newspaper
permiso   permission
pero   but
perro   dog
perseguido   persecuted
persona   person
pesar   weigh (to)
pescado   fish
peso   weight
pestaña   eyelash
pezón   nipple
picadura de abeja   bee sting
picante   spicy
  comidas picantes   spicy foods
picar   itch (to)
picazón   itching
pie   foot
piedra   stone
piel   skin
  cáncer de la piel   skin cancer
pierna   leg
pijamas (las)   pajamas
pila   battery
píldora   pill
píldoras anticonceptivas   birth control
  pills

pimienta   pepper
piña   pineapple
pintor, pintora   painter
pintura   paint
pinzas   tweezers
piojo   lice
piojos   lice
piorrea   pyorrhea
pisalengua   tongue depressor
piso   floor
pista   lane
placa   plaque
placenta   placenta
plaga   plague
plan   plan
planificación   planning
planta del pie   sole
plata   silver
plátano   banana
plato   plate
playa   beach
plomero   plumber
pobre   poor
pocos   few
poder   be able (to)
podiatra   podiatrist
polen   pollen
policía   police officer
polio   polio
pólipo   polyp
póliza   policy
polvo   dust
pollo   chicken
pómulo   cheekbone
poner   put (to)
por, para   for
por eso   therefore
¿Por qué?   Why?
porcelana   porcelain
porcentaje   percent

porque because
postizo false
postración heat stroke
postración nerviosa nervous breakdown
postre dessert
potasio potassium
practicante orderly
precio price
pregunta question
preguntar ask (to)
prematuro, prematura premature
preocupado, preocupada worried
preparar prepare (to)
présbito far-sighted
presión de la sangre blood pressure
presión directa direct pressure
préstamo loan
prevenir prevent (to)
prieto dark-skinned (coll.)
primavera spring
primer nombre first name
primer piso first floor
primero first
primeros auxilios first aid
primo, prima cousin
privado, privada private
problemas emocionales emotional problems
proceder proceed (to)
procedimiento procedure
proctología proctology
proctoscopía proctoscopy
producto químico chemical
productos lácteos dairy products
profundo, profunda deep
prohibido prohibited
prohibir prohibit (to)
pronto soon
protector dental mouthguard

proteger protect (to)
proteína protein
protuberancia(s) bump(s)
proveedor, proveedora provider
pruebas tests
  prueba de CAP CAP test
  prueba de Holter Holter scan
psicólogo, psicóloga psychologist
psicoterapia psychotherapy
psiquiatra psychiatrist
puente bridge
puerta door
pulgada inch
pulga flea
pulmones lungs
pulmonía pneumonia
pulsante throbbing
pulso pulse
  pulso irregular irregular pulse
  pulso lento slow pulse
  pulso rápido fast pulse
punción lumbar spinal tap
puntos stitches
purificar purify (to)
puro cigar
pus pus
¿Qué? What?
quedarse stay (to)
quemante burning
quemar burn (to)
querer want (to)
queso cheese
¿Quién? Who?
quinto fifth
quiropráctico chiropractor
quiste cyst
quitarse take off (clothes) (to)
radiografía X ray
radiología radiology
radiólogo, radióloga radiologist

radioterapia   radiation therapy

raíz   root

rápidamente   quickly

rápido   fast

rascar   scratch (to)

rasguño   scratch

rasurar   shave (to)

rata   rat

ratón   mouse

rayos equis   X rays

raza   race

readmitir   readmit (to)

receta médica   prescription

recibir   receive (to)

recibo   receipt

recién nacido, recién nacida   newborn

recomendar   recommend (to)

reconocimiento   checkup

recordar   remember (to)

recto   rectum

recuento   count

recuento de la sangre   blood count

recuperación   recuperation

recuperar   recuperate (to)

recursos   resources

referencia   referral

refresco   soft drink

refrigerador   refrigerator

regalo   gift

registrar   register (to)

regla, período   period (menstrual)

regresar, volver   return (to)

relaciones sexuales   sexual relations

relajado, relajada   relaxed

religión   religion

reloj   watch

remedios   drugs (legal)

remplazar   replace (to)

reparar   repair (to)

repollo   cabbage

resfrío   cold (illness)

resistir   resist (to)

respiración   breathing

respirador   respirator

respirar   breathe (to)

responsabilidad legal   liability

restaurante   restaurant

restricciones   restrictions

resucitación cardiopulmonar   CPR

revista   magazine

rezar   pray (to)

rico, rica   rich

riñón   kidney

rinitis alérgica   hay fever

río   river

ritmo cardíaco   heartbeat

rodilla   knee

rojo   red

romo   dull (edge)

ronquido   snoring

ropa   clothing

  ropa interior   underwear

ropero   closet

rosado, rosada   pink

rótula   kneecap

rubéola   German measles

rubio, rubia   blond

ruptura   rupture

sábado   Saturday

sábana   sheet

saborear   taste (to)

sacar   remove (to)

sacarse   take off (to)

sacerdote   priest

sal   salt

  sal de epsom   epsom salt

sala   room, unit, ward

  sala de conferencias   conference room

sala de cuidados intensivos   Intensive Care

sala de emergencia   Emergency Room

sala de espera   Waiting Room

sala de maternidad   Maternity Ward

sala de meditación   meditation room

sala de operaciones   Operating Room

sala de partos   delivery room

sala de recuperación   Recovery Room

salida   exit

salir   leave (to)

saliva   saliva

salón   lobby

salón principal   main lobby

salsa   sauce

salud   health

¡Salud!   Bless you!

salud mental   mental health

sangre   blood

  sangre en los excrementos   blood in the stool

sarampión   measles

sarpullidos   rashes

sarro   tartar

satisfecho, satisfecha   satisfied

seco, seca   dry

secretario, secretaria   secretary

sedante   sedative

sedantes   depressants

sediento   thirsty

seguir   follow (to)

segunda opinión   second opinion

segundo   second

seguridad   security

seguro (a salvo)   safe

seguro   insurance

  compañía de seguros   insurance company

  seguro de accidente   accident insurance

seguro de salud   health insurance

  seguro de vida   life insurance

selva   jungle

semana   week

semen   semen

sencillo   simple

senos, pechos   breasts

sensibilidad   sensitivity

sentarse   sit down (to)

sentir   feel (to)

septiembre   September

séptimo   seventh

sequía   drought

servicios   services

servicios de salud   health care

servilleta   napkin

severo, severa   severe

sexo   sex

sexto   sixth

sí   yes

SIDA   AIDS

  prueba del SIDA   AIDS test

siempre   always

sien   temple

siesta   nap

sífilis   syphilis

signos vitales   vital signs

siguiente   next

silbido en el oído   ringing in the ear

silla   chair

simpático   cute

sin   without

sin embargo   however

síndrome   syndrome

síndrome de muerte infantil súbita   SIDS

síndrome del alcohol fetal   fetal alcohol syndrome

síntoma   symptom

sistema inmune   immune system

sistema nervioso   nervous system
sobre   about
sobre (de carta)   envelope
sobrina   niece
sobrino   nephew
socio   partner
sodio   sodium
sofocación   suffocation
sol   sun
solo, sola   alone
soltero, soltera   single (person)
solución   solution
somnífero   sleeping pill
soñoliento, soñolienta   sleepy
sonido   sound
sonograma   sonogram
sonrisa   smile
sopa   soup
sordo   dull (sound)
sordo, sorda   deaf
sorprendido, sorprendida   surprised
sótano   basement
sostén   brassiere
su   her/his/your
subir   go up (to)
sucio, sucia   dirty
sudar   perspire (to)
sudor   sweating
sudoroso   sweaty
suegra   mother-in-law
suegro   father-in-law
sueños   dreams
suéter   sweater
sufrir   suffer (to)
suicidarse   to commit suicide
suicidio   suicide
sunami   tsunami
superficial   shallow (person)
supositorios   suppositories
sutura   suture

tableta   tablet
tablilla   splint
taladro   drill
talco   talcum powder
talón   heel
tamaño   size
también   also
tapar   cover (to)
tarde   late
  por la tarde   p.m.
tarjeta   card
  tarjeta de crédito   credit card
  tarjeta de saludo   greeting card
  tarjeta postal   postcard
taza   teacup
té   tea
técnico   technician
tejido   tissue
teléfono   telephone
teléfono celular   cell phone
televisión   television
temperatura   temperature
temprano   early
tenazas   forceps
tendón   tendon
tendonitis   tendonitis
tenedor   fork
tener   have (to)
tener que   have to (to)
terapeuta   therapist
terapia   therapy
terapia física   physical therapy
terapia hormonal   hormonal therapy
tercero   third
terminar   end (to)
termómetro   thermometer
termostato   thermostat
terremoto   earthquake
testículos   testicles
tétano   tetanus

tía aunt
tiempo time
tienda store
 tienda de regalos gift shop
tierra dirt
tijeras scissors
timbre bell
tío uncle
tipo de sangre blood type
tiroides thyroid
toalla towel
toallita washcloth
tobillo ankle
 tobillo torcido sprained ankle
todavía yet, still
todo all
tomar take (to)
tomate tomato
tomografía computarizada CT
  scanning
tonsilitis tonsillitis
tornado tornado
torniquete tourniquet
toronja grapefruit
torta; bizcocho cake
tos cough
 tos dolorosa painful cough
 tos ferina, tos convulsiva whooping
  cough
toser cough (to)
trabajador social social worker
trabajar work (to)
tracción traction
tragar swallow (to)
traer bring (to)
traje suit
tranquilo calm
transfusión de sangre bloodtransfusion
transporte transportation
trapecio trapeze

trasplantar transplant (to)
trastorno disorder
tratamiento treatment
 tratamiento del nervio dental root
  canal
tratar try (to)
trauma trauma
tren train
triste sad
tristeza grief
trompas de falopio fallopian tubes
tu your
tuberculosis tuberculosis
tubo tube
úlcera ulcer
úlcera en la boca canker sore
último last
ultrasonido ultrasound
un, una a
uña nail
uña encarnada ingrown toenail
una vez once
ungüento ointment
unidad neurosiquiátrica neuro-
  psychiatric unit
unos, unas some
uretra urethra
urólogo urologist
urticaria hives
usar use (to)
usted, tú you
ustedes you (plural)
útero uterus
uva grape
vacío empty
vacuna vaccination
vacuna contra la influenza flu shot
vacunar vaccinate (to)
vagina vagina
válvula valve

vapor steam
varicela chicken pox
vasectomía vasectomy
vaselina vaseline
vaso glass (drinking)
vejación sexual, molestia sexual molestation
vejiga bladder
 infección de la vejiga bladder infection
vena vein
 venas varicosas varicose veins
vendaje bandage
vendedor, vendedora salesperson
veneno poison
venir come (to)
ventana window
ventilador electric fan
ventrículo ventricle
ver see (to)
verano summer
verde green
verificar check (to)
verificar verify (to)
verruga wart
verrugas genitales genital warts
vestido dress
vestirse get dressed (to)
víbora venenosa poisonous snake
vida life
viejo old
viento wind

viernes Friday
VIH HIV
vino wine
violación rape
violar rape (to)
viruela smallpox
virus virus
virus del Nilo Occidental West Nile virus
visión vision
 doble visión double vision
visita visit
visitante visitor
visitar visit (to)
vista sight
vitamina(s) vitamin(s)
vivir live (to)
vivo, viva alive
voltearse turn oneself over (to)
vomitar vomit (to)
voz voice
vulva vulva
y and
ya already
yerno son-in-law
yo I
yogur yogurt
zanahoria carrot
zancudo mosquito
zapato shoe
zona postal zip code